PRAISE FOR *A SINNER IN MECCA*

"Parvez's heroism is rare and his courage well documented. Putting his own life at risk, he takes us on a surprising and compelling journey through the frontlines of his much-contested faith. A brilliant follow-up to his films, *A Jihad for Love* and *A Sinner in Mecca*."

—Reza Aslan, #1 *New York Times* bestselling author
of *Zealot* and host of CNN's *Believer*

"In our lives, we face a choice of whether to live with judgment or reach deep within ourselves to find an inner moral compass that leads us to a metaphorical Mecca of unconditional love. With his powerful, brave book, *A Sinner in Mecca*, Parvez Sharma takes us on his hero's pilgrimage, teaching us of an ethereal truth: the Qibla, or direction of Mecca, resides within each one of our hearts."

—Asra Q. Nomani, author of *Standing Alone in Mecca*

"Sharma's gripping journey unfolds with cinematic splendor, giving those of us who will never experience the Hajj firsthand the next best thing. This book examines modern Islam's beauty and its ugliness with an unflinching gaze and a hopeful vision for its future."

—Cole Stryker, author of *Hacking the Future*

"Parvez Sharma's Hajj pilgrimage is not only a journey to Mecca but to his deepest self. Both a Muslim and an out gay man, Sharma writes bravely and brilliantly. His religion is ancient. His story is timeless."

—Kevin Sessums, *New York Times* bestselling
author of *I Left It on the Mountain*

"As a gay man and a Muslim, Parvez Sharma's unique personal journey is reflected in this powerful examination of faith, sexuality, and gender. In a divided world, Sharma fearlessly crosses the boundaries and barriers that separate us from each other and finds common ground in the search for love and truth."

—Cleve Jones, author of *When We Rise*

PRAISE FOR *A SINNER IN MECCA* (THE FILM)
(ASINNERINMECCA.COM)

The New York Times Critics' Pick: *"Mr. Sharma has created a swirling, fascinating travelogue and a stirring celebration of devotion . . . we emerge from his film more enlightened."*

The Hollywood Reporter: *"Wrenching . . . gritty . . . surreal and transcendent; visceral and abstract . . . an undeniable act of courage and hope."*

The Los Angeles Times: *"Challenging his own faith in the face of adversity."*

The Washington Post: *"Complex . . . Revelatory . . ."*

The Village Voice: *"Next time you hear politicians or right-wing broadcasters asking why 'moderate' Muslims don't denounce terrorism, show them this movie."*

Thompson on Hollywood: *"Combines the political, personal and spiritual in a remarkable way."*

The Guardian: *"With poetic simplicity . . . a delicately personal story and a call to action."*

NBC News: *"The talk of the documentary circuit . . ."*

New York Daily News: *"Takes its audience where no movie has gone before."*

The Daily Beast: *"Goes undercover . . . A rare look . . . Sure to be controversial."*

Vice: *"Brilliant . . . Rare . . . Takes aim at Wahhabi Islam . . ."*

Slant Magazine: *"A work of vital political and social import."*

Paper Magazine: *"Surreal . . . Bold . . . An incredibly rare insight . . ."*

Yahoo News: *"A rebuke of Saudi Arabia."*

Indiewire: *"Powerful, illuminating . . . a remarkable examination of contemporary Islam."*

BBC Persian: *"Shocking and courageous."*

Screen International: *"Unprecedented . . . surreal."*

Globe and Mail: *"A first-hand look at the Amazing Muslim Race . . ."*

The Toronto Star: *"A deeply personal film about faith and forgiveness."*

DocGeeks: *"Moving . . . Brave . . . Visceral . . . Insightful . . ."*

Screen Daily: *"Meaningful . . . A testament to courage . . ."*

The Daily Mail: *"Powerful."*

Jahan News (Iran Govt.): *"An attack on Islam."*

* Also visit http://nyti.ms/1gRQPhl for a full-feature profile on the filmmaker in the *New York Times*.

A SINNER IN MECCA

A SINNER IN MECCA

A GAY MUSLIM'S HAJJ OF DEFIANCE

PARVEZ SHARMA

BenBella Books, Inc.
Dallas, TX

All the events and people in this book are real and told accurately to the best of the author's memory and ability. Many names and identifying details have been changed for the individuals' safety and mostly per their request.

BenBella Books, Inc.
10440 N. Central Expressway, Suite 800
Dallas, TX 75231
www.benbellabooks.com
Send feedback to feedback@benbellabooks.com.

Printed in the United States of America
10 9 8 7 6 5 4 3 2 1

Library of Congress Cataloging-in-Publication Data:
Names: Sharma, Parvez, author.
Title: A sinner in Mecca : a gay muslim's hajj of defiance / Parvez Sharma.
Description: Dallas : BenBella Books, Inc. 2017. | Includes bibliographical
    references and index.
Identifiers: LCCN 2017008521 (print) | LCCN 2017021631 (ebook) | ISBN
    9781944648404 (electronic) | ISBN 9781944648374 (trade paper : alk.
paper)
Subjects: LCSH: Sharma, Parvez. | Muslim pilgrims and pilgrimages--Saudi
    Arabia--Mecca. | Homosexuality--Religious aspects--Islam. |
    Wahheabeiyah--Saudi Arabia.
Classification: LCC BP187.3 (ebook) | LCC BP187.3 .S5155 2017 (print) | DDC
    297.092 [B] --dc23
LC record available at https://lccn.loc.gov/2017008521

Cover and insert photography © Yousuf Zafar   Text design and composition by Aaron
Copyediting by Brian J. Buchanan   Edmiston
Proofreading by Kimberly Broderick, Amy   Cover design by Sarah Avinger
    Zarkos, and Rachel Phares   Printed by Lake Book Manufacturing

Distributed by Perseus Distribution
www.perseusdistribution.com

To place orders through Perseus Distribution:
Tel: (800) 343-4499
Fax: (800) 351-5073
E-mail: orderentry@perseusbooks.com

**Special discounts for bulk sales (minimum of 25 copies) are available.
Please contact Aida Herrera at aida@benbellabooks.com.**

For Dan, my very life, and for a magician called Andy Tobias.

"Whoever performs Hajj and does not have sexual relations with his wife nor commits sin, nor disputes unjustly, then he returns from Hajj as pure and free from sins as on the day on which his mother gave birth to him."

—A hadith attributed to Prophet Muhammad and compiled in *Sahih Bukhari*, arguably the most influential book in the Sunni canon

CONTENTS

Map of the Middle East   xiv
Map of the Indian Subcontinent   xvi

Prologue   xix

Chapter 1: Li Beirut   1
Chapter 2: An Alien with Extraordinary Ability   30
Chapter 3: Pube Face, Towelhead, Camel Fucker, Cave Nigger   52
Chapter 4: The Garden of Paradise   80
Chapter 5: Shoot Me in Here   107
Chapter 6: The Naked Believer   119
Chapter 7: The Satanic Verses   131
Chapter 8: Mecca Vegas   145
Chapter 9: Muslim Boot Camp   152
Chapter 10: Mecca's Many Muhammads   169
Chapter 11: My Passage to India   189
Chapter 12: Islam 3.0   221

Glossary   252
Bibliography   272
Thank Yous   277
About the Author   280

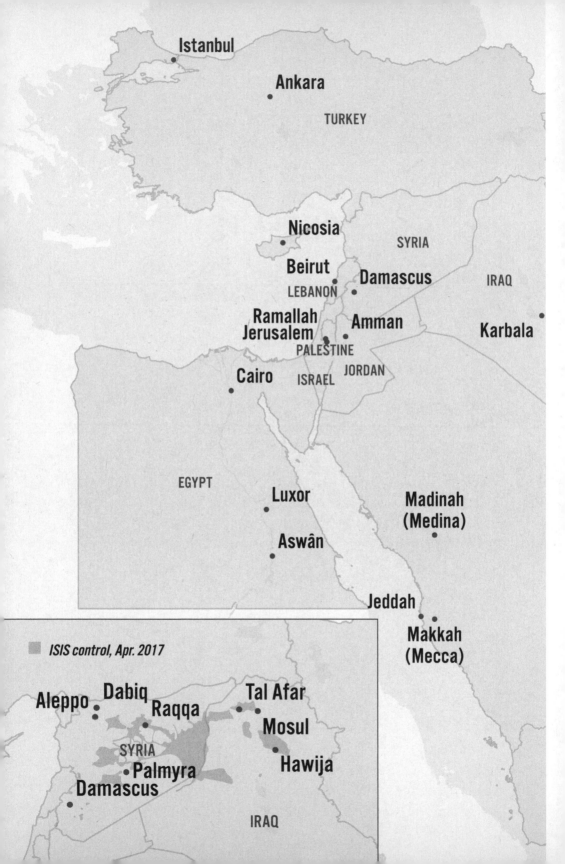

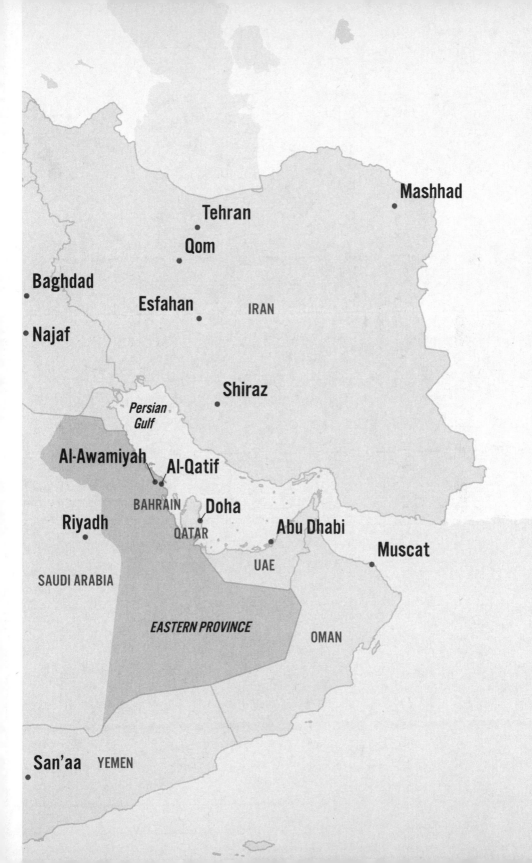

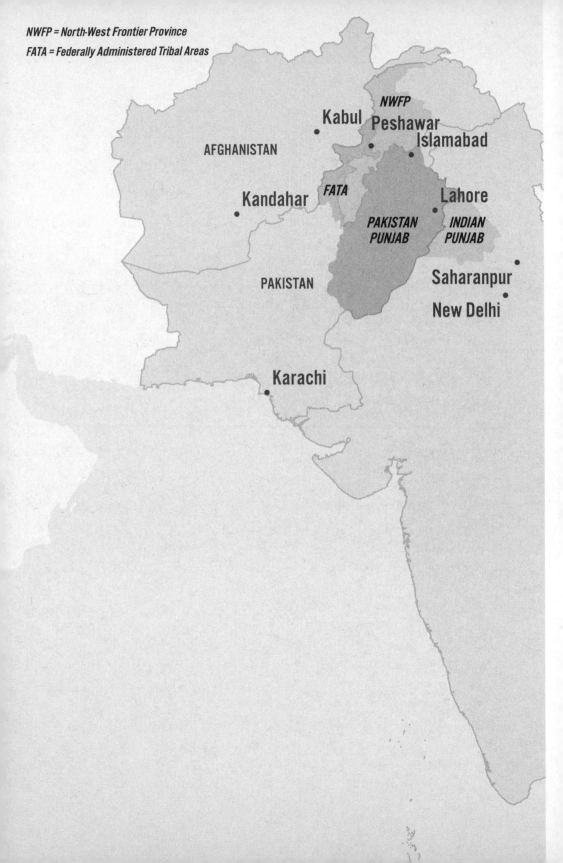

NWFP = North-West Frontier Province
FATA = Federally Administered Tribal Areas

Kabul

AFGHANISTAN

NWFP
Peshawar
Islamabad

Kandahar

FATA

Lahore

PAKISTAN
PUNJAB

INDIAN
PUNJAB

PAKISTAN

Saharanpur

New Delhi

Karachi

PAKISTAN
KASHMIR

Line of
Control

INDIAN
KASHMIR

NEPAL   Kathmandu   Thimphu
Lucknow   BHUTAN

                    Dhaka
        Calcutta
INDIA   BANGLADESH

SRI
LANKA
Colombo

PROLOGUE

"What's his name?" I asked my more-awake husband on a Sunday morning as he told me about the carnage in Orlando, Florida. It was a little less than five months, almost to the day, before America would elect Donald J. Trump to the presidency of the United States.

America's largest mass shooting—and it was a deranged lone-ranger, again. The target? A gay nightclub, Pulse, in Orlando. Odds were it was yet another psychopathic white male with the typical easy access to guns Americans unfortunately enjoy. But my instincts were different this time.

"It's going to be a Muslim," I said. It was similar to the certainty I had been expressing for months with friends and Keith, angered by my belief that a Trump presidency was inevitable and imminent.

"Why on earth would you say that?" said Keith. "The majority of these shootings are carried out by unhinged white guys." I just repeated my sad premonition as we swiped through various websites on our phones. Hashtags like #Orlando, #OrlandoStrong, and others were spreading faster than the Zika virus, and Facebook "stati" were rapidly changing. The tweetology of Orlando was building up fast.

"I am doing it for ISIS," or a similar statement, is what this mass murderer allegedly claimed in a call to a stricken night-shift producer at the local News 13 of Orlando. The CIA would later debunk the theory of any connection between the shooter and the Islamic State. It was said the gunman even managed to call 911 in the middle of his massacre. He lay dead at 5:53 a.m. according to this tweet from Orlando police: "Pulse Shooting: The shooter inside the club is dead."

Hours later, I was proved right. It was a Muslim name, Omar Mateen, a probable self-hating gay Muslim who some claimed had a profile on Grindr, a gay-hookup app. Heavily armed, he had walked into Pulse at 2:02 a.m. After three hours of absolute annihilation, forty-nine lay dead. And fifty-three were seriously wounded. I remember thinking to myself that we Muslims in the West bore some responsibility. Our time for victimhood, as far as I was concerned, was over. More Islamophobia post-Orlando? And why not? Butchery in the name of Islam has been carried out almost every single day in the years following 9/11. History will forever mark our times as a period of a violent Islam.

My pledge of allegiance was just a year old and America's rightward spiral was well underway. This fascist American summer was a mere foretaste. Trump had built a coalition for whom a "Muslim registry" was just one of many hateful battle cries.

"There will be scores of new Mateens," I said to the printed press that called, saying no to cable producers. I just didn't know how to make a case in pithy soundbites.

Using an ugly-face Kimoji, oversize blue teardrop falling from exaggerated false eyelashes, I texted Adham, my friend in Saudi Arabia: "Trump will win. And now it will be years of Muslim psychos saying they killed for ISIS." Sitting in his Jeddah home, he too replied with a sad-face Kimoji.

To my husband that morning, I said, "Muslim check. Daesh check. This is a war that will never end. They can all invoke the Quran for violent jihad and they do and they always will."

"But don't you espouse reading the Quran in context? Isn't that hypocritical?" Keith asked. He had lived through years of my making a very public case against Islamophobia, using the Quran as my primary tool. I had always been a Quran defender. Had I changed so much?

"Not even nearly," I replied, "The Quran is an almost schizophrenic text."

"What on earth is that supposed to mean?" he asked.

I told him about how the book that took twenty-three years to reveal was not revealed sequentially and to some could even seem discombobulated. I told him how its Surahs (chapters) were seen as either Meccan (revealed in Mecca) or Medinan (revealed in Medina). The latter, some said, were more "violent" because the Medinan Muhammad had tasted war. Pre-migration, the Meccan Muhammad had been a haunted and broken man. A pacifist, and thus the nature of those revelations.

"It's almost as if there are two different Qurans all mixed up," I said. "And I would even dare to add that it's almost as if there are two different Muhammads in the Quran and the later canons of Islam."

"Stop saying that in public. I think that's dangerous," he said, hugging me tightly.

Was there safety in my little island of Manhattan? "It sits off America's coast and should be an independent nation," I used to joke. In this changed America, would I dare to publicly wear that T-shirt I had once bought in a Southall shop in London? The T-shirt was Saudi-flag green and in bold letters proclaimed: "Don't Panic. I'm Islamic." I treasure it to this day.

Trump's spooky campaign was racist and misogynist. It made PC obsolete. Millions of American tongues were suddenly untied. America's dark side was becoming its visible one. On this June 12, 2016, massacre, Trump tweeted twice. One tweet went, "Appreciate the congrats for being right on radical Islamic terrorism, I don't want congrats, I want toughness & vigilance. We must be smart!" Neither tweet had any state of grace or condolence. We were going to "elect" a cold-blooded monster. His voters preferred brown, dead gays anyway.

The nihilistic ISIS allegedly celebrated his ascent. Almost five months later as Trump won the US presidency, *USA Today* quoted an entity called "the al-Minbar Jihadi Media network," affiliated with the "Islamic State," saying, "(We) rejoice with support from Allah, and find glad tidings in the imminent demise of America at the hands of Trump." For other Islamic anarchists, Orlando, Brexit, and finally the US election were all "proof" of the "demise of the West" that would bring "civil war" and "destruction." As I continued to troll the dark web, I found others claiming affiliation to ISIS, saying this would all fuel "recruitment." Islamophobia is a real thing, and I continue to live it. But the more "moderate Muslims" invoke it, the greater the power ISIS gets to recruit against what it sees as the Christian West, the enemy of Islam, against whom violent jihad is a religious duty. Trump, for ISIS, is a blessing like none other.

I wondered if Trump knew that his idea of a violent, misogynist, and offensive Islam was eerily similar to how ISIS or Saudi Arabia's ruling Wahhabi ideologists interpreted and presented the faith. This felt like the beginning of the Talibanization of America. Like the Taliban, Trump and his followers would turn the clock back.

If there had never been an Obama, there would not be a Trump. The profound hatred of the former by the racist supporters of the latter was finally naked. This all-white bigotry actually started in 2008. The line that runs from Sarah Palin through the birthers and the Tea Party to end up with the Trumpsters is a straight one. Mostly everyone ignored the fact that a significant percentage of White America never accepted a Black man as their president. They never accepted a Black family living in what had always been a very White House, which Michelle Obama eloquently reminded us was "built by slaves." For some it was as if the Obama years didn't even happen. Did that percentage vote for Trump? Absolutely. But even they probably could not have foreseen a near future where strange phrases like "the alt-right," "fake news," and "alternative facts" would enter common vocabulary.

Barack Obama was not allowed to create a post-racial America. The "Black Lives Matter" campaign was only one example. Trump made racism and all flavors of intolerance acceptable again. The white majority in this country knew that by 2020 the majority of children under five would be from a racial minority. And in mere decades America would be a majority-minority country. For now, the fearful and intolerant parts of Trump's white-male majority clung to power as ferociously as they could.

As Trump headed to victory, an almost forgotten affliction called the "alt-right" grew insidiously stronger. This white-supremacist fringe movement that preferred Nazi salutes, shouted Hail Trump! at his rallies, and flashed other Third Reich–style accouterments was part of Trump's winning coalition. Even the traditional Republican right had never seen anything like it. Initially on the shoulders of his right-hand man and alt-right hero Stephen Bannon, Islamophobia, anti-Semitism, and hate in general would all become unlikely brothers in Trump's Nixonian Oval Office. This was the (viciously) Separated States of America. Europe was keeling rightward and there was no reason for America not to do the same. Like millions I felt it strongly. This crowd was entering the White House to alter history and maraud our future. At the same time I reminded myself that Islamic supremacy was but a mirror of white supremacy.

A few months post-Mateen and during the Trump transition, a friend who is on the senior staff of a prominent senator reminded me, "Be careful. What you say. What you write. You are Muslim. The registry will probably never happen. But it's a time for vigilance, Parvez. We feared it and now it's here."

At public events, I said that I, too, was a "radical" Muslim but of a very different kind.

Radicalization had been the word of the moment for a while. Orlando had attacked my core. I was a devout Muslim. And I was gay. I ended up writing an op-ed for the American news site called *The Daily Beast*, which it unfortunately titled, "Gay Muslim: Islam Is No Religion of Peace." Thankfully there was a sub-headline, "Like the two other monotheisms that precede it, Islam has blood on its hands."

A burden had been lifted. The apologetic "Islam is a religion of peace" was forever wiped from my vocabulary. After years of getting my hands dirty throughout the Muslim world, filming guerrilla-style in dictatorial regimes with no government permission, after literally risking my life to complete and film the harsh and ultimate Muslim journey, the Hajj, I finally had earned the confidence to say this. I had battled for the truth of my words. For Islam, I had literally put my life at risk more times than I could count.

"Read it. Loved it, man! For the first time imo you are speaking the complete truth. I told you all your Islam stuff is bull-shit!" reliably texted my Jeddah BFF Adham.

I texted him that a reread would tell him that I was not damning Islam. I was just asking for necessary self-contemplation amongst all Muslims—a generalization, but not one without precedent within the faith. Are all Muslims "terrorists"? No. But are all terrorists Muslim? The majority seem to be.

In Trump's America I would be one of many with a target on our backs. We would come to realize again that there is no real understanding of American political culture without race at the center of it. Was it as simple as Muslim being the new Black? For those like me, the facts don't help: Islam is seemingly at war with a large chunk of humanity. It is also at war with itself. And I have always fought hard not to be a casualty.

CHAPTER 1

LI BEIRUT

You have no idea how many rich Saudi fuckers come here," Babak said. "We Beirutis fuck well. The Saudis? They walk around like they are so butch, but once naked they are all bottoms." I laughed.

Babak was the twenty-something founder of Arabian Bears, who organized "Bear" tours of Lebanon, Syria, and Jordan for Western gay men keen to sample the delights of the region. Bears, for those not initiated into the ghettoization of Western homosexuality, are the gay men who do not conform to "body fascist" stereotypes and flaunt the hair on their bodies and the ample meat on their bones. Or, as a friend said, "They are just gay men who have given up."

It was Ramadan 2010, almost the end of Islamic year 1431. The year 1432 would be momentous, but I didn't know it then. I was in Beirut to talk to the Lebanese about God and sex. My film, *A Jihad for Love*, was two years into its run. Our calculations, based on theatrical release in the US and Canada, a huge number of film festivals, good television ratings in countries like India, and thousands of DVD sales, added up to the film's reaching hundreds of thousands of people. I was traveling fast and furiously through twenty countries. Was this my fifteen minutes? The flood of journalists seeking interviews never seemed to cease. The highs had been many. And the fatwas came fast, as did the online hate. Our publicist had taught me well in the school of "there is no such thing as bad publicity."

Beirut was a city finding its feet after years of civil war. A month earlier an Egyptian feminist organization had organized a screening of the film in my beloved Cairo, but I had been unable to attend. So this was the first time I had shown up with my producer in an Arab capital. It was a big deal for me, like a major milestone had been crossed. Getting to Beirut as a servant-class Indian was quite the story.

It had taken months for the Middle East offices of a German non-profit foundation affiliated with the German Green Party to get me a visa. A proud, green card–carrying nonresident alien in the US, I still held an Indian passport. The women at the foundation were even asked by the Lebanese authorities to sign a guarantee that I would not marry a Lebanese woman in an effort to become a citizen. It was typical Lebanese racism toward people from my part of the world, who form a substantial chunk of the indentured-labor class for wealthy Beirutis. But they finally did stamp my passport. Getting to any other Arab country had never been a problem. I had innumerable Egyptian visas. But Egypt was a poor country that did not import its toilet cleaners from the Indian subcontinent. They were abundant in its own majority, living in wretched poverty. Egypt was the poorest of all Arab countries, but it had remained the cultural heart of the Arab world for centuries. Here in tiny Lebanon, there had always been a wealthy upper class composed of Christians and Muslims alike. The former, with many sub-sects, were almost the majority. The latter were equally sectarian, split between different schools of Sunni and Shia Islam.

Religion was always a complicated issue here. A perilous democratic structure had been formed after two decades of civil war. It was designed to placate all groups. Constitutionally, the president had to be a Christian and the prime minister had to be Sunni Muslim. The speaker of Parliament was always Shia. And then there was Hizbullah ("The Party of God or Allah") that wove into the power structure in complicated ways. For many of the Shia Lebanese, Hassan Nasrallah was a revered sheikh and freedom fighter. For the West, Nasrallah was a terrorist. I understood both sides of the argument, which put me in a tight spot with my Western colleagues.

In Beirut, I was joined by my Jewish producer, David. Like me, he encountered Lebanese border officials surprisingly examining passports at the boarding gate of the Beirut-bound flight while we were still in Frankfurt. Like mine, his passport needed to prove he'd never been to Israel. He'd been to Israel more times than anyone I knew. In any case, to me it was clear: I was entering a police state. I am sure the Iranian visa on my Indian passport did not go unnoticed and was probably a positive. Fortunately, David had always been smart enough to get his numerous Israeli entry and exit visas on separate pieces of paper—a luxury the equally paranoid Israelis offered at their equally aggressively policed borders. I would not know either way because Israel was never on my map of countries to visit. At the time, I was a proud supporter of the BDS (Boycott, Divest, Sanctions) movement against Israel—a panoply of boycotts that were intended to combat what many of my Facebook friends called "Israeli apartheid." David was excited to be in Beirut. I told him he was a masochist but respected his curiosity.

Within my first twenty hours in the country, I had walked past Beiruti graffiti featuring a Star of David with blood oozing from it. Equally without nuance was the hurriedly scrawled "Fuck the Jews" on a nearby wall. I prayed David missed it. Both of us were gay and proud of our Jewish-Muslim partnership.

We'd split up to do different things, as usual. David and I mostly met at screenings and our joint interviews. I had a Grindr date that night. Grindr, the gay hookup app, was blazing a trail on smartphones worldwide. Everyone seemed to know about it, and for the ultra-fashionable gay Beiruti men it was a must-have. The other popular hookup site, called Manjam, had not yet developed an app like Grindr that told you, right down to the number of feet, where a potential hookup waited. Its heterosexual equivalent, Tinder, was a while away.

Standing in the small lobby of our hotel, the Mayflower, I wondered if David had noticed the map on display. We didn't have an opportunity to discuss it. Perhaps neither of us wanted to. There it was: what I had often seen on many maps of the world in Islamic textbooks when growing up. Lebanon's neighboring country on this map was labeled Palestine and most of its newer Jewish cities, such as Tel Aviv, had been obliterated. Jerusalem was in bold with its Arabic name, Al Quds. There was Lebanon, there was Syria, even Jordan and Egypt, but the entire nation of Israel had been wiped off the face of this version of earth.

My Grindr hookup was getting closer. At 600 feet I told him I was coming down to receive him. Only hotel guests with room keys could ride the elevator.

He was a beautiful and muscular manimal with a perfectly groomed black beard and mustache. The sex was unbelievably good, and predictably he was a bottom, as all Arab men I had ever bedded were. We discussed Beirut, smoking our post-coital cigarettes. He said he would be happy to take me for a walk on the fabled Beirut corniche. I remembered it from a '60s Bollywood thriller called *Ankhen* ("Eyes"), which was set entirely in Beirut—a city that at the time was cinematically living up to its reputation as the "Paris of the East." The film had built a world of intrigue and glamor. I asked him if he had ever been to Dahieh.

I had spent time studying the geography of the ancient capital of this sliver of a country. Achrafieh, Hamra, and Dahieh were neighborhoods of this divided city, where the fault-lines of religious conflict ran deep. The first was a majority Christian district, the second a mix of all religions, and the last was Hizbullah-land. There was even a Beiruti West Village in Achrafieh's Sassine Square. That's where the artsy crowd hung about.

Four and a half million people of eighteen different sects sharing about 6,000 square miles would be a recipe for trouble anywhere. Did fifteen years of civil war change that?

"Can you take me there?" I asked.

He took several moments before replying, "Why? Are you curious about Hizbullah? Are you a journalist? Or some kind of spy?"

I assured him I was not and told him about the screenings of my film. I told him I hoped he could come.

"I am married with two children. I can't go to a film like this in public," he said. And then he dropped the bombshell: "I should tell you, because you seem like an honest guy. I actually go to Dahieh every day. I work for Sheikh Nasrallah. I help them with their Facebook and tweets and all that, because I am very good with computer stuff."

I had just hooked up with a member of Hizbullah. This was a first.

We continued talking. I told him how I had studied the extent of the support the organization had in Lebanon.

"A lot," he said.

I told him how I knew that even people in the government supported it as a legitimate resistance movement that had stood up to the Israeli army. He said he was proud and that it was a good fight. I asked him if they paid him well. He said it was enough to support his family of four. Like many anonymous tricks gay men hook up with, I had not even bothered to ask this trick his name.

"Rafik," he told me anyway. "Just like Hariri, our Sunni prime minister the Syrians killed in 2005."

I questioned him about the extent of Rafik's popularity.

"It was nothing compared to Nasrallah," he said.

I asked him if he knew that Hariri was once employed by the Saudis.

"Those Saudis, always fucking things up. You should see them in the summer here. Fucking everything in sight in the fancy hotels. Yes, I know Hariri made millions in Saudi. Everyone in Lebanon knows this."

I repeated my maxim to him: "One person's terrorist is another person's freedom fighter."

"Nowhere is it truer than it is here, Parvez," he said. "Look back at your own history in India. I am sure the British would have called the Indian freedom fighters, like even Gandhi, terrorists."

I could not disagree with that kind of logic. I liked Rafik and agreed to walk the corniche with him.

"So you are not Muslim?" he asked.

On Grindr Rafik had lamented the only way to get "uncut men" was by hooking up with an "Achrafieh Christian."

"I am Muslim. But Sunni," I replied.

"An uncut Muslim? How is this possible?"

"We Muslims come in all colors, shapes, and sizes, don't we, my friend?" I gingerly put my arm on his shoulder. Lighting a cigarette, he gently removed it. We walked some more. He was clear that he would not take me to Dahieh, because it would be too dangerous. He urged me to "maybe find a journalist type" who could take me. After the balmy Mediterranean breezes of our corniche walk-and-talk, Rafik and I exchanged emails and promised to stay in touch.

We didn't.

Later in the trip, I befriended a man called Mo, named after the Prophet like hundreds of thousands of Muslims. He was one of the few who fashionably shortened it this way. Western journalists covering this volatile region often used Mo as a fixer and he was a good one. I learned he was planning to marry his British Jewish girlfriend in Cyprus, a favored practice amongst many young wanting civil marriage. Interfaith marriage was like inviting trouble in this sectarian state. Thus many young couples ended up in Cyprus and the government looked the other way.

"We inherited this religious system—we didn't choose it," said Mo.

So much here seemed oddly familiar to notions I had grown up with. One of the young pro-Palestine activists who organized the film screenings introduced me to her buff gym-trainer friend, Bassam. He commuted to Hamra daily from the Bekaa Valley. Distance didn't mean much in such a tiny country. He told me he kept a secret apartment in downtown Beirut for weekend sexual trysts, "with girls so beautiful you cannot even imagine it!" This suggested money. Almost sensing my thought, he said his family was one of the richest contractors in the region. He told me that the only *halal* ("permissible") form of intercourse was anal, because the hymen remained intact. And the hymen has always remained that most-prized virtue amongst the believers, both Christian and Muslim.

He told me about his girlfriend studying in Cairo. "I promise you I have never touched her," he said. "She is the woman I am going to marry." This was Arab hypocrisy on full display.

"You can butt-fuck all the women who are available," said Bassam. "But you only marry a virgin." I remember being offended by his poor word choice.

As a woman, if you had made the mistake of allowing a man to deflower you vaginally, there was a solution. Vaginal reconstructive surgery thrived in the region. Traditional Arab women got most respectability when they were married into a "good family" and hopefully reproduced. The Arab matriarch is an all-powerful ruler of the household. To her, the son will always present a virgin. My mother would have expected nothing less.

It was 1 a.m. When I left India a decade ago, I thought I had left the polytheism of the Hindus with their 10 million gods behind me. But as I walked into the cavernous confines of the "only gay" nightclub in the Arab Middle East, the Hindu form of the God Shiva doing his tantric dance to shake up the universe seemed to have followed me. Beirut was expensive. I paid $20 (US dollars are circulated as a parallel currency in Lebanon) to get in. The club was inexplicably called Acid. I saw the Nataraj statue immediately. He loomed behind an impossibly long bar. Right below him a sign proclaimed, "Open Bar till 5 a.m."

I looked around. There was erotic-looking, Khajuraho-like kitsch—probably plastic sculptures—on an enormous wall. I wondered why this bar's design was so influenced by Hindu iconography from the erotic temples of Madhya Pradesh. Everyone said it was just the way it had always been.

"It is Ramadan and that is why it is not so crowded," Babak said. He leaned in to be heard over the blaring techno remix of the popular Egyptian song, "Habibi Nour el-Ain."

"If it was not for all the fasting and no-sex rules at this time, otherwise you could not move here at this hour." Babak said he had recently invited an "opportunistic" *New York Times* reporter to this bar to take pictures for what he called a "horrible and lying article." The piece claimed Beirut was "the Provincetown of the Middle East." Local gay activists I met were unanimously furious about the piece. In truth this police state and Beirut had a long way to go in all possible realms of civil rights.

Babak told me he was half-Armenian and half-Palestinian. "Therefore, I am fucked from both sides," he said. This was true. The Lebanese, it was said, gave equal hate time to both those ethnicities.

Later we stood outside Acid, sharing a cigarette, and Babak looked at what closely resembled a Hummer pulling up.

"That's a gay Saudi prince," he informed me. I had no way of confirming this, but the tags on the car did have the Saudi flag. "He comes here sometimes to pick up boys. Everyone knows." Babak stated this like well-established fact.

A short, pot-bellied man got out of the car, surrounded by a posse of either security guards or sexual conquests. They walked confidently to the entrance and the bouncer bowed obsequiously, allowing them in for free. It looked like they'd been here before. I stared. I thought of my favorites, the Kardashians, filmed entering nightclubs. "Fag time," said one boy loudly, lighting a cigarette. He had already been introduced to me at a gay bar called Bardo we had visited earlier that night, where he seemed to be the belle of the ball. He flashed his many bracelets at me, including one that read, "I Heart Beirut," stylized like the "I Heart New York" shirts.

"Barbie!" I hugged him. This magical creature of the night could be anything; more Barbie-like than Ken or perhaps a combo of both, in the shortest shorts I'd ever seen and a thick layer of mascara. He posed flamboyantly for my phone and stuck his ass out right in the street. A passing driver whistled.

Babak pointed at the hills that rose above Acid. "There's the Haftoor Grand Hotel. All the journalists were staying there as Israel was bombing us in 2006." With a flourish he swiped his arm down to point at the shimmering valley of lights below. "And that is Dahieh." Babak didn't know how keen I was to go there, to Hizbullah-land. I didn't bring it up since he was a Christian. He told me how Israel bombed Dahieh to rubble. The journalists at the Haftoor had front-row seats.

"The gays did not stop dancing even one night here at Acid during the entire war," said Babak. "Israel's drones soared across the sky and cluster bombs fell right down there in Dahieh. These guys were dancing to techno trance through the whole fucking mess."

"Bless the un-bombable gays," I said. We both laughed.

I considered titles for future op-eds I never wrote. I landed on "Love in the Time of Ramadan." I took notes on my phone as I'd always done in my travels with *A Jihad for Love*. It had only been a few hours since I was in bed with Rafik, and here, outside Acid, I was discovering the unsettling geography of this contested capital.

"Did you ever see *Men of Israel*?" asked Babak as he drove me on another gay bar–hopping night.

"No, what is it?" I replied. "Sounds suspicious."

"It's the hottest porn of these sexy Jewish men. I am sure the Israeli government must have funded it!" he joked, alluding to what gay activists call "pink-washing." With his reliable sarcasm, Babak said I would be a much richer man if I decided to be a porn filmmaker.

It was through Babak that I learned a little more about pink-washing in some of the most contested real estate on the planet. He, in his own unique "non-activisty" way, was trying to build an Arab alternative for "detested" Tel-Aviv. Pink-washing was the term used by many gay activists to refer to the deliberate stance of the Israeli government in claiming Israel was the only country in the region to support gay rights. Tourist agents published entire brochures highlighting how the sun and the sand, the gay bars and the nightlife in cities like Tel Aviv, made Israel a *chosen* destination—a haven for gay tourists eager to sample hedonistic Mediterranean life.

"There's a ninety-million-dollar budget available to push the gay Israel agenda," claimed Hassam, another gay activist I met in Beirut. "This is one of their real government programs to avoid discussions about Israeli apartheid against Palestinians, and to deflect attention away from the occupation." Other activists argued that Israel was a far cry from a gay paradise. Gay Pride marchers were routinely attacked and vilified in cities such as Jerusalem, where the ultra-Orthodox Jews proliferated their homophobic intolerance just as they did in their illegal settlements.

The public argument I made in interviews I gave in Beirut was simple: Nothing but homophobia could make Israel's chief Sephardic rabbi and two other chief rabbis; the heads of the Roman Catholic, Armenian, and Greek Orthodox churches; and three senior Jerusalem imams sit together at the same table as they did in 2005 in a famous *New York Times* cover picture. These otherwise bitterly divided religious figures made probably their only public appearance together to protest that year's ten-day Jerusalem World Pride Festival that would include a Pride Parade. During the parade, it was an ultra-Orthodox Haredi Jew who stabbed three marchers with a sharp kitchen knife. His name was Yishai Schlissel.

During a police interrogation, he described the motive behind his actions: "I came to murder on behalf of God. We can't have such abomination in the country." He was practically speaking like a Wahhabi cleric. Wahhabi Islam is the ultra puritanical form of Islam in Saudi Arabia, with much influence in the rest of the Muslim world. Claims have been made that in Saudi Arabia Wahhabis are a minority. I disagree.

As I told a journalist at the time, this is what happened in my own India when religious Hindus and Muslims united publicly against lifting the gay "ban" in Article 377 of the Indian penal code. This article made "sodomy," "carnal intercourse against the order of nature," and "bestiality" part of a punishable list.

"Nothing better than a good old-fashioned round of gay-bashing to bring the Hindus and Muslims together," I told him, trying to explain the similarities. This was because Lebanon had its own 377 in Article 534 of its penal code.

I hung out with members of the openly gay group Helem, funded mostly by European nonprofits. Like Istanbul, Beirut served as a waiting room for Middle Eastern gays seeking asylum in the West. Helem helped them to navigate a complex Lebanese bureaucracy for temporary visas.

Although islands of tolerance like Acid existed in Beirut, nobody was waving rainbow flags from their apartment windows.

There was always the danger of government crackdowns. Local activists told me of retrogressive practices like rectal exams, which were common for men detained for "unnatural behavior." Hardly a Provincetown, I thought to myself.

At the Turkish-style bathhouse Hammam al Agha, a lot of cruising was going on. In just a few years it would be raided. The anal-probes of the men arrested at the Plaza Cinema for "unnatural behavior" were soon to return. Helem was taking a strong stance on the freedoms that had not yet arrived constitutionally, religiously, or socially. There was no San Francisco–style Castro Street or New York's Chelsea neighborhood to be found in Beirut. The activists at Helem were right about their perilous freedoms. Later, I gave them a bunch of unmarked DVDs of my film. They said some of them traveled regularly to Damascus, Aleppo, and Amman and would make sure the DVDs ended up in "the right hands." I was thrilled—I had successfully managed to send DVDs of my contraband film to many Muslim countries including Pakistan, Iran, and Saudi Arabia. And there would be many more.

Fouad, a Palestinian-American writer and activist, invited me to a raucous party at his apartment in the Christian enclave of Achrafieh. He worked for the US-based pro-Palestine website "Electronic Intifada." There I met fixers and filmmakers, correspondents and bankers—even a sixty-year-old former soprano. They drank, smoked hashish, and talked all night. I participated in the drinking but not the smoking. My one experience with hash as a younger man had left me paralyzed with paranoia. A twenty-something French woman performed an architectural analysis on Beirut's downtown. She described it as plastic and soulless. It had been commissioned by the billionaire former Prime Minister of Lebanon Rafik Hariri.

We lingered on the balcony of the apartment. I rested my arm on a ledge and noticed that it was riddled with bullet holes.

"Bullets in Beirut," I said.

"Par for the course," she replied.

At 2 a.m., no one showed any signs of leaving. Sensing my exhaustion, the host's sister, Sayida, approached us. She worked with Palestinian refugees in Lebanon.

"Don't worry," she said. "This is normal. In Beirut we always party like it is the apocalypse tomorrow. You need another drink." At the time I still drank alcohol. Most of the Muslims I knew also imbibed. I didn't know it then but total sobriety lay in my not-so-distant future.

"Right now there are Israeli drones above us," she continued. The fatalism of the Beirutis was familiar by now. Even if some or maybe all of the people at this party were not religious, they seemed to share the idea that "the end of days" was always just over your shoulder.

My Saudi friend Adham texted me one day while I was in Beirut. I had met him at an *A Jihad for Love* screening in Toronto in 2007. Since then we'd become great texting buddies. He lived in Jeddah, but the frequency of our correspondence meant he never seemed far away. "Only you know," he had once said to me about his attraction to both men and women.

"Did you see this?" It was a link to an English-language Arab weekly called *Egypt Today,* read mostly by expats in Cairo. It was from 2008. Moez Masoud, a young Egyptian *daa'y* (caller to Islam) and media expert who had studied under the grand mufti of Egypt, Ali Gomaa, was quoted in this article about my film:

> The [documentary] is correct in its use of the term of jihad but defines it incorrectly. When people who have homoerotic desires struggle against their inclinations, they are struggling against an act that satisfies their physical body but is against their spiritual self . . . jihad is to struggle in the cause of good. It's a struggle for the sake of goodness, beauty, justice, and truth. Homoerotic activity is not a manifestation of these universal principles; it's a violation of them and is in antithesis to the spiritual dimension. I love the title [of the movie] but when defined differently. We need to have jihad against extremism in society so we can learn to love the sinning person that is struggling, even though we hate their sin. And so, I too, call for a "jihad for love."

Although he was not ready to welcome gays into the religion with open arms, it felt like Masoud was meeting me halfway.

"LOL!" I texted back, "He is calling for a jihad for love! Like really?! Anyway, why are you sending me such an old link?"

"I was googling you! I love Beirut btw. Kiss it frm me."

Adham and I texted almost daily. Over the years we have physically only met a few times, but I count him as one of my closest friends. There is practically nothing I have not told him. Just a few days after the Egypt protests—which I reported on extensively—erupted, I asked him rhetorically if revolution was coming to Riyadh. He had texted back, "Are you kidding me? Parvez, unlike the Egyptians, the Tunisians, the Egyptians, and others who may follow, we Saudis just don't suffer enough." At the time, I thought that was a very succinct way to address a fairly complicated question. He continued, "It's always been Al Saud. It will always be Al Saud."

Over the years, just like mine, Adham's life changed. Just months before my Beirut schlep he acquired a fiancée. My friendship with the bisexual Adham is unusual, and I never asked if he had ever acted on his desires. He would never reveal it to his family. It was cultural. I understood because I grew up in small-town India. I have never dared to say the three words to my dad—I am gay. For Muslims like Adham and me, as far as family was concerned, it was "don't ask, don't tell," which suited all parties.

In that 2010 Beirut winter, Adham, as always, was a daily presence in my life. By extension it seemed that Saudi Arabia itself was a daily presence as well. The #Jan25 hashtag was still not the most-used on the planet, and even Tunisia was a few weeks away, but there "seems to be some unease here, I don't know why," he once texted me from a Dunkin' Donuts in Jeddah, a popular cruising area for gay men. I wondered how long Adham could sustain all the charades, but I refrained from upsetting him.

Adham's engagement to Zubeida, a second cousin, was "arranged" by his pious mother, in a practice familiar to all Muslims. Surprisingly, the two are still not married. Zubeida and Adham only met when she visited family in Jeddah or when he went to Riyadh. Meeting itself was a complex negotiation because of Wahhabi views against *ikhtilat* (gender mixing), which was reliably the most explosive subject in the kingdom.

Zubeida attended Thursday Quran-study circles. The Prophet, it is said, called them "Halaqah." Religious as she was, Zubeida was completing a PhD at the Princess Nora University in Riyadh, where her family lived. Opened a few months after bin Laden's death, PNU, as the Saudis called it, was the largest and "most modern" female university in the world, they boasted. At its opening, King Abdullah and other male dignitaries sat in a mixed-company room with women whose faces were uncovered. The clerics were furious. But Abdullah stood his ground. And yet in 2012 this same king introduced a system whereby husbands were "informed" on SMS when their wives or children were leaving the country.

PNU's campus was proof of the country's need for good architects, beyond those supplied by the bin Laden family. This was a tasteless marble, glass, granite, and central air structure. Women would enter wearing ordinary sneakers; their *abayas* when taken off would expose heavily made-up faces and stilettos. An abaya is a baggy black sack that covers every inch of a woman's body. Some abaya-clad women, like a female *mutawa* (religious police), will also cover their feet with socks and wear black gloves.

There is much erotic power in covered female flesh. A good example is Rita Hayworth's one-gloved striptease, singing, "Put the blame on Mame" as Gilda in the 1946 Hollywood noir of the same name. It lives forever in YouTube fame. Just in the act of taking off her glove, Hayworth becomes hypersexualized, with every straight man in that Buenos Aires nightclub mentally undressing her. A woman in an abaya or other styles of veiling is also a hypersexualized entity. A carefully revealed ankle, when the mutaween are not looking, is enough to stir lust. There is nothing more threatening than a sliver of female hair or ankle to the discipline of the male armies of the devout, in conservative Muslim minds, such as the duplicitous enforcers of morality in Saudi Arabia—the mutaween.

Adham often probes to determine whether Zubeida has a mind of her own. About the ruling Sauds, she had said, "We don't talk about these things. But in my opinion our king is from God's will. He listens to us."

Were women like Zubeida the majority? Never challenging the status quo? Did they truly believe that if they held the hand of their mahram (a male guardian from within her direct family) they could achieve stellar education and careers?

I asked Adham when the wedding was. I was eager to attend. He said it would be a while yet because "PhD students take forever." I gasped when I learned what her thesis was: "Sharia in the twenty-first century." This "super-pious" woman entering an "arranged marriage" with her closeted bisexual fiancé was certainly obeying the absolute command to exercise intellect that lay at the very birth of the Quran. Muhammad, its vessel of revelation, was illiterate, after all, a condition Zubeida would clearly not tolerate.

"I would die to read her thesis," I said to Adham.

"ISA I will send it to you when she is finally done." He was using the shorthand for everyday Arab terms as Muslims often do. An ISA is *Inshallah* ("If God wills").

"I understand why your shameless Saudis love to summer here," I texted Adham. The more I walked its streets the more I loved the city. I felt that, except for my beloved Istanbul, Beirut was the most cosmopolitan Muslim environment I had ever experienced, though many Beirutis would be offended at the characterization of their city as Muslim. It recalled the openness that I imagined permeated Muslim societies during centuries of Ottoman rule. As I left a café locals called "Facebook," with an exact replica of a "like" as its prominently displayed sign, a writer friend informed me, "I think this may be the only café called 'Facebook' in the world."

In central Beirut, a few hours after Adham had texted me about Zubeida's surely fiery PhD topic, one of two evening screenings for my film was held in a fashionable café-turned-screening-room. It was packed to the rafters. The post-film question-and-answer session went on for at least an hour, probably more. I tried to be witty, saying, "Clearly Hizbullah were not invited to this." Just a few nervous laughs. This was complicated territory and jokes about this audience's fellow inhabitants were not welcome. I was learning fast and my mind kept on drifting to Adham's revelation about Zubeida's thesis.

An audience member spoke up. "Why are these people in your film so religious? In Lebanese culture religion traumatizing gay people like this is unheard of."

I responded, "Thanks. That's an interesting way to look at the film. I hope the film answered your question? I always hope that the film speaks for itself, better than even I can." She persisted and I said, "Maybe things will change? These days we even have Saudi women doing PhDs!" Raucous laughter. I didn't offer the stock Islam 101–style responses I used with Western audiences. I was being hypocritical. I avoided a discussion I would have welcomed in any other country. This was probably because I didn't know enough about how religion lived in the twenty-first century Beiruti environment. I already knew well the history of religion's role as the deep-est possible divide in this civil war–torn country. But I hadn't really taken up the opportunity for any contemporary religious discussion with anyone, even Rafik, for example, that night we walked on the corniche.

Post-screening, Aisha, a butch lesbian activist, told me, "I loved it! In any case, how much of Beirut have you seen? Will you allow me to be a guide to something no tourist gets to see?" I took up her offer and we arranged to meet at noon at my hotel the next day.

"I have been waking up late, I must confess," I said to her. "This is such a city of the night."

What I didn't tell her was that one of the reasons I couldn't meet early was that my hookup the previous night had deprived me of sleep. He was a tongue-tied Saudi Grindr trick who called himself Ahmad. I always wanted to know something about the person I was hooking up with, so there was some semblance of honesty in a purely sexual encounter neither of us would probably tell anyone about. Few people realize the enormity of promiscuity amongst gay men compared to other sexualities and genders.

Ahmad was ready to cancel when I told him about my film. "I don't want to be interviewed about all this, man," he texted. I told him he had nothing to fear because the film had already been made. He traveled fre-quently from Jeddah to Beirut for a financial group he said he worked for. As he left that night I gave him an unlabeled DVD of the film. I used to do this often, sending DVDs through friends (and in this case a trick!) going back to Muslim countries, where the film could never be seen officially. Two years before I came to Beirut, a Dubai gay friend of mine, Salman, whom I met at American University when I was a professor and student there, emailed and said he had been to Lahore in Pakistan and seen pirated DVDs of the film being sold on the streets of the bustling Anarkali market. Salman had already made many copies for friends in and around Dubai and once organized a private screening in his living room. It was an "Underground Railroad" of distribution I was trying to build, without actually putting the film on YouTube.

I had already added Aisha as a Facebook friend when we met the next morning. She took me on a tour of the subversive graffiti that lined the walls that had once delineated the outer boundaries of the city and the beginning of its Armenian quarters. One said "Berlin" in Arabic, allud-ing to that city's divisive wall. Snow White brandished a Kalashnikov in another with the words "Say no to Lookism" in English spray-painted next to her. *But why the gun?* I thought to myself.

"That is about the obsession of the Lebanese for boob jobs, tummy tucks, liposuction, and general desire to be flashy and beautiful all the time," she explained with obvious disgust.

Aisha also told me that both Lebanese sexes were also obsessed with nose jobs. I found a lot of Lookism graffiti. Right next to it, some of Hizbullah's rallying cries were displayed in beautiful Arabic calligraphy. "God let us meet Husayn in the afterlife," it said, referring to one of the most revered Shia imams and the Prophet's grandson. For Shias, Husayn was the second caliph, right after Ali. For Sunnis, the second caliph after Ali was Abu Bakr. And in this deceptively simple fact about Muhammad's lineage and succession lay the beginning of a sectarian Islam bloodily divided into Shia and Sunni. As I studied the Hizbullah graffiti on this wall, I was reminded that there was nothing simple about this deep divide that had finessed into two essentially separate religions in the centuries following the Prophet's death.

"I hate them," Aisha said, breaking my reverie as she referred to Hizbullah.

I had always been fascinated by graffiti in the bathrooms and streets of foreign cities. For me, the graffiti were always an indicator to how a society actually lived. I felt unique access to the minds of the city's individuals whenever I studied the graffiti.

We drove down 22 November Avenue, and Aisha pointed to what she called "the Horsh." The Horsh El Snoubar was a legendary park the Israelis had bombed to smithereens in 1982.

"For reasons we Beirutis have never understood," said Aisha. "It was always locked up since I was a child." This park had been off-limits to mostly everyone for almost twenty-five years, even though it had been reconstructed after the fifteen-year-long Lebanese Civil War ended in 1990. Aisha told me that Beirutis wanting to visit the park had to apply for special permits, and that it was apparently easier for Western tourists to get in.

"This is very strange," I told her. "A locked-up park? But let me tell you that in Manhattan we, too, have a locked-up park called Gramercy Park. It's only for residents who live around it."

"This is not like that," Aisha said, adding it was just one of the things that made Beirut mysterious and inexplicable. "Look there. It's a Russian prostitute." She pointed to a Caucasian woman in a tight-fitting dress and stilettos. "This has now become a popular place to pick them up," she said. I wondered what treasures lay inside the Horsh's boundaries that made it so special.

"Do you know that you are named after the Prophet's favorite wife?" I asked, changing the subject.

"Of course I know. Though I don't know if all Muslims would agree with you," she replied. Aisha's legacy has not escaped Islamic sectarianism.

As we drove I learned more about her. She had a girlfriend in Damascus, and it was often hard to visit. Syria's role in the civil war and the continuing "interference" into Lebanon's affairs was well-established fact. Aisha was part of the population that had not lived the civil war and probably thought of Syria differently from the way her parents did. Aisha's father was Syrian Alawite, like Syria's tenacious dictator Bashar al-Assad, and her mother was Lebanese Shia. The Alawites are considered a sect of Shia Islam. The al-Assad family that ruled Syria would soon face a state of chaos, unprecedented in its history. Aisha seemed to hint about it. She was a frequent blogger and wrote about regional issues. She must have been privy to knowledge I didn't have as an outsider, even though I prided myself with how hard I worked to be up to date with events in the region.

"Things are changing very fast here," she said cryptically. "If you follow all the blogs and news as I do, I think it's like a time bomb waiting to explode."

The latter sentence I had said every single time I had been to Cairo in the past several years. And at this time, the explosion was mere months away. I asked her if she was talking about the more general Middle East.

"Yes," she said. "For example, you could make the argument that Bashar al-Assad's days are numbered."

I was surprised. Assad seemed so solid and even a voice of secular pluralism in my mind. I would be proved more than wrong.

"Nothing here is stable anymore," she continued. "If you heard the talk on the streets of Damascus like my girlfriend does, you would wonder. She is also deeply thinking about politics all the time, like me. She, too, has a blog. But mark my words—nothing in Syria or anywhere else in this region is ever going to be the same old acceptable way again. And the whole world will be shocked."

At my second screening I met Safa, a Christian who was a longtime resident of the place I had been dying to visit: Hassan Nasrallah's fiefdom, the Shia suburb of Dahieh. In a less surreal city, a Christian woman like her, not dressed with Islamic modesty and living in a deeply conservative neighborhood, would not be possible. But Beirut surprised me at every turn. I told her how everyone seemed afraid to take me.

"I will take you," she said. "Just Facebook me and we will make a plan."

A day later, Safa and I sat in her Toyota Landcruiser. "Big family," she explained.

Dahieh's sprawl was less posh than either Hamra or Achrafieh. Shabby, bombed-out apartments in various stages of construction and destruction piled atop each other. Clothing hung out in the alleys to dry. We were completely immobilized by the traffic. There was a lot of graffiti and the familiar yellow Hizbullah flags. I recognized the logo. I told Safa what I knew about it, because the Iranian religious police, the Basij, had similar flags that I had seen in my one-and-only trip to Tehran.

Around twenty-five, I told Safa, while still working briefly as a reporter for a news aggregator, I had been to "Shia-central" Tehran for two nights to do a story about the Fajr Film Festival. It was my first foreign trip ever, and I found Tehran to be a Delhi-like (albeit with mountains), very polluted, and traffic-logged city. Nowhere in the world is there greater reverence for Imam Husayn than in Tehran. The non-pictorially averse Shia made sure his murals abounded. Mayors of the city (Ahmadinejad used to be one) had repeatedly said there never could be enough murals of *shaheeds* ("martyrs"), Ayatollah Khomeini, and even Islamic events on all possible walls. The Iran-Iraq war was a still recent memory.

I had passed a cemetery called Behesht e-Zahra and my cab driver allowed us to shoot. Dressed in all black chadors, groups of women stood lamenting around graves unlike any I had ever seen—each had been built with a framed photograph of the dead "martyr" and these huddles of black scarecrows wept. It seemed like they were worshipping them. Is this what made them so undesirable to Sunnis?

Safa's voice broke my Iran story. "Where do they all have to go? Have you ever seen traffic like this? This whole country is a fucking prison anyway," she said while honking loudly at a swerving motorbike that was zipping through the snarl and almost hit us. Nothing but this dude was able to move, it seemed.

Safa and I started chatting about the Hizbullah logo. It was bright yellow with elegant calligraphy saying *Hizb-Allah* ("The Party of God") in Kufi-style script. The first Arabic letter, Alif of the Allah, rose up to hold an AK-47. It was a clever design because it depicted this political party well. Some versions of the logo boasted a sword, a globe, a book, and what looked like a branch of a tree. The text above was from Surah 5 of the Quran, which said, "Surely the party of Allah are they that shall emerge triumphant." Underneath the logo were the words that identified the movement: "The Islamic Resistance in Lebanon."

Safa was impressed with my knowledge. "Did you know it comes in other colors, too?" she asked. I said I didn't, but then we passed a green-on-black version.

"See those?" she said. I spotted an unusual English green-on-yellow flag that said, "Our Blood Has Won."

"I guess that refers to the 2006 Israeli bombings?"

Safa nodded. She was not wearing a headscarf. "Don't worry, they don't bother me," she'd said. "Hizbullah has eyes everywhere. They know exactly who I am."

Her tank top and jeans in Lebanon's arguably most religious neighborhood seemed like a deliberate act of defiance. I said as much. She said, "I dress like this every day. I live here. Why should I change?"

Hasty rebuilding was evident in many unpainted brick walls. She said Iranian money had made Dahieh "rise up like a phoenix" virtually overnight after the ceasefire. I already knew that Hizbullah had come to be seen as a viable and necessary resistance even by Christian youth in 2006, which she confirmed. I told her how India's ultra-Hindu right wing had a similar "organization" called the RSS. They made themselves indispensable after tragedies and natural disasters to gain more followers.

"Nothing brings the Lebanese together more than our hatred for Israel," she said.

I noticed the empty streets. Safa said, "It's Ramadan. Everyone is sleeping at home. You should see it at night when all the *fanoos* are lit up and the food stalls fill the streets."

I had grown up with a rich Ramadan nightlife. And I had been in Cairo one Ramadan to see the pretty, festooned lanterns called fanoos light up festive alleys and homes. While the daytime rigor of Ramadan was an absolute, the nights of the month were a pan-Muslim version of the

American holiday season, building up to Eid al-Fitr, the Muslim Christmas. After a month of abstinence-filled piety, it was the most joyous of festivals. I remembered it fondly as a time of gifts and ice cream. For adults, it importantly meant the return of a sex life. My Ramadan 1431 Beiruti Grindr hookups must surely have assigned me a very special place in hell, reserved for the worst sinners.

"Oh, I thought that they only have fanoos in Cairo. And how do you eat during the day as a Christian in this part of the city?" I asked.

"Egypt is not that far, so there are fanoos everywhere. Eating—it's simple. Just don't do it in public."

Safa pulled up in a corner. "Let's wait a few minutes and let them all go in to their mosques," she said. She was not particularly drawn to religious ritual. She had informed me as much when we first met.

"This reminds me of a slightly cleaner version of Manshiyat Nasser," I said, referring to one of Cairo's largest slums, also known as "garbage city."

"That's totally not fair, Parvez," she said. "I have been to Cairo. This is heaven compared to that dump!" In hindsight and after visiting Manshiyat several times after, I realize she was right. Hizbullah-land could be compared to typical middle-class suburbs from Delhi to Cairo. A conspicuous difference was the Hizbullah flags and the unctuousness of countless printed odes to "martyrs," with their prominently placed pictures.

As everywhere else in the Shia world, and much like the Behesht-e Zahra cemetery in Tehran, the representation of the face of a shaheed was of extreme importance. We drove past murals of Ayatollah Khomeini, father of the Iranian revolution, and Hassan Nasrallah, Hizbullah Chief. I refrained from comment. I didn't know then that I would be in a land of unmarked graves in less than a year. The Shia had no problems with idolatry. The only worship that seemed to be allowed in the land of the Wahhabis, I would soon discover, were visages of the king and other prominent royal family members always waving and smiling benignly at the populace. These murals were accompanied by florid and obsequious Arabic. Unlike Saudi Arabia, Lebanon had no problem displaying countless faces of martyrdom. Beirut felt like a schizophrenic city and that's why I fell in love with it.

The call to Zuhr (early afternoon) prayers began from mosques across Dahieh. I was silent.

"You won't pray?" Safa asked jokingly. "Everyone in your film is doing it all the time."

I paused. "These will all be Shia mosques. I am forbidden in them," I replied, not knowing at the time how very closely the Shia and I would be aligned in just a few months.

We were in what looked like an ordinary residential alley. A mangled tangle of power lines and air conditioners perched precariously above most windows. Jumping out of the car, Safa directed my attention to a nondescript two-story building. Its only ornamentation were two more pervasive Hizbullah flags.

"So that there is the Media Relations Department of Hizbullah," she said gesturing. I took a photo of the street sign.

"No way," she said. "You don't do that here. Major trouble."

She said she had a chatty friend there called Ibrahim Mousawi, who, I learned later, was the head of that department in the well-oiled machine that was Hizbullah. "He is the best gossip ever and knows everything that is going on," she said. Asking her how and why she knew someone in Hizbullah bureaucracy seemed inappropriate. But I noted down our location on my phone in any case. We were on Bir al-Abed street. (In Dahieh, street signs were mostly in Arabic. In many other parts of Beirut, they were in Arabic and French).

"If you want to ever pay them a visit, just ask any taxi in Dahieh about the Fawaz Building. They will know immediately," she said, drawing a smiley face in the air. "Who knows? You might one day want to make a film about the soldiers of the Party of God." She laughed.

Safa then brought me to the strangest place I had ever seen: a Hizbullah gift shop! All around us, in every conceivable form, lay what I could only describe as Hizbullah kitsch. "It is a Hizbullah memento store," laughed Safa. I could have spent an hour or more there.

Shia icons of the "Made in China" cheap plastic kind were neatly laid out. "Wow, these guys are smart! People in China are actually employed to make coffee mugs with Nasrallah's mug on them! This could be a global Shia franchise!" I said. I was delighted and couldn't resist posting a photo of a Nasrallah coffee mug for a Facebook status update. I captioned it, "If you had told me that I would be standing in a Hizbullah souvenir store in Southern Beirut, I would have said you are crazy." I posted another photo of a T-shirt saying, "I heart [Hizbullah logo]."

Both Keith and I were eager purveyors of kitsch. Just like graffiti, I feel kitsch offers me some unvarnished insight into a society. I had gathered a significant amount in my travels across Muslim countries, but this beat everything. The yellow T-shirts with the green Hizbullah sign stopped at medium. I should have bought more for my many Jewish friends in New York who shared my dark sense of humor. I bought yellow Hizbullah keychains. I bought two coffee mugs with waving Khomeini and Nasrallah pictures on them. I bought pens and miniature Iran and Hizbullah flags on pedestals. The swag was endless. I got all manner of Hizbullah tchotchkes, even a battery-powered cheap glass knickknack featuring the Hizbullah logo that glowed a lurid green when turned on. I wondered how the shop could remain unshuttered during prayer time, but clearly for this store owner capitalism trumped religion. He did not accept credit cards. Only cash. And then, too, only the almighty US dollar.

After shopping, I told Safa, "Why don't I send your buddy Mousawi an email saying I am a freelance journalist doing a story about Beirut and want to write about all the different parts of the city. Harmless, right?"

Safa gave me his direct email address. Standing there a few feet away from the office itself, I sent him an email, calling myself a freelance journalist from India. I was asking for what was probably the unthinkable—an interview with Hassan Nasrallah. It would stay away from "political matters" and discuss the "reconstruction and modernization of Dahieh," I said. I did not—this was important—identify myself as a permanent resident of the US. If I got permission, I would probably be blindfolded and an Indian passport would help with the many checkpoints. Where was he living in this sprawling suburb, anyway? Was that a question that perennially remained unanswered for even the most-seasoned Mossad agents surely embedded here in Dahieh?

Safa and I bid goodbye when she dropped me outside the Le Commodore Hotel, where I was to meet a journalist at the Benihana restaurant. Over sushi and sake, which the flashy Lebanese seem to covet way more than their own delicious and abundant local cuisine, the culture critic of the pro-Hizbullah and leading leftist newspaper *Al-Akhbar* peppered me with questions about the documentary and why I did not film in Lebanon.

"You Beirutis are not religious enough," I laughed as he took notes. He told me why he had to move back to this "troubled land of [his] birth" from London, giving up a high-paying job with the Saudi-owned *Al-Hayat* newspaper. He could no longer stand its pro-Saudi politics. He said as he grew older the "Beirut in [his] heart" called him back. He told me the feeling of the apocalypse I experienced at Fouad's party was a permanent Beiruti emotion. The civil war and the presence of Hizbullah, which led to the frequent Israeli bombings, were two examples of why the city was "fascinating." I agreed, telling him I had felt at the edge of some abyss since I arrived. He offered to take me to a well-known bookstore on the main Hamra drag. I said I had just been shopping at the "Hizbullah Store" in Dahieh. I showed him my purchases. He gawked and hurriedly asked me to put them away. Clearly, Beirutis did not want to acknowledge their militant fellow citizens.

"I know this won't give me an easy time if US customs decides to examine my checked baggage, but I like danger and thrive on it," I said. The article that appeared prominently placed my account of my visit to Dahieh. At the time, while I still had several days left in the country, it troubled me.

Later I met up with two new pals, party host Fouad and Mo the fixer, who helped Western journalists covering this volatile region, at a popular Hamra hangout called Café Younus. They had a symbiotic relationship. Mo gave Fouad story ideas and the latter got him fixer jobs. Fouad was obviously an American, but he was searching for his Palestinian identity. Lebanon was the closest he could ever get to his ancestors' homeland. Israel would never let him in because of his inflammatory writing.

Mo was super-connected with all things Beiruti, including the local politics and Hizbullah's antics within that constantly changing realm. Beirut was competing with Cairo in becoming a haven for reporters on the Mideast beat. In just three months everything would change. Both Fouad and Mo barely made enough to survive in this expensive town. But rents in the areas they lived were still cheap. Writing for *Electronic Intifada* was not a monetary pursuit, so Fouad had started writing for the *Guardian Online* and other paying sites. I had written for them too. I happily shared my other contacts, while telling him how, post-film, I too was unemployed.

"Maybe you can become a reporter for *Al-Manar*!" laughed Mo. *Al-Manar* (*The Beacon*) was the Hizbullah-run television channel banned in most Western countries. In my hotel room, all it ever seemed to broadcast were Hassan Nasrallah's speeches. He laughed when I told him they put me to sleep. I reminded Fouad of a promise he had made at the party.

The next morning, we made a motley crew: Fouad, Mo, and I, with my trusty SLR hanging around my neck, disembarked near the lower-middle-class neighborhood of Sabra, which borders the abjectly poor Shatila, a slum to most of the Beirutis we had hung out with. It felt like a pilgrimage because it might be the closest I would get to the Israeli-Palestinian conflict. The area was home to the world's largest concentration of Palestinian refugees. Fouad advised me to put the camera away in my backpack.

"I don't want to remember this experience as poverty porn," I told them. "When we were in Rio, they had guided tours through the favelas and I refused to go. So you are probably right, Fouad."

The residents were wary of cameras and journalists. This was a very volatile place where politics and poverty were intertwined. Another ticking time bomb, I thought to myself. The Maronite Christian Phalange party, cheered on by the Israeli Defense Forces (IDF), had hunted and killed Palestinians in the little alleyways of Shatila in the eighties. The Lebanese civil war was on then and every neighboring country, especially Israel, had taken sides. Fouad first took us past what he called "the wall of death," where he said men had been lined up and executed in cold blood by the Israel-supported Phalangists.

"There are many such walls. They killed more than three thousand people here. My people. Yasser Arafat and the PLO (Palestine Liberation Organization) were still alive then. I was just a child, but growing up, my parents and grandparents explained it all to us." He tried to explain the complicated history of the civil war as we walked. I tuned out because I'd heard it many times before. We entered a slum that seemed a cleaner version of Dharavi in Bombay.

"That's Martyrs Square." He pointed to a gravesite with marked graves. Many bodies were dumped in mass graves, but some of the important PLO functionaries were buried here. "Hizbullah controls this gravesite now," said Fouad, unverifiably. I could see one flag, perhaps used only as a territorial marker. There was no memorial except a lonely red-painted concrete column that misspelled the word "massacre." The alleyways of Shatila grew smaller, and we were soon walking single-file past many Palestinian flags and posters of Yasser Arafat with the backdrop of the Temple Mount in Jerusalem, which Muslims know as Al-Aqsa, "the furthest mosque" and Islam's third holiest. It is said to contain the stone (thus "Dome of the Rock") where the Prophet Ibrahim (Abraham) placed his son Ismael for divinely ordained slaughter. There was even an Arafat with the Kaaba behind him, direct proof of why Palestine unified the *ummah* (the worldwide "community" of Muslims) even beyond sectarianism. There was no dearth of Stars of David oozing blood.

There were newish posters praising Turkish President Erdogan. I thought about how my newfound love for Beirut felt like my love for Istanbul. The latter was way more familiar. Turkey was the "stable Muslim democracy" of the region. At the time Erdogan had "heroically" challenged Israel and the US about the former's attacks on a flotilla on a humanitarian mission to Gaza.

We passed a little school where unsegregated boys and girls engaged in a drawing class. I bought a bottle of water at a store, which had a prominent display of a variety of condoms. Right next to it was a small mosque.

"See, here is proof that Islam likes sex! Condoms and mosques right next to each other," I said, trying to lighten up the somber mood. The shop played Fairuz, one of the Arab world's greatest chanteuses, as she sang her fabled ode to this city that had created her, Li Beirut. This time we came upon yet another massive mural of Yasser Arafat with Al-Quds (Jerusalem) spread behind him. The gold-plated Islamic dome is the Empire State Building of Jerusalem, making the city's skyline recognizable worldwide. Massive Arabic letters said, "What is more worthy of battle than this, which is ours." The message in Sabra and Shatila was clear everywhere I turned. Israel was the biggest enemy and its existence was contested. And Jerusalem belonged to Islam. I remember thinking how religions and civilizations are always built atop each other—historically destruction has always predicated construction.

Slipping away from my group, I came upon an entire wall of handsome young Palestinian men, painted as a giant mural. "Shaheed," read part of the text, the Arabic, Urdu, and Farsi word for *martyr*. I wondered how many *intifadas* (often translated as "uprising") remained. How many wounds would forever fester? For the Palestinians, the second intifada had ended and the third was yet to come. But the *Nakba* (literally, "the catastrophe") of the 1948 war when almost a million Palestinians were forever uprooted from their homes by the new nation-state of Israel had never ended.

I would have loved to find a T-shirt version.

On my last afternoon in Beirut, I visited the newly built, "fake," "plastic" downtown. It was built with the assassinated Rafik Hariri's fortune, to the chagrin of the Beirut intelligentsia, who seemed unanimous in their disapproval. The call to Maghrib (evening prayers) began. I felt drawn to the nearby Mohammad al-Amin mosque that dwarfed all else. It reminded me of the Blue Mosque in Turkey. I later learned that it was deliberately built in the Ottoman style, with two blue domes and Ottoman-style minarets, with their sharp conical ends.

Indoors the mosque was spotless, with gold calligraphy and soaring ceilings. An enormous chandelier hung at the center of the carpeted praying areas, with a beautifully appointed *mihrab*, a niche found in every mosque that points to Mecca. The mosque, like many, was named after the Prophet Muhammad. But even in its transparent efforts to replicate centuries of Islamic architecture, the mosque felt like a hastily built twenty-first-century Taj Mahal.

I prayed with an intensity I had never known. We formed just one line because there were so few of us. It was peaceful. A bearded old man came and sat next to me. He said I didn't look like I was from here. I told him I was visiting from America. He offered no invective.

"I only pray here because it is close to the shop where I work," he told me. "Otherwise, it is ugly. You should have seen all this in the seventies. It was much grander."

"Yes, many people have told me that," I said.

"Have you been on Hajj? You should see the wonders of the Masjid al-Haram in Mecca. That is true Islamic history. You should go. It's sunnah." I wish I could have told him how the Saudis were actually the most destructive force upon Islamic history. I shook his hand and sat there for a long time, making a quiet resolution that would forever change my life.

That evening our raggedy bunch, including David, Mo, Fouad, Safa, Aisha, and I, reunited and arrived at an allegedly Hizbullah-run restaurant. The smell of za'atar was everywhere. And an enormous buffet filled with ful, tabouleh, hummus, falafel, labaneh, baba ghanoush, plus all manner of mezze. South Asian waiters scurried around. Entire families were breaking the fast with dates, Coke, and appletinis. Women in hijabs filled their plates right next to women dressed like the skirt-wearing Safa. Was this Lebanese-style pluralism? My phone lit up. Safa, who shared my black sense of humor, burst into laughter when she saw the email. My request for an interview with Nasrallah had been denied, citing a "heavy travel schedule." It was signed off with "The Media Relations Department of Hizbullah wishes you a productive stay in Beirut."

"Where on earth would *he* be able to travel?" I whispered to Safa.

"Tel Aviv, of course! They are waiting to welcome him!"

Muhammad Saad al-Beshi raised his slender sword. Four feet of steel, gently curved at the end, gleaming in the merciless sun. Muhammad squinted at the sky, as if seeking approval from the Almighty. He then looked down at the figure, shrouded in white, kneeling beneath him. Muhammad commanded him to recite Islam's testament of faith, the *Shahadah*: "There is no God but Allah and Muhammad is his messenger." The scene unfolded outside Medina's Mandarin supermarket in a dusty plain roughly the size of a football field. A hundred yards away, a hushed crowd of about fifty men watched.

A white-robed figure with a red-checked head cloth read out a long sharia sentence, including "engaging in the extreme obscenity and ugly acts of sodomy." Six long-bearded men recited Quranic verses. One of them nodded at Muhammad, who stepped back and took his position to the left of the condemned, stretched his right leg forward, his left leg back and raised both arms in an elegant, almost yoga-like posture. And then, a clear, efficient blow, cleaving the neck swiftly. His head fell with a hollow thud that ricocheted across the entire field. Done with the macabre deed, Muhammad shouted, "*Allahu Akbar!*" ("God is great") and wiped his blade on a white cloth, which he tossed away. Some of the assembled witnesses murmured, "*Allahu Akbar,*" in response. The headless body swayed forward before momentarily snapping up, as if to attention, and then slumped finally to the right. My hand trembled. I dropped my iPhone onto the sand. I stifled a scream. A mutawa turned and headed toward me.

"Let's run and get lunch," said my companion, picking up my phone. "There's an Al-Baik nearby."

I awoke to soaked sheets. Keith, my husband, the man I loved more than life itself, snored softly beside me. His warm breath startled the hairs on the nape of my neck. His hand moved to my shoulder as if to comfort me—even in sleep he could sense my nightmare. I gently extricated myself.

Another sleepless night? I walked to my laptop. Dozens of windows were already open from my last session. Google searches from the prior night: "Homosexuality, Saudi Arabia," "Beheading Saudi Arabia," "Hajj Saudi Arabia," "Camera, filming Mecca," "Shia prayer, Sunni prayer," "Beshi, Riyadh," "Hajj, death, stampede," "Wahhabi, punishment, Hajj." Beirut was six months ago.

"You should call me Mo," Muhammad had said in a chatroom window, "like all my friends." Friendship seemed impossible on this page of naked selfies that would put Anthony Weiner to shame.

Buttfuck11 also reached out, "Want my pussy? Im in Hamra and u?"

"Not in Beirut," I typed back.

"Where r u then?"

I clicked block. Buttfuck11 died an instant death on my Manjam—a hookup site gay men in the region used. I looked for Mo786. He was not online.

I walked to the kitchen and lit a cigarette, recalling the second-hand events that inspired my nightmare, which seemed to have traveled into the surreality of a sleep-walk. Muhammad had walked away while sheathing his sword. Men in blue jumpsuits scurried from the sidelines and threw the bodies onto stretchers, grabbing the heads by the all-white cloth tubes that covered them, and carried the executed to two waiting vans. The crowd dispersed, and a lone man hosed the blood down a drain.

My hands shook violently and the cigarette fell. I considered brewing some coffee. It was 3 a.m.

A twenty-six-year-old Saudi man lingered. He was an accidental witness to the slaughter. Born and raised in Medina, Muhammad al-Din knew to avoid this place on Monday mornings, the designated time for capital punishment. But this was a Friday, when usually only a list of the condemned was published in the papers. His mother sent him out to buy groceries, but when he arrived at the supermarket, the shops were shuttered. He had become distracted while texting friends and was soon swept up in the crowd headed to the mandatory Friday afternoon prayers. In Saudi Arabia, the unfaithful have nowhere to hide at prayer time in public; the disobedient go to prison or are sentenced to public lashings. Five times a day, in every Saudi city, town, and village, the baton-brandishing religious police patrol all public places to command that all business stop and all shops close until the prayers finish.

I had met Mo in a chat room on Manjam two years before. I was using the site for grassroots promotion for my film. I had to get the word out to the closeted Muslim world. These chatrooms were the only places they could "congregate," assuming a false sense of safety. Mo had recognized me from my profile picture and told me how he had watched my film, *A Jihad for Love*, on a smuggled DVD with a few friends in Riyadh. We stayed in touch. He wanted me to help him get enrolled in a US university—"Anything to get the fuck out of here." One night he told me of the execution. He seemed strangely calm and expressed surprise about the choice of executioner. Muhammad Saad al-Beshi was Saudi Arabia's executioner-in-chief and normally carried out his beheading or amputation duties at the infamous "Chop-Chop Square" in Riyadh.

In an *Arab News* interview that Mo had also sent me, al-Beshi crowed that as Saudi Arabia's lead executioner he was "proud to do God's work," and that he kept his sword, "a gift from the King," razor-sharp with nightly polishing sessions, assisted by his seven children. In the interview he had boasted, "People are amazed how fast it can separate the head from the body."

"Parvez," said Mo, "most of the world will not learn about this one. They chose al-Beshi for this execution, so it must be important, but doing it on a Friday in Medina, it's all very strange. I was not meant to see this man. No announcement, nothing. I need to get the fuck out of here, man!"

Back at the computer I searched our chat history and found the execution conversation with its links. I found phone footage of the execution, or a similar one, on LiveLeak. I could not find the QuickTime file he had sent me. I played and replayed the video. Daesh, known to some as IS, ISIL, or ISIS, though it had existed even before 9/11, was a while away from worldwide beheading-and-massacre infamy. For now, this is what the Saudis did and I would soon be their unwelcome guest.

Still sweating, I returned to the bedroom. I was consumed by anxiety. I reached to my nightstand. Not my old friend Advil PM. No, it was an Ambien kind of night.

CHAPTER 2

AN ALIEN WITH EXTRAORDINARY ABILITY

Islam's story went like this: Four thousand years ago, the Prophet Ibrahim (known to Jews and Christians as Abraham) was asked by God to bring his Egyptian wife (some claim slave) called Hajjar (Hagar) and his first-born from her, Ismael (Ishmael), to the barren deserts near Mecca. Ismael's name means "God will hear." Clearly, God had heard the need for Ibrahim to have progeny. What he might not have heard were Hajjar's presumably unstated (because they are not well documented) desires not to be an abandoned mother and spouse.

We were told that the Jews and the Christians believed Hajjar was dumped in the desert because Ibrahim's first wife, Sara, wanted to get rid of her. For the Muslims, Hajjar is allowed to understand her own misery because as Ibrahim is leaving her and his infant firstborn basically to die, he informs her that it is God who has commanded him to do so. And *this* is supposed to make her feel better. Many Muslims also believe that both Hajjar and Ismael are buried right next to the Kaaba in Mecca, the holiest place on earth.

Hajjar is central to Islam and, for my adult self, is one of the most sacred, compelling, and mysterious figures in the faith. However, she is conveniently left out in many narratives and in our childhood stories. Her only purpose is that she gives birth to Ismael, who crucially would father the tribe (the Quraysh) that would give birth to the Prophet Muhammad. But her legacy is vast.

When first dumped, Hajjar ran between two hills called Safa and Marwa, desperate for water to save her suckling infant's life. After the seventh run, a sacred, life-giving spring called Zamzam appeared. The story is told in many different ways, but this is what I was taught. Zamzam flows to this day, and the Saudis have with great fanfare brought in global "experts" to testify its purity and "extraordinary" mineral content.

Only as a young man did I learn that Hajjar was in fact "the Mother of Islam." One of Islam's greatest Shia scholars, Ali Shariati, even exclaimed, "See how special she was. God chose a black slave woman from all humanity to be buried next to the Kaaba! Not even our Rasool (messenger) gets a place there. God gave one of his most humiliated and weakest creatures a room in his house. Never forget her!"

In Mecca, I would realize that some of the primary rituals of the Hajj are a memory of Hajjar's difficult life. The word *hijrah* ("migration"—the Islamic calendar begins with Muhammad's hijrah from Mecca to the city called Yathrib, later Medina) has its root in her name, as does the word *mohajjir* ("immigrant"). It was even claimed that the Prophet said, "The ideal immigrant is the one who behaved like Hajjar."

But it was mostly men who wrote the canon of Islam, like its two predecessor monotheisms. It helped these misogynists that Hajjar was not directly mentioned in the Quran. They were constructing a patriarchy. They have tried to diminish her. In truth, this woman is the very center of Islam. To obliterate her is impossible.

If women wrote the history of Islam, Hajjar would get credit for what she really is: Islam's matriarch, a monotheistic first. If Ibrahim's behavior were analyzed in present times, many would say he was a deadbeat dad and a sadistic husband.

Ibrahim was also an authoritarian father, who never took no for an answer. He forced Ismael to divorce his first wife but was happy with the second. He was an absentee parent. Yet, when commanded by God again, as he often seemed to be, it was this son he ordered to help him build a cube-shaped room right next to his well at Zamzam. That room, the Kaaba, would become the center of a flourishing trade capital called Mecca and today the central point of my religion.

Ibrahim famously dreamt that God had commanded him to sacrifice Ismael. He recognized the urgency, because only prophets received divinely inspired dreams. Even *Shaitan* (Satan) attempted to dissuade Ibrahim from carrying out this brutality. Ibrahim hurled seven stones at him thrice, driving him away. The pious Ismael agreed to be sacrificed. Just as Ibrahim raised his knife to kill his own firstborn, God intervened in very timely fashion. He told father and son that they had aced this test of faith, and Ibrahim could sacrifice a goat instead.

This father's readiness to murder his son was heartbreaking to me as a lonely child, craving parental affection. This mental image, alongside the bloody streets, contributed to my anxiety before and during the festival of Eid al-Adha, the Feast of Sacrifice, that commemorates this act.

For so many men who control the narrative of Islam, a Muslim woman's body is a contested space. The women who shaped my life and my mind at different points in my life tried in their own limited ways to reclaim their bodies from the men who claimed ownership over them. In this, these women were all rebels. But in the ridiculous logic of the Wahhabis, for example, there is nothing more dangerous and distracting to the obedient (male) armies of the pious than an exposed strand of female hair.

In the early eighties, the center of my favorite Eid al-Fitr was a distant aunt we called Khala, which literally means "aunt." She was wise and wrinkled and funny and really thin—her bones would peek out of her modest and plainly colored clothing. In this quality of an almost emaciated, bony scrawniness, she was the opposite of my voluptuous mother, whose curves were never quite hidden by any *dupatta* (a long, multipurpose scarf) she would drape over them as a nod to propriety. And this, perhaps, in my mother's case, was by design. There was little about my mother that was not a carefully considered detail.

Khala is the greatest storyteller I ever knew. She brought a world of adventures and brave (Muslim only) heroes alive to the motley crew of kids sitting around her. On top of that list was the *Rasoolullah*—that's what she called Muhammad. We knew already that this meant "Messenger of

God," and this is how we were respectfully to mention him, avoiding the utterance of his name. And then we were to append the tongue-twister *Salallahu Alaihi Wa'salam* ("Peace be upon Him").

"But why do we want to wish him peace every time, Khala?" I asked.

"Because he would wish the very same for you, Parvez."

And then, "Khala, what did Rasoolullah look like?"

A question that has created much worldwide mayhem. But it was safe to ask Khala. Each time she would add newer, magical details until, for my childish imagination, Muhammad became real. A rather handsome man—even in my pre-sexual mind these descriptions of him would evoke a forbidden longing I could not explain. I somehow knew that any articulation of this complex longing was forbidden enough to conceal, even from Khala.

Khala's descriptions of the Prophet began with her reminding us that Islam was the best religion because, amongst so many other good things, it also forbade us from any kind of idol worship. (This idea of Islam being the most superior religion creates dangerous duality worldviews when in hands not quite like my childhood Khala's.) We were forever forbidden to depict Muhammad, the Rasoolullah, pictorially. The consequences, she would emphasize, were divinely dire. Ironically, ask most devout Muslims, and they will be able to describe what Muhammad looked like in great, often poetic detail, but they know the line that can never be crossed. So we children often drew pictures of Khala's stories, but never of Muhammad.

Once Khala was convinced that we would not attempt to draw any pictures of the Prophet, she would begin. "Rasoolullah, peace be upon Him, was tall. He had a sturdy build with long, muscular limbs and tapering fingers. The hair of his head was long and thick and wavy, just like your curls, Parvez." When she directly referenced me in these stories, a thrill of recognition and blissful affirmation rushed through my body. This proved that I was better than the other children.

"His forehead was large and prominent, his eyelashes were long and thick, his nose was sloping, his mouth was large, and his teeth were well set. His cheeks were spare and he had a pleasant smile. His eyes were large and black with a touch of brown. His beard was thick, and at the time of his death, he had seventeen gray hairs in it. He had a fine line of hair over his neck and chest. He was fair of complexion and altogether was so handsome that Abu Bakr, peace be upon him, composed this couplet about him: 'As there is no darkness in the moonlit night, so is Mustafa (Muhammad), the well-wisher, bright.' Now, children, who is Abu Bakr?"

I would raise my hand before she had finished asking the question, informing everyone that Abu Bakr was our first *khalifa* ("caliph"), and he was also the Prophet's father-in-law and one of his senior *sahaba* ("companions"). Khala would smile approvingly at me. And in an instant, my Eid was made. In just a few years, I would know that my version of Islam's history was heavily influenced by Sunni (Hannafi) ideology, and for the Shia there is a completely different line of Muhammad's inheritors.

In her little sessions, Khala made sure that we understood that the Quran was divided into chapters called *Surah* and each chapter was made up of verses, which were called *Ayah*. This was hardly Quranic study. I was just being taught the basics and the eight essential Surahs. Khala's Quran came heavily edited.

I now hope she might even have been proud of the man I have become. She made sure I would never forget her. I never have.

In 1998, I set forth on my first pilgrimage to what I would now probably call the land-of-the-not-so-free. We couldn't make the connection to JFK, our intended destination. After some commotion, Kuwait Airways put us in a hotel near Kuwait International Airport for a night's unanticipated layover.

So on June 17, 1998, I set foot on foreign Arab soil, the soil likely once trod by Prophet Muhammad. It was only my second time out of India. Looking back, I feel this was no coincidence. The airport was a surreal display. Glitzy marble and brass columns, glistening so clean you could eat off the floor. Kuwaiti sheikhs in their flowing white robes glided around as if floating on air.

A stern-looking official took our passports and told us we could collect them in the morning. I didn't know it then, but this would not be the first time an authoritarian Arab regime would confiscate my passport. We were herded into an air-conditioned bus, drove through the barren desert, and there it was: fancier than anything I had seen. The oil-rich gulf monarchies' endless thirst for tall towers had begun. In the not-so-distant future, Dubai's Burj Khalifa, the world's tallest building, and the Kingdom

Tower in Mecca, the world's third-tallest, would prove that Gulf Arabs loved their skyscrapers, given that they didn't really have much else for topography. The former provided enough glam to draw the Real House-wives of Beverly Hills in as they gamboled around Dubai in a future season finale. Kuwait had similarly tall ambitions but could never really catch up to Dubai.

My room was a *nouveau riche* wonderland of gold faucets and a mas-sive shower. In my Delhi apartment, I'd used a bucket to wash. Within a few minutes of entering the room, I used the glitzy shower with all manner of controls and settings. I also saw my first Jacuzzi bathtub and bidet. I had no idea what they were. The wonders of Google and a laptop had still not arrived in my life.

Faux-gold carvings with arrows pointing toward Mecca had been engraved on the bed-stands, so the faithful would know where to direct their daily prayers. I was not a supplicating Muslim at the time, so I paid no heed to the calls for nighttime prayers that rang out from several mosques around my hotel.

I flipped channels on an enormous TV. The new Al Jazeera network was hosting an interview with the Saudi "jihadi" Osama bin Laden. At the television channel where I worked in Delhi, Al Jazeera was monitored constantly and that network was almost single-handedly making Osama a global celebrity. His fame rested on what he called his "jihad" in Afghani-stan against the Soviet occupation, which was long over. In a sense, he was a jobless terrorist. His movements between Afghanistan and the abhorred Pakistan provoked much fearful debate among the hardly neutral senior journalists at my channel. And *jihad* was a few years away from becoming the most famous word on the planet.

Bin Laden was framed off-center with carefully placed Kalashnikovs. Despite being in what appeared to be a cave, he had a carefully controlled media persona. His thoughts seemed disjointed. At one moment he railed against the wrongful occupations of Muslim lands by infidels and then moved to boasting about his father's renovation work in Mecca, in "the Prophet's holy site," meaning Medina and at Al-Aqsa in Jerusalem. He spoke of the injustice of "that" Jewish occupier (deliberately not naming Israel) of Jerusalem, of Palestine, and of the torture of hundreds of thou-sands of innocent "Muslim Palestinian lives." And then there was familiar anti-American and anti-British rhetoric.

I had followed bin Laden's story with interest ever since it broke on Indian television. He seemed always to be giving interviews. Osama bin Laden's soothing voice lulled me to sleep that night.

"What brings you here?" asked the black border agent once I made it to New York. I had never seen a black person, growing up in racist and classist India. My first visit to my mythical America was beginning!

"To visit my family and vacation," I replied.

"Welcome to America. Enjoy." It was like she was serving a massive ice cream sundae. She stamped my passport. Strangely clad men in long black coats and tall hats stood at the baggage carousel. The Kuwait Airways bags were coming out on a carousel shared by the Israeli airline El Al. I had never seen orthodox Jews or met anyone who was Jewish. The irony of the shared carousel is only in retrospect.

In later years my cousin who picked me up said, "You came out and bent over to kiss the soil." I always say I have no such recollection, even though part of my brain thinks I might melodramatically have. It was the soil of Bill Clinton's America: I hope history will not remember him merely as the president who was impeached for getting a blowjob.

"F-O-B—that's what you are," said my cousin. "Fresh Off the Boat! Knows nothing! We will even have to get you new clothes! And some deodorant to make you smell better!" he laughed.

New York dazzled me. And if the central thesis of the uber-phenom *The Secret* is true, I must have put a super-strong intention into the universe because it would become home. Manhattan, years later, strangely felt like an island that trapped yet protected me.

The next night, I was taken to my first-ever gay club. My straight cousin and his straight friends joined. They were comfortable enough in their sexualities not to be threatened. I stuffed dollar bills into two butts gyrating on the bar. All of my gay activity in India had happened while my mother lay dying and thus was furtive, fast, and, to my mind, filthy. She'd always told me sex was shameful in her indirect conversations on the subject.

I followed an unattainably handsome black man into what looked like a back room with heavy curtains. Inside it was my mother's definition of sex. Filth.

The evening after that, my cousin and I schlepped to the Bronx for a game at Yankee stadium. America was large, floodlit, and filled with giant colas and heaping baskets of fries and Coke. I bit into my first hot dog and then in shock asked, "Is it pork?" My cousin confirmed it was kosher, the Jewish version of halal.

I could not follow the game. My cousin explained the rules, but my mind wandered back to my earliest memories of the Eid of the Sacrifice and how they were mixed in with India's favorite sport: cricket. Cricket for me was a blood sport. The crack of the baseball bat could only send my mind back in time to the cricket games of my youth, where my childhood effeminacy evoked reliable bullying. Children can be cruel like no one else.

I recalled the rivers of blood that ran through my childhood neighborhood as goats were slaughtered during Eid al-Adha. Then my mind brought up a memory of another bloody annual—exclusively Shia—ritual on Ashura, the tenth day of the Islamic calendar's first month, Muharram: Bare-chested Shia men self-flagellating to commemorate the martyrdom of one of their greatest ancestors, Imam Husayn, who was killed in the Battle of Karbala in what is now present-day Iraq. Little boys, many my friends, played cricket in the bloody soil, caused by the procession. I joined them hesitantly, aware of my fear and the trauma of ridicule at my inability to excel in the national obsession. Shirtless Shia men, sinewy and drenched in sweat, walked past us in their annual *Tazia* ("mourning") procession. I watched them, fascinated, perhaps feeling my first sexual arousal. They had metallic chains in their hands, which they called *zanjeer* (a type of chain), and they repeatedly and rhythmically whipped themselves. As zanjeer hit skin it left a trail of blood, which was oddly arousing. Trying to focus on my cricket and failing miserably, I could only stare at these muscular, hirsute men. Sectarian Shia-Sunni riots during this time often broke out.

For a moment, I was back in the baseball game. My cousin cheered the Yankees on, and I noticed how big and sexy some of the players were. He had generously kept us out of the bleachers.

I was back in India. Hindu-Muslim raged again. The dots connected in my nine-year-old mind. Some Hindus, as in years past, had left the carcass of a pig—that unholiest of unholy animals—for the Muslims in the local mosque, and the enraged Muslims had set fire to the homes of a Hindu community of primarily lowest-caste cobblers. My fear of cricket and my fascination with these men and the violence they created mingled and formed the momentary tapestry of an unusual childhood mind. Cricket was the one supreme religion both India and Pakistan shared. One particularly violent riot had erupted near our school when it was discovered that the Muslims had celebrated with sweets and firecrackers after the Pakistani team defeated India. *"Katuas"*—(circumcised) bastards—my school friends would spit out. Katua for them was the racial slur for Muslims.

Generations of Indians had grown up obsessed with cricket, and there was nothing more exciting than an India-Pakistan match. Some Muslim families in the neighborhood distributed sweets when Pakistan won, while my parents told me to "be secular." We were to root for the Indian team, because not doing so is unpatriotic. But I always secretly rooted for the Pakistani team, admiring their taller, and in my eyes more masculine, physiques.

Besides my homosexuality, I would also grow up ashamed of the part of me that was Muslim.

Years later, as a journalist in Delhi, I had befriended a cricket-obsessed hack whose theory was simple: the reasons the Pakistanis sometimes did so well against the Indian team was that they had the focus that can uniquely be instilled by Islam alone. The Hindus, he told me, just did not have that dedication. I challenged him with the names of Indian Muslims in the national team. But the question remained. *Does the discipline of a good Muslim life make a Pakistani cricketer superior to a Hindu, Indian one?*

"Isn't this just the most fun thing you have ever done?" yelled my cousin over the din.

I smiled and nodded my head. I could not bear to tell him that none of it made any sense and therefore my mind was busy visiting other places.

The intense intersections of ritual violence—sexualized in my prepubescent mind—with the real inter-religious violence I experienced and many insecurities of a lonely childhood never went away.

I asked myself: *Implausible as it sounded, was the discipline of Islam and indeed of jihad partly a genetic trait passed on from Muslim to Muslim, through blood ties?*

The blood of animals and humans flowed and swirled in my mind's eye when the Yankees hit yet another home run.

"Awesome game!" shouted my cousin. "This is the best of American sport that you just saw! Even better than cricket!"

During that same 1998 trip, my cousin bought me a special ticket to San Francisco, which I fast realized was hardly the capital of Planet Gay. My pilgrimage to the fabled Castro Street revealed just a short city block. A theater, a few restaurants, a gay bookshop, a coffee shop, and that was it.

Pride arrived and so did I. The enemy nations of India, Pakistan, and Bangladesh mingled here in a single tent. They were South Asian LGBT's in this label-loving land. Or Desis ("from back home"). Growing up in India, it's rare to meet a Pakistani or Bangladeshi, unlike in NYC, with the yellow-taxi cabbies who would be so abundant in my future home.

San Francisco was a fast education in everything that lay between twink, bear, and dyke. Did this endless bacchanalia and exposed behinds, with some floats sponsored by corporate giants, really herald anything prideful?

Night fell and brought with it a return to the sexual abandon of the shadowy, sweaty back room I had experienced at NYC's Splash. This one was called the Power Exchange and was advertised as a bathhouse. I had never been to one. Rooms upon rooms spread out before me. Their doors ajar, naked men waiting, usually with their butts in the air. All you needed to do was walk in. I came upon a nude man in a leather sling—he was positioned such that his legs were up in the air. There was a line of semi-naked men waiting. It was dark but it was clear that this leather bottom was in it for the long haul. I did not join the line. No condoms were in sight. By day, I imagined these cubicles could easily transform into a call center for a tech company.

Leaving, I wondered aloud to my friend, "What is there to be proud of?"

I killed my mother when I was twenty-one. She lay dying of a painful cancer in the Indian city of Calcutta. I was busy coming out in far-away Delhi. Horny and thoughtless. Eager to experience the shabby kind of hedonism that a young, gay lifestyle could offer in third-world India, I traveled to what was billed as India's first gay conference in Bombay despite her protestations. I barely saw her those last few months. And I never got to say goodbye.

She had once spoken longingly of unmade pilgrimages, unfulfilled resolutions. And a place she called "God's House," where sins could be prayed away. I wondered if I would ever fulfill her dreams. I wondered if we would reconcile in earthly physical space or in the afterlife. I wondered if I could get her Urdu poetry published in a land more receptive to her language, in Pakistan, where it was their lingua franca.

I did not cry at her funeral. I felt that the shame of my sexuality killed her. I knew that she died angry. The guilt of murdering a parent is an immense burden to carry. Mine felt particularly heavy.

New York's Columbia University had granted me admission with no financial aid for the first year. I entreated the film department chair for a scholarship and his firm no meant I just couldn't afford it. So I fell back on my second option, DC's American University. In that town I could even stay for free with extended family. But they were daily reminders of my unfinished business with grief.

By 2001, I was on triple duty. I was a full-time graduate student, an adjunct professor at American University, and a part-time employee in the media division at downtown DC's World Bank. It was there that I had front-seat views to the smoke pouring from the Pentagon. I called my cousin. In a few minutes, cellphone reception would stop.

"You have to come home right away," he said. "We remember what went down in school in '79." Of course everyone remembered the Iran hostage crisis, which predictably generated hate in America. My school-going cousins had been mercilessly bullied for appearing Iranian, just because of their skin color. Children can be particularly cruel. "Just get home. Your beard and your skin color don't help!"

Rumors flew faster than fighter jets. George W. Bush and gang had disappeared. Hijacked planes were flying all over DC. One would hit the Capitol at any moment—a Capitol that was uncomfortably close. Another was well on its way to flying into the White House. I thought of thousands of TV-segment producers struggling to place accurate lower third infographics on a live calamity unfolding on cameras in real-time. Soon we were in split-screen mode—Towers and the Pentagon. I knew it was he. To date I don't understand my prescience.

Clearly the Feds, Langley, and Foggy Bottom were either glued to Osama bin Laden's most melodramatic attempt to live in worldwide infamy forever or busy rushing home or to government bunkers. Osama bin Laden had pulled together the greatest show on earth, without resources like the US had. I wondered if he, too, watched it live and what his preferred network was.

People had spilled into the streets from all the office towers. What was eerily common: cellphones to ear, almost everyone had eyes peeled to the sky. I was in hyper-sensitive mode, my nerves probably as frazzled as anyone else's when I boarded the Red Line on the Metro, which miraculously was still working. Were all these panicked people looking at me? Did that blonde woman just move away from me deliberately? To readjust my position on the impossibly crowded train, I put my backpack on the floor for a moment. A murmur arose from all corners—or was I imagining it? I hastily retrieved the backpack and put it back where it belonged.

By the next morning it was official. It was Muslim hands that did this. America would never be so safe to so many ever again. 9/11, they would call it. History would forever be divided into a before-and-after narrative.

Almost a planet away from the Muslim neighborhoods of my childhood that ricocheted with calls to prayer five times a day, I realized: Islam had American blood on its hands. And just like that—in less than twenty-four hours—I had no choice: I "came out" as a Muslim.

"Fuck you, Arabs!" a group of white boys yelled from across the quad of American University. "Go home!"

It was as if the word *Muslim* was branded on my forehead. The beard and skin color didn't help. The fuss of coming out gay in India seemed a lifetime away. Xenophobia was hip. Beards, unlike today, were not. Ignoring the daily stares and comments, I focused on very special pleasures like seeing snow for the first time. I stuck out my tongue to taste a flake. It tasted like magic. Did it smell as pure as it looked?

"I don't feel sorry for y'all," my friend Katy had said. "See what black people go through every day. Intolerance and racism? We have known it for decades." We agreed, though, that Muslim was the new Black.

It was only a year since I had moved to DC in 2000 to do double duty as an adjunct professor and master's student. One of my friends, Fayaz, was a natural leader and told me about the group he headed of what he called "LGBTQI" Muslims, provocatively named after a chapter in the Quran. An interesting and dangerous choice. At the same time, I needed a thesis film. Osama bin Laden was Islam's spokesperson. My thesis film, I grandiosely thought, would offer an alternative. Islam's unlikeliest storytellers, gay and lesbian Muslims, were going to tell the story of the faith. And I started filming for what was called *In the Name of Allah*. Every chapter in the Quran begins with the phrase *Bismillah* ("In the name of Allah"). I, too, wanted to be a provocateur, and this could be the perfect vessel.

A filmed silhouette said, "You have to understand what life is like growing up as a gay person of color in this country."

None of these LGBTQI types wanted to show their faces, so I was making a film of darkness where shadows talked. And pretty soon it would start feeling like a bad idea.

"What do you mean, 'person of color'?" I said. It was honest, because I had no idea what he meant.

"You don't know what a person of color is? It's an appropriation of identity in a majority-white society. The rest of us are persons of color. There are entire movements based on this principle. I am surprised you don't know," said the silhouette condescendingly. In my opinion, white was also a color.

My subjects, the label-loving gays who were born and raised in the West, continually presented themselves as warriors of an "inclusive" Islam. They loved having all manner of conferences, funded perhaps by the same patrons who sponsored me. I became a familiar face. I attended conferences in DC, Toronto, and London. I filmed it all. Endless panels about "queer identity," about "gender," about "liberation theology," about "a gender-neutral reading of the Quran." Hours of wasted footage and money.

Whatever their behavior in their daily lives, these LGBTQI Muslims seeking newer labels every day became super-religious at conference time. Many, like me, consumed alcohol at gay bars after Isha (the final mandated prayer of the day), but during the day, conference time meant a daily performance of at least four or five communal prayers. Optics mattered to these conferencing Muslims. I filmed it all. Did they hook up? Frequently. In fact, I doubt that any were sober to wake up for Fajr, the dawn prayer. I certainly wasn't. It was a strange rainbow utopia built in a suburban outpost of a cheaper hotel franchise. Anybody could be an *imam* (a leader of prayer), and then there was something I had never dared to conjure up: Men and women prayed together! This was a gay Muslim Disneyland that most Muslims on the planet would never recognize and would reliably condemn. Did these LGBTQI types know this?

What particularly turned me off was that some of the women would not even cover their heads while praying, and I remember being shocked and turned off too by the many visible female butt cracks of these devout

Muslimahs decked out in tank-tops and tights. A part of the yoga-like praying in Islam involves bending down and resting your head on earth. The supplicants form neat lines behind each other. The Islam I had grown up with, at the very least, demanded a state of purity and the covering of the head as a sign of being in sacred space. Dressing modestly was ordained for both men and women. These people were like Muslim hippies! Perhaps I was too naïve or judgmental, as an FOB ("Fresh off the Boat").

My thesis film, as expected, was a film about silhouettes and panel discussions. It would never have a life in the real world. I needed to be a real filmmaker. And I needed to make a film about the kinds of Muslims I would recognize with greater ease. That other film is what became *A Jihad for Love*. I had narrowly escaped being lost in the endless jungles of identity-politics-created acronyms like LGBTQIFOBPOC.

For sexual contacts online I also upsold myself as "Middle Eastern" since Indian, to me, meant unattractive. Surprisingly, Arabs were now hypersexualized anyway and the flavor of the month. And I looked like them!

I got my degree and I was done with DC. It seemed like a small town where racism and Islamophobia reverberated louder. My fellow graduates all seemed to be getting jobs in nonprofits and lobbying firms. This was not a future I had imagined for myself, even though it offered the security of a paycheck. I could have gone back to journalism, but I did not desire to be a mere interviewer. I wanted people to interview me. It was time to move to what had always been the Mecca of my dreams. The megalopolis that had teased my tongue with freedom, hope, and desire during my first US trip in 1998. I was New York–bound like millions before me had been for two centuries.

I'd received a job offer as TV producer for *Democracy Now!* It was a New York–based, leftie, "progressive" public TV and radio show, flush with post-9/11 and Bush-bashing rhetoric. We hosted people like Norm Finkelstein, Arundhati Roy, Michael Moore, and Cornel West.

Democracy Now!'s anti-"neo-con" harangues were familiar. The music of Nigerian bandleader Fela Kuti filled newsbreaks (no sponsors or commercials). The staff was made up of mostly white do-gooder Brooklyn hipsters. The kinds who would later perform their designated roles in what I can only call the 99-Percent Show near Wall Street. I was their proud acquisition. A Muslim immigrant POC gay man. A diversity hire! This crowd became tiresome quickly.

My long-distance Parisian boyfriend allowed me to occupy a tiny, musty room in his rent-controlled East Village garden apartment (for free), which he "shared" with a painter called Paul. In truth he visited only twice a year, and Paul (and now I) had it mostly to ourselves. In retrospect I cannot believe my fortune. Only a chosen few get to live for free in a private garden apartment in one of the most desirable NYC neighborhoods for almost three years. And it didn't matter that my room was barely more than a hole in the wall.

Paul was HIV-positive, and I always had to remind him to take his daily cocktail of pills. I was not just his part-time caregiver and roommate. I cared deeply for him, emotionally. Paul finally succumbed to AIDS-related illnesses. My heart was broken. My soon-to-be-ex Parisian boyfriend lost the coveted lease. In New York losing a rent-controlled East Village apartment such as this was like losing the keys to the Taj Mahal. But then I had a new boyfriend named Keith and we moved in together.

My new job included filming protests. I heard familiar angst such as, "Dictator in Chief," "Bush out of Iraq," "What do we want? Peace! When do we want it? Now!" The anger was palpable. But it lacked one basic cause, a rallying cry, and it's a mistake the American (presumably Democratic) left makes all the time. These were disorganized leftie-warriors. Thousands gathered for a march on the East Side of Manhattan, many of them leftovers from the Seattle World Trade Organization protests of 1999. Many were rag-tag revolutionary anarchists, smelling of weed and body odor. *This is why the right is dominating in this country*, I thought, and even said as much to colleagues. They put on power suits and lobby and schmooze with DC power brokers. How could anyone take these lefties seriously by comparison? The DNC tent was big, but with these types, it could easily collapse. Years into the future the "Left" remained a disorganized cacophony, undisciplined and leaderless, slogan-poor and without *one singular cause,* allowing Donald Trump his win.

I hated my job and was lucky to find both a producer and a seed grant for the film I truly wanted to make. So I worked hard at making myself completely unnecessary at the station, and they did exactly what I wanted. They fired me.

I jumped headlong into shooting *A Jihad for Love*. My first stop was Egypt, via France. It was not my first time in either country. Filming began haphazardly. There was no script and the subjects took years to find and convince. I remember meeting Ziyad, an escapee from a Cairo prison, who talked about the comfort the Quran gave him while he was imprisoned. Incongruously, we sat at Le Depot, a sex club near the Marais in Paris, talking about Islamic verses.

I filmed a lesbian couple, Maha and Maryam—the former a hijab-wearing second-generation French Moroccan who is one of the most devout Muslims I've ever met, and the latter her veil-less, less religiously inclined partner—in Cairo. Maha opened my mind immeasurably when she said, "People feel that a woman wearing hijab is either an extremist or oppressed, but for me, it sets me free."

Maryam would become a prominent woman's voice during Egypt's revolution, though she never revealed her sexuality. Maha, in the early days, had told me she couldn't even allow the word "lesbian" to slip past her tongue. Her shame and the spiritual violence she experienced was profoundly sad. It would take two years till Maha allowed me even to set up a camera.

Pretending to be a tourist, I filmed them surreptitiously in one of Cairo's many tourist traps, Mokattam Hill, famed for its Saladin or Citadel mosque. They were more loquacious when I recorded interviews at a friend's apartment in downtown Cairo. Maha yearned to go on Hajj but believed she couldn't without somehow finding a mahram.

I challenged Maha with the 34th verse from the Quran's fourth chapter, *An-Nisa* ("The Women"). This provocative Surah has been used by both Muslim scholars and Islamophobes. Referring to how husbands were to treat their wives, it in part said, "Beat them lightly." Maha pointed out how *dharb*, the word that meant "beat," was used in various other ways in the Quran, so it was contested. She was hardly the first Muslim I had met to use semantics and the context of the seventh century, which is when some Sunni Muslims believe the business of putting the scripture together, pen to paper, allegedly began. Using their own lineage, Sunnis say the third Caliph Uthman oversaw the completion of this enormous task two decades after Muhammad's death. For the Shias, within six months of Muhammad's death, his son-in-law and caliph number one, Ali, had a complete physical transcript of what until then had been entirely oral revelation to Muhammad. I told Maha how I felt the book needed to be immutable.

At the Madbouly bookstore near the soon-to-be-world-famous Tahrir Square we bought a thick tome called *Fiqh al Sunnah* ("Jurisprudence in the way of the Prophet"), surprisingly on the not-religious Maryam's recommendation. Laudably she found a vague reference to female same-sex activity, and we even found a word for it—*al-Suhaq*. The punishment was "to let them go." She squeezed Maha's hand and said, "See, there is no punishment." Maha's reply surprised me: "Sometimes I want to be punished."

They would later come to New York because they had final-cut privileges. I took them to the historic Malcolm X Mosque in Harlem. I gave them an abbreviated history of the Nation of Islam. I told them why I was not taking them to the $17 million, partially Saudi-funded glitzy marble mosque on 96th Street. Its first imam, Sheikh Muhammad Gemeaha, was an Egyptian who fled the US after claiming that 9/11 was a Jewish conspiracy, adding, "If it became known to the American people, they would have done to Jews what Hitler did." His anti-Semitism went further, blaming Jews for the spread of "heresy, homosexuality, alcoholism, and drugs." Anti-Semitism is distilled into many Muslim minds at a very young age. So is the idea that Muslims and Islam are superior to the rest of the world.

My film needed to tell the stories of men like Ziyad, too—people who actually lived with the consequences of their lifestyles. I would seek them out in Muslim countries. I couldn't ask for government permission. I would film guerrilla-style. I was afraid and yet thrilled to be on an adventure that would take me to twelve countries. I would always hide my tapes in my checked baggage with a prayer. Because this was raw footage, the faces of my interview subjects were not yet concealed. In Egypt, for example, there could be real consequences for Maryam and Maha. Taking even greater precautions, I filmed several minutes of touristic footage at the beginning and end of every tape, in the unlikely event that custom agents in these countries would seize and watch the tapes.

Funding came in spurts. The stories I filmed spanned the many geographies of Islam, different cultures, different languages, and different kinds of Muslims. I would not allow my work to paint Islam as a problematic monolith.

After years of paperwork, US immigration services finally allotted me the coveted designation of an "alien of extraordinary ability." This was no joke—it was a real visa category that many sought and only a few got. John

Lennon and Yoko Ono were aliens of extraordinary abilities just like me! The Brazilian soccer phenom Pelé was one, too.

I started appearing on panels again, categorized as "brown," "Muslim," "progressive Muslim," "immigrant filmmaker," "queer activist," "person of color." Invitations piled up. One panel described me as someone whose work "addresses a critical force field." I was flattered. They said my work addressed "Muslim sexual diversity, community, voice, and rights" and "raises a number of thorny questions about political representation and commercial support." Heady stuff.

I was the compliant Uncle Tom or the house-Negro of gay Muslims. I could conveniently be put on display as a last-minute inclusion of "diversity" into leftie events that were still very white. Was the "white man's burden" a real thing?

I had no particular admiration or patience for the ivory towers of the academy. But I hypocritically basked in the attention coming from them. In truth I was penniless, surviving only on rent-free luck. And I was not even a proven filmmaker yet. I hid my shame by dressing smart in designer hand-me-downs from my DC cousins.

Many labels making me a novelty could be stuck on my back. Thus at the conferences they invited me to, I purposely decided not to use the "academese" that they didn't know I knew so well. I told stories instead. I happily shared memories about the delights of Muslim festivals like Eid al-Fitr and the Eid I feared, Eid al-Adha, while growing up in my tiny North Indian hometown, which was a twenty-minute ride away from one of the world's most puritanical schools of Islam.

The hosts were gratified to find the "real thing." I had actually *lived* the abstractions and concepts that existed for them only in books and Wikipedia. Major plus! I spoke with an accent! A Muslim Uncle Tom?

We took money kindly provided by Jewish funders and foundations. The "LGBTQI Muslims of color"-types raised questions about my political intent. I was part of a Jewish propaganda machine, they claimed. I was familiar with anti-Semitism. Anyone who grows up Muslim is. And if they claim they have no idea where it comes from, they are either lying or are ignorant of the complex history of our faith's relation to Judaism. But I was surprised it came so openly from these enlightened lefties who claimed they were fighting the good fight. I was proud of my Jewish-Muslim collaboration! At fundraisers we held for the film, my producer David and I joked, "We are an unlikely Jewish-Muslim collaboration. And it's mostly nonviolent!" On cue, it always brought laughs and, we hoped, larger checks.

"You are naïve," said the indignant Muslim LGBTQI. "You will do great damage to the truly Islamic content of your work, because it will be labeled a Jewish conspiracy." These same people later said the finished film was "too Islamic"!

Imran, one of the conferencing Muslims, did become a close friend. One day we sat sharing our first-time stories. "You go first," he said, "mine will take forever."

"I got to choose it," I told Imran, and in an instant I was transported to the eighties. "It was a class thing. Muhammad was a lower-class Muslim. I loosened the drawstring on his trousers because I wanted to. The pitiless summer sun scorched everything, but our small white room was cool, and there was nothing I wanted more than to take off his white trousers.

"There had been an argument at home and I had driven the ten kilometers on my father's Bajaj scooter to the Nau Gaza Peer, a Sufi shrine. The heat and the dust clouds were overwhelming. Only a few sickly and dehydrated pigeons had dared to venture out with me.

"Nau Gaza Peer was a mystic's mausoleum. Legend had it that the mystic was nine meters tall. Another said that the grave's size changed every time it was measured. The mystic was a magic man of infinite wisdom, my mother told me, because he was both Hindu and Muslim. I was a sickly child, and my mother, with her head carefully covered, would bring me to the shrine often so that we could observe the ritual of covering the mystic's grave with a piece of fabric, which she hoped would cure my bronchitis!

"But then there was Muhammad, the hirsute and handsome caretaker of the shrine. He knew me.

"'Your mother has not come with you,' he said. I said I was alone because I was angry. Muhammad gave me some water and we chatted.

"'Khuda Baksh is what my parents call me, but you should call me Muhammad, because that is my proper name,' he said. I giggled, telling him that doing that in English this would become 'Muhammad, Forgive Me God.'

"'Oh, I am always asking God for forgiveness,' he said, and then, 'You go to St. Mary's school, don't you? Will you teach me English, Parvez?' I promised him I would if he would allow me to see the small room where he lived a few hundred feet away from the grave.

"What we did in the room involved pleasure and pain. At thirteen I did not know how to distinguish between the two. But I knew that I wanted Muhammad with every fiber of my young being. I did not know his age, but I knew the feeling was mutual. I had never kissed a man before and as we lay in the room, spent and wordless, he caressed my face and kissed me again.

"Shadows grew longer. I mumbled about needing to leave but he put his hands to my lips as the call to the evening prayer spread across the roofs of the hundreds of mosques in Saharanpur and entered our private little world through the room's lone window.

"'We must pray, Parvez,' he said.

"I told him I did not know how to pray properly.

"'Well, now you will learn. I will teach you to pray the *Namaz,* just like our Prophet did, and you will teach me English. Deal?'

"We stepped outside as the *muezzin's* voice exhorting the faithful to pray reached a crescendo. As afternoon faded to dusk, Muhammad taught me the proper ways to perform the ritual cleansing before prayer, stressing that because of what we had just done we would need to do the longer *ghusl,* a ritualized bathing of our private parts, instead of the usual *wudu,* which was a simpler ritual.

"He unfurled his blue-and-green prayer rug and I sat a few feet behind him so I could follow his lead. Muhammad was leading me in my first complete Namaz prayer. He was thus becoming my first imam, literally, a learned man who knows how to lead Muslims in prayer. I wondered if he was asking for forgiveness. I knew that, for me, the thrill of our afternoon was greater than my shame of it. When we were done, Muhammad held my hand.

"'Why did you not get circumcised in the Prophet's way, Parvez?' In Hindi, the question would have been crude, but Muhammad spoke in the more elegant Urdu using the metaphorical way of describing the mandatory Muslim male circumcision, *Sunnat* ("circumcised preceding in the Prophet's way").

"After that, I would always excuse myself from my mother's frequent desires to visit the shrine together. Just days after my secret afternoon with Muhammad, the shame of my uncut penis had been discovered at a urinal while at school. I would often return home in tears. I strangely remained ashamed of my uncircumcised penis. In India, you could go either way. But the boys who instilled the shame were circumcised. For them it was confirmation of my 'girl-boy' status, and on me they practiced the kind of cruelty only children possess.

"Weeks passed and when I finally dared to tell my mother, she forbade me ever to reveal this 'uncircumcised' status, adding again that 'this kind of talk is dirty.'

"She could have chosen to confront my pain with a different choice of words. But she was bequeathing the legacy of shame and of secrets that she had grown up with. The rest of my life would be marked by it. For example, my notion of sex being shameful came from my mother, and could not be solved by therapy.

"The only way to escape this childhood of shame was to leave home. And as soon as I knew I could, I did. Only years later did I realize that some of us go on journeys hoping that we can be transformed into better selves, but sometimes we discover that we never needed to leave home in the first place. For as long as I can remember, I have always been escaping home. And each time I left, I was searching for it."

"So basically, your first trick taught you how to pray," said Imran, laughing.

Those conferencing, label-loving Muslims applauded my thesis film, *In the Name of Allah*, which we played later that day. Imran hated it.

"You are very brave," said a white Muslim convert covered in decidedly un-Islamic tats and piercings as he shook my hand. "I saw your film." I did not tell him that I would forever hide that "film" monologue of silhouetted Muslims. And that he should forever cover his arms!

I wondered what form of masochism made this Caucasian (presumably Christian?) man convert to Islam. There was much I could have said, but I didn't want to break his heart. I thanked him and sought Imran, telling him about the encounter.

"Do these guys even understand the destructive forms of Wahhabi, Deobandi, and other styles of Islam and how much damage they have done? Their version of Islam would never be taken seriously by almost the entirety of Muslims on the planet!"

"This utopia will remain in this suburban hotel!" Imran replied. "Fools!"

My friendship with Imran was a precious thing. Back home, Pakistan and India were not exactly BFFs.

CHAPTER 3

PUBE FACE, TOWELHEAD, CAMEL FUCKER, CAVE NIGGER

In 2005, I started filming Zahir, who called himself a "gay imam," in Johannesburg. I joined him and his partner in what was to culminate as a journey to Mecca for the *Umrah* (the lesser pilgrimage—a Hajj-lite) via a tourist trip to Egypt. I did the latter and filmed voraciously. We traveled from Upper Egypt (which is the south of the country) toward Lower Egypt (surprisingly, the north) on the Nile. Floating through the country, I vowed I would never again go on a packaged river or ocean cruise—a tightly regimented week of tourist-trap-filled horror, with nowhere to escape. But a semi-interesting pharaonic history of the land through Aswan and Philae and Luxor unfolded from the mouths of a medley of avaricious tour guides. My fear of the Umrah to Mecca was growing. I had started filming Maryam and Maha in Cairo earlier that year. So far Zahir was allowing me to film his grand voyage.

I lingered at Luxor, wanting to engage him in a discussion about anything but the Quran. Zahir, who knew absolutely nothing of modern politics and the history of Islamic terror, showed little interest. His knowledge seemed to begin and end with the Quran. I was always trying to test his real-world intelligence.

"Do you know any derogatory post-9/11 slurs?"

"What's a slur?" he asked

"Like Muslims in America being called towelheads and cave niggers." Ironically, I did have a towel on my head that day—Luxor was in a heat-wave. "Same in Joburg?"

"Nigger like Negro? Of course." That enormous slur rolled off his tongue nonchalantly.

For someone who had lived (and, some would argue, continues to live) through apartheid, he showed surprising naiveté. We were wandering the immense spectacle of the female pharaoh Hatshepsut's temple, the scene of the horrific massacre in 1997 that saw more than sixty tourists dead and hundreds injured. While he clucked about how pre-Islamic Egypt was Islamically wrong, I countered with how absolute feminine power had historically never been a religious or political novelty.

"That's true," he admitted.

I explained that Egyptian President Hosni Mubarak had exiled leaders of a political Islamic movement called *Al-Gamma'a al-Islamiya*. And they were behind the attacks in '97.

I told him that Mubarak the dictator was always afraid of the Islamists and had jailed hundreds belonging to the *Ikhwan al Muslameen*, the Muslim Brotherhood, founded on the extremist teachings of a schoolteacher, Hassan al Banna, in the 1920s. An *Ikhwan* government would one day briefly rule Egypt, but that was inconceivable at the time. I asked him if he knew that the Ikhwan used slogans like, "Allah is our objective; the Quran is the Constitution; the Prophet is our leader; jihad is our way; death for the sake of Allah is our wish." I asked if he knew they, too, had been accused of terror, even in Saudi Arabia. He had no idea of the former or what I was about to say. The Ikhwan had an on-again-off-again relationship with terror, and many from their brotherhood, including Ayman al-Zawahiri, broke ranks to join al-Qaeda. I asked if he knew that al-Qaeda had finally been held financially responsible for the massacre. Could his knowledge of the Quran answer any of the violence and terror that was being used in its name? This was a post-9/11 world. Surely he had to know. Surely his Quran was different from bin Laden's.

"You know, I try and stay away from politics," he said. "That is better left to people like you. My wisdom comes from the Quran. Let's go back to the boat. It will soon be time for Maghrib prayers."

Obedient, though disappointed, I followed. We ended up where we had started, in the chaotic megalopolis of Cairo. I took a Bombay-style auto-rickshaw to the nice neighborhood of Garden City. The driver asked me in broken English where I was from.

"Min al-Hind," I replied.

"Wow! Amitabh Bachchan!" he said, showing me CDs of the Bollywood megastar he kept in his auto. In a surprising act of generosity, he refused to charge me for the ride. Cairo reminded me of Bombay, a name I defiantly clung to because Hindu right-wingers had changed the name to Mumbai; using Bombay for me at least was a political choice. Driving in Cairo was certainly similar: no rules. Accidents were common, and yet the city somehow functioned. The auto was taking me to meet Bassam, an old dissident journalist friend whose latest piece tore Mubarak apart, listing just a sampling of his crimes. As the auto careened, I thought about how long Mubarak's Mukhabarat, Egypt's version of the FBI, must have watched him. Every Arab dictator has a Mukhabarat. People often disappeared overnight, forever. I had always worried for Bassam.

Later on that balmy Cairo night, I was back at the hotel. Zahir said we should start "spiritually preparing" for our next stop, Mecca, for the Umrah. But indescribable terror and guilt had filled me as the day of departure to Mecca drew closer. Tickets had been bought. Hotel booked. I was wasting scarce production dollars. But I just could not go to our planned final destination in Saudi Arabia.

I had said it to Zahir every night on the boat. By now he was furious with my refusal—my absolute inability—to go to Mecca with them.

"You have to understand my crisis of faith!" I said.

"What crisis? You were always meant to come with us to Mecca. That was the plan all along."

"I know I am failing you. But I am not feeling the religious devotion that brings millions of Muslims to Mecca."

"We will be with you. It will be fine. The Kaaba changes everyone who comes into contact with it."

"You have to understand. I feel like I am going there for the wrong reasons. I am going there to film you. I am not coming *with* faith. I am not coming *for* faith, either." I would be letting down the memories of my mother and Khala by making a journey this important with no faith in my heart. Not going to film Zahir in Mecca for a one-minute scene in the film hardly had the gravity of defiling my mother's memory.

So I backed out. My first opportunity to go to Mecca and I did not have the courage to take it. What I really felt was immense terror—that the Saudis would find out. And I would never be able to get out. Zahir and his partner would be going to Saudi Arabia for almost two weeks. My producer was livid when he heard. "We will not have a film without Mecca," he said.

This imam, Zahir, told me he would need a detailed document proving my faith so we could continue filming upon his return.

"You can change your ticket and go back to Johannesburg," he said, offering me a magnanimous solution. "The housekeeper will let you in. I will call her. Stay there and meditate on why you could not make this journey and then when I return I shall have an answer and hopefully so will you."

Initially my guilt was brutal. I had turned my back to the Kaaba. My damnation was complete.

I had two more nights at the Ramses Hilton, whose balconies would provide perfect backdrops for Al Jazeera's cameras to film the goings-on at Tahrir Square and the nearby Qasr al-Nil bridge as revolution arrived in Cairo's streets almost five years later in January 2011. I changed my ticket after Zahir left. I wanted a few more days in one of my favorite cities. I moved in with Garth, an old Cairo hand, hack, and, more important, dear friend. We discussed the dangerous work he had helped me with during a brief trip in winter 2001. As always, he urged me to "be careful." Garth was straight, but because he had helped me find gay subjects a few years ago, both he and I knew deeply that this was probably the world's most dangerous city for gays. In summer 2001 the Mubarak regime's pogrom against gay men that came to be known as the Cairo 52 made worldwide headlines. In order to placate the restive religious establishment, Hosni Mubarak arrested fifty-two men at a floating gay nightclub called the Queen Boat. Fifty were charged with "habitual debauchery" and "obscene behavior," while two were charged with "contempt of religion." They were treated like "terrorists." They were tortured and raped repeatedly after being subjected to "forensic examinations" of their buttocks. Ziyad, whom

I later met in Paris, was one of the fifty-two. He finally escaped the horror to end up in unfriendly France. (I wish all asylum-seekers knew that the West was hardly a "promised land." Refugee status is rarely the key to an easier life.) Egypt's newspapers had in 2001 published all the arrestees' names, addresses, and photos, intentionally provided by the dictatorial regime. Ziyad was included.

"What shame to my poor widowed mother," he wept.

"Satanic Cult," screamed those headlines. Homophobia, as on most of our planet, is deeply entrenched in Egypt. Mubarak had often successfully invoked "Islamic morality" to keep his Muslim "subjects" suppliant. Once it was a debate about hijab, and the latest threat to Islam was rampant homosexuality. To this day, Mukhabarat types troll websites like Manjam to "entrap" gay men. It is said the police know if someone is gay by the color of his underwear. White is straight.

I hung out in Zamalek cafés with Hamza, an old friend. This wealthy neighborhood was old money. And many of its residents had no idea about the dire straits just a few miles away in Manshiyat Nasser, home to the infamous Garbage City. Zamalek residents didn't venture there, but Hamza had once taken me. He knew, even more than I did, why this country was a ticking time bomb. Now he was producing some chic Arabic T-shirts that, while playing with language, indirectly talked of change. One said *hurriyah*, the Arabic word for freedom, on the back, and on the front was a big question mark. He gave it to me.

Nothing ever changed in Zamalek. Ladies lunched, many of them expat European wives married to rich Arabs, and they gathered at places like the Gezira Sporting Club to share cocktails. Membership was coveted. They were Cairo's version of the Real Housewives franchise. Zamalek's schizophrenia about the real Egypt was decades old.

Later, back with my host, I reminded Garth how he and I had met a "gay" man a few blocks away at the Hardee's, which would in just a few years become a crucial trauma center for the Tahrir Square revolutionaries. Garth and I visited old haunts. He told me getting bylines from the region was getting harder, meaning it was hard financial times for freelancers like him. That, too, would change in just a few years.

Cairo was always the (broken) heart of the Middle East—its political, historic, cultural, and even political center, but the majority of its residents lived in abject poverty. Cairo had given the Arabs some of their richest cinema and, later, television. Gaudy telenovela-style soaps called "Ramadan Specials," manufactured in Cairo TV studios, got big Arab audiences in entertainment-starved Saudi Arabia, for example. For some, Cairo was the center of Islamic thought and theology because it contained Al-Azhar University, the Harvard of Islam. Unfortunately for me, not far behind was the Wahhabi-taken-over Darul Uloom Deoband of my childhood, probably Islam's Princeton. It seems that the latter has won the battle of theological supremacy given the enormous impact Wahhabi ideology has had in the Sunni Muslim world. But Al-Azhar, which even includes seven Sufi schools in its curriculum, remains the largest. Its impact cannot be underestimated. It implements gender segregation and yet disdains the Wahhabis. I always wonder how history would be different if Al-Azhar's "Islam-lite," relatively speaking, were at the center of worldwide Sunni opinion. The even larger campus of the American University of Cairo did not have gender segregation, but it did not claim to be a religious school.

I had time to visit Al-Azhar's campus, where as expected men and women were separated, Saudi ikhtilat-style. Long Saudi-style abaya garments on women were a rarity in the Cairo of my memories, but unfortunately I now saw many, a dramatic increase since prior visits. More women, especially the younger ones, were embracing the hijab, fashionably covering the head and part of the neck, miles away from a Taliban-style burqa or Saudi-style abaya. Print magazines like *Hijab Fashion*, the *InStyle* for the fashionable young hijabis of the American University of Cairo, were the rage, as they presented chic prêt-à-porter versions of the headscarf. The Prophet Muhammad's wives could never have envisioned this haute-couture takeover of his simple command for modesty in dress for both genders. This was not oppression; it was clear that the women who covered chose to do so. There was no sharia here. But like everywhere else, the extent to which a woman would go when choosing to cover herself was, in many minds, a marker of conservatism. Hijabs wrongfully equaled extremism in the West's mind already.

I had built a wide network of journalists, writers, and filmmakers in Cairo. Years later this network would embrace my film. Its members would also form a crucial source of minute-by-minute information when I would report about the unfolding revolution in 2011. Every bit of information they

gave me formed a tweet or Facebook status. At this time, in 2005, my network included a favorite of the film-festival circuit, Yousry Nasrallah. Over
tea and coffee at his downtown Cairo office, he was in recovery from his
four-and-a-half-hour epic *Bab el Shams*, or *The Gate of the Sun*. Based on
celebrated author Elias Khoury's fabled novel of the same name, it was a
vivid, epic-like history of the Palestinian people. At its core was the word
every Muslim knew, *Nakba* ("the catastrophe"). For Muslims, it was the violent 1948 occupation of Palestine by the newly created state of Israel. From
bin Laden to Mubarak to the Ayatollah Khomeini, every Muslim zealot or
politician had used the Nakba as Islam's never-ending injustice, a rallying cry
to Muslims around the world. For many the Nakba had never ended at all.

Yousry would have laughed me out of his office if I had had the power
to look about a decade into the future. In 2017 the new US President
Donald Trump would name a fanatical bigot called David Friedman his
ambassador to Israel.

When they blithely promised they would move the US embassy to
Jerusalem a chill went down my spine. Did this man and his gang have
absolutely no idea of the worldwide repercussions of this incendiary move?
And these repercussions would not be felt only by 1.7 billion Muslims.
There is a reason that Jerusalem and the occupied West Bank and Gaza
remain the world's most-contested real estate. The city of Jerusalem as the
possible capital of Israel is just one issue that lies at the heart of the world's
most unsolvable problem. Al-Quds, as Jerusalem is known in Arabic,
home to the world's third-holiest mosque for Muslims worldwide, is the
most visible symbol of Islamic oppression and all the power of empire that
the Muslims lost. Many Muslims are taught this.

But at the time, Yousry and I just shared our common woe about how
funding was scarce, and then I told him about my still-unfinished film.

"Islam and homosexuality? A film? It's just going to be a black screen!"

I met many old friends at my favorite Café Riche on Talaat Harb Street
in downtown Cairo. We exchanged stories about future dangers we shared
prescience on. "If Mubarak falls, everything falls!" said an older writer
friend prophetically. Neither he nor I could ever have predicted that this
very café would become a triage center for revolutionaries in a little over
five years. I made sure I bought Garth a big box of pastries from the bakery

of Cairo's storied Café Groppi downtown. The famous statue of Talaat Harb, a renowned Egyptian economist of the 1900s, marks Groppi's location and the modern name of this square. But it is still known as Soliman Pasha Square to what I called "the triple Cs"—Cairo's crazy cabbies. Until the early 1950s, the area was named after Soliman Pasha (born Joseph Anthelme Sève and the top army commander during Muhammad Ali's reign). It was renamed Talaat Harb Square by Gen. Gamal Abdel Nasser, who was eager to erase all evidence of the monarchy he'd toppled. Tahrir Square lay a few minutes away. This entire area had not been a stranger to revolutions, including the one that was coming.

One night, Garth took me to a casual bar that most Mideast correspondents gathered at to exchange gossip, careful never to reveal their own scoops. So off we went past the Odeon cinema to the Odeon Palace Bar atop the "Odeon Hotel" on Abdel Hamid Street. I didn't know if it was still a safe meeting-place for gays. Garth said it was the "favorite stop" for the many hacks who made up Cairo's (not official) Foreign Correspondents Association. This was the kind of place only Cairenes knew about. It was a no-frills, expansive space for a restaurant that also included a shabby rooftop "garden" bar. But it all had the aura of history. No one seemed to know for sure if this building was a "real" hotel.

Boozy journos are purveyors of the best kind of gossip. "This town is a ticking time bomb," I said, as I had on every single visit to Cairo in the past. The journos agreed. This was a police state, after all. Mubarak, a dictator fashioned after many in the region, had stayed in power for over two decades, walking a tightrope between the "secular" Cairo elite, many of whom owed much of their offshore wealth to his brutal regime, and an impoverished, still-silent majority, for whom Islam was their only weapon. It was within the latter where the Brotherhood had spent decades quietly building its political machine. The Ikhwan (brothers) took care of the desperate whom everyone else had forgotten. Mubarak, much like his dictatorial predecessors Nasser and Anwar Sadat, had perfected the art of suppressing the most organized political force in the Arab Middle East, the Muslim Brotherhood. Much of the leadership of the Brothers, all devout Muslims who had the silent support of the Egyptian masses, had been incarcerated in Mubarak's torture chambers for decades.

The conversation veered into a discussion about recent stories of a man who trained as a medical doctor but was anything but, who was moved from a Sanaa prison in Yemen to Mubarak's notorious Tora prison in Cairo after 9/11 to serve a life sentence. This notorious man used the moniker Dr. Fadl, which stuck. His real name was Sayyed Imam al-Sharif.

There were about eight of us. After swearing us to secrecy about his name and affiliation, Azhar, a Gulfie journo at our table, passed around a bunch of densely written photocopied pages. He claimed this was Earth-shattering content. Azhar had somehow managed to get regular access to the incarcerated doctor, whom he said he had known since the mid-nineties. We were getting, said Azhar, a scoop. In truth, most of what he told us did not unfold publicly till 2007–08. Azhar said this doctor was in essence the "father of al-Qaeda." He said these pages would form an important and decisive book, and "the sheikh" (Fadl) was thinking of calling it *Rationalizing Jihad in the Modern World.*

"You have to pay attention to this man," said Azhar. "Like his title?"

There was some discomfort at our jolly table. Surely no one wanted to say the name of this "book." I didn't tell Azhar that I had known of Fadl for a while. Anyone who studies Islamic extremism and terrorism as I had for years knows Fadl. They also would know names like Hassan al-Banna and Sayyid Qutb. Books like Fadl's *Essential Guide to Preparation* (seminal for violent jihadis) laid the theological foundations of al-Qaeda. This upcoming *Rationalizing Jihad in the Modern World* would take a historic, unexpected turn: It would be an about-face on the use of violence.

Books like these are not like regular books from publishing houses. They used to travel in hundreds of thousands of bound photo-copies around the globe to recruit future violent jihadis—an underground rail-road of Islamic terror. Now we have the web, as do al-Qaeda and ISIS. Like Osama's mag, *Inspire*, ISIS has two of its own. None need newsstands. Fadl's new book was first published in the *Al-Masry Al-Youm* newspaper in six parts in winter 2007. Fadl's captors (the feared Mukhabarat) also made sure a six-part interview of Fadl's 180 from being the "father of jihad" to peacenik was arranged for the pro-Saudi *Al-Hayat* newspaper, which is the Middle East's *New York Times*. But always looking over its shoulder, it is a mere shadow of its American behemoth, which Trump and his cronies would venomously attack as "false press" in the not-so-distant future.

I wondered how this man's name was totally unfamiliar in the Western press. His incarceration and the preparation book got a lot of Arab press. The US National Security Agency does a great disservice in not diligently following every single word published in Arabic or Urdu papers and online forums. Fadl is a living Islamist ideologue who provided fodder to extremist Islam and its ideology of violent jihad. In fact this man is the true "father" of modern violent jihad. This incarcerated Fadl, Azhar reminded us, laid the Quranic basis for al-Qaeda in his 1988 opus, *The Essential Guide to Preparation*, which claimed violent jihad was the natural state for all Muslims, who should always be in conflict with nonbelievers. That book is still a bible of violent jihad. It came into existence after Fadl and Osama bin Laden had considerable hang-out time in Peshawar. All this "literary" output? Right under the noses of the Pakistani government, which definitely knew where both men were.

On this night atop the Odeon, I wondered, if a mere Gulfie hack like Azhar knew about this Dr. Fadl and his new criminal literary output in 2005, then why did it take the world and especially the US to discover him in a *New Yorker* article dated June 2, 2008? The ideological father of al-Qaeda had been (comfortably) writing away in the prison of a dictator who was a US ally for years.

According to Azhar, while writing in prison Fadl had undergone a 180-degree turn in his ideology and some pages of that were in our hands. Because he met Fadl frequently, Azhar described a cell filled with earlier books of Islamic thought and the Sahih's (Sunni canon) and more: Clearly Fadl was following due academic rigor, because he knew his content would be attacked by the likes of his former students Ayman al-Zawahiri and bin Laden, and it was Zawahiri who famously produced a 200-page response mocking Fadl. In the not-so-distant future, his new book we were passing around would be widely available because it was regime-approved. Cairo rumors had started—it was available to be bought from Egypt's Ministry of Interior for 150,000 Egyptian pounds.

"I usually carry them in my backpack," Azhar said, taking more copies out. "Too unsafe otherwise." Azhar read a part where Fadl confessed he had been wrong all along. He was using the same Quran he had used to sanction bloody jihad to say that "there is nothing that invokes the anger of God and His wrath like the unwarranted spilling of blood and wrecking of property." The book said that terrorism of all kinds was not in compliance with sharia.

To Zawahiri and Osama's chagrin, Fadl denounced al-Qaeda in this *Rationalizing Jihad* book. In a direct nod to 9/11, he said that "the blowing up of hotels, buildings, and public transportation" was not permitted. He laid out strict conditions for the "rare" occasions a jihad would be called for. Most important, he alluded to the "Greater Jihad"—the kind I had always known about and longed for. It was a struggle of the spirit. Fadl now claimed there was no Islamic sanction for killing in the name of Allah, even if the victims were non-Muslim. He repudiated even *takfiri* doctrine—the idea of one Muslim declaring another to be an apostate. Osama was born into a Wahhabi ideology. It's a ridiculous view because it makes more than a billion Muslims infidels. Historically, takfir and violence often went together. Fadl took Quranic aim at the 9/11 hijackers, saying they "betrayed the enemy," because the visas the "enemy" had given them was a contract of protection. He reserved a great deal of rage for al-Qaeda, whose very foundations were built on his words, saying, "The followers of bin Laden entered the United States with his knowledge, and on his orders, double-crossed its population, killing and destroying. The Prophet—God's prayer and peace be upon him—said, 'On the Day of Judgment, every double-crosser will have a banner proportionate to his treachery.'" He raged that the Bush administration's decision to bomb Afghanistan was what al-Qaeda deserved. He didn't stop there: "People hate America, and the Islamist movements feel their hatred and their impotence. Ramming America has become the shortest road to fame and leadership among the Arabs and Muslims. But what good is it if you destroy one of your enemy's buildings, and he destroys one of your countries? What good is it if you kill one of his people, and he kills a thousand of yours?"

"Fadl is a big deal, isn't he?" I asked the assembled journalists, all of us shocked.

"Yes, he is. Here in the Arab world," replied one. "I wish America would pick up on it, but they don't even care." By 2007 many Arabs were reading and talking about what was an earthquake. Did US intel even know that Fadl was the theological founder of al-Qaeda, not to mention kind of hiding in plain sight in the most prominent prison of the country that was a long-term Arab ally?

Did the Americans realize that this father of modern jihad was now a peacenik and available to talk? Was the Bush White House listening? More important, had anyone in the CIA ever read *The Essential Guide to Preparation*—and, yes, between its lines as well?

Rationalizing Jihad in the Modern World desperately needs accurate translation. It answers thousands of questions, all from the inventor of violent jihad. It helps us understand parts of ISIS. It took the *New Yorker* story of June 2, 2008, written by Lawrence Wright, to finally acknowledge this man.

I was reminded that sinister police states like Egypt acted as gate-keepers to the dark world of terror by imprisoning men like Fadl. Like him, some seemed to do a 180.

This was clearly a gang of night owls. It was 1 a.m. and they got even more fun and loquacious. Edward, from a big British newspaper, began to talk about Egypt's popular fatwa-on-demand television shows. He told us how on one such show, a Dr. Izzat Atiya of Al-Azhar University pronounced an otherworldly fatwa in response to a woman who wanted to know if she could reveal her hair to male colleagues at work. Atiya used perverted Islamic logic to say that if she breastfed the colleagues five times, she could reveal her hair! This would make the men related to the woman and thus preclude any sexual contact. There was enormous out-rage. The grand mufti of Al-Azhar denounced it as un-Islamic. Mubarak's minister of religious affairs at the time, Mahmoud Zaqzuq, decreed that future fatwas needed to be compatible with "logic and human nature." Atiya did a swift turn around and said he had misinterpreted a hadith. This was the kind of stuff that these foreign correspondents reported about in Mubarak's Egypt. It was either hilarity or revulsion. Revolution, often the subject of boozy discussions, was not part of their journalistic oeuvre. Mubarak's stranglehold on society seemed impenetrable. His Mukhabarat did the dirty work of making people disappear overnight.

With dread, I returned to lonely and soulless Johannesburg. Zahir's house-keeper Thambi let me in to the mansion, conveniently located in the majority white and thus rich Sandhurst neighborhood, which Zahir could only afford because of his rich doctor husband. It came with a swimming pool and Thambi. Black women in post-apartheid Africa had no option but servitude to the white or sometimes colored rich. In subsequent trips, South Africa struck me as one of the most inequitable and oppressively racist places on the planet. While the government was quick to remove the signs, apartheid had mostly not gone away. How on earth was this considered an equal nation? Clearly its much-touted constitution did not affect decades of hate.

Thambi, who used a *kanga* (a cotton sling favored by African women) to hold her newborn as she cooked, cleaned, and shopped, was just one visible symptom. A Baby Björn was beneath her status in this still unequal country. Thambi and I didn't share a language and I didn't drive, so there was nowhere to go. I read the books of Islamic thought and theology I had bought in Cairo.

I prepared a long document, telling Zahir how he could be at the center of this evolving LGBTQ universe around the western world, hoping that it would appeal to any narcissism he had. I centered my argument on the principle of the greater jihad, reminding him I was going to call it *A Jihad for Love*. He returned from Mecca, read my work, and was impressed with the effort, research, and thought I had put into the proposal. He agreed to be in the film.

Neither the imam nor I knew at the time that the film would bring him worldwide fame and enable funding for his future pastoral career, as all manner of foundations flocked to him. I regret presenting the *ijtihad* (independent reasoning) Zahir favored as solution for the Islam-homosexuality conundrum at the end of that film. It was false logic. Audiences love happy endings. I gave them one.

I am sure Zahir didn't know that al-Qaeda, *Dar Al Saud* ("The House of Saud"), all Wahhabi and Deobandi logic, and perhaps even Daesh loved the concept of ijtihad. I would never share a table with them.

I wondered if I needed to film talking heads to understand the historic and theological disarray created by Islam and its ever-changing and also bygone relationship to homosexuality. In the early years of the eighth-century Abbasid Empire, in a region that would include present-day Baghdad, the Arab poet Abu Nuwas, a favorite of the caliphs, flourished. Nuwas wrote a kind of verse that would not easily be accepted in a moralistic society like America. A scholar called J. W. Wright had published some of it in translation in a book called *Homoeroticism in Classical Arabic Literature*. In the often-florid Arabic of his time, Nuwas wrote verses that would shock even the organizers of my (first-ever) 1998 San Francisco Gay Pride. It was claimed Nuwas even wrote verse that would be considered pornographic in puritanical America:

Oh Sulayman, sing to me and give me a cup of wine . . .
And if the wine comes round, seize it and give it to me!
Give me a cup of distraction from the Muezzin's call
Give me wine to drink publicly
And bugger and fuck me now!

Nuwas's risqué verse got the better of him eventually. He died in prison. During a particularly prolific period of writing, he went on to take Ayahs 17 and 22 from Surah 56 of the Quran and transform them into a homoerotic fantasy. Ayah 17 said, "Round about them will (serve) youths of perpetual (freshness)." These youths were clearly male. Ayah 22 said, "And (there will be) Companions with beautiful, big, and lustrous eyes." Nuwas was being homoerotic before the concept even existed in the English-speaking world. Poetry lay at the heart of Islam. What was the Quran if not a deeply spiritual, enormous, and eloquent poem? The tribal Arabs in Muhammad's time had always turned toward poetry in difficult times, both sanctioned and from the lips of wandering minstrels, and no subject was off-limits for them. Today, all good Muslims, including unfortunately the ones who blow themselves up to get a direct ticket to heaven, would dismiss Nuwas's poetry as fiction. While the seventy virgins "bearing wine" were often mentioned, the fact that amongst them in this paradise there would also be a sizeable number of youthful boys was conveniently forgotten. Clearly Nuwas was far ahead of his times. His rejig of Quran 17:22 was genius.

I started filming with Ziyad, whose first encounter with me was in Le Depot, the Paris sex club. Ziyad was brutally and repeatedly raped during his incarceration. Condoms were never used. He managed to escape prison and flee Egypt. He was granted asylum in France when I first met him. Unfortunately, the French system granted him nothing beyond that. He was treated with contempt, living a penniless life on the streets of Paris while trying desperately to learn the language of his new country. At the time, it was inconceivable that he would be allowed to return to Egypt—the freedom of an EU passport was far away. The young man was clearly suffering from PTSD. And unfortunately that was not the only illness the regime of his homeland given him. Ziyad tested positive for HIV soon after he arrived in France. It was no doubt a result of repeated anal rape by prison staff in Tora prison. In the film, we transcribed every word he said. He repeated the same story, almost word for word, for an excellent report Human Rights Watch did on the subject, so I was sure of his veracity:

I go inside. Asthagfirullah! A scary cop sat on a chair. I had a position before I was arrested, in the family, in the neighborhood. The biggest asshole called me Mr. Ziyad. And this man spoke to me like a child. The worse head man, Fakhry Saleh, walks in.

"Strip, kneel."

He talked to me like a dog. I got down on all fours. I must have done the wrong position because he said, "No, no, this will not do. Get your chest down and your ass up."

I said, "I can't," and I was crying.

And he said, "All these things you are doing will not cut any ice with me. Be quick about it, we've got work to do." He shoved my underwear almost up my nose. "Red, you bitch, you sharmuta! Red? Do you have no idea? Real men wear white or sometimes black. Fucking cocksucker." He said, "Shut up, everything is clear in front of us."

First, he looked and felt me up. Suddenly, six doctors came in. What is there about my anus? They all felt me up, each in turn, pulling my buttocks apart. They brought this feather against my anus and tickled it. After the feather came the fingers. Then they stuck something bigger. I begged for mercy as it was hurting a lot. I could now feel that my ass was bleeding. Fakhry instructed the men to wear gloves to avoid touching the blood. I wept, but these men had no emotion, none at all.

Fakhry said after, "Why didn't you cry when men put their things in you?" I wanted to spit on him. But I was still crying.

A Jihad for Love was released in late 2007 to great success: good reviews and free worldwide travel. I got the blessing of free travel to twenty-two countries. I tried to learn to forget the death threats, emails, trolls, and fatwas calling for my death. There would be more in the future.

But my own spiritual damnation lingered.

My years of study had taught me that practically no one knew the fact that a sexual revolution of immense proportions came to the earliest Muslims, some 1,300 years before the West had even "thunk" it. This idea of carnal plurality was exactly the kind of unthinkable, unimaginable Eastern innovation the prudish Christian world feared and derided. It was Islam's at least fourteen-centuries-old sexual revolution, which had included equal gender rights. Post-colonization, a political Islam was on the ascendant. That traditional sexual candor was lost in the rhetoric spewing from loudspeakers perched on mosques in cities from Riyadh to Marrakech to Islamabad. It is often said that, unlike for some of the Catholics of our time, sex has never been (the original) sin for Islam. This is *one more* reason Islam supremacists have to gloat. Islamic "Homophobia," which the West needs to understand, is really a post-colonial construct left behind by the hastily departing empire builders after the Second World War. India, for example, had 400 years of sexually tolerant Muslim rule where eroticism was celebrated in many forms. This celebration went back even further when you look back at the supposedly Hindu versions of many Indian cultures that gave us the Kamasutra and Khajuraho. Then came the British colonizers for 200 years, who singlehandedly destroyed centuries of sexual freedom. When they were departing with their prudish, Victorian-style values declaring sex dirty, they left a penal code that makes homosexuality punishable to this day. For centuries, the prudish Occident, all the way up through Victorian and Edwardian scholars of the Orient, while writing about Islam's Ottoman Empire and other Eastern peoples, had spoken about the "licentiousness" and debauchery of the caliphs. Beautiful young lads were being used for sexual pleasure, they fumed. Clucking around with notions of racial superiority, these Occidental ancestors to white supremacists and the alt-right believed everything that was non-Caucasian needed to be colonized or destroyed.

I imagined most returnees from the lavish courts of Muslim empires would have been emissaries and ambassadors and must have always returned home with longing for what they were leaving. Yet these sated returnees publicly depicted a distinctly un-Christian sexual hedonism of "a lesser people."

In my Q&As for *Jihad* I talked about the wrongs of history. The colonizers left, but in practice their sex-averse penal codes remained. Islamic societies saw a religious revivalism greater than ever before. Theocracies like Iran were born. The discussion about sex and sexuality moved from what had been in the realms of courtly life, poetic fantasies, and even other arts, to the bully pulpits of the mullahs. The policing of morality by the state and, if applicable, the religious state, had begun. The increasingly loud theocracies or even your neighborhood imam were erasing centuries of sexual freedom. The same Islam that had not only tolerated but openly celebrated homosexuality was now being used to justify the 2001 government-sanctioned pogrom against gay men in Egypt—America's "enlightened" friend in the Middle East.

In the middle of my travels with the film, in December 2007, I got a text from a friend in Lahore. Former Pakistani Prime Minister Benazir Bhutto had been assassinated. CNN showed footage of Bhutto's last rally at Rawalpindi's Liaqat Ali Park. Her microphone was branded with its manufacturer's logo, *Shahid*, which means "martyr" in Urdu. Bhutto's death was the final nail in Pakistan's political coffin. The world had never seen a Muslim woman like her. A United Nations report concluded, "Ms. Bhutto's assassination could have been prevented if adequate security measures had been taken." Pakistan was a land of rumors. Some said that the president at the time, Pervez Musharraf, deliberately ignored her repeated requests for additional security. But because Musharraf's son and daughter-in-law had been early supporters of my work, I chose the rumor that said al-Qaeda was responsible.

Benazir was my mother's icon and thus mine. Celebrity, geographical proximity, the charismatic impact only a beautiful and powerful Muslim woman can have on a formative gay male mind—all of these were contributing factors. I was fifteen when Benazir, whose name meant "like none other," entered my imagination. My mother had just bought the autobiography of the Dukhtar-e-Mashriq, or "Daughter of the East," and insisted that I read it as well. I was soon swept up in a world of intrigue and the violence of feudal politics that had spelled doom for her father when he was hanged by the tyrannical, soon-to-be dictator Zia ul-Haq.

My mother had often spoken of wishing to visit Pakistan, a land where ancestral history was left behind in mindless violence. Whatever happened in Pakistan was important to Indians, and vice versa. Many years later, when I was a student in Washington, DC, Ms. Bhutto and I actually (un-Islamically) shook hands as she finished speaking at my university. I told her how my Indian mother idolized her.

"That's very special," she said in her impeccable Oxford English.

Her life was a testament to the latent strength of all Muslim women. Benazir ruled the very-Muslim country of Pakistan twice. Her death struck me as a loss for Islam. The religion had surprisingly proved that women could lead nations. She was the first to do so. This was the beginning of a period of both success and despair for me.

We had all survived the Bush era and we were in 2008. Globally loved, *A Jihad for Love* was creating minor celeb status for me.

"Enjoy it, won't last," my friend Adham texted sagely. One morning in late October, I turned the pages of a dog-eared Quran to prove a point to Keith, who did not have a religious bone in his body.

"There is no compulsion in matters of faith, Surah 2, Ayah 256," I said. "See! There! Islam doesn't force anyone to become Muslim or to have faith, even. Muhammad built the region's, and Islam's, first democracy."

He laughed at my need for him to know this. I merely wanted us to be able to quash a rumor (that was already rife) if someone ever asked us. The 2008 Democratic presidential nominee, Barack Obama, shared his middle name, Hussein, not only with the Iraqi tyrant Saddam but also the most revered Shia imams. His opponent, John McCain, fielded questions about Obama's faith, despite the latter's insistence that he was a Christian.

I knew this would happen. Using Islamic patriarchy, a sheikh could make the argument that children inherit the father's religion. But Obama Senior was an atheist. Barack met him only once and was raised by his white Kansas grandparents among Protestants. If rigid rules of Wahhabism were followed, both father and son could be considered apostates for having left the religion. In Saudi Arabia apostasy carries the death penalty.

On November 4, 2008, as New Yorkers sensing history being made euphorically poured into the streets, it seemed for a night that the race divide was forever shattered. In Harlem, 125th Street was filled with thousands, including Keith and our friends, glued to giant TV screens that had been set up at a few public places or in bars and restaurants. It was almost like everyone was united by a sense of prescience that Obama would win. I stayed home, kneeling before our television set. I prayed in the Muslim way, formally, repeatedly, for Obama to have God's favor. As NBC called the result, I heard firecrackers and shouts of jubilation from the streets. Barack Hussein Obama had won the biggest US presidential victory in history with 69.5 million of the popular vote.

Some evangelicals saw him as the coming of the Antichrist. For others, he was the Black Jesus. In a few years, he would become a fallen prophet. I always believed that humanity's last battles would be fought on the front lines of race and religion. And as every single Republican tried to block any decision Obama ever made, I realized once again how deep the fault-lines of prejudice and racial injustice ran in this country. The birth of the Birthers and the subsequent Tea Party were all you needed to realize that Obama, a brilliant and charismatic orator, tactician, and president, was trapped in the racial-paranoia cycle that these new entities were mere fronts for. Segregation was just a few decades gone, yet many in America's right wing could not tolerate a black family in a very White House built in part by slaves. For some, it was as if Obama never existed. For others, he was the "uppity Negro," and the KKK needed to be brought back. Thus, the racist Tea Party and the Birthers were born. Donald Trump was one of their heroes.

For me, America's most storied black ghetto, Harlem, was home. And Harlem was changing. Young white couples with fresh babies seemed to be migrating uptown in hordes. Keith and I found a sticker outside our building. It had an ominous "X" sign with the words "Whites Out Of Harlem" printed on it. There must have been others. We laboriously peeled it off and trashed it.

In my corner of this neighborhood, what I sometimes jokingly called Upstate Manhattan, I lived surrounded by black ladies who churched. Those were heady days. For me personally, Barack and Michelle's very own Camelot is a forever kind of thing.

It was still too early to realize that Obama in the long term would be seen as the black president who was unable to heal Black America's long-broken heart. How could this one man correct such enormous historical wrongs? Was just his elevation enough? It was too early to know how much the majority-white Republicans would cripple him by refusing to sign *anything* that had the name Obama on it. They made his name poison, and his race lay behind *every single time* the Republicans said no to him. Obama's rise was directly proportional to the rise of racism. Some on the right were now reorganizing like never before with even a catchy new name, The Tea Party, and predictably all their events were almost all-white. As this nation's first black president, Obama was already carrying an immense burden. Yes, history would remember him. But would it be just for his race and how much it affected his ability to achieve?

Two weeks after Obama's election, my feared Eid of the Sacrifice arrived. Bullets ricocheted in my beloved Bollywood. Bombay, a city of 20 million people, was taken hostage by terrorists for three nights. One hundred sixty-four people were killed. This strategically scattered killing spree struck terror into every heart and would form just one of many blueprints for future attacks in Brussels and Paris.

The terrorists came from Pakistan. Lashkar-e-Taiba (ironically, "Army of the Pure"), the group responsible, shared some of the Wahhabi ideology of the future ISIS. I felt torn between my two identities as an Indian and a Muslim. The thought that these men had timed their attack to coincide with the Eid that marks the end of the Hajj sickened me. Bollywood was ruled by three megastars—all Muslim. Shahrukh Khan, Amir Khan, and Salman Khan were quick to denounce the carnage. They were uber-sensitive of their public Muslim identity. They wore black armbands and didn't celebrate the festival. In Hindu-majority India, these Khans had transcended religion. Their soundbites, like those of hundreds of Muslims on TV, were attributed not to Islam but to "the minority community." This phrase had always been a subtle but reliable way to prevent unrest in post-partition India.

The bloodbath in Bombay shook me to my core. India, with its more than 140 million Muslims, was number three on the highest-Muslim-population nations list. This was India's 9/11.

NYC entered the holiday season with its endless parties. At one of them, I listened in horror to a diamond-and-daiquiri-dripping Indian socialite opine on how the blasts in Bombay would improve box-office numbers for everybody's new favorite movie, *Slumdog Millionaire*. She was just one of the many "deeply concerned" Indians and Pakistanis in the room that night pledging to hold marches and benefits.

It would have been easy for me to pontificate from thousands of miles away.

Benazir and Bombay, which both broke my heart, also gave me an opportunity to realize the parts of me I was wrestling with to build my public
identity. I was already one of the world's most public homosexual Muslims.
The United Nations courted me for a speaking engagement. The EU was
not far behind. I got to meet Michelle Obama. Powerful stuff.

A Zionist group within the UN invited me as a symptom of how bad
Islam really was. I was naïve. This event unfolded in Geneva on UN ground.
Hours after landing I discovered the real agenda. Sitting on a panel where
this group wanted to showcase me as one of the other oppressed Muslims
sharing the table, I launched into why my hosts were against any view I
held of Palestine and Israel. I made a strong case against the occupation
and was politely asked to leave. It was a crash course in how my words now
held weight and had to be used responsibly.

But my notoriety expanded among the conservative Muslims. I was a
marked man—publicly labeled an infidel for my blasphemous argument
that Islam and homosexuality could coexist. Following the release of the
film, some religious opinion condemned me for the sin of apostasy. One
fatwa provided extensive, supposedly Quranic evidence and quoted from
the "Judgment on Apostates" section of the curriculum used in Saudi
schools:

> An apostate will be suppressed three days in prison in order that he
> may repent. Otherwise, he should be killed, because he has changed
> his true religion, therefore, there is no use from his living.

Reacting to the fatwa, me, and the film, a commentator on a Saudi
website posted, "If I could kill him with my own hands I would. But I am
sure Allah will take care of that."

I was doing well on the speaking circuit but was also tired of "the gay
Muslim" that always prefixed my name.

My internal alienation from the activism scene, the assassination of
Bhutto, the attacks in Bombay, and more made me feel far removed from
my heritage as a Muslim. I knew I had to do something about it. I felt like
a minority in multiple ways. I was gay among disapproving Muslims. I was
Muslim among xenophobic Americans. And I was Muslim among gays
who could never relate to the power of a faith that burned inside me, despite
many of its leaders naming me a *kafir*, a disbeliever, a big sin in Islam.

I decided it would soon be time to make good on my Beirut resolution from 2010: to go on the Hajj.

The devout Muslim subjects of my film longed for and feared the Hajj. I felt as though I owed my going to myself and to them. Unquestionably millions of gay people had performed Hajj over the centuries. But none had made a film about it, using mainly an iPhone, and with no government permission from a regime that would love to imprison or behead me. If I could pull it off, it would be a world first. There are hundreds of thousands of Hajj videos online, but to construct a film by being inside the 3.5-million-strong crowd all by myself is one of the most dangerous things I have ever done. My agenda for the film was clear: I would reveal the real—what until now had been an almost "secret"—Hajj. This would be truth-telling without a Saudi minder or fixers or even a crew. If I were to succeed, this footage needed to be unlike anything the world had ever seen. It would be from inside the grit, sweat, and tears of my pilgrimage. It would essentially be the Saudi Arabia they, the House of Saud, don't want you to see.

There are only a very small number of visual accounts that exist of the Hajj and call themselves films. I, like several other journalists, accurately refer to them as "junket films." They amount to nothing more than the Saudis showing off. I know the process. First make sure you are an all-Muslim crew. Then get "permission" papers by providing IDs, pretending to be or actually being real journalists, and adding obsequious letters of intent: all sent to the (universally despised) Ministry of Hajj. Final product— "the film" of the Hajj is exactly how the Saudis want it to be seen: the greatest show on earth, and they (the Saudi monarchy) are pulling it off every year. One of those junket films even included talking heads of various departments in the Saudi bureaucracy, including the all-important Ministry of Hajj. The so-called "filmmakers" who make these videos are usually accompanied by a minder.

There was no doubt in my mind that the Saudis had me on some no-fly list. I slipped in only because they are processing millions of visas at Hajj time. You would not expect the man who had made the world's very first film on Islam and homosexuality that generated a huge amount of (Google-able) news to head to Saudi Arabia, where beheading was a weekly ritual for crimes that included homosexuality (with some sharia stipulations met). And here I was, deciding to do exactly that. As a Muslim

I was embarking on the greatest journey of my life. The filmmaker part of my brain said: There was no way I would not film it.

Something even more urgent and personal was at stake. I had felt like a sinner for years because I thought I had "killed" my mother with the shame of my sexuality. This pilgrimage would be in her honor. Maybe she (and I) could find a place of forgiveness in Mecca? It would also be a way for me to silence my Muslim critics who called me an infidel. *A Jihad for Love* was about my coming out to the world as a proud homosexual. This pilgrimage would be about my coming out as a prouder Muslim. But I was always a troublemaker and thus the pilgrimage was timed perfectly, a few months after the Arab Spring and bin Laden's death. I was walking into the jaws of danger defiantly and willingly again. This penchant for real, raw menace has always been part of who I am. The Saudis rightfully were terrified of their populace's catching the revolution bug. I intended to be right there if it happened. Hajj after all brought millions together.

But first, there were a few things that needed attending to.

My lawyer said Keith and my getting married would be a good idea. The possibility of being "found out" in Saudi Arabia was real and the consequences unimaginable. We knew the Indian embassy would do nothing to protect me. She said a marriage and the "alien with extraordinary abilities" green card might help get the attention of the US consulate in Jeddah, in case anything happened. In a backhanded way, I was obeying Islam's recommendation to be married before going on the Hajj. I would "fulfill all worldly obligations."

Keith and I were able to tie the knot in Manhattan's City Hall on the historic first day that it was legal. We approached marriage with a blasé attitude. A reporter who knew me approached. After he agreed to keep us anonymous, both Keith and I told him, "We are doing it just for taxes!" He did use the quote. I was paranoid. I was slowly creeping back into the closet. My Saudi visa was still in process and I had to be careful not to be photographed or mentioned as a gay Muslim this or that. My sins, my crimes were a mere Google search away.

On my wedding day I carried my decades-old Quran with my mother's passport photo inside. This day was the polar opposite of the bacchanalia of Gay Pride. The latter was all about big penises, bubble butts, six packs, and corporate sponsorships. This day was about commitment, wholesomeness, love, and history.

I proudly showed Keith my mother's photo inside the Quran.

"She wouldn't have approved, you know," he said, "and neither would this book."

"It's not just a book," I said tersely.

He put his arm around my shoulder. "I know. But I'll never understand your need for it."

We kissed for the first time in public. We'd been together for eight years, and it was my first PDA. I felt safe. And I felt loved.

I now knew where home would forever be. It was wherever Keith was.

But a pre-Hajj obligation evoked terror.

The platform of the 125th Street station on the 1 train is one of my favorite places in Manhattan. It is above ground, and in winter, as the snow softly falls, I sometimes get off there for no reason at all. The snow creates an effect such that the surrounding apartments seem to float in the air and almost touch the platform. Through the windows, warm young Columbia University undergrads are unaware that I can stare at them staring at their laptops.

But that's winter. I was headed downtown on a super-hot August 2011 morning to obediently submit myself to Islam in the harshest manner possible. I had carefully planned the date to coincide with Eid.

New York was the fabled Mecca of freedom. Her trains roared underground through the world's greatest example of diversity. Their routes marked a geography, which often on ground level easily changed into different realities, even nations. On the subway, just like Muhammad's Ummah, everyone was equal.

On the downtown 1, the spectacle of New York was always visible. Sometimes there would be perfect parents bringing their perfect children to and from school. They had fulfilled their mandated roles. Ordinary people, whose children would be their only legacies. *Would they leave a mark on history or would it be people like me*, I thought arrogantly.

As the Quran droned in my headphones, I sneaked a few longing stares at the white boys who had just boarded exposing their youthful, superior skin color, in thrall of the last days of summer. Were they unaware of their youthful beauty?

At the end of every day I sat and Islamicized my new iPhone. It was coming with me as my primary hope and tool for filming with some ease.

Sadly, the screensaver picture of Keith had already been replaced (though I did keep several in my photos app) by the green (Islam's color) Saudi flag—sword, testament, and all. Why would this nation choose to put an instrument of absolute violence on its primary national symbol? Allegedly it was visual evidence of how strictly the country enforced Wahhabi sharia. To be safe, my iPhone's playlist was fast filling with recitations of various Quranic Surahs instead of hip-hop that used the C- and D-words.

As I turned my worldly possessions halal, I was constantly aware that Islam's scalpel of disciplining sexuality had missed me by a hair's breadth when I was a child. I was spared the blade owing to some "medical problems" that remain unexplained. My research terrorized me. Google reliably threw up strangeness. One website claimed the Prophet had said, "Prophet Ibrahim circumcised himself at the age of eighty, using a hatchet." And then there was a more obscure Sunni hadith that says that one should not pray for a dead Muslim who is uncircumcised.

As a Sunni, my decision to go on Hajj with Shias instead was unusual. For the Wahhabis, the Shia are worse than Islam's bastard children— infidels, as much as I was, but for different reasons. The hatred is mutual. But even they, my fellow infidels, agreed with their Sunni oppressors on this one thing: The uncircumcised Muslim male was damned. Thus, the religious opinion that terrorized my soul the most came via Grand Aya-tollah Ali al-Sistani, Iraq's highest Shia authority. The year before my Hajj he had allegedly pronounced the death penalty for all gays in US-occupied Iraq, leading to a pogrom that lasted for years. And unfortunately I had publicly dared to investigate and write about the ayatollah's call for the killing of gay men.

About circumcision, this ayatollah opined: "If an uncircumcised pil-grim in *ihram*, be he adult or discerning child, performs a *tawaf*, it is invalid. Unless he repeats it, after being circumcised, he will, as a matter of precaution, be regarded as a person who has abandoned tawaf." The tawaf is the obligatory counterclockwise circumambulation of the Kaaba, per-formed several times during Hajj. For my fellow Shia pilgrims, al-Sistani's word is usually like God's word. It is al-Sistani who is also credited with a famous fatwa about depicting Muhammad:

"If due deference and respect is observed, and the scene does not con-tain anything that would detract from their holy pictures in the minds [of the viewers], there is no problem." No Sunni would dare say this.

An uncut penis could be a dangerous thing in the small Indian town I grew up in. The fractures of intolerance rarely surfaced amongst the Hindu and Muslim communities coexisting mostly peaceably as they had for generations. But once there were riots. During this mayhem, we barricaded ourselves. The adults whispered about how the mobs of either religion identified whom to kill. My grandfather was staying with us during one period of these clashes, brought on by a Hindu mob that had dumped the carcass of a pig in a mosque. The Muslims retaliated by slaughtering a cow outside a temple. My grandfather had lived through the death trains of India and Pakistan's partition. He recounted how his two best friends were stripped, genitally identified as Muslim, and hacked to death. I hid to hear this whispered adults-only story.

As the train screeched to a halt at the 86th Street station, I was rudely reminded of the purpose of my journey. A fully veiled woman boarded the train with her festively dressed little girl. It was Eid, after all. I got up immediately to offer them a seat. I would never know if she smiled in gratitude; there was no face to be seen. But the mind of a sinner always wanders. As the imam musically intoned the Quran in my headphones, I stared sexually at yet another cute hipster boy.

My urologist, Dr. Stein, said I was a "brave man." In that moment of trauma, as he began the procedure, I felt safe telling him what I had told no one but Keith. During my pilgrimage, I would be wearing the ihram, two seamless pieces of white cloth with no underwear. In my many nightmares, my ihram would fall off in Mecca, subjecting unsuspecting pilgrims to my un-Muslim penis.

Dr. Stein laughed and said, "The two Valium and Percocet you took should be kicking in now. Does this hurt?" as he jabbed at what must have been my penis. I yelped in pain. But soon I seemed to be in some kind of waking dream.

In Arabic, the word *Islam* means "submission." For its obedient followers, this is a religion of meticulous discipline. Osama bin Laden's jihadis feel superior to all other Muslims in their belief that only they know how to live by the harshest strictures of our religion. A distant uncle in my family refused to even swallow his own saliva during Ramadan. He used to lecture us as children, "We are superior to all other people."

This uncle was the only unmarried adult relative I knew, and now I wonder if his doctrinal adherence to some of Islam's harshest strictures masked the shame of his own sexuality, which I imagine he never acted upon. The morality of sex is tightly controlled in Islam, as in all patriarchies, and women's bodies are primary targets. But penises and male dress (modest—no sleeves rolled up) are also technically controlled. I was leaving for the holy land as a fearful pilgrim. If my sexuality was my primary sin, then surely its most visible marker was my penis, which I had failed to discipline. This, perhaps, was my chance to undo some of the sin that marked my penis, by irreversibly altering it.

"You have a new penis, Parvez," said Dr. Stein. "This looks perfect. But you don't have to see it quite yet."

I was taking all of the dissonance of my twenty-first-century life into an almost seventh-century Saudi Arabia. Siri and my new penis were coming along. All that remained on my i (for Islamic) Phone was a hidden picture of Keith.

"It will take eight weeks to look normal," said Dr. Stein.

Friends said my circumcision proved I was "crazy" and they would never take such an irreversible, life-altering decision. I had no choice.

Now that my penis was halal, it was time to tackle the last few preparations for my journey to Mecca. Alcohol was out but sleepless nights Googling every possible Saudi atrocity were in. There needed to be a crash course of the vast Shia canon. One of my prophets, Steve Jobs, died a few days before I left, but he bestowed a final gift that would accompany me on my journey—the iPhone 4S. With it I would document my journey in the hopes that I could use the footage for a new documentary film. Tension between Iran and Saudi Arabia was ramping up over an alleged Iranian plot to assassinate Adel al-Jubeir, Saudi Arabia's ambassador to the United States. The day before I left, Muammar Gaddafi was assassinated. Everything seemed to be telling me to stay put.

I tried to remind myself of the purpose of my journey of the spirit. I assuaged my fears by reading famed Iranian scholar Ali Shariati's famous rumination on the Hajj. The book, originally in Farsi, was simply called *Hajj* and translated into many languages. Shariati is considered the ideological father of the Iranian revolution and is one of the loudest progressive voices in recent Islamic history. In his book, he said:

Now take off your clothes. Leave them at Miqat. Wear the Kafan which consists of plain white material. You will be dressed like everyone else. See the uniformity appear! Be a particle and join the mass; as a drop, enter the ocean.

Shariati is also famed because he was one of the first Iranian scholars to view the Shia religion through a revolutionary lens, making him in a sense a "father" of the idea of a Shia political Islam. A revolutionary lens to view an entire religion? I held onto that. I was a revolutionary too and this Hajj was my jihad.

Years ago I had been introduced to Shariati's work by a friend who left France for the UK to do a PhD at Oxford. I had always admired her. Rereading Shariati reminded me of Shahinaz. I emailed her about a possibility. Her response thrilled me.

CHAPTER 4

THE GARDEN OF PARADISE

Here a ninja
There a ninja
Everywhere a ninja ninja!

I hummed my made-up ditty in my head. I was surrounded by them. Ninjas. Not the combative kind, but the Saudi version. Some women on my flight were women no longer! Their Hajj gear—black sheaths covered every inch of their bodies. I understood that women in Saudi Arabia were commanded to cover their bodies, but why, oh, why, in the beating hot sun, were they forced to wear all black? Were these foreign women masochists, or did fear of retribution on Saudi soil compel them to suffer this way? The men looked comparatively comfortable in their civvies. They felt no need to change, at least not until they entered the area of Miqat (the many standing places outside Mecca where ihram needs to be worn) in Mecca. In addition, we were flying to Medina first. The Quran itself only called for modesty for clothing for both men and women. Nowhere in the book were there references to these tent-like black (or Taliban blue) sheaths, and this question of dress is subject to heated modern debate. Those who enforced the morality of the hijab quote from various parts of the Quran, like Ayah 59 of al-Azhab, Surah 33:

Oh prophet tell your wives and daughters,
And the women of the faithful,
To draw their wraps a little over them.
They will thus be recognized and no harm will come to them.
God is forgiving and kind.

There were curtained prayer rooms fitted right next to the toilets. Many in my party decided to pray. What time zone? Which prayer? I stayed where I was. I thought it was absurd to pray on a plane, but my TV screen reminded me, with its Mecca arrow, which direction to point my supplications should I be overcome with a need to show off my piety.

My Shia group leader, Shafiq, distributed pamphlets and prayer books. The Shia were entering a butchered land. The Wahhabis had destroyed broad swathes of Shia history and culture, most notably the graves of their ancestors. We were given maps that marked the names and locations of these burial sites. This was remarkable. It was a feat of diligent, secret cartography.

A week before my circumcision, I had emailed my friend Shahinaz in London and asked her to join me. Being adventurous, she agreed. Shahinaz was an old friend whom I also filmed for my first doc. She, like me, was gay. She was "Allah conscious," like her Somali parents in Paris, but Islam's strictures were not for her. They had emigrated to France when she was five. She was my Shia, African, and French cousin! I always introduced her as my London "cousin." Later, we were destined to become husband and wife, Saudi style.

It was karma that a real cousin of hers in Birmingham was coming on Hajj the very same year with the UK contingent of my very same Hajj group—we would all become one big group upon arrival. What are the chances! We both felt it was meant to be. Especially because as her cousin he became her mahram, or male guardian—a practice that many Hajj groups still follow, to allow women to perform the pilgrimage. In some modern Shia and Sunni practices, it is not necessary, as the group leader becomes the mahram for "unaccompanied" women. I paid for Shahinaz's Hajj—it only seemed fair. She knew I was planning to film and also write a book.

Shahinaz and I reunited at Doha International Airport where the British contingent had joined us. We were not able to sit together on the connecting flight, but we checked on each other often.

Medina Airport was dated and dingy, boasting only a few squeaky luggage carousels—hardly the ostentatious display of Saudi excess I expected. Men and women lined up separately to retrieve their baggage.

As far as I and many in my group were concerned, our Hajj began at touchdown. Even though the formal Hajj took only five days, my journey of the spirit started here.

A naked fear filled me as I walked toward Saudi immigration. I wondered if I was Muslim enough to be allowed in. I was at the doors of the nation I most feared and loathed: Wahhabi-land. Wahhabism is the cruel and puritanical form of eighteenth-century Islam the Saudis practice. In 1744, a struggling and ridiculed desert cleric called Muhammad Ibn Abd al-Wahhab made a pact with an also struggling tribal leader called Muhammad Ibn Saud. Wahhab would be allowed to make his version of Islam the law of the land that Ibn Saud was trying to create. And he and his followers in exchange would accept Wahhabi dogma as Saudi sharia. The land and country that would be created would be a monarchy composed of Dar Al Saud, "The House of Saud." They reserve the death penalty for people like me. Beheading and being flung off a tall building were the punishments of choice.

Immense faith had brought me here. I was obeying my highest calling as a Muslim, to embark on the Hajj pilgrimage. This was my journey of the spirit. I prayed I would be allowed to finish it.

"Muslim?" said the balding border guard scrutinizing my Indian passport.

"Yes," I answered with a confidence I did not feel. He typed into a tired-looking PC. Had he Googled me and already known who I was?

Stamping my passport with his grubby fingers he said, "*Ahlan al Hag*" ("Welcome, Hajji"). Premature, I thought. The greeting was reserved for those who had already fulfilled Islam's highest calling.

"*Inshallah,*" I replied. He smiled. My response contained a reservation—I did not yet feel like a true pilgrim.

I had dreaded this moment for months, fearing that my status as an out gay man would prevent me from entering the holy land. I had built the moment up in my mind to such a degree that the actual event could only feel anticlimactic. I was not thrown in jail or barred from entry.

Instead, the guard's warm greeting felt as though he had stamped the word "Muslim" on my forehead.

"Bonjour Monsieur! Welcome to the land of the unfree," read a text from Adham.

"Inshallah, I will meet God!" I replied, tongue firmly in cheek.

"Inshallah, for everything! The best Muslim excuse there ever was!"

"Just put it all in God's hands LOL!" I replied.

At the time, I thanked the late Steve Jobs for the iMessage function of my 4S. I got unlimited free texts riding on the kingdom's largest network, Mobily. I created a Keith, Adham, and Shahinaz MMS group for general texts.

"It will all be fine. I love you," Keith texted. He had dealt with the enormity of my fears preceding this pilgrimage. His love would sustain me in the weeks to follow.

"Have they taken your passports yet?" Adham asked.

A few minutes later, on our bus, they did.

The following morning, I overslept and missed Fajr, the first prayer of the day. Big mistake. I had already opened myself up to the condescension of my roommates with my careless disregard for ritual. These judgmental men in my room were forming a schoolyard-like clique at breakfast. I was subtly excluded from their camaraderie. Pretending to sleep, I would sometimes hear conversations. One of them, a hypochondriac called Abdullah, had a bagful of medication and Epipens. One morning he said that if he became a martyr in Mecca, he would consider himself and his entire family blessed. He had earlier looked disapprovingly when I prayed in the Sunni way. So I kept my eyes shut.

He audibly whispered to the others that he worked for the US military in Virginia, where he lived with his wife and newborn son. He operated drones over his native Pakistan.

"How do you know you aren't killing your Shia brethren?" asked a roomie.

"I don't know for sure, but I always hope it's the evil Sunni jihadis and not one of my own."

Shahinaz and I walked toward Medina's heart, which was the Prophet's Mosque right across the road. In the light of day, it felt otherworldly. It is impossible for someone of my generation not to think of Tatooine, the desert planet where a young Luke Skywalker discovers his destiny. The sand and heat did call Tatooine to mind, but it was also the architecture and the people.

A mutawa thwacked us. "Marry?" he said.

"Yes, of course!" we both exclaimed.

"Proof?" he snarled.

We made great show of searching our belongings and then said we had left them at the hotel. "You'll just have to take our word for it, brother. Why would we lie in Medina?" Probably illiterate, he left us alone, and Shahinaz set off to find the women's corrals.

A quarter of humanity is Muslim, and they all gathered here from every corner of the globe during Hajj season. Mecca and Medina are the United Nations of Islam, showcasing the diversity of the world's fastest-growing religion. The rest of Saudi Arabia is a monoculture of "ninja"-style abayas for the women and the *dishdasha* or *thawb*, a long, flowing, usually white robe, for the men. Here, it was a rainbow of colors and styles. I saw Chinese men wearing teal vests and white caps, Kenyan women in bright pink scarves, and Somalis in dazzling block-printed fabric. Every group was color-coded so members could easily spot one another in the crowds. In a cosmopolitan place such as this, it's not always easy for the Saudis to enforce a tight dress code. The immensity of the Hajj promises a strange freedom that can only come from strength in numbers and hiding in plain sight. There was an occasional all-black abaya-trapped woman floating around, but this was really the United Colors of Islam. I started taking photos surreptitiously, with the goal of documenting these styles on an imagined Tumblr I would call "Hajj Couture," but then I remembered that I could be hauled to prison for taking pictures of women here. In a Twitter-obsessed country I was ironically afraid to send out tweets from my Hajj, because that would be a sure-fire way to invite the attention of the wrong kind of Saudis—in my case, their Interior Ministry and their Mukhabarat. Biggest concern of all: I was not a US citizen but an Indian one. Both the Saudis and the Indians would want someone like me gone. In retrospect, it feels like a small and petty fear, but the reality of it then seemed big. The chances? Fifty-fifty.

Massive retractable umbrellas bloomed over our heads from unassuming marble columns, shielding us mercifully from the mid-morning sun. We were periodically spritzed by mists of cool water. Just like I'd experienced in Palm Springs! All of this across miles and miles of pristine marble. Gulf excess was not new to me but this was quite the sight.

Did my fellow pilgrims realize that this comfortable microclimate came at a heavy price? In the two holy cities, the bin Ladens colluded with the House of Saud for the biggest reconstruction project in the history of Islam. Countless artifacts, burial sites, objects the Prophet loved, and historic structures were steamrolled to make way for the high-tech yet tasteless glitz and marble. It's difficult to imagine a broader tragedy of cultural erasure in modern history. The Al Saud gave the Mecca and Medina reconstruction project, predictably, to one of the world's richest construction companies, the bin Laden Group. One of the family's many sons was called Osama. He worked briefly at the Mecca office, to oversee the destruction and would later lament about all that the Al Saud destroyed, never mentioning his own family who *actually executed* the destruction.

This was the Masjid al-Nabi, the "Mosque of the Prophet." He was buried here, and Medina represented, for me, a student of Islam, the birthplace of Islam's democracy. Exiled by his own tribe from Mecca, Muhammad had laid down the foundations of the religion's first constitution. At its center was the principle of Tawhid, the oneness of God. This was *al-Madinah al-Munawwarah*, the "Radiant City," primarily because Muhammad built Islam's first society of peace and tolerance within its boundaries. In seventh-century Yathrib, as the city was called then, women had real rights. Jews existed harmoniously alongside Muslims. The first Muslims, the ones we'd always been taught to emulate, came from Medina. They called it the city of *Sukoon* ("Peace"). A peace of the spirit.

Inside the mosque, a maze of striped archways stretched out before me. The melodious, drawn-out call to Zuhr prayers echoed through the halls. This is the only semblance of music that is allowed in the entire country. All else is forbidden. A country without music? To many this would be inconceivable. But for young Saudis, music can be a dark secret whose volume is always set low.

I had not come to my Hajj unprepared. The history between Saudi Arabia and Iran and Sunni-Shia conflagrations through the centuries had been part of my research material all my adult life.

It was the night of the Shia prayer, the long *Dua'a Kumayl*, a supplication of a man who was, for them, the most devout follower of the Prophet's son-in-law, Imam Ali. The latter for all Shia was the rightful successor to the Prophet because he was married to Fatima, the Prophet's youngest daughter. She gave birth to the next two imams, Husayn and Hassan, as the Shia lineage progressed from the Ahl al-Bayt (Muhammad's family). For Sunnis, the Prophet's inheritor was a *sahaba* (close companion) called Abu Bakr. And that lineage rift would forever separate Shia from Sunni.

In this Shia prayer, Ali's faithful servant Kumayl speaks for Ali. The faithful recite this prayer in order to seek fulfillment of "legitimate" desires, to request safety from enemies, to request the forgiveness of sins and to ask for wealth, and more. My new group-friend Hossein marched with me toward this redoubtable scene with a confidence I didn't feel. He was Iranian and, as often happens, we bonded over a cigarette.

There is a political element to this prayer ritual. The Iranians deliberately gather in large numbers to recite the extremely long supplication near the Prophet's Mosque in Medina. It's a Dua that can happen only on a Thursday night. That night there were, by my estimate, about 2,000 Iranians. Ironically a much greater number of Saudi riot police corralled them. Shia protest would be intolerable mobocracy. Post-revolution Iranians often used the Hajj for protests against many matters, including the Dar Al Saud. Iranians have been frequently banned from the Hajj, either by their own government or by the Saud who fear them.

Islam's deepest schism is about who inherits the Prophet's wisdom. He would not recognize the sectarian Islam of today. The most-visible symbols of this divide are the nations of Sunni Saudi Arabia and Shia Iran. The greater Middle East has always been their playground. The fleeing colonizers in the mid-twentieth century left gore and hastily carved nations in their wake. To this day, both Iran and Saudi Arabia compete for hegemony in countries such as Iraq, Jordan, Lebanon, and more recently Syria and Yemen. Revolutionary Iran in 1979 married political power with religion, filling the Saud with terror. Their utopia was of a Wahhabi-Saud marriage, where the clergy were left alone as long as the monarchy stayed in power. The head honchos of that clergy even issued fatwas on command to enable the monarchy to continue wielding political power. Iran's revolution turned logic like that upside down, because, most important, it toppled a monarchy—the shah of the Pahlavi dynasty that had ruled Iran since 1925.

If this could happen in a nation that had had monarchy for 2,500 years, what would befall the House of Saud if the same winds of revolution blew Saudi-ward?

In the sixties, the Iranian shah sent a series of open letters to the Saudi king, Faisal. In one he famously said, "Please, my brother, modernize. Open up your country. Make the schools mixed women and men. Let women wear miniskirts. Have discos. Be modern. Otherwise, I cannot guarantee you will stay on your throne." Miniskirts were forever banned from the Iranian mind just a decade later. In any case, the Saudis were skittish because of history. In winter 1979, as the Iranian revolutionaries were taking the US embassy hostage, the Masjid al-Haram (Noble Sanctuary) in Mecca was overrun by revolutionaries. They were led by one Juhayman al-Otaybi, who declared the Mahdi (Islam's redeemer; in this case, his brother-in-law) had come.

Much blood was shed in this city where the Prophet had forbidden even the killing of an insect. The mayhem lasted two weeks and infidel French troops ended the siege. This seizure at the Kaaba while revolutionary Iran jubilated fueled eternal terror in the House of Saud.

The newly anointed Ayatollah Khomeini spoke out on Tehran Radio on November 21, 1979: "It is not beyond guessing that this is the work of criminal American imperialism and international Zionism." He knew he was beginning a decades-long tirade against the "Evil Satan," often represented by the US and Zionism. In Iran, anti-Western rhetoric grew. At the same time, Saudi Arabia solidified its ties with the US.

Not only was the ayatollah expressing the hatred his revolutionaries were carrying out at the US embassy in Tehran, he was also during that time of innumerable daily fatwas making the claim that monarchy like the government structure of Saudi Arabia was un-Islamic. The rise of the Khomeini's *Velayat-e Faqih* ("Rule by the Jurists") would be akin to Saudi King Khalid's handing over power to the Wahhabis' grand mufti.

In Islamic eschatology the arrival of the Mahdi signaled that the Day of Judgment was fast approaching. Both Shia and Sunni believe in this end of times, with the arrival of this Mahdi. But for most Sunnis, the Mahdi has not yet come and exists only as a theological and theoretical concept. For the "Twelver" Shia, the Mahdi (basically their twelfth and final imam) has always been there and can manifest at any time (with Jesus)—he just went into a state of occultation 1,200 years ago. Both Shia and Sunni call him Muhammad al-Mahdi, after the name of the Prophet. It is interesting that some Shia believe the Mahdi's coming out will have several portents, including massive war in Syria, destroying it, and in Iraq fear and death for its people. I would love to see the faces of Wahhabi-inspired ISIS terrorists when they learn the despised Shia share their thinking about this critical truth we are actually living.

Iran and Saudi Arabia are the world's most prominent examples of sharia law, and yet they couldn't be more different. Iranian zealots have never let go of their idea of their utopian, pan-Islamic revolution, which is abhorrent to the Saudis. The fight is about both oil and ideology. In the Iran-Iraq War, the Saudis plied Saddam with $25 billion. Their temporary love of Saddam was disingenuous. He conveniently kept the country's Shia majority in check, while retaining an important geographical and cultural divide between them and Iran. In 1984, the countries came to the brink of war as Iranian planes flew over Saudi soil. Khomeini, who was never at a loss for words, declared, "These vile and ungodly Wahhabis are like daggers which have always pierced the heart of the Muslims from the back." Using the familiar and time-tested idea of *takfir* (Islamic excommunication, where one Muslim accuses another of being a *kafir*, a nonbeliever), he made the claim that Mecca was in the hands of "a band of heretics." All Saudi kings took immense pride and earned most of their legitimacy by appending the title of "Custodian of the Two Holy Mosques" to their names. The ayatollah was attacking that basic precept.

Since 1981, Iranians had held yearly Hajj protests against the US and Israel in Mecca. The Saudis tolerated this. But in 1987 troops arrived to stop them. This led to riots that killed 400. The Saudis conveniently blamed the trouble on *shirk* (idol worship). Angry protesters, always easily conjured up by the Iranian religious police (the Basij), ransacked the Saudi embassy in Tehran. All Iranian pilgrims were banned until a 1991 thaw.

Later in Mecca, our group's *mutawif* (Hajj guide) would show us the exact overpass where the clashes occurred. As with their unusual maps of unmarked graves, the Shia would inherit the memory of what happened at this overpass.

Ayatollah Khomeini was the only reason Indian novelist Salman Rushdie (*The Satanic Verses*) earned worldwide fame. When the gang of Iranian jurists, with Khomeini as their leader, issued a death decree against Rushdie, the Saudis wanted a piece of the action as well. The Saudi Wahhabis pronounced that Rushdie would have to appear before a sharia-sanctioned tribunal before he could be sentenced. It was an exercise in foolishness—both countries trying to outdo each other as to whose Islamic condemnation of Rushdie was the valid one.

In 1988, King Fahd called for ceasing all anti-Iran media campaigns. Was it détente? It was clear that the Al Saud dynasty controlled what passed for Saudi media. They would later even go to great lengths to launch Al Arabiya, their reaction to the often anti-Saudi, Qatar-based Al Jazeera. In 1990, both countries rejected the use of force in the Persian Gulf and came out strongly against Saddam Hussein's invasion of Kuwait. Détente again? A brief one, yes, this time. Official ties between the two nations were even restored in 1991. Iran's foreign minister, Ali Akbar Velayati, visited Riyadh. Flashbulbs popped and hands were shaken.

Real evidence of rapprochement would come from the Hajj. The Hajj operates on a quota system. The kingdom of Saudi Arabia claims that Hajj visas from different countries are directly proportional to their Muslim populations. Iran is a nation of more than 80 million Muslims. Saudi Arabia, in comparison, has about 30 million. In 1988, a determined King Fahd had allotted Iran only 45,000 pilgrims. Protesting this quota, Iran boycotted. Thus, with much fanfare the Saudis announced that they were letting in 115,000 Iranian pilgrims in 1991. The ayatollah smiled.

In Medina later that Dua Ku'mayl night, I couldn't help but notice Iranian flags outside certain hotels.

"That's where the Iranians stay. They put the flags so that they can find each other," said my Hajj guide when I asked about it at a daily *majlis* ("gathering"). My group, like all Shia, regularly held these where they mourned the injustices brought upon them by the Sunnis and commemorated their greatest imams, including the Prophet's grandson Husayn, the second in the succession line after his father Ali. Husayn's butchering and death at the Battle of Karbala in the seventh century was mourned as if it had happened yesterday. In India, as in Iran, it was even a national holiday. I would sit on the side trying my best to visibly commiserate.

I wondered if the majlis of my Khoja group was the same as other Shia? The Khojas are yet another example of Islam's great diversity. They are one of the many subsets of Shia Islam, with ancestry in Western India and East Africa. It seemed my group had both Twelver Khojas and Nizari Khojas. The former believed in twelve imams, with the last being in occultation and scheduled to reappear as a Mahdi who would rule for five, seven, nine, or nineteen years (according to whom you talked to) before Yawm al-Qiyamah (the Day of Judgment) and rid the world of all evil.

The Nizari Khojas in my group placed great emphasis on the Islamic principle of ijtihad, or independent reasoning. I was always drawn to their discussions throughout my Hajj. They seemed a reasonable lot and I wondered—would they also leave my homosexuality open to the ijtihad they so revered, if they found out?

As far as the Wahhabi-Salafi establishment was concerned, all Shia, including Sunnis like me who choose to travel with Shia, were infidels. Much had changed from those heady days in 1991, when the Saudis also agreed to an Iranian request to allow 5,000 relatives and friends of the 412 "martyrs" of the 1987 riots to attend the Hajj. Our group was told to stick together and march under the Canadian flag—to display a US or British flag during Hajj was unthinkable. Did Saudi BFF US presidents even know this? Every other nationality during the Hajj, including the (despised) Iranians, marched with its national flag.

To worldwide surprise, Iran's President Mohammad Khatami came on a state visit in 1998, the first since the '79 revolution. And in February 2007, the biggest surprise of all—the often-reviled Iranian President Mahmoud Ahmadinejad performed his pilgrimage at the invitation of King Abdullah. I had come on the Hajj as an educated pilgrim. My decision to be there in 2011, the year of the Arab uprisings, which I very openly reported about (especially from Cairo), and the death of Osama bin Laden, was a deliberate one. Less than a week before my departure, the FBI uncovered an Iranian plot to assassinate the Saudi ambassador to the United States, Adel al-Jubeir. "Operation Red Coalition," as the FBI had named it, produced headlines. Stuxnet, the malicious computer worm, had struck Iran recently.

The political part of my brain wanted to know if the Shia upheavals in the eastern part of the kingdom had penetrated Mecca and Medina. For Saudis, it was normal to call 10 percent of their country the pejorative *rafidah* ("rejectors"), the most used anti-Shia Arabic slur in the region. Saudi Shia are concentrated in the east, inconveniently close to the major oilfields. In Saudi Arabia's geographical curse, oil and the reviled Shia live in the same land. The Al Saud feel more in control of what used to be the western Hejaz region that contains Mecca and Medina, and even the neighboring Nejd. But it is the Shia in the Ash Sharqiyah (Eastern Province) that they fear. Even Adham texted that all

Shia of Qatif, referring to the governorate in the Eastern Province, are "trouble-makers." The indoctrination of this kind of internecine hatred went deep. Qatif's geography is inconvenient, too close to Iraq, Iran, and the contested Persian Gulf for the often-jittery Saudi monarchy. By 2015, the Saudis had mandated that pilgrims had to state whether they were Shia or Sunni on their Hajj visa applications—basically religious apartheid, Saudi style. Post-Hajj I would come back home with both derision and disgust for the Saudi Wahhabi machine and devour every piece of news that came from the region. But on this night as all these historical milestones met in my brain, I walked determinedly with Hossein, eager to be a part of the Iranian Dua.

In 2011, when I entered Saudi Arabia, Shia youths protested on the streets in the east of the country. An ignored, maligned, super-connected, and majority-under-twenty-five populace is a highly combustible mix; even one event can ignite revolutionary fire. The release of political prisoners and an end to the years of a state-sponsored sectarianism were the primary demands of the protesters. I had seen protest videos and read about the restive Saudi Shia population. Pre-Hajj, I had visions of exploring Qatif and its dissent. When there I became a prisoner of the Saudi regime. As a passport-less pilgrim, I could go nowhere but Mecca, Medina, and Jeddah airport.

I knew of the Saudi Shia underground, strangely through friends in Tehran. Traditionally, many Shia follow a *marja al-taqlid* (exalted source of emulation). In Iran, that person is Ayatollah Khameini, who like his predecessor Khomeini makes *Velayat-e Faqih* the very fulcrum of governance and all foreign policy. For the Saudi Shia, their marja is the less-influential Ayatollah Ali al-Sistani, whose penile fatwa had filled me with much fear. Preaching from Najaf in Iraq, he is uncomfortably close for the Saudis.

The influential Saudi cleric Muhammad al-Arefe had once called al-Sistani an atheist, un-Islamic, and debauched. The Shia world reacted with predictable fury. But the cleric the Al Saud really feared was Sheikh Nimr al-Nimr, who preached from the Qatif-al-Awamiyyah region, their own soil. Imprisoned several times, Nimr had called for the end of the regime, free elections, and even the secession of the Eastern Province. Shia youths, who were his largest support base, saw him as a "secular reformist." I had followed Nimr's outspokenness on Twitter carefully, beginning in 2010. Riyadh feared he would generate *fitna* (the undesirable Islamic state of civil strife). In truth, he was a Quran-inspired pacifist, rallying protesters to "use the power of the word" rather than violence. The "word" in Islam always means the Quran.

In Medina, on the night of that Dua, as my Iranian pal/smoking buddy Hossein and I passed the Prophet's grave on the way to the mass of Iranians, we were getting close to the Jannat al-Baqi (Garden of Paradise) cemetery—the setting for major Shia-Sunni clashes in 2009, when the mutaween were caught filming Shia women praying at the graves. The religious police denied it, arguing they did not condone filming of any kind, and filming women would be unspeakable. Many religious figures the Shia mourned were buried here and the Saudis had destroyed the graves forever.

After the clashes, Nimr gave a particularly inflammatory, viral sermon, saying, "Our dignity has been pawned away, and if it is not restored, we will call for secession. Our dignity is more precious than the unity of this land." Nimr had become "a prominent Saudi Shia reformist."

Two years after my Hajj, in October 2014, Nimr was sentenced to death. In 2015, the Saudis executed a record-breaking 157 people, most beheaded by sword. Nimr's sentencing was a global Shia phenomenon. On January 2, 2016, the Saudis executed forty-seven people and casually mentioned that Nimr was amongst them. The shock caused global headlines and protests. In Tehran, using now-familiar tactics, protesters ransacked the Saudi embassy. The ever-growing number of what I call the Twitter Sheikhs of Saudi Arabia reacted immediately in different ways, depending on whose pleasure they served at. Protesters in Qatif dared to use a slogan they had rarely used, "Down with the Al Saud." Nimr was a rallying figure. Many feared that the Shia youths will fall back into a predictable state of complacency. In Saudi terms that usually means not questioning the ultimate authority of the king, but openly complaining about everything else—usually on Twitter and YouTube. Filled with tweets and YouTube videos, my mind expected to see revolution erupting even that night as thousands of Iranians gathered. I was wrong.

This Dua Ku'mayl gathering of Iranians was close to the Prophet's Mosque in Medina, surrounded by Saudi riot police. Hossein confidently walked right into the phalanx of security.

"Let us through. We're Iranian," he said in Arabic to one of the Saudi guards surrounding the praying mass of Iranians. He grabbed my hand and led me defiantly past the ring of Saudi police. I had spent months studying Shia Islam. It was almost like learning a new religion. But this prayer could take up to an hour. I was not sufficiently indoctrinated, so I mumbled what little I could remember of the prayer and bowed my head to avoid suspicious glances. I felt one with the Iranians. Like them, I was an infidel. Thankfully the Iranians did not know why, or they would have rejected me as handily as the Saudis rejected them. "We have shared something momentous," said Hossein, "so I must tell you a secret—I was part of what you guys in America were calling the green revolution in 2009." I squeezed his hand tight, knowing how much it would have taken for him to tell me this.

There was no point in sleeping that night. Saudis open the gates to the Garden of Paradise cemetery at 4:30 a.m. Was it called paradise because all its nameless occupants were firmly settled there? We waited with a bawling Shia supplicant soundtrack. These meek mourners were the "warriors" of Ayatollah Khomeini's revolution that the House of Saud feared so much? I had to laugh.

"Pay attention to this," said Hossein, swatting me with his map. "It's places like this that we really need it." I pulled my map out of my bag.

I knew the history. The cemetery had existed since the Prophet's time. Many religious figures the Shia mourned were buried here and the Wahhabi Ikhwan forces of the Saudis had demolished all the graves by 1926. The desecrated al-Baqi lay in ruins. It contained the remains of many of Islam's ancestors, including some in the revered Ahl al-Bayt (Muhammad's direct family). Grave-marker destruction, as for Daesh today, has remained a favorite Wahhabi pastime.

Finally, the gates to "paradise" opened and thousands of pilgrims rushed through. It was hard to get past the formation of mutaween. These feared creatures blocked the wailing Iranians like a face-off. This was the front line of a divide that I'd previously only understood in theory.

"*Bida!*" they yelled, adding "*Shirk!*" to good effect. The former means "heresy." The latter, "idol worship." For these Wahhabis, the mere attempt at praying graveside is idol-worship. They point to Muhammad's destroying pagan idols contained in the Kaaba. The Shia argue that they are not literally praying *to* graves. They are merely praying to God *at* the grave. This is an important distinction. But for the mutaween these reviled infidels are praying to graves. It's kind of like how many modern Protestant Christians, unlike their Catholic brethren, avoid decorating their homes with crucifixes. But you don't often see Protestants policing Catholic prayer. The mutaween take it a step further: Any depiction of the human form at all is considered un-Islamic.

About 4,000 of these illiterate guys are on the payroll, but thousands more patrol the streets as volunteers. This is what happens when years of Wahhabi indoctrination meet joblessness. Their goal is to ensure total compliance to Wahhabi ideology. Many are young and angry, and, given power for the first time in their lives, they predictably abuse it. It's a dangerous combo. They fine and imprison people without evidence, and their accusations of apostasy can even lead to an execution. Their power seemed limitless, and I reminded myself to be careful, for my green card wouldn't protect me in a sharia court. I would soon experience their terror. All these thugs really know are bits of the Quran. They direct much of their ire toward women going about their daily business who dare to display any skin or hair, intentionally or not. And thus my so-called ninjas.

I had Googled the mutaween and was already petrified. Their notorious barbarism is on full display on the web. You just need to type "Mecca school fire" as search terms. In 2002, a girls' school in Mecca caught fire. Worldwide media also lit up. What followed was a global tragedy and an enormous PR fiasco for the monarchy. The mutaween barred the doors, preventing the girls' escape, because they were not properly covered, and they barred the male civil-defense forces from rescuing the girls because they claimed that direct contact with the girls' bodies would arouse the men sexually. And so, rather than risk such impropriety, the mutaween shoved girls trying to escape back into the inferno. Fifteen of them burned to death. More than fifty were severely burned. I find it difficult to imagine a more despicable example of a zealotry that encourages adherents to follow the letter of the law at the expense of its spirit. The subsequent global outcry was so loud that the incident marked one of the rare moments the US government publicly reprimanded the Saudis.

I had grown up with gender segregation. I had spent time in states that police morality. Even Iran's feared religious police, the Basij, paled in comparison to the barbarism of the mutaween. In 2007, the mutaween beat a man to death when they caught him selling alcohol in Riyadh. In

2013, two men died when their car drove off a bridge, chased by mutaween for singing patriotic songs about their country. Videos of mutaween abuses proliferate on YouTube.

As dawn broke above the graves, the green dome of the Prophet's grave appeared on the horizon. Saudis have tried to destroy this dome for years. Swarms of pigeons took off into the desert sky. The wailing mourners had moved on, and an eerie silence replaced the din. The prayers I now heard were whispered. My companions discussed the quality of the lighting for photographs of the unnerving landscape. I broke away, seeking a solitude more appropriate for this place of death. Some poor pilgrim, who must have died here, was being buried. At that moment it occurred to me that no one in this man's family would ever know where to find his remains. This was no headstone land.

I had thought I had forever lost my ability to cry after my mother's funeral. In part I had come to this strange land to look for those lost tears. I was glad to be alone.

Muhammad, for many Muslims, chose the spot where the vast Baqi exists today. *Do the Saudis still mess with it?* I wondered. That morning it felt like a city of the dead. Schools of Islam dispute where the Prophet's daughter Fatima is buried near here. Muhammad had no male heirs, so Fatima's presence in Islam's lineage is central. For some, she is buried under the green dome. Others argue that she is buried in Baqi.

I walked back to the Prophet's mosque. I prayed Fajr. I felt more in tune with my faith than I had for a long time. I was meant to be here.

After a nap, Shahinaz and I (luckily without incident) went to the mosque again for Zuhr (noon) prayers. Our happiness was short-lived. Soon a mutawa appeared, saying she couldn't sit with me. Ignoring my protestations and Wahhabi law on not touching strange women, he scooped her up and dragged her away.

She texted, "It's fine, let's text after Zuhr and we will find each other again."

In the Tatooine area, it seemed men and women could walk together. What looked like miles of ceiling closed in to shield the pilgrims from the morning sun with nary a squeak. More bin Laden gadgetry installed to ensure our comfort. Here, the discipline of Islam was on full display.

Perfectly formed rows of supplicants stretched for miles. We were emulating the Prophet's *sunnah*, his way of life, which all good Muslims are taught. The Prophet, or one of his companions, must have decreed that not even one believer should break formation, physically, and by extension, spiritually. At this time, I noticed that all the women, including Shahinaz, had suddenly disappeared.

I lingered at the green dome under which Muhammad was buried. Since the eighteenth century its existence had been contested, and yet it stood firm. *This is the divine in action*, I thought.

I reunited with Shahinaz and we explored our surroundings. This Prophet's Mosque is Islam's second-holiest mosque. The first obviously is the Masjid al-Haram at the Kaaba's ground zero in Mecca. As a child, I knew there were secret messages and signs in the heavily calligraphed columns that surround Muhammad's grave. This was Islam's Da Vinci code. For the Shia, it was of utmost importance: The Prophet's daughter Fatima, who would lay forth the lineage of Islam through her husband and their first Imam Ali, had her "room" here. The very foundations of the Prophet's Medina home lay within this mosque.

Sunnis believe that the rightful inheritors of Muhammad's legacy, the earliest two caliphs culled from his closest companions—Abu Bakr and Umar—were also buried there.

"For me, this is not a mere mosque," I whispered to Shahinaz. It was where long-lost memories became sacred. It was where the first Islamic nation and community were built, as close to the concept of democracy as could possibly exist in seventh-century Arabia. During Muhammad's life it was a home, it was a center for community to gather, it was a university, it was a place of refuge for the homeless, and yes, it was also a mosque.

Our Hajj guide described a fatwa from the nineties that came from the particularly cruel Saudi Grand Mufti ibn Baz. It partially decreed:

> There is a specious argument put forward by those who worship graves (code for Shia), namely the fact that the grave of the Prophet is in his mosque . . . It is not permissible for a Muslim to take that as evidence that mosques may be built over graves, or that people may be buried inside mosques, because that goes against the traditions of the Prophet, and because it is a means that may lead to shirk . . .

Baaz came in a long, destructive ideological Wahhabi line. The father of the "third Saudi State," ibn Saud, captured the Hejaz (that contains Mecca and Medina) in 1925. His ISIS-like *ikhwans* ("brothers") used their brutality to demolish nearly every tomb or dome in Medina in order to prevent their veneration. The job was finished on April 21, 1926, on a day that some Shia mark as *Yaum e Gham* ("Day of Sorrow"). They never dared to touch the Prophet's grave, which determined pilgrims were almost stampeding to touch.

Many Muslims believe an empty grave next to Muhammad's is reserved for Jesus, who will return near the Day of Judgment to kill the *Daijal* (Antichrist, false messiah). Gold-plated Ottoman-style columns surrounded this area, with gold-inlayed Quranic verses. The grave itself was invisible because it was covered with gold mesh and black curtains.

Our Hajj guide also described a Grand Mufti al-Shaykh–signed pamphlet during Hajj 2007. It said that "the green dome shall be demolished and the three graves flattened in the Prophet's Masjid." The hypocrisy of the Sauds was clear. No bejeweled ornamentation, they said. But this was it: a mausoleum with a disagreeable medley of faux gold, marble, and more. Why would a Muslim not pray to his/her Prophet at such an ornate mausoleum? The bin Ladens claim they spent $6 billion here. Shahinaz and I snickered at their faux, gaudy results. We both knew the Sauds are petrified of the worldwide outcry the destruction of this dome and Prophet's (mausoleum-like) grave would cause.

I lost Shahinaz as the orderliness broke into religious fervor closer to his grave. With their canes, mutaween whacked pilgrims who were daring a moment of graveside prayer. And yet they persisted. I felt peace in the pandemonium. Every believer wanted to get as close as possible to the grave. We were united in our forbidden longing. Even the incessant harassment of the mutaween could not take that away from us.

"Let's meet after Baqi in the hotel. I am safe," Shahinaz texted.

The crowd dispersed. The heat was unbearable. Over lunch at Al-Baik, a Saudi KFC, Shahinaz and I confabulated. A terrible incident had occurred: A woman in her tent had diarrhea and her period simultaneously. She had soiled her sleeping bag. With the exception of Shahinaz, who gave her Imodium, she was being treated like a pariah. Shahinaz helped her move and clean up. The sleeping bag needed to be replaced and the group leader had one. Where was simple compassion? Piety required it. No one except for Shahinaz seemed to possess any. And she said a few women were barely literate, probably products of "arranged marriage."

Life in Saudi Arabia could be described in a sentence. Constant prayer, interrupted periodically for daily life and beheadings. But forcibly shoving religion down people's throats never worked. I told Shahinaz what Adham had said. The majority of young Saudis hated prayer, and yet it was inextricably wound into the fabric of their lives. It was best not to be caught stationary outdoors during prayer time, anywhere. I had slept through Fajr on my first day, after all, and no storm troopers beat down my hotel room door. But we were experiencing judgmental fellow pilgrims. A woman had told Shahinaz to wear socks and gloves when she went out. Once, when I was praying just outside my packed hotel room, two guys said, "Praying in a corridor is haram." This I knew: Laughing mid-prayer was haram—forbidden.

My desi-dar was going off frequently. *Desi* literally means "from the homeland," which is South Asia. Many unskilled workers here were desi. Later, I sat down next to a younger man I immediately recognized as Pakistani owing to the shape of his close-cropped beard and his fairer skin. His skin tone matched mine. Muslim Indians, and by extension Pakistanis, generally have lighter skin than their Hindu neighbors.

"*Assalamulaikum,*" I greeted him in the Muslim way. Peace be with you.

"*Alhamdulillah,*" he replied. Praise be to God.

"Your name means merciful," I said after we exchanged names. "Do the Saudis treat you that way?"

Rahman smiled. "I am lucky to work here so close to the Prophet's grave."

I probed further. "What's it like to work for the Saudis?"

"Hell," he said quietly. He told me they'd taken away his passport five years ago when he'd entered the kingdom. In exchange, he received an *iqama*, a work permit. This legal slavery permeates all Gulf monarchies. Rahman had not been able to visit his family for years. His employment was indentured servitude.

In this Rahman and other immigrant laborers were not unlike female citizens in Saudi Arabia, who need "exit visas" after receiving "permission to travel" from their male guardians—a husband, father, or son. They are prisoners in their homeland, victims of a patriarchal servitude. Many find a way around it. Saudi women hide in gated palaces. Rahman lived in a hovel.

"We sleep six to a room," he said. "Often there is no running water." Rahman slept at most four hours each night, working multiple shifts to make enough money to send home. At night he swept the marbled floors of the mosque, and by day he worked in a tiny watch-and-mobile shop. He would save almost a week's wages to buy phone cards to call home. For me, he was proof of the dirty little secret of oil-rich countries. Despite the rampant displays of wealth and conspicuous consumption among the kingdom's elite, many live below the poverty line. A majority of this demographic is composed of immigrants robbed of their passports, like Rahman.

I wondered if he had any glimmer of faith in political change. Had he seen any graffiti that hinted at dissent? He became taciturn. He must have feared I was an informant.

"Walk around your hotel," said Rahman. "You will find what you need to see." That's all he would say.

I asked if he was on Facebook in this hyper-social web country. He had a mobile, after all.

"What's that?" he replied. We said goodbye. I knew he knew.

My extensive reporting on the Arab Spring was easily searchable on the web. Was I naïve to hope I would find people eager to be filmed or talk to anyone who knew of Saudi dissent? My text bud Adham was the only real "source" I had here. With him and his web of contacts, I could easily film in Jeddah and Riyadh. But it would be harder to get to Qatif, where the protesting Saudi Shia lived. Passport-less I could do nothing outside of Mecca and Medina, and my lens was a religious one.

I did keep a watch on the Twitter feeds of Saudi sheikhs and opinion makers I followed. The kingdom had Twitter's densest user base in the Arab world. As for Egypt, through my writing I had tried to clear up the misconception that Cairo 2011 was a "social media revolution." Egypt is the poorest country in the region, with more than a quarter of its people living below the poverty line. Many of the revolutionaries were far too poor to own smartphones or even have access to social media. A significant number definitely used social media, but to make it the primary catalyst of the revolution was specious. Saudi Arabia, on the other hand, is the richest Arab country, and smartphone penetration is vast. The insurrection-terrified Saud tolerated Twitter and more. Most places, including both of Islam's two holiest mosques, had wi-fi that occasionally worked. Twitter was a rare place where ikhtilat ("gender mixing") "existed" freely. Men and women hung out as equals here. And the Sauds know the importance of keeping their country's under-twenty-five majority happy. Princess to pauper, everyone is already on or trying to jump aboard the social web train.

A Saudi "Day of Rage" was announced on Facebook for March 11, 2011. It was deliberate because it was a Friday. As in Cairo, mosques were rightfully seen as rallying places for the mandated once-weekly communal prayer. Some reports said that only one protester, Khaled al-Johani, showed up in Riyadh. He was sentenced to eighteen months. Adham, who was in Riyadh, kept me updated hourly. Police presence was unprecedented, with helicopters in the sky. There were police checks on cars and individuals headed for mosques. Fridays in mosques were dangerous. So regimes from Tunis to Tripoli to Damascus rushed to police the Friday variety of devout thousands with potential to be incited. In Cairo, revolutionary imams had used Friday sermons to rally the faithful against the "un-Islamic" Mubarak regime.

Obeying the Al Saud, Riyadh's grand mufti fatwa-ed, "Islam strictly prohibits protests in the kingdom because the ruler here rules by God's will." He invoked the familiar Fitna ("chaos"). Compliant ulema (religious scholars) also tweeted on point.

There were more protesters in Shia towns such as Awammiya in eastern Qatif. According to Adham, people were being fined, flogged, having their passports confiscated, and even being exiled in the Shia east. I would have given anything to go and film.

In 2009 and 2010, there had been huge floods in Jeddah, leading to a high death toll and a subsequent groundswell of anti-government sentiment. A hashtag went viral across Saudi Arabia: "#JeddahIsDrowning." This term captured widespread rage against how the regime handled the floods; however, it never led to any street protests. Were the Saudis afraid or complacent? Soon, protests exploded in Bahrain, Kuwait, and Yemen, meriting worldwide media attention.

Saudi King Abdullah did not want Mubarak's fate. As usual, he simply threw money at the problem, unveiling a $37 billion welfare program.

Sycophantic billboards sprang up to welcome Abdullah returning home from a medical trip to NYC: "Welcome, King of Humanity," "If you are well, we all are well." The second of the powerful Sudairi brothers, Salman, became king after Abdullah died in 2015.

I did find some graffiti in an alleyway near our hotel. Nothing political. Perhaps the promise of the Arab Spring had faded into a bleak Islamist Winter.

We had been in Medina a few days, and sitting in the malodorous bus, I tried to drown out the sound of our Hajj guide with my headphones soothingly playing the melodious voice of an unknown qari. He was reciting Medinan Ayah 21 from Surah 33 (Al-Azhab, or "The Allied Troops"). I loved his intonation. There is music to be found in Wahhabi Islam, even if it lies only in prayer intonations and calls to prayer.

"You have indeed in the Messenger of Allah a beautiful pattern (of conduct) for any one whose hope is in Allah and the Final Day, and who engages much in the Praise of Allah." My mind wandered as the recitations lulled me into a space of quiet reflection.

In this parsed little portion of the qari's recitation lay all the evidence any Muslim would need for emulating the Prophet's life and traditions that the sunnah comprised. But those seeking perversion knew exactly where to look, even young Daesh types who didn't know how to pray correctly. Jump to verse 64 of the same chapter, and you'll find: "Verily Allah has cursed the Unbelievers and prepared for them a Blazing Fire."

An overworked Fox cub reporter hopefully got a raise after finding a Surah like this. It must have taken a lot of Wikipedia-ing. Fox network's Sean Hannity allegedly had claimed the Quran forbade Muslims from taking Jews and Christians as friends. Hannity, Trump, and Islamophobes in general treacherously provide endless recruitment fodder for the Daeshes and Boko Harams of the world.

My mind also wandered to the history I had studied. It was the Quraysh *jahils* (pre-Islamic ignorants) who worshipped idols (shirk and thus *mushrikun*, those who commit shirk) and who initiated war with Muhammad. He survived assassination attempts. His followers were routinely raped, killed, and tortured. They called him a madman, and as he walked the streets, they even threw human excrement on him. After Khadija died, a heartbroken

Muhammad, then a pariah and not a prophet, was forced to flee Mecca, the city of his birth. He was a hunted man running away like a coward shamefully in the dark of night. This outsider and outcast survived years of hatred and ridicule. It was in Medina that he found shelter and started to build the earliest community of Muslims, whose numbers only multiplied. His enemies were nonplussed.

What of the book? Many claim the Quran only calls for conflict in self-defense. Arguably, Muslims historically fought monarchical, not civilian, armies. Is this emulated in part by the Saud-abhorring Daesh?

I had learned to carry my expanding bag of scriptural evidence to my speaking events. I always wanted to give my audiences proof of Islamic pluralism like in Ayah 62 from the Quran's second Surah, *Al Baqarah* ("The Cow"):

> *Those who believe (in the Quran), and those who follow the Jewish (scriptures), and the Christians and the Sabians—any who believe in Allah and the Last Day, and work righteousness, shall have their reward with their Lord; on them shall be no fear, nor shall they grieve.*

Jews, Christians, and Muslims are equally rewarded in the Quran.

The Medina bus on which I had allowed myself to wander jolted to a stop and my mind re-entered the present. We were in a logjam. Hundreds of immovable buses. For me, it was additional evidence of Saudi disregard for the comfort of the pilgrims.

Our mutawif was talking about how exemplary the life of Muhammad was. He serendipitously was using a Surah that I remembered from my childhood with Khala. Even though he gets only four direct mentions in the Quran, Muhammad lies at its heart. There would be no Quran without Muhammad. All of Islam's rituals and traditions are based on ancestors like him. Muslims are required to try to emulate his life, thus the sunnah. The 21 Ayah of the Medinan Surah 33 says, "Ye have indeed in the Messenger of Allah a beautiful pattern (of conduct) for any one whose hope is in Allah and the Final Day, and who engages much in the Praise of Allah."

After hours, we reached Masjid Quba, the mythical first mosque built by the Prophet. This is not a sectarian entity, but is mentioned both in the Quran and the sunnah. It was said that just praying two *rakat* ("movements") of prayer here amounted to the blessings of an entire Umrah, the lesser pilgrimage. The Saudis had destroyed the original mosque. This was an austere Wahhabi version.

A few stragglers in my group expectedly prayed to what looked like unmarked graves outside a shrine of some sort. The mutaween were quick to arrive and disperse these infidels. I was recording.

"Shirk," he said grabbing my iPhone. "Password?" I had no choice but to give it.

These were early days, but this vicious mutawa went through my footage methodically and deleted every single video and photo. He shoved his right hand and the phone into my face forcibly, as if to make sure that I'd lose my balance. I did and fell backward, thankfully on a small dune, which cushioned the impact.

Our group leader rushed to me, pulling me up.

"Don't ever mess with these guys. You will soon be able to spot them because their beards and dress are different. At all costs, stay away from them and their sticks," he advised, adding, "And whatever you do, don't ever record or take pictures at places like this!"

The violence of those moments had struck terror in my heart.

Adham replied after I texted him what had happened.

"Remember habibi this is not your lovely Cairo. Be careful."

"Why?"

"You have to remember that those winds from the Nile don't blow here. Nothing changes. We change nothing especially these fucker mutaweens, you have no idea Parvez. BE CAREFUL," he ended in all caps.

To comfort me, Shahinaz sat next to me in the bus. The group leader whispered audibly, "Right now it's OK, but most times you will both be separated."

When the mutawa grabbed my phone and pushed me to the ground, he was giving me an early lesson on how cruel, rigid, and pervasive the Wahhabi control of this country was. And its feared foot soldiers of morality had the run of the land. The Wahhabi tenets forbidding depiction of the human form were clear. But later in Mecca it was impossible for them to control millions taking Hajj selfies. I hid in plain sight and yet got into trouble often. Recording a shot for a hoped-for film needs more lingering and deliberate "camera" movement than a quickie selfie.

Our next stop was Masjid Qiblatain, the fabled mosque where the Prophet changed the Qibla (direction of prayer) from Jerusalem to Mecca. Al-Aqsa (the Temple Mount in Jerusalem) had always been "the furthest mosque" in the world's most-contested real estate, Al-Quds in Arabic and Jerusalem to those who acknowledged Israel's existence. Muslims worldwide have always mourned the "loss" of Jerusalem. Politically adept elders when I was growing up blamed its forfeiture upon "the treachery of those corrupt Arabs." For thirteen centuries, Jerusalem was ruled by Muslims and the sites sacred to Christians, and Jews in the city were never willfully destroyed in the name of Islam. Was it the world's best example of a religious plurality that did once exist between the three faiths?

I knew Al-Aqsa from childhood. In Jerusalem, in the year 621, the Prophet ascended to heaven several times and negotiated with God on a night Muslims commemorated as *Lailat-e-Miraj* ("the Night Journey") and prayed more to get extra brownie points from Allah. Muhammad rode, on a heavenly steed called Buraq, from Mecca to Jerusalem (Al-Quds) and then multiple times to heaven. A flying horse? Wondrous to any child. There were always lots of *tongas* (horse-driven carriages of a very particular South Asian style) on the streets of Saharanpur, and as a child, I clamored for rides, wondering if they, too, like Buraq, could ascend into the heavens. I was always discouraged because traveling in tongas was what "poor people" did. Out of all of Islam's stories I grew up with, this was my favorite. Muhammad's job was to be our negotiator-in-chief with God, so he could bring down the number of required prayers from an unreasonable fifty to five.

"Fifty? Oh my god!" exclaimed Shahinaz when I told her.

On his way, it was said the pragmatic Muhammad met and discussed matters with Jesus, Moses, Ibrahim, and even Adam. Muhammad knew these figures were necessary. He needed them on his side. That day, I lingered at Qiblatain as long as I could, knowing that perhaps I would never get to visit the modern Al-Quds.

Muhammad was a man of skill, wisdom, and moderation and could be a crafty diplomat when needed. He did not believe in harm. His lifetime was a time of respect for the other monotheisms, and the Quranic revelations relied on them to build the Quran's own expansive and poetic text. Jews and Christians were not hated—they were to be respected as "people of the book." Muslim men could marry Jewish or Christian wives. And all Muslims could eat Jewish food. The Quran made kosher and halal mono-theistic brothers. I wondered how the unhinged evangelicals back home would react if they knew Jesus gets more mentions in the Quran than Muhammad. And it's all positive.

It was day four in Medina, and I was wary of filming. Spiritual-tourism shifts had been arranged, and Shahinaz and I, thankful to be reunited, had a lot to share. She told me a fight had broken out in her tent between two camps: One believed that full-face abayas were de rigueur. The other said faces needed to be exposed as the Prophet commanded. There was no détente. We disembarked at Uhud, where the reluctant warrior Muham-mad lost. In his only other battle at nearby Badr, he won. The third, "The Battle of the Trench," was or was not a battle, depending on whom you talked to.

An area the size of half a soccer field had been walled off. It contained what looked like a grave. All you could do was peer through crude lattice-work. Groups of Shia, both genders, stood lamenting. I felt one with the pain of the abaya-wearing women. It was more than 100 degrees. Import-ant companions of the Prophet who were martyred in the battle of Uhud were apparently buried there.

"Film this," my group leader, Shafiq, encouraged me, adding, "We need all the evidence we can get, because before long even this will be destroyed by them." I promised to share the footage with him. Afraid to this day that someone would figure out it was I who made the pilgrimage with the group that year, I never ended up sharing it.

I focused on the women. A shirt-and-trouser-style Iranian pilgrim passed them with the boombox reminiscent of the extremely divided New York City of the eighties, where the racially charged slur "ghetto blaster" was used to describe these contraptions. And boom this one did: with rec-itations of long Shia lamentations. Out of nowhere, a group of mutaween approached the wailing women—one busied himself with grabbing the Iranian's boombox. As one of them seemed to notice me, I hastily put the phone in my fanny pack, which would in a few days do double duty as an ihram-holding belt, and walked away as fast as I could. The other mutaween used their familiar wood staves to hit the abaya-clad women with gay abandon. Clearly these illiterate philistines had missed the many Islamic missives about not disrespecting women.

In spite of these barbarians, strangely, I had never felt safer. I texted my MMS group, "It's hard to explain, but surrounded by millions of Muslims from every nation on earth gives me a sense of safety I never felt before. I am not even afraid of the mutaween!"

And then I got an unlikely text from Hossein, my pal on that Dua Kumayl night at Jannat al-Baqi. "Please never mention the green revolution thing to anyone, Parviz. It's our secret."

"Sure," I replied.

CHAPTER 5

SHOOT ME IN HERE

Saudi Arabia was in a panic yet again because of "those damned Iranians, always creating trouble," Adham had texted me one summer. Iran almost savored the sweet taste of "revolution" again in June 2009. It was three decades after Ayatollah Khomeini's return from exile in France when Reza Shah, the last US-supported Pahlavi monarch, fled a country that would change forever. The triumphant ayatollah had established a theocracy that some believed would be toppled in what came to be known as 2009's brief "Green Revolution." Thousands poured out into the streets contesting the irrepressible Mahmoud Ahmadinejad's re-election. The protesters said he had stolen the election from a reformist called Mir Hossein Mousavi. Allegedly, 1,500 died as the Iranian Basij (Iran's version of the Saudi mutaween), with Arab militias flown in, quashed the protesters. Neda Agha Soltan, a young girl, *died on camera* on Tehran's Kargar Avenue. The horrific video still remains in circulation.

To support the marchers, Tehranites used to gather on rooftops at dusk to cleverly shout *Allahu Akbar* ("God is great!"). They were smartly appropriating the religion that had been forced down their throats for three decades to express unanimous disapprobation. *Marg Bar Dictator!* ("Death to the Dictator!") and a cacophony of other challenges to the regime proliferated. Directly referring to Hizbullah and Hamas, a sign said, "Gaza and Lebanon were not enough, now they found Yemen to send money too!" Iranians often complained that their tax money was used to fund Lebanon, Yemen, and other Shias.

I reported this brief uprising through the eyes of friends who were pounding Tehran's streets. Long prison sentences awaited them, but at the time it seemed impossible. The protesters felt an impending victory. One of my friends was a forty-year-old poet called Arash who wrote to me sporadically from proxy servers. (The regime was trying, obviously, to control the web.)

> The Iranian people are experiencing one of the widespread civil movements in modern history. Every day, near to the end of the protests, people get informed of the next move and the next venue for gathering. According to the word of mouth, which was the most reliable means of communication available, people were supposed to gather in Haft-Tir Square and march toward Valiasr Sq. at 5 p.m. Wednesday, June 17, 2009.

This was word-of-mouth-style insurgency.

At another time, Arash said, a young man had attached a piece of paper on his chest that read: "Shoot me in here." In solidarity that year, Iranian Olympic athletes sported green arm-bands.

Arash said some of the more common placards included:

- "My green vote was not your black name!!"
- "Liar, where is your 63 percent?"
- "Ahmadinejad beware! We are a nation, not criminals."
- "We want revolutionary people, we don't want bystanders."
- "Where is my vote?"
- "The song of those killed echoes in our souls."
- "Iran mourning over its heroes."
- "Congratulations to the Murderers."
- "We are outside the time, with a bitter dagger in our backs."

Revolution 2.0 died as fast as it had started. That's because it never was one. In 1979, Khomeini's Islamic revolution happened because millions willed it. This short un-revolution of the twenty-first century was primarily about disenfranchisement. Mir Hossein Mousavi's supporters believed that Ahmadinejad had stolen the election. But they lacked the nationwide fervor and revolutionary spirit against the Shah that in 1979 brought Ayatollah Khomeini with it and a brand new name, for what for all purposes was really a new nation: The Islamic Republic of Iran. One of the first actions of that new nation would be the siege of the US embassy.

After praying a few times in the Saudi version of the Prophet's Mosque, on a lonely morning, I returned to Jannat al-Baqi, the historic graveyard bordering the mosque. My spirituality was on the ascendant. It felt as if my mother and I had forgiven each other. The question of my sexuality seemed distant and improbable in surroundings such as these.

"Why should anybody care what gender I prefer?" I asked the Prophet Muhammad while walking the wasteland. The answer I got was simple. "It's nobody's business but yours, and if you want a religious solution, Islam made the path open for all of us. We talk directly to God and never through intermediaries." I had been sitting at the Prophet's Mosque for hours. Time seemed to have stopped. Surprised, I heard Hossein's voice again, saying it was strange we kept on running into each other. I wondered if he knew who I was and had followed me. In any case, we made our way to our hotel to freshen up, promising to meet in the lobby in half an hour.

"I have something to show you," he had said conspiratorially.

Our two-star and shabby Al-Ishraq Hotel was near the fancier Ramada Inn a block away. But it was all about location, because we were across from the Prophet's Mosque. And this is why not waking up for Fajr prayers a couple of days ago had felt like such a crime. Even with its two elevators swaying dangerously, this hotel seemed to function. The shared rooms were filthy. We had four to ours. I generally kept quiet around them. Friendship was not really an aim. And if they Googled me, the results could be catastrophic.

I glanced at a group email from our Hajj leader before leaving the room:

I had a lot of thoughts that I wanted to share with you in this email but I am really running behind in my own preparations . . .

Inshallah, we will talk a lot during the trip. However, I do need to start this journey with a clean slate. So my dear brothers and sisters, if I have said or seemed to have implied anything that may have offended you, I seek your forgiveness as it is an important part of the journey.

He was so right. It had to be a clean slate. And forgiveness played a vital role. My homosexuality, once again, seemed to be a non-issue with either God or his Prophet.

"Are you still able to go to Iran? Do they know you were one of the protesters in the Tehran streets of 2009, protesting Ahmadinejad's reelection?" I peppered Hossein with questions as soon as I found him smoking downstairs. He confirmed my suspicions and said he hoped they did not have him on a list. But he reminded me what I already knew: It is rare to find an Iranian in Tehran who does not have a police record of some type. The list of punishable infractions is long, idiotic, and convoluted. He lived a dual life between Amsterdam and Tehran, where his wife and children were. He hoped to get them out of that "fucking hole," he said, adding he was the guy who had the "shoot me in here" painted on his chest in the 2009 protests.

I was eager to change the subject, which could easily move into a problematic discussion. It seemed so was he. I told him how on the way down in the always-filled-to-capacity elevators I had noticed that someone had his possessions in a large Budweiser tote with the beer-company logo and beer bottles emblazoned all over. We laughed at the consequences if it actually held the forbidden liquid.

"Why are normal people like us so afraid of these fucked-up governments anyway?" said Hossein. I remained silent.

We walked down Al Manakhah Street lined with small shops selling all conceivable products from watches to ihrams to abayas to money belts to *atar* (perfume). The last was soon to be forbidden.

Iranian flags abounded. We passed the fancy-looking Medina Mövenpick Hotel.

"This is where the fancy Iranians with money live. We are going second-class!" He laughed, outside the grungy Zowar hotel that also flaunted the Iranian flag.

"Looks like Medina's version of Valiasr in Tehran," I joked to Hossein, who was pleased to learn I had once visited Iran and knew this major avenue that divided the city. For extra bona fides I lied and expanded my two nights there to a week.

"Hardly! That's the longest street in the Middle East," he said. I was surprised he used the term because most Iranians I knew did not consider Iran as Middle Eastern.

We were shortly gliding up an escalator in Hotel Makarem, which put my Al-Ishraq to shame. And I was pretty sure that this part of town was heavily surveilled. Hossein confirmed it by saying, "We are watched." I felt reckless.

We knocked and entered Room 701. The door was ajar. Compared to mine the accommodations were plush. There were two double beds.

There were about ten men in this room. The majority were younger Western-style Iranians. Some of the younger men sipped coffee—they were dressed in what I was to discover was traditional Iranian Hajj garb—no flowing thobes for them. The men wore khakis and collared (no tie) shirts with Ahmadinejad couture.

There were two who had everyone in rapt attention. They wore black turbans and robes I had always seen on Shia *marjas* (revered Shia-style ayatollahs) or *syeds* (literally, "descendants of the Prophet Muhammad"). But for them to be hanging out in 701 probably meant they were just mere mullahs. I deliberately introduced myself as Parvez Hussein, using my middle name. For Iranians it immediately became Parviz—which in Persian means strength. And my first two names actually made me one of them. If I dared reveal I was a Sunni in 701, the consequences would not be pleasant. Hossein and I sat on the floor. It seemed they were engaged in high-level discourse and our role was perhaps to ask questions but never challenge them.

They opined on the destruction of Shia history by the Wahhabis, the real *munafiqun* (plural for "hypocrites"). Be strong, said the duo. We can already see their behavior at Baqi and at Dua Kumayl tonight, they said. They encouraged us to be on the lookout for coded questions that would primarily come from mutaween. They want to know if you are Shia or Sunni, said Turban #1. Turban #2 added that they do this with questions like, Where do you live? How do you pray? What is your name? Do you listen to music? What kind?

As with others I met in Mecca, there was a sense of foreboding. Turban #2 said, "Our Shia brothers in Iraq, in Sham (Syria), in Yemen, in

Lebanon, in Bahrain, and in Iraq will soon face grave dangers. We will need to help them. It's coming," he ended ominously. In just a year, the Daesh followers of Wahhabi Islam would use all these questions and more to identify Shia innocents and brutally kill them in front of GoPro-like cameras, the videos to be uploaded to YouTube.

At the time I just wondered, *How did they know what was coming?* I didn't know it then, but exactly the same kind of premonition of Daesh would come again during my Hajj. In a tremulous voice, I asked Turban #1, "Honorable Marja Taqlid . . ."

Turban #1 laughed and cut me short. "He is the marja, I am a mere syed." Then for a minute the Turbans played the uniquely Iranian game of *taarof*, a half-fake, half-real merry-go-round of obsequiousness and propriety, common to every Iranian I had ever met. Finally Turban #2 looked in my direction.

"Exalted Marja Taqlid," I began, still tremulous, "The Imam Khomeini," and I over-obsequiously added, "our Rahbar Inquilab, said that, 'We are in Oneness with Sunni Muslims. We are their brothers. It is obligatory for all Muslims to maintain unity.'"

I asked, "But then why do some ordinary Iranians use insults like *Arabe soosmar khor* ("lizard-eating Arabs"), saying Wahhabis are sponsored by America, and they call us *rafidah* ("rejectors")? In India and Pakistan, our Shia brothers are *khatmals* ("bedbugs"). "

I was proud I had actually quoted the ultimate leader, the rahbar ("leader") Khomeini.

But Turban #2 didn't seem pleased, staring contemptuously at me. "Parviz, you said?" I nodded. "For matters like this, we should always obey our rahbar. So many quotes are attributed to him that sometimes it is hard to know what is true or false. I just want you to know that we Shia are sitting now in the land of the enemies." For "enemies" he used one of thousands of words shared by Persian and my native Urdu, namely *dushman*. Frequently someone in the group would decide it was time for the *Salawat* or *Darood Sharif*, a supplication praising the Prophet. I had frantically learnt it in Arabic rote-style before I left, knowing that the Shia invoked it all the time. It said: "Oh, Allah, let Your Peace come upon Muhammad and the family of Muhammad."

Chai was served. We sipped it Iranian-style by putting a sugar cube in our mouths. It was going to be a long night. The Turbans opined a great deal. Their revulsion for their Wahhabi hosts was on full display. Much more egregious behavior than plain old lizard-eating was assigned to them. It was also an occasion to lament the evils of the Great Shaitan, America and its inextricable ties to these Saudi monsters. The year 1987, when Shia-Sunni riots in Mecca killed four hundred people, was relived in great detail. As were many other Hajj slights and wars over the years, including the biggest: Iran and Iraq.

At one point Turban #1 whispered, "As you know, many of our Beirut brothers are staying in Anvaralzahra and Darolrahmah. They are the true warriors and we will gather tomorrow."

I knew "Beirut brothers" was simple code for Hizbullah.

Time for another salawat. And then, conspiratorially, Turban #2 said, "We have to protect their identity at any cost. We meet them only in times like this and we must find time to sit together and properly strategize, nothing like face-to-face."

Another salawat! To this day, I regret not trying to finagle my way into that coming meeting.

The young men in the room seemed to be interested in other things.

"How long are we separated from our wives?" asked one.

Turban #1 hurled an angry torrent of Persian at the questioner, who looked ready to disappear. The Turban, from what I could discern, was using a mixture of religious (sharia) law, a passage or two from the Quran, and quotes from a list of rules. He added, "Remember you have to work on *intezaar*." In both Urdu and Persian, the word meant "waiting."

Since my arrival, I had been taking notes on my phone and sometimes on pieces of paper (in Hindi—in case they were ever discovered). In this room tonight I did not dare. What I did know was that Hizbullah operatives were using the Hajj to meet their Iranian supporters, including this seemingly high-level duo. Had al-Qaeda done the same?

More chai and another salawat later, there was a dispute over *ziyarat* (literally, "visit"). Turban #1 claimed he had a theory that even the rahbar would approve. Ziyarat to holy places, just as I had grown up with in South Asia, was also central to Iranian identity. Iranians used it for everything. From visiting Karbala, most famous as the shrine of the revered Imam Husayn and the most-performed Shia pilgrimage on earth, to the shrine of Fatimah Masume in Qom, the second-holiest city in Iran after Mashhad—it was all ziyarat. My mother used to take me, a sickly child with frequent bronchitis, on a ziyarat to the mausoleum of a peer (Sufi mystic) called the Nine Meters Peer. You had to cover his grave in nine meters of satin every time you visited. You would also light incense and pray. Sacred to both Hindus and Muslims, shrines like this are common all over South Asia. As they are in Iran, Pakistan, and other parts of the Muslim world. Regardless, here in Wahhabi-land, the very utterance of the word "ziyarat" could land you in prison. For Turban #1 and many Shia, including the Iranians, Hajj is a ziyarat that often begins in Medina and ends in Mecca.

The grave-despising Wahhabi masters of the Saudis tolerate the semi-circular area denoted by a short wall near the third column of the Kaaba in Mecca as being "Hajjar's skirt," knowing full well that for most of the Muslim world this is where Hajjar and her son, Ismael, who began Islam's lineage, are buried. If they tried to destroy these graves there would be global mayhem. This is also the reason they haven't destroyed Muhammad's grave. For many Shia, this Hajjar's-skirt area, known as *Hatim* in Arabic, also contains many other graves of Islam's ancestors. So for them, said Turban #1, the sanctity of that grave site was primal and constituted a ziyarat. The Wahhabis know this, and every Hajj accuse the Shia of performing *shirk* even within the Masjid al-Haram (Islam's holiest mosque, home to the Kaaba, and translated simply as the Noble Sanctuary). *Haram* when pronounced with an emphasis on the "A" becomes the word for everything that is forbidden in Islam.

Turban #2 decided to quote from Khomeini, reminding us, "Even if we forgive Saddam, even if we forget Quds and forgive Israel, and even if we forgive America's crimes, we will never forgive Al Saud."

I triple-texted my safe MMS group comprising Adham, Keith, and Shahinaz: "You up? I am hanging out with Hizbullah!"

"Wish you were here dude," replied Adham. "Amazing jam session in Jeddah. The beer is flowing like Zamzam!"

I choked on my laughter at his reference to Islam's holiest water. Keith's reply sobered me up.

"Don't do all this, honey. I can't sleep at night with worry. Just do the Hajj and get out of there. Nothing political. PLEASE."

But I know he knew that I thrived on the dangerous and loved politics.

There was a lull and then another young Tehrani type, who looked like he was forced to come (he was, as I later learned), looked at Hossein and me.

"Hossein, have you told Parviz about what will happen at Jamrat?"

I knew that Jamrat was one of the last, most feared, and deadliest rituals of the Hajj. It had claimed thousands of lives. Pilgrims got to stone columns representing devils, re-enacting what the Prophet Ibrahim had allegedly done. Stampedes, injuries, and death (literally by stoning) were common.

"Ah!" laughed Hossein. He told me that in Iran pilgrims had schools for training for Hajj. When they were taught how to stone, they were told to say, "Death to America!" at the largest column, "Death to Israel!" at the second column, and "Death to Britannia!" at the third and smallest column. The room burst into laughter. So did I. Hossein told me later that some "poorer" Iranians actually practiced this at the Jamrat columns during Hajj.

In room 701, no one showed signs of leaving, each staring at his glowing smartphone, pretty much like anywhere on the planet. I made an excuse that it was time for my Fajr wudu and they wished me well. The night was proving what I had always suspected. The Iranian Hajj, like the Shia Hajj, was a political and spiritual act. I was back in the closet as a filmmaker and homosexual. If either Turban had Googled me, 701 would have been a very different space. Yet I felt solidarity with them.

"The Hizbullah shit is true, Parviz," Hossein said. It could well be true. Medina and Mecca at Hajj time, when the Saudis were processing millions of visas, was the perfect time for the supposedly "bad" Muslims to get in and confabulate.

For an instant, I thought I should come out to Hossein and also tell him about Shahinaz. But my rational side told me that our friendship would be brief: Hajj buddies in Medina, but drifting apart naturally as the pilgrimage progressed.

It was still two hours to Fajr. Shahinaz joined me for a dangerous cigarette, hiding in an alley. If a mutawa was crawling at this hour, I would say she was my sister. I was not very savvy—these were early days. We did the unthinkable! A sleepless gay man and a bare-headed woman sharing a cigarette. We discussed roommate woes. She said her rudest roommate took the largest bed and claimed a superior piety. "Makes me want to vomit!" Earlier, she'd also texted, "It's pray 24/7 in the tent every day, but then they form little cliques bitching about each other."

She was my eyes and ears to peer into a forbidden world. I was eager to know what happened to the women on Hajj. We had never imagined this extent of segregation. She asked if my burden of faith felt lighter. We were opposites. She, like Keith, did not have a religious bone in her body. She respected how I was putting life and limb at risk, so she had also come wanting to "watch my back." Pretty soon we had realized how impossible that was. The shared cigarette on that "Hizbullah Night" was a moment we needed to cherish. Shahinaz would suffer so much more, being a woman smoker on Hajj. In the best of times, even in India, smoking women were derided and labeled.

A menacing mutawa approached from the darkness. I was glad that Shahinaz had a small, boyish frame with a frizzy, afro-like mop of hair. From afar she could pass for a boy. We ran. This poor night-shift mutawa never got a chance to use his cane and write us up. Or worse, haul us to a Saudi dungeon.

The next morning was a flurry of activity. Younger Hajjis like me rushed between rooms of the second-timers. The day was upon us. We needed to don the ihram, the mandated dress for male pilgrims that consists of two seamless pieces of white towel. Two pieces, one for each half of the body. Both halves were about two meters long. The tying of the one over the lower part of the body was particularly challenging. The upper part was just like draping a shawl. Underwear was forbidden, so the lower half was challenging. My circumcision was still not healed. The terror I experienced over accidentally exposing it was unspeakable. One false move and my shame would be public. A kind uncle invited me into his room. He was already in full-on Hajj couture. The uncle looked at ease, wearing it around the waist, running to the ankles, which had to be exposed. His was held in place by fabric folded over without a knot.

"This is the Burmese style," he said, "easier because you are not too fat." He showed it to me, draping it over my pants.

"They will tell you not to tie a money belt around it, because it is not *sunnah*, but don't listen to them. You will need that belt after you have worn this for even a day. So do it secretly when no one is looking," he whispered. Sage words because they were true. I bought several. In Mecca, word spread that Parvez had extra fanny packs. This was no Christmas. Yet I felt like Santa Claus dolling them to the desperate men whose ihram's were in danger of falling.

Upon donning the lower part of my ihram, after performing all rituals and making sure I wore no underwear, I realized the sexual potential of an unsheathed penis rubbing against this Made in China towel fabric.

"A horny gay man into mid-eastern types would be in paradise here, with all this man smell and exposed genitalia," I texted Shahinaz, who replied, "The burqa vs Hijab vs Niqab vs Abaya wars are on here, my dear!"

I banished thoughts of the sexual implications of each man around me, separated from nudity by just a towel. We looked like the men I had seen in gay-hookup saunas during my first trip to the US in 1998. Also, fragrance was part of the long list of the forbiddens while wearing ihram, making for an unpleasantly malodorous Hajj.

I focused on the spiritual. The ihram was much more than a mere garment. A long list of restrictions came with it. I know the Prophet had deemed it as Hajj couture because he imagined an equal Ummah, in white, dressed in exactly the same way, facing their maker, naked on Judgment Day. The ihram was supposed to signify Muhammad's equal Hajj. I had grown up listening to many opinions about ihram. Some elders used to say the word "ihram" meant abstention—abstention from war, hunting, the sexual, and so much more. Donning this garment, I entered an ineffable state of grace and piety. Faith had brought me here and it would protect me in the weeks that lay ahead. From this point on, even killing an insect was forbidden.

The terrors of walking thirsty for miles, with underwear-less thighs rubbing against each other in humid weather that feels like the 100s, lay in the future. Caused by walking with these brutally chafed thighs, the Hajj rash no one talks about is hell on Earth. I wish I had known that since 2007 the Saudis had offered pilgrims the option of "seamless trousers." The English-language *Saudi Gazette* had written a piece on it on July 16, 2007, saying, "Pilgrims often complain of sore thighs because of friction as a result of long walks. The trouser will protect the thighs."

I texted Shahinaz, "What is your Hajj couture, Madam? No underwear?"

"I will leave that to your fertile imagination darling," she replied snarkily.

We were innocents, she and I. No one had ever dared to tell us the unspeakable horrors that unfolded when unsheathed male genitalia rubbed against the bodies of hundreds of thousands of women, not separated in the holy mosque in Mecca. At peak time, the tawaf was violent. The majority of these men had never been in such extreme proximity to the bodies of women. And not every male pilgrim had the discipline of piety.

Going down for my first fag in my brand-new threads, I took a pathetic-looking selfie for my MMS group. An older pilgrim looked on disapprovingly. I winked at him. There was no way on Earth I was going on Hajj without cigarettes. And thankfully I was not the only one with tobacco on his mind and breath.

CHAPTER 6

THE NAKED BELIEVER

Subject: URGENT!!! Tim Hortons!
 I would like to thank a brother for giving me this information
Salam Alaikum, Brothers and Sisters.
 I asked my owner a question about if the Ice Capp has alcohol
or not. My owner gave me a specific number for me to call because
he was not sure. So I called that number. It turns out that the Ice
Capp does have "ethyl alcohol," which is the same thing that is used
in drinking alcohol. So the Ice Capp is now confirmed HARAM
for us Muslims. They said that anything that usually contains any
artificial flavoring at Tim Hortons will likely contain some trace of
ethyl alcohol.
 I also asked them about all other products like smoothies,
lemonade, french vanillas, and hot chocolates. And they said that all
of them have artificial flavoring, which will end up in all the drinks
also having alcohol. So then I asked them about all the baked goods
(donuts, timbits, bagels, etc.) so they gave me a list, please look at
the list to see.
 Al Hamdellah rubal alameen that inshAllah all of us will be
granted a spot in paradise for following the laws of islam. InshAllah
we will all be granted rewards.

Mixed Berry Smoothie
Anything in can or bottle
Food:
12 Grain Bagel
Wheat & Honey
Sesame Seed Bagel
All donuts/timbits are HALAL except the following:
Lemon Cake Donut
Apple Cinnamon Donut
S'mores Donut
Red Maple Leaf Sprinkles Donut

Razia Sultana, the author of this edited email, was a newly married immigrant to Canada who had "forced" her husband Rashid to come on the Hajj. We had sat next to each other on the plane from Doha to Medina. Rashid made sure he sat in the middle. This friendly couple had already acquired the Canadian "eh" and the earnest jovial manner I had always admired in the people of their adopted homeland. He told me that he was a nonbeliever and that she had forced him to come so he could quit smoking. Seemingly possessed of only religious bones, and dressed in the opaque ninja body armor of her deep black abaya, Razia gently admonished him through her full-face niqab. I stared straight ahead.

When the plane had landed in Saudi Arabia, and as Razia moved to be processed in the female pilgrims' line, Rashid asked if he could bum a few cigarettes from me.

"Don't tell her. We will smoke in secret when the women are not around." As if Shahinaz were not enough, I now had the added burden of another secret smoker and unfortunately one of the opposite sex who could face unthinkable consequences if caught.

As it turned out, for most of our Hajj, the women were corralled out of reach.

I told Razia she shared her name with a historic Indian warrior-queen, played to seductive perfection in a famous Bollywood film from the eighties. By this time Rashid and I had become smoking buddies and

I knew he was fifty and had another wife and two daughters, as old as the much younger Razia. She didn't know of their existence, he said. He had married wife #1 only for immigration reasons and then his parents found him Razia in Bombay. With a Canadian passport he was an eligible bachelor, a perfect match. I did not tell Razia. I also did not tell her that her famed namesake had taken on many women as lovers during her short but tumultuous reign in India. Thankfully, Razia had not seen the film or she might have remembered a provocative song sequence where the voluptuous Muslim actress Parveen Babi was bathed in camel milk by a harem of young women, who like their queen were in various stages of undress. Meanwhile the real Razia now wore black gloves, extreme even by Saudi standards.

Men and women are not separated in the Noble Sanctuary in Mecca, so-called because it contains Islam's center of gravity, the Kaaba. Both genders get equal face-time with God in this, his "house." During our Hajj, many women around the Kaaba chose to defy the Prophet's own edict not to veil. Perhaps word had spread about the indignities women suffered from the underwear-less male pilgrims, most of whom had never been in such close proximity to so many women. Toward the end of our Hajj, Razia, like so many of the other women, would approach the Kaaba covered in the black sheath and even socks!

Six days after we left the holy land, I to America and Rashid and Razia to Canada, the latter started an email list-serve. Exercises like haram-halal studies of the Tim Hortons' menu made her its most prolific poster and I perhaps her most loyal reader.

All Muslims know that Hajj is a pilgrimage that most of the world will never be permitted to make. For centuries, Mecca, sitting at an ideal crossroads between the Indian Ocean and the Mediterranean, was the city into which desert tribes weaved their caravans to trade and to pray. The city had always welcomed the thirsty and the weary, the believers and the merchants whose primary religion was money. No one was turned away at the doors of Mecca, it was said. Not true in the Mecca I went to.

Muhammad did only one Hajj during his lifetime. Returning triumphant as the Prophet to the city he had been banished from, and accompanied by 100,000 newly minted Muslims, he spent the night in a desert oasis called Dhul Halifa, had a bath, and put on his own ihram. He then went straight to the ancient mosque and, on seeing the Kaaba, fell to his knees, proclaiming, "Oh Allah, You are Peace. With you is Peace. Our Lord, keep us alive with peace." However, his next acts were not exactly peaceful, as he set about methodically destroying the idols that had been placed and worshipped in the cube for hundreds of years. He needed to lay down the foundations of Islam: The idols needed to go. He knew that the sanctity of the young religion he was bringing to this city's inhabitants needed protection. Non-Muslims brought idols with them.

Preparing for my departure I was thankful that it was my mother's courage that ran through my veins. But I had also spent most of my own adult life afraid of my own faith, tormented by what I believed was certain: I was just not Muslim enough to ever be allowed into the holy land. For me, Islam had always been a faith of fear. Perhaps I was here to conquer my fear of faith. Access to twenty-first-century Saudi Arabia is tightly controlled, and Mecca is perhaps one of the world's most secret cities.

Large signs on all roads that led to Mecca warned "Muslims Only." Well-marked exits to get off this Islamic highway to heaven make sure that all sensible unbelievers leave while there is still time. But I already knew that Chinese construction workers, for example, had become quick converts to Islam so they could be allowed to enter, just like the French soldiers who liberated the grand mosque in 1979. It helps that Islam's testament of faith, the Shahadah, takes less than a minute to articulate: "I bear witness that there is no God but God and that Muhammad is his Prophet." The five days of Hajj are all about Mecca and it is here that the keys to heaven are supposedly made available to each pilgrim. But for me, like many, the Hajj was every single moment we spent on Saudi soil including, especially, Medina.

Our Shia-filled bus sped toward Mecca. At the time, I thought I was the only Sunni in my Hajj group. I shared this secret with our group leader. My bigger secret I dared not share. That stayed in my Hajj closet.

"We Shia welcome you, brother Parvez," said Shafiq. "But if it were the other way around, it would never happen. A Shia pilgrim in a Sunni group? Never!"

Shahinaz and I sat together at the back of the bus. As in Medina, I wanted to establish that she was my cousin. We shared our fears at what lay ahead. She was close to being ninja-like, but it was at least a practical white and best of all her face, as the Prophet had commanded, was uncovered. Her real cousin Abdellah from Birmingham snored softly next to her.

In the middle of the night, as my Mecca-bound bus had filled with fellow pilgrims, all of us announced our arrival to God at his own house by chanting, "*Labbaik Allahuma Labbaik!*" ("Here I am, oh God, here I am!") As we smoothly passed through each of Islam's checkpoints, my heart lightened. No one had dared to stop me entering Mecca.

The Prophet I knew, the Muhammad whom I came here to seek, would have fought valiantly to prevent the schism between Shia and Sunni, which violates every single principle of the united Muslim Ummah he had worked hard to create. As we chanted, I realized that, just as Islam belongs to nobody but its believers, Muhammad and his Quran thankfully belong to all Muslims. I was following in Muhammad's footsteps, entering a city that in so many ways had been forbidden to all of us on the bus, just as it had been forbidden to him, to try to take back ownership of Islam. Perhaps our Hajj itself was an act of subversion? There was a strange comfort in knowing that these fellow pilgrims sharing my bus were, like me, Islam's outsiders.

Many truths, though, were uncomfortable. It is clear to most Muslims that many of the September 11 hijackers, trained in the kind of Islam the Saudi monarchy ordains and survives because of, must have performed this very pilgrimage. Why? Because, they were Saudi, and that's what (the religious) Saudis do.

I had been doing all five prayers for months, but that was hardly prep for what lay ahead. It was 3:40 in the morning when we arrived. We had been on the bus for a grueling eight hours. Under normal circumstances—not during Hajj—the trip from Medina took about five. After we deboarded, Rashid, Razia, Shahinaz, Abdellah, and I approached the Noble Sanctuary together, in the hopeless hope we would do this together. But within a few minutes it became clear we could not stay as a group, and the couples disappeared into an urgent mass of humanity larger than anything I had ever seen. I tried to hold Shahinaz as long as I possibly could.

And then I was left alone. My solitude amongst the millions who surrounded me was incongruous and immense.

I was wearing my ihram, Burmese-style. The ihram was about the democracy of Muhammad's vision of the Ummah. The Saudi Hajj of the twenty-first century, however, is an unequal pilgrimage. For many it plays out in posh five-star comfort. As I entered the boundaries of the holy mosque that is home to the Kaaba, I felt a profound sense of accomplishment. I was here as a rebel, one who would never be allowed in by the Saudi brand of Islam, which thrives on inequality and oppression.

The image of the Kaaba is imprinted on every single *janamaz* (prayer rug) I ever saw. As with most Muslims, the image had been seared into my memory since childhood. For a religion that does not like images, that of the Kaaba is the most sacred.

My first thought was that I was not supposed to be here. And then, transfixed by the sight of the cube, I was reminded once again that it was just an empty room. Its geometry ensured that it had no direction. Instead, one-sixth of humanity was commanded to face it five times a day for their entire lives. Was this it, the center of my faith, of my prayers, of love, of life and death?

On this night as I looked at the black cube for the first time in my life, I wept. The tears that were stolen from me at my mother's funeral returned in a violent and unstoppable tide. I wept like a newborn child. But here she was, holding me, breathlessly, in a complete and loving embrace of some kind of final acceptance. She whispered how much she loved me. In that moment of grief and of recognition, of loss and of discovery, I did not realize that I was about to begin the most violent night of my life. I declared my *niyat,* my formal intention of performing Hajj. And then, like a drop entering the ocean, I joined the moving mass.

The strict rules of Islam here in Mecca were enforced by several thousand mutaween. Post-Medina I could spot these orange-beards—some dyed their facial hair with henna—in their loose-fitting red headscarves, patrolling the crowds with their thin wooden canes, ready to arrest anyone they found breaking the rules—from dress-code infractions to sexual acts, alcohol possession, consumption of un-Islamic media, and various other forms of Western behavior including smoking. The last they merrily did themselves.

The mutaween also enforced the prayer times. I had seen them in action, prowling around, making sure that all the shops selling kitsch closed their shutters five times daily, and making sure that each of us was praying "the right way."

They had to make sure we maintained proper posture during our daily prayers, and even during the sometimes hours-long wait times before those prayers. According to the mutaween, my right foot needed to be arched upright under my right buttock and my left foot needed to lie horizontal between the various ritual prostrations of prayer. This was a torment to my unaccustomed body, and the longer I knelt during my daily prayers, the more acute—and familiar—my pain became. I had recently realized that I was suffering from the recurrence of my old pilonidal cyst, developed two years earlier after countless hours sitting with bad posture at my computer. It was what they used to call "Jeep's disease" during World War II, the painful result of prolonged rides in bumpy Jeeps. I needed a heavy course of antibiotics and some women's sanitary pads for any bleeding, and most of all, I needed to keep pressure off my coccyx. At this moment, as I approached the Kaaba, built up in billions of Muslim minds like mine as a moment of lifelong immensity, I had none of those options.

In my right hand I clutched a *tasbih,* the prayer beads Muslims favor. It, too, was made in China. This tasbih had exactly ninety-nine ugly plastic beads. The tasbih that hung on the knob of my mother's closet had 100 beads. The hundredth, she would say, just reminds you that you are a very good and blessed person when you come full circle after reciting the ninety-nine names of Allah.

I did not know the ninety-nine names of Allah. On a good day I could muster eight or nine. Today had not been a good day at all. So I decided to go with what I knew best. I mumbled *Allahu Akbar* with a ferocity I did not know I possessed. It was a whispered, almost inaudible ferocity. It would amplify and even reach screaming level, though that moment had not yet arrived. Sometimes you need to be at your loudest for God to hear your faith.

I was to perform seven rounds of tawaf as mandated. Because I was performing the Shia Hajj, I knew I would need to get as close as I possibly could within the first few circles, competing with hundreds of thousands of pilgrims jostling for space. I could see women getting molested and I even heard their screams.

My tasbih beads were soon slick with sweat. So was the rest of me. A dripping line of sweat seemed to have formed around my still-unhealed penis. On my lower back, I felt something dripping, slowly, incessantly, and shamelessly. I hoped it was not blood.

There could not be blood. It would stain my white ihram, turning it *najlis* ("impure"). The same ihram that is supposed to be the surest symbol of the ideal democracy of Islam. And then, once again, I would have to carry out the complicated *ghusl,* or ritual washing and purification. I would somehow need to find my way back to the hotel and re-do all of the many ablutions, each moment prescribed and written down. A prayer for every drop of divinely sanctioned and cleansing water on my body. I had spent weeks memorizing the right Shia prayers for the moment the right hand passes over my navel, for when I wash my arms exactly the right way. I had tried so hard to get this right, to get this just right so that later on, when my having been here became public, I could not possibly be questioned about my intentions or the legitimacy of my journey. But a bloody ihram would be proof of my dirtiness, my sin.

The ihram was not just two seamless pieces of white cloth. It was a state of mind. As Muslims we had been taught that this simple white clothing was intended to make everyone appear the same in the eyes of God. This teaching, of course, showed the much-vaunted democracy and oneness of the Muslim Ummah, the worldwide brotherhood of believers.

My mother used to say that the ihram was the *kafan*—the shroud. That going on this journey was a preparation for death. And if we were lucky enough to die in a state of ihram, then we would find a one-way ticket to heaven by being buried in the holy land. If a person returned alive, she explained, he was required to bring the ihram back with him and keep it safe, to be used only upon death and to be buried in. Blood would be shame greater than I could imagine.

It was the *Allahu Akbars* that helped me focus. They each formed a complete and extremely long moment, concentrating only on the immensity of God. That was how I had trained my mind in the last seven months of real preparation. Quietly, hopefully, and unobtrusively, I moved my left hand slowly to my backside. I was soaked with sweat. But there was no blood. The next few *Allahu Akbars* out of my lips quivered with gratitude.

My ego, which I was hoping to lose, forget, or leave behind someplace around here, led me to imagine that each pair of these millions of eyes could pierce through my sinning soul and read every twitch of doubt that clouded my carefully arranged face. I did not realize at the time that the business of getting the approval of Allah is busy and all-consuming and not conducive to much else besides a kind of obsession with only oneself. I did not realize that a mere demonstration of faith is never enough and that for many of the worshippers around me, the preoccupation with a lifetime of sin had been a full-time job.

In a momentary distraction from my focused repetitions, I remembered the feature filed by an intrepid reporter much before September 11, who had visited a US prison and found Muslim inmates being allowed to use their prayer beads for therapeutic effects. In the nineties, the meditative properties of clutching prayer beads had been used for the "successful recovery" of thousands of prison inmates, said the reporter. She added it had become controversial when gang members began carrying their differently colored prayer beads inside the prisons to identify themselves. The idea of Muslim prison inmates and gang members in the US using prayer beads, no doubt purchased from some Walmart in the meth-addled heartland, in some sort of Islamic cleansing ritual, brought a smile to my face.

My iPhone lit up. In a nation where women cannot even get into the driver's seat and are pretty much denied any form of voice, the rather talkative Siri would be a revolutionary. The problem was, she had not been talking much lately—she required a Wi-Fi network to work. But now, suddenly, she had found a network: It was called "The Saudi bin Laden Group." I busied myself trying to log on. I tried variations of passwords. Osama, Jihad, Jihad911, Kafir, Kafir786, Tawhid 1432, and many more, conjuring up all the weird Islamic combinations I could think of. None worked and much still needed to be done on this night. But I found another variation of the bin Laden construction group, which I joined and it was free. I missed talking to Siri, but, allowing more distraction to crowd my mind even as I continued to mumble *Allahu Akbar*, I wondered if the ever-so-smart Siri knew that that dignified feminine silence was just the way to behave in the holy land.

I texted my husband, "I am here, my love. It's strange but the Kaaba is protecting me from now on. You may not hear from me for the next few hours but don't worry. I will be safe."

Keith replied, "I love you. So, so, so much."

Perhaps only one New York minute had passed as I stood there with my crowded mind, typing on my phone. Not that a New York minute would ever mean the same to me again. Every second seemed to last a lifetime these days. I would probably, after this longest and perhaps most miraculous night of my entire time on this planet, measure my life in Mecca minutes.

And then I plunged willfully into this ocean of believers. On this night of magic and torment, I would not be alone after all. *I clutched my mother's hand with my right hand. In my left hand, I held a passport photograph of hers, with her hair defiantly uncovered. Tonight, though, she was wearing a bright red dupatta scarf wrapped tightly around her head. The cancer that had ravaged her once-proud frame had also taken away all of her hair. Even though she had no hair left to hide, the same hair that was deemed dangerously powerful enough to distract the believing men around us from their arduous tasks of faith on this long night, I took a breath and adjusted her scarf. She smiled knowing that I had finally embraced faith. I was the capable son bringing her to this place of faith, poetry, and longing. As she squeezed my hand back, I could feel the pride running through her own frail hand into mine.*

I could see the black burqa, inlaid in gold with Quranic verses, that covers the door of the Kaaba. The unstoppable river of humanity that surrounded me heaved toward it, trying to touch it, to reach and kiss it. This was Islam's mosh pit. And on that first night, for me it became a space imbued more with violence than with any notion of spirituality. I was going to lose so much on this longest of nights. I tried unsuccessfully to touch the Kaaba. The tears that I did not think I even possessed anymore returned as my breath almost touched the surface of the black stone. A surface made smooth by millions, each hoping for that touch that would cleanse the filth from their sinning hands and souls. The successful pilgrims around me were desperately rubbing their hands and often even prized personal possessions on the surface, hoping also to carry some of the power of this surface back home with them. We had worked very hard to get this close.

But my group's Shia Islam of martyrs also dictates many acts of self-deprivation. In the nights and days ahead I would marvel at the amount of pleasure a Shia Muslim could derive from renunciation and denial. Martyrdom seemed so well suited to them. In this mosh pit of Islam, Shia jurisprudence seemed clear. We were to get as close as possible and yet, unlike the Sunnis, we were to refrain from touching the stone or even looking at it. *My mother, who had always called the Shia "khatmal"—bed bugs, who reproduce prolifically in sinister and secretive ways—was still by my side and touched the black stone for a fleeting second.* I couldn't.

I simply faced the Kaaba and did my mandated *istilam,* a flying kiss-like greeting to the cube, as I began each new round of the tawaf. Dawn was breaking as I ended with my two *rakats* (movements of prayer) at the Maqam Ibrahim, the standing place of the Prophet Ibrahim, marked by a small golden kiosk. *Mother and son, we prayed together.* This was the only mosque in the world that did not separate its male and female believers. At this moment, bowed down in what should have been introspective prayer, I received an unholy thwack from the cane of a mutawa. I needed to move on.

In a manic stampede I was pushed toward my next ritual, *Saee* (ritual walking), at the hills of Safa and Marwah. Just like Hajjar, the desperate mother who centuries ago searched among these hills for water so that she could save her son Ismael's life, I disobediently walked briskly between the hills, like women were commanded to do for "modesty." Men were supposed to run in the same area of that section highlighted by green fluorescent lights. *As my mother walked with me, I knew she, like Hajjar, was trying to save my life.* Two kilometers apart, both hills were now encased in glass cages which pilgrims, especially the Shia among us, may no longer touch.

I felt her hand slipping away. As I lost my balance and fell a man stopped and helped me up, this time gently pushing me into the mandated jog. He and I jogged the stretch together. But I had lost my mother's photograph.

Broken and haunted, I searched for it as I left. In that mass of humanity, I had lost one of my most treasured possessions, one which I had hoped would get to touch the Kaaba with me. Later, I wondered if this really was how it was meant to be. It belonged there and I left her there where she was probably trampled into a million pieces by the feet of the manic pilgrims. Perhaps she would have wanted that image of herself to be left right there, near the Kaaba that had haunted her.

I looked up at the sky, if only to escape the madness around me for a moment. I was searching for evidence to prove a childhood theory right. Elders used to say that even birds would never dare to fly over the Kaaba. Mecca's many pigeons were waking up and taking flight. Just as they had predicted, they did not fly over the cube but rather, like us pilgrims, circled it.

Dawn was breaking, and with it rang out the *azaan,* the call to prayer, as melodious as I had been promised it would be when I was a child. Music is banned in Saudi Arabia, one of many prohibitions in a long list of what the authorities claim is "Islamically" forbidden. In that moment, I felt that these rather unmusical Saudis had managed to create a perfect song in the call to prayer. The voice of the *muezzin* was loud, clear, and beautiful, and he drew out each Arabic word into a melody:

> *God is the greatest.*
> *I testify there is no God but God.*
> *I testify that Muhammad is his messenger.*
> *Come to prayer. Come to success.*
> *Prayer is better than sleep.*

The Wahhabis call music un-Islamic. Do they understand that calls to prayer and recitations of the Quran are music to millions of Muslim ears? Did they conveniently forget the rich history of music in these sands? I would kill to see a mutawa do the Harlem Shake at one of Jeddah's thriving underground music concerts.

CHAPTER 7

THE SATANIC VERSES

D id you make it?" I texted Shahinaz.

"Barely," she replied.

"Adham said there is a Baskin-Robbins in the big mall across from Haram. Meet there at 10 a.m.?" Shahinaz was also in a group chat with me, Keith, and Adham, so she knew him well.

"I think this King Fahd gate is better."

"OK. Let's get three hours of sleep and meet there!"

The pitiless sun was already on full throttle at 10 a.m. as Shahinaz and I rendezvoused at the King Fahd gate. Her attempt at not letting one strand of hair escape the hijab was comical, almost.

I wished her a good morning.

"Nothing good about it, sweetheart," she said. "It's my birthday today and see my state!"

She was shocked by what I told her next. Wahhabi doctrine had robbed generations of children of the delights of the annual ritual. Celebrating birthdays, they said, was *bida*, an un-Islamic innovation. Celebrating the Prophet's birthday, Mawlid al-Nabi, for example, was forbidden, unlike in most parts of the Muslim world.

This was for me the ultimate example of Wahhabi malevolence: Entire childhoods were robbed of the balloons, cakes, gifts, and mirth of birthdays. The ones who dared to celebrate did so in secret. At the turn of the millennium, posters signed by the "highest authority" surfaced saying birthday or anniversary celebrations were "heresy."

We both started walking to the Abraj al-Bait Mall across from the Kaaba. A mutawa approached us. "Mahram?" he asked ominously.

"She is my cousin," I said. He asked for IDs. Recklessly, once again we made a great show of looking for them, informing him we had left them in the hotel. We showed him our matching denim messenger bags that had all the information about the Hajj group. He made notes with his mucky fingers and let us go. As if he was ever going to check, we laughed later. Was I no longer afraid of them?

Inside the mall was a wondrous nouveau-riche Alice's Wonderland. I realized that what was ugly and in bad taste for us educated pilgrims was novelty and a spiritual experience packaged in luxury for pilgrims from countries like Sudan and Somalia. For many, it was their first-ever flight that had brought them here. For others, an escalator was a novelty they had never seen. Baskin-Robbins, Dunkin' Donuts, and Hardee's competed for attention with Chanel and Givenchy stores. Everything that filled Shahinaz and me with distaste was splendorous to many others. And then the ultimate. A Starbucks! I didn't know then that I would return many times. It was divided into singles and family sections. We went into the family section knowing she could never enter the singles section.

I launched into a tirade on everything that was wrong with this country. All these malls and cranes constructing multimillion-dollar apartments with views of the Kaaba were built on destroyed history. Dar-al Aqram, the first school where the Prophet taught, lay flattened under marble tiles. The home he was born in, Bayt al-Mawlid, was demolished to build a "library." The house of one of the greatest Quyrash tyrants opposed to Muhammad was replaced (rightfully, some said) by toilets. The dome covering the original well of Zamzam water was said to have been demolished. Abraj al-Bayt itself sat on the ruins of an Ottoman fortress. Many Ottoman architectural flourishes had been dynamited to smithereens. We had seen it in Medina.

Shahinaz said that, super-inconveniently, her period had started. There were various opinions on the matter, including denying menstruating women pretty much anything including access to the Kaaba. The influential canon Sahih Bukhari outright forbade it. Was there sectarian unanimity?

"Misogynist bastards," she complained. Later on in the pilgrimage she would tell me that women for whom it was that time of month were treated despicably in the tents in Mina, pushed to far corners as if they had Ebola and not allowed to participate in religious activity. Mina was the tent city of indescribable proportions set up on the outskirts of Mecca, used only for Hajj. It was notoriously unsafe. Many fires had started there, killing hundreds of pilgrims.

We decided together that she would not report her menstrual cycle to her group leader. We were probably playing with fire or utter damnation at the very least. But there was no way either Shahinaz or I wanted her to be confined for several days as if the plague had infected her.

Shahinaz was angry as we sipped our special birthday Frappuccinos. "Pure? WTF. I am pure. Period or not! It's part of being a woman."

We marveled at the edited Starbucks logo—there was no mermaid. The Saudis had made sure this giant corporation complied with their silly religious logic on faceless women. Was a mermaid a woman, even? The edited logo was on the coffee mugs they were selling that said "Starbucks Makkah."

On another note, I was now clearly bleeding; my ihram needed sanitary pads. We had texted and Shahinaz had carried them in her bag. I hid them in my backpack before going through the very complicated procedure of untying the ihram, properly positioning the pad as she had instructed me, and then putting it all on Burmese-style again. The location for all of this was a Starbucks bathroom cubicle. These sparkling bathrooms had thankfully not been discovered by many pilgrims. I did many pre-prayer ablutions there.

"How long was I gone?" I asked as I emerged now equipped with my comforting pad.

"Oh, about half an hour," she said.

"*Je suis désolé,*" I answered using her native French.

"Don't worry. With your strange cyst you are now discovering what it means to be a woman bleeding once every month!"

We ventured out of the mall into a cheaper bazaar selling mostly Chinese-made Islamic tchotchkes. Curiosities abounded. A shop selling colorful women's abayas called itself "Caribbean Hajj." Another shop sold "I heart NY" shirts. There were cheap plastic toys like buses and trains to Mecca. The merchants were careful not to display human, and especially female, faces anywhere, and yet we passed a storefront brazenly selling the non–Victoria's Secret unmentionables for probably the poorer pilgrims. That other franchise probably did exist in the iridescent malls of the Saudis, but this country, like its Hajj, was unequal. Here, purple, red, and pink bras hung openly in what I imagined would be a big, shamelessly brazen anti-Islam display to the Wahhabis. Had a mutawa seen it? Was he bribed to shut up? Shahinaz went into the shop alone.

"You won't believe it," she said coming out. Apparently collections of condoms, tampons, and sanitary pads were displayed prominently under a glass cover in the back.

A shopkeeper invited us into a nondescript clothes-and-bags store. It was true Meccan enterprise on display—this town for at least fourteen centuries had been home to a fiercely competitive merchant class. He was proof. At the back he had photocopying, laminating, and scanning machines. There was also a flat-screen Hewlett Packard monitor. He spoke fluent Arab-lish, as I had taken to calling it.

"You not her mahram? I make life easy for you."

He asked for 500 riyals, about 50 US dollars. He took passport photos. Within minutes he had made what looked like two authentic Saudi IDs. Shahinaz, whose Arabic reading was superior to mine, said they looked authentic.

"From this day, Parvez Hussein, I, Shahinaz, am your wife!"

I couldn't believe it. We could be together all the time. For her cousin Abdellah, I remained a friend. For our Hajj group, she, like him, was my cousin (and Abdellah understood the reason for the lie). And now for these Saudi brigands, we were husband and wife with the IDs to prove it!

One day, sitting with Shahinaz in a sliver of shade contemplating the Kaaba, I started to tell her a story of an unlikely Prophet. I knew that while nonreligious, she was interested in the intellectual sparring about what was academic to her and spiritual to me.

It was a moonless night in 610 and a forty-year-old Meccan merchant called Muhammad sat meditating in a cave called Hira on a mountain called Jabal al-Nour. In Urdu, *hira* means "diamond." In Arabic, *Jabal al-Nour* means "the mountain of light." Muhammad had been suffering for months from what a modern-day psychiatrist would perhaps diagnose as a bipolar depression accompanied by hallucinations. He trudged regularly for two hours to this cave for some silent contemplation. Islam's oral and written history tells us that Muhammad took some water and simple food with him.

Mecca's still *jahil* ("ignorant") residents were busy worshipping 360 idols, all kept within the black cubical room built by Ibrahim and Ismael. This room would become the center of a religion that had not yet been revealed to this illiterate man who was not yet named Prophet.

On a particularly difficult night, the angel Jibreel appeared to Muhammad.

"Ikra!" commanded the angel. *Read!* Muhammad was naturally petrified and told the angel he was illiterate. The angel held Muhammad in a stranglehold, now commanding him to recite. Finally, the angel burst into verse and revealed the first of what would become twenty-three years of revelation. This would become the 96th Surah of the Quran, called *Al-Alaq* ("The Clot").

> *In the name of Allah, the Most Beneficent, the Most Merciful.*
> *Read: In the name of your Lord Who created.*
> *Created man from a clot of blood.*
> *Read: And your Lord is the Most generous,*
> *Who taught man the use of the pen,*
> *And taught man that which he did not know.*

As I had been in childhood, Shahinaz was as fascinated by the idea of an illiterate man being asked to read/recite. I told her that as an adult I would ponder the significance of the first revelation in so many ways being about knowledge and education. It was God who "taught man the use of the pen," the verse was saying. Surely the religion that would follow would be about intellect, literacy, freedom, and wisdom. This verse being revealed first is not an accident. Islam would need an intellectual submission to God. Had the power of that pen been lost forever?

Shahinaz understood that *islam* ("submission") came with the intellect of the *qalam* ("pen").

After receiving his revelation in the Hira cave, not far from us, I told her how Muhammad knew he could not dare report it to anyone in his community of the Quraysh tribe. He ran from the cave into the arms of his now sixty-five-year-old wife, Khadija, and begged her to "cover him." Here was a young husband seeking protection from a wife who was older and the breadwinner in a society that was ruled by polygamous men with wives who had no rights. His shameful revelation needed to be kept secret that night, from everyone but her. She believed him, as she always had and would until the end of her life. Muhammad and Khadija's love story always lay at the heart of the birth of Islam, I told Shahinaz.

The story we discussed next was dangerous territory here. It was little known. The Quraysh allegedly worshipped three female goddesses: Al-Lat, Al-Uzzat, and Manat. At the time, the central characters in Muhammad's life were all women. Guided perhaps by their feminine energy, he headed to the Kaaba on a cold night in 616, hoping for new revelation, for new converts.

It was said he found himself chanting some verses about the three daughters of God: "Have you ever considered what you are worshipping in these three Goddesses—these are the exalted *gharaniq* ("cranes") that fly higher than any bird and their intercession is approved?" These were reprobate verses—and Muhammad's later biographers, mostly male, concluded that Satan had put them on his lips. The Quraysh were electrified and ready to embrace this new religion that would include their beloved female goddesses. But Muhammad remained troubled that the Quraysh were not learning the humility, submission, and democracy of his new religion.

Allegedly, Jibreel came back to him and said, "You have recited to those people something I did not bring you from God." Muhammad was contrite and Jibreel said that all the previous Prophets had made "Satanic" mistakes, mistakes that could be easily rectified.

The few Muslims who even know this story are told that Surah 22 was now revealed: "God renders null and void whatever aspersions the Satan may have cast and God makes his messages clear in and by themselves." The important precedent of revelation's being progressive was set. God could alter revelation.

The biographers claim that Muhammad now chastised the Quraysh. Why did they attribute daughters to Allah when they themselves preferred sons? These so-called goddesses were simply empty names and fabrications. Thus, these "Satanic verses" were obliterated forever from the canon, and Muslims now four years into Islam could no longer take the old religion of idolatry seriously.

"Patriarchal bastards," again murmured Shahinaz, whose attention I still held.

The God the Muslims experienced was harsh and powerful, "meteor-like," I said to her. Shortly after this repudiation of the Satanic verses, chapter 112 of the Quran, the Surah of Sincerity, was revealed: "Say He is God, one; God forever; not begetting, unbegotten and having as equal none." This brought the central crux of Muslim spirituality: the principle of Tawhid, or unity. It was not a mere metaphysical abstraction of the singularity of the divine; it was a call to action. God had taken charge of previous transgressions and was commanding and ordering, "Say."

Biographers say Muhammad brought respect to women in a society where they had had none. Having up to ten wives whom he treated respectfully was proof. The widows and divorcees he married would have otherwise been the dregs of society.

"I can't deal with the ten wives," interrupted Shahinaz, "just as much as I can't deal with the polygamy in the Mormons." I told her it was a product of the times, but she remained unconvinced.

Unfortunately, the same men who obliterated the Satanic verses from the Islamic canon also got to write Islam's history. Sitting there, we both wondered if Muslims like her and me would have found a better place in Islam if the women of the faith had been allowed to control its destiny. Our female Muslim ancestors, other than Hajjar, celebrated mostly during the Hajj, were conveniently forgotten. The few who did make it into this male narrative are there for very particular reasons. Virgins, for example, fit perfectly into the narrative of the ideal Muslim woman because their sexuality has been controlled and they become paragons of virtue. For the Sunnis I grew up with, therefore, the Prophet's second wife, the virgin Aisha, became his favorite wife after Khadija died. The Saudis, we both realized, had no room for Khadija and Muhammad's rebellious marriage.

For most Sunnis Aisha is the best woman of her time and she gets to be called *Umm al-Mu'minin*, the mother of all the believers, and she is the most important woman in the Ahl al-Bayt, the sacred core family of the Prophet Muhammad. Aisha's virginity at the time of her marriage to the Prophet is what makes her an object of so much reverence. But she is also divisive.

Shia, Shahinaz reminded me, never include Aisha in the *Ahl al-Bayt*. For them the most revered woman within the Prophet's family is his daughter Fatima, who was married to his rightful successor, his cousin Ali, and the Shia's first imam, and bore him his two beloved grandsons, Hassan and Husayn, who would also follow as imams and the rightful caliphs. Shia theology, which at its heart is about a great deal of public mourning, made sure that the women in Shahinaz's group openly wept nightly when a famous hadith called *Hadith e Kisa* ("the Hadith of the Cloak") was narrated. It is a particularly moving hadith. Muhammad takes his daughter Fatima, his son-in law Ali, and their two sons under his cloak, raises his right hand, and speaks to God:

> O Allah, these are the people of my Household (Ahl al-Bayt).
> They are my confidants and my supporters.
> Their flesh is my flesh and their blood is my blood.
> Whoever hurts them, hurts me too.
> Whoever displeases them, displeases me too.
> I am at war with those at war with them.
> I am at peace with those at peace with them.
> I am the enemy of their enemies and
> I am the friend of their friends.
> They are from me and I am from them.
> O Allah! Bestow Your Blessings, Benevolence,
> Forgiveness and Your pleasure upon me and upon them.
> And remove impurity from them and keep them thoroughly pure.

I told her why this hadith was so powerful to me. It conveyed a very visual image of a man protecting his family and claiming them powerfully, using a blanket-like cloak. It spoke to the kind of blanketing warmth of parental safety I never knew as a child.

As we talked, hundreds of wheelchair-pushing young boys (you would *not* want to cross their path) raced past, allowing the old and infirm to do their tawaf on the second level of this beyond-mammoth mosque, which its bin Laden builders said was almost ninety acres. Theirs was a civilized tawaf. There was no way they could be in the mosh pit of thousands around the Kaaba. Shahinaz laughed at my word choice. After a Zamzam water break, we returned to our miraculously still-empty spot at Starbucks.

Changing subjects, we spoke of how the France she grew up in, once a violently colonial power, like much of Europe, suffered from what I have always called a "reverse colonialism." In Britain, the colonizers of my ancestors, colonialism was manifested in its largest minority: the immigrants from the Indian subcontinent. In France, said Shahinaz, the immigrant flood came from the colonized soul of North Africa.

Historical memory is short. Or were the shadows of the horrors that followed Weimar Germany just too hard to erase? It seemed that this Europe forgot that immigrants included impoverished souls fleeing the demons of poverty, ignorance, and illiteracy—byproducts of a particular kind of Islam that resurged only after the colonizers abandoned their nations to many uncertain freedoms. My prescience was right. In only a few years there was a helpless flood of those escaping Daesh terror, arriving in indescribable pain.

Xenophobia was hardly a novelty to Europe. As a descriptive for this impending terror, the media invented the catchy phrase "Eurabia." Less than a century ago, the expansionist and seemingly unstoppable Ottomans intent on creating Islam's greatest caliphate had been turned away at Europe's doors. Panicked pundits opined on TV. A carefully built edifice of Caucasian Christianity that often masqueraded as secular could forever be destroyed by a new wave of dark-skinned immigrants from Turkey and North Africa—the inheritors of the blood-thirst of the once-powerful Ottomans!

For Osama and later Daesh, fears of the impending doom of a new "Eurabia" were a godsend: a strange reaffirmation of the perverted logic and stated desire to reclaim Islam's lost glory.

Shahinaz reminded me about how I had begun filming her in 2005 for *A Jihad for Love*. I had arrived soon after the riots that followed the electrocution of two unemployed French Muslim teenagers at a Paris electrical substation. They were escaping a xenophobic police force that loved chasing Muslim youths through the streets.

It was the stuff of urban legend. Touring the burnt remains of the destruction, Nicolas Sarkozy, then the interior minister, decided to channel the revered French author and philosopher Albert Camus, who was raised in colonized Algeria. In 1947, in perhaps his most influential and enduring work, *La Peste* ("The Plague"), Camus wrote: "If we put all this lowlife in prison, honest people could breathe."

Camus referred to these "lowlifes" as *racaille*. And Camus, being one of the most influential wordsmiths in the language, finds his quote immortalized in the authoritative *Le Petit Robert*, which defines the word variously as "contemptible populace," "rejects of society," and more.

Sarkozy was already anointed for many as the worthy, if controversial, successor to French President Jacques Chirac, as he toured the troubled suburb of Argenteuil. This was once a rural retreat for well-heeled Parisians, immortalized on canvas by Claude Monet, among many illustrious others. Monet would not recognize the contemporary Argenteuil, where I would become a frequent visitor and which for all intents and purposes was Europe's largest slum for the nation's Muslim "scum." Mile after mile of what in New York would be "the projects" was an overflowing cauldron of immigrant discontent and now allegedly sinister, planned dissent.

In 2005, a resident of one of these public-housing towers that Sarkozy toured, perhaps nostalgic about the Argenteuil Monet had painted, called out to the future president from a precarious perch on his balcony: "*Quand nous débarrasserez-vous de cette racaille?*" ("When will you get rid of this scum?")

Always in campaign mode and very aware of his upcoming ascension, Sarkozy did not skip a beat and declared: "*Vous en avez assez de cette bande de racailles? Eh bien, on va vous en débarrasser.*" ("You've had enough of this group of scum? Well, we'll get rid of them for you.")

In this almost royal "we" was his arrogant certainty that in the not-so-distant future he would be forming the government of the Republic. In his emphatic restatement of the problematic racaille, Sarkozy was successfully creating his brand-new avatar: The president who would save this nation from the religion (code for Islam) and the impurity of foreign dogma that was oozing like a coming plague from the once-infallible towers of an increasingly shaken Fifth Republic.

But this was Hajj 1432 (2011). We were at Islam's ground zero. Shahinaz reminded me of what I had said in Paris: "Part of the Islam that lives in Europe will be a problem." But I did not want to damn my religion here in Mecca so I added, "Has France forgotten its recent revolutionary past? The savage Jacobins were using the guillotine to chop heads at the end of the eighteenth century when Islam was at its highest intellectual powers!"

"Wow, this will explode," I had said once to a friend driving me around pre-9/11 Marseilles. It was a bizarre premonition, but I needed to explain my perspective about the sheer numbers of unemployed, disgruntled, primarily North African men who just hung about at squares, sharing cigarettes, fashion, and a constant yearning for sexual contact with women their mothers would never approve of. These were rightful citizens; France is where they were born. "Protection Sociale," though mired in socialist bureaucracy, was a good-enough monthly check. Who needed a job in those circumstances? Unlike their parents or grandparents, these were no "refugees" who would have to fight to win their passports through a complicated asylum officialdom. For many of them, as in atheist France, the mosques their mothers hoped they would attend, but which they had scant interest in, had been moved to basement levels and their lives seemed purposeless. Like their families they had never quite risen from the poverty line and lived in shabby tenements in well-hidden, graffiti-filled suburbia. Nanny states like France put food on the table and a roof over your head. Clearly Europe was ripe for "recruitment."

I reminded Shahinaz of how we had first met. On a chilly late December morning, I got off the Paris metro stop called Barbès-Rochechouart, a short walk away from le marché Dejean, a familiar open-air market, rich with the smells and flavors of the Maghreb, which is North Africa west of Egypt.

This neighborhood, which was, as always, buzzing with the calls and whistles of merchants trying to attract customers, is called *La goutte d'or*, which translates into "drop of gold." The French call it Little Africa. The open-air market is not the only famous feature of this neighborhood, much celebrated in many a backpacker's guide to Europe. Most of them, however, do not mention its other special qualities beyond the enterprising immigrants who seem to make it rich enough to be on the tourist circuit. These would be its flourishing crack-cocaine trade and its high crime rate: all visible markers of the otherness that frightened some Caucasian natives.

Simply put, it crawled with a large, colorful assortment of racaille.

The woman I was meeting introduced herself to me with a question: "Parvez, am I the first of the racaille you have ever met?"

Like many of her fellow disenfranchised young French friends, she had appropriated the derogatory term.

I did not tell her that no one had ever introduced herself to me in quite that way before. Born in Somalia, Shahinaz, under her strikingly frizzy, Afro-like mop of wild hair, had a life force that was infectious. She became my guide to all of the racaille hangouts in her troubled and ever expanding city.

Shahinaz had grown up in this Paris version of the projects. Like most immigrants anywhere in the world, her family in France had arrived in waves, with already-settled family members helping the newer ones. Some of her younger male cousins had been able to develop significant running skills sharpened by the French cops intent on chasing them.

Shahinaz was enterprising, though. She was able to capitalize on her intellect, surprising to so many of the elite in a woman from her background. Her racaille-ness therefore became a strength. In addition, being an articulate non-hijabi Muslim in a country that had just banned the Islamic headscarf made her the perfect Muslim who could be molded into a crusader. She did not speak like the racaille or even dress like their women, and therefore she was easier to understand and it was safer to allow her into conference rooms and human-rights cocktail events.

"Ha!" she laughed, as we sat in Mecca. "Look what you have turned me into now. Your very own ninja!"

In 2006, Shahinaz had told me that she was horrendously circumcised as a child, soon after her parents returned from Hajj, transformed by the puritanical, Wahhabi Islam they experienced. They seemed to have a renewed Islamic purpose as they migrated to France, soon after her circumcision.

"They distributed sweets when I told them I was going on Hajj," she said that evening in Mecca.

I had admired her since way back then, I told her.

This young woman possessed remarkable powers of articulation and an ability to place the story of her own life into complicated historical contexts.

Months after our first meeting, she would, with just one simple sentence in Arabic, get to the very heart of my film and the intractable question I was attempting to answer in trying to figure out if Islam and homosexuality could peacefully coexist. To my camera then, she said, "*Ya Allah. Ya Wahad. Ya Ahad. Ana Habit Bas.*"

"Oh, God," she was saying. "My only God. I only loved."

The turn of phrase was remarkable. She was responding to my rather convoluted question about the conversation she might want to have with God on Judgment Day. Central to Islam is the concept of Tawhid, the "oneness of God." The Shahadah, the testament of faith that makes one a Muslim, reiterates the concept: "I testify that there is no God but Allah and that Muhammad is his messenger." Nothing in Islam is more sacred than this tenet of a single divine entity who cannot be replicated into any other form.

Shahinaz, in that breathtaking sentence, took this sacred and central concept of "only" not just to affirm her faith as a Muslim but also to grant affirmation to her forbidden love. Surely the usually not-merciful Allah present in both of our childhoods would find it hard to turn this beautiful and articulate woman away from the doors of heaven. "My *only* God." "I *only* loved." During salat, namaz, or prayer, whatever you choose to call it, there is always a moment given to Tawhid, and it is when the supplicant raises his or her right index finger while whispering, "*La ilaha Illallah.*" There is no god but God.

With her own inimitable wisdom, Shahinaz looked back at her genital mutilation with a political acuity that placed it right in the middle of a still-unresolved debate. She described it as an act of rape, not just of her body but also of her innocence. She added that it was certainly not consensual and was a very visible and enduring symbol of an oppressive patriarchy that did not want women to have a sexual being.

My own genital mutilation, years away at the time we were filming *Jihad* in 2005–06, would, unlike hers and that of most others, be a voluntary act. It would be the most visible, entirely self-inflicted marker of my complete, very-conscious submission to all of the tenets of my faith. It was also the most radical step I would ever take to tame the primary tool of my sinning self. Islam was surrender. And surrender, I did.

I told her how blessed I felt that she was on the pilgrimage with me. She already knew about Adham, my text companion, and Keith, whose atheism she admired.

I then came out to her about the recent circumcision. She said my piety was "remarkable" and she just could not imagine an adult doing something so drastic to prove it. I told her I had no choice. She held my hand. An intimidating mutawa approached. We had our IDs ready. He skulked away like a dog with its tail between its legs. No mutawa could touch the hand-holding Parvez Hussein and Shahinaz Mousaoui! They were married!

Later, Shahinaz said the Prophet *would definitely* have been much kinder to women, their bodies, and their lives than his male biographers.

She said her faith was always either on or off. If she decided to become "religious all the time," she would crave a time she believed was most emblematic of the religion, that the Prophet Muhammad would have most recognized, which was the time within his own life when he was able to be the much-tormented vessel of divine dictation and to move on to creating an egalitarian faith, far ahead of its time.

Her idea of this Prophet was unlike any other I had ever heard. I admired her because I had never really dared to say the things she would so easily say. He, she said, would never have allowed genital mutilation to happen to her.

"Muhammad was a feminist," she repeated in Mecca, just as she had once said in France.

I had never heard any Muslim say something so remarkable. I did not know how to react. But I made sure it was on camera and in my film, recording her in Paris years ago.

"You and I need to figure out his feminist credentials one day," I said. She nodded.

And then, as the call to Maghrib prayers began, we furtively avoided the ritual-heavy wudu. It would have involved a schlep. We prayed right next to each other, of course, directly facing the Kaaba—the real thing. Did God notice? An openly gay (intermittently bleeding) Muslim man was praying right next to a menstruating lesbian, who was his fake wife. Each Muslim was equal here and the spirit of the moment meant that God accepted us here. My homosexuality felt like a smaller burden. Who cared? I needed to come out as a Muslim. And every moment here, I was.

"They are driving me batty," Shahinaz texted the next night. "And it's like giggly school cliques. Somehow I am never invited. There is this really hot woman, married of course ;-(. We hang out though. Her husband beats her. Muhammad's his name, obviously. Let me know if you find him!"

Muhammad is the most-used first name on the planet. Half my group probably comprised Muhammads.

In Islam, God has ninety-nine names even though He can only be one. Many here could rattle them off in less than a breathless minute. I never knew them all.

Muhammad, though, usually just goes by Muhammad.

CHAPTER 8

MECCA VEGAS

From this point on, my time with Shahinaz became increasingly impossible. It was almost as if the women were deliberately being taken further away. Shahinaz sent me frequent dispatches from the women's group—how they would tell tales on one another and yet be there for each other when things got challenging, like a simple menstrual cycle. She said they regularly held the Shia majlis, and tears were abundant.

On this morning, I was Shahinaz-less—she was taken on a "women only" tour of Mecca's Saudi destruction; we men were soon to have our own. Pretty soon I would start escaping the male-only tours.

The other woman in my life, Siri, seemed confused. She and I rode on the sometimes password-free Wi-Fi network kindly provided by Osama bin Laden's family, the biggest construction conglomerate in the holy land. Siri was babbling about not knowing the geography of where we were. I had just finished Facetiming with Keith back in New York, assuring him I was safe. I was still transfixed by an ancient sight—hundreds of thousands of chanting pilgrims from nearly every nation, all circling the Kaaba. From my vantage point, on the second level of the largest mosque in the world, the Masjid al-Haram, the pilgrims seemed to float. *Haram*, depending on how it is pronounced, could mean both "forbidden" and "sanctuary."

I was yearning for a nice cup of joe. *Asr*, the afternoon prayer, was a while away. On the escalator I glided down past an ascending group of abaya-wearing women, presumably on their way to get their one-way tickets to heaven, along with extra brownie points from Allah. I didn't dare tell them that they were defying the Prophet's edict on behavior in Mecca. Men and women were supposed to be equal here. Women actually have to expose their faces, so that God would see them! But this was Wahhabi-land. As I got off the escalator, I noticed a sign: "WATCH OUT ABAYA." Some thoughtful engineer must have considered the constant danger that would accompany women on these escalators, their abayas dangerously dangling below the ankles they dare not expose.

I was a bit shaken. Yesterday I had chatted with an older Yemeni man called Mohamed at Al-Baik, the Saudi version of KFC or Popeye's. I told him how the bin Laden family got worldwide fame only because of one out of more than fifty children. He referred to that Osama as "Sheikh Osama." Sheikh was often reserved for a learned Muslim. I asked him why. I learned once again that one person's terrorist could be another's freedom fighter.

He told me how Osama's father had been a Yemeni. He rose to become a multibillionaire, BFFs with the ruling Saud.

"What do you think of the new Kingdom Tower?" I had asked him, referring to the monstrosity that dwarfs everything in Mecca. "Isn't it like King Abdullah's having an erection?"

Mohamed laughed. "But remember, Parvez—Sheikh Osama destroyed America's two biggest erections." I had difficulty sharing his mirth.

"How can you live in that country as a Muslim?" he asked. I changed the subject and we parted company.

On this day as I continued walking out of the mosque, I was in a dystopian, Ayn Randian landscape. Dozens of skyscrapers and innumerable cranes leapt into the heavens. Crowds of pilgrims, transformed now into eager shoppers, seemed to be oblivious to the obliteration of Muslim history that predicated the new construction. Chinese workers, hastily converted to Islam, were among the burgeoning armies of builders. More indentured servants from India, robbed of their passports and hope, also toiled here. In the past five decades, Saudi authorities had allegedly destroyed more than 90 percent of Mecca's Islamic history in the form of buildings, graves, and artifacts. They built a row of toilets over the home the Prophet shared with his first wife, Khadija. In the nineties, Saudi architect Sami Angawi fought to save this home. He made other attempts at conservation, even directly appealing to the king. But the clout of the bulldozer-happy bin Laden family was no match for one man's protest.

As a young man, Osama bin Laden was briefly his family's executive assigned to Mecca. He oversaw the early stages of the demolition his family was carrying out. Years later, when he finally gathered the courage to speak openly against the Saudi-sponsored erasure of Islam's history, he omitted this major detail. As Osama's list of grievances against the Al Saud grew exponentially, he never referred to that time in Mecca.

The Saudi king insists upon the title, "The Custodian of the Two Holy Mosques." This is his only way to reinforce his authority throughout the Muslim world. The Al Saud, and their builders, the bin Ladens, exert a sense of ownership over these holy places, which should theoretically belong to all Muslims. Change is inevitable, but change at the expense of history is tragic.

The bin Ladens claim they are creating space. Fair enough. I certainly understood the need for more open space, more transportation, and more lodging. But a deliberate government and Wahhabi-sanctioned project to rewrite the history of Islam is egregious. Brand-new trains ferrying pilgrims across the desert, in true Saudi apartheid, were only open to citizens of the Gulf Cooperation Council. So much of the new construction was for the rich, since they provide the most tourism dollars. Another example: An enormous Al Saud palace, complete with helipads, hid behind massive concrete walls, just a few hundred meters from the Kaaba. Why do the Al Saud need a palace so close to the Kaaba even though they possess the keys to it—opening it only for their "special" guests?

Till I got to Mecca, I used to think that the excess and hedonism of the Saudi ruling family were reserved for salacious gossip rags. But Saudis love monarchical gossip and much arises from the deeds of King Salman's son, who shares his father's name.

Still Shahinaz-less on that day, I went into the singles section of the Starbucks in this crass megaplex. I had to chuckle again at the company's logo. The voluptuous mermaid was replaced by a star shining over a sea. This total censorship was better than giving the mermaid an abaya, I supposed. Some years later, a Starbucks in Riyadh would temporarily ban women from entry, putting up a sign reading, "PLEASE NO ENTRY FOR LADIES ONLY SEND YOUR DRIVER TO ORDER THANK YOU," after their literal gender-segregation wall collapsed.

A fellow pilgrim broke my reverie, asking for a light. His name was Abdullah. We bonded over our shared Siri problems. She was refusing to talk to either of us.

Repeating what I already knew, he said how women unaccompanied by men dared not enter any public space here. "Let's go to the family section. I want you to meet my wife and sister-in-law."

"But I'm not family," I protested.

"We are brothers on Hajj," he said, putting his arm around my shoulder.

Abdullah's wife Aisha, who was certainly no virgin like her seventh-century counterpart, was visibly pregnant. For all three monotheisms, virginity is a virtue. For most Sunni Muslims, the second-purest woman is the Virgin Mary, whose son Jesus gets more Quranic mention than Muhammad. Beating even the New Testament, Mary, who gets seventy mentions in the Quran, is the only woman directly named in the holy book. Too many Christians have no idea about the high esteem Islam reserves for them.

This Aisha wore a black niqab that sheathed the lower part of her face. I wondered how on earth she could sip her coffee through the veil. Her sister Maryam was similarly clad. The trio had decided to embark on the Hajj when they discovered Aisha's pregnancy. They described their long car journey from Sharjah to the Fairmont. This was Gulf money in action. The women did not satisfy my curiosity—their cups remained on the table. Not even a sip!

Abdullah told me of his first night at the Masjid al-Haram. The threesome began the sacred tawaf as soon as they entered Mecca. He was separated from Aisha and Maryam early on. I immediately understood his fear.

"My experience was the most violent night of my entire life," I told them. The mass of believers all heaved toward the Kaaba in attempts to get ever closer, and even to touch it, leaving no room for the weak of will. It was a mosh pit. A survival-of-the-fittest situation. Most of these men had never been in such close proximity to so many women ever in their lives, I'd thought. The screams of women rising above the Quranic chants from that night still haunt me.

Abdullah described his experience in detail. He was unable to find Aisha and Maryam for hours. He prayed their piety would protect them. "Un-Islamic things happen there, brother Parvez," he says, shaking his head. "Un-Islamic." Aisha and Maryam were silent. As my chai tea latte arrived, Abdullah was quick to change the subject. "Maryam is an unmarried student," he told me. "You should talk to her about New York. She is fascinated."

Was he matchmaking? Pleased with myself, I launched into a description of the five boroughs. The women, if they were fascinated, never uttered a word of response. Abdullah smiled. At any rate, my "Hajj butch" was clearly working.

On cue, the call to afternoon prayer rang out. I assumed the mutaween would soon be running around with their canes to shut down all the shops, but I was wrong. As in India, this mall had its own class system. A mutawa wouldn't dare enter the Chanel store.

This mall is built squarely on top of the eighteenth-century Ottoman Ajyad Fortress. Turkey was among the few Islamic countries that dared to protest its destruction. The Saudis have successfully bullied most of the Muslim world into silence. The mall is housed inside a 120-story clock tower, the fourth-tallest building in the world. The clock faces are the world's largest. There are 98 million pieces of glass embedded into the four clock faces. Apart from the mall, the tower complex also houses a five-star hotel and hyper-luxury apartments costing eight figures, advertised in British newspapers such as the *Guardian,* as the world's most-coveted Islamic real estate. A single night in a royal suite in one of these hotels can cost close to $6,000. Mecca contains some of the most expensive land in the world, with ten square feet in some areas selling for well over $100,000.

My educated Shia group considered it particularly obscene. In our group tours of the city, they clucked their tongues at this symbol of unfettered capitalism. In the circular whirl around the cube, at times it almost seemed like people were praying to the looming tower instead of the Kaaba. On the other hand, the clock tower served as a helpful beacon, since it's visible from anywhere in Mecca and miles around. I was often lost, and the tower, not Siri, guided me back.

I realized that my point of view about the crass consumerism on display was in the minority. I approached Mecca with a critical mindset. The Gucci shops and escalators were quotidian to me, but to a poor pilgrim from Somalia who had just disembarked from his or her first-ever flight, these would be perceived not only as unimaginable luxuries but also as encouraging markers of an ascendant Islam.

Muhammad's Hajj of equality lay in tatters, at Saudi hands. Clad in white, all were supposed to be one and the same before God. The richest prayed next to the poorest and performed the same rituals. But now brutal dictators from African regimes could rent out entire suites in the Fairmont Mecca Clock Royal Tower. The website advertises:

> Fairmont Makkah Clock Royal Tower offers unmatched hospitality throughout the ultimate exclusive hotel experience with Fairmont Gold where our discerning guests have the privilege of choosing their rooms showcasing unrivaled views of either the Kaaba, Haram or to The Holy City of Makkah.

Their jacuzzis, saunas, and steam rooms promised "a guaranteed way to melt away stress." This Hajj experience was quite different from mine, to say nothing of those of the poorest pilgrims, many of whom slept on the streets throughout their Hajj.

Abdullah, like me, had discovered the spotless Starbucks bathrooms and together we performed our wudu there.

Then he said, "Now let me teach you how to pray in a shopping mall."

"But the Kaaba is right there," I replied, pointing to the entrance to the mall.

"It's hot," he said. "It can't be 'Kaaba, Kaaba' all the time." We took sanctuary in the air-conditioned mall, kneeling with others in neat rows below beckoning neon signs. I was one with the mall-praying lazy pilgrims.

Later, I obeyed my maxim: If in Mecca, head to the Kaaba. The Hajj is a harsh pilgrimage that is fundamentally about faith and surrender. My moments spent praying to and contemplating the Kaaba offered great succor. The hungry hands of sinners, over centuries, had made its grainy, granite surface a vessel of forgiveness. It radiated a strength that filled me. Drawn to it like a magnet, I would return night after sleepless night. If Islam offered redemption to its sinner-pilgrims, it was to be found right here.

"Parvez?" It was Younes, a thoughtful, mild-mannered doctor from Montgomery, Alabama, who was part of my group. I'd instinctively liked him—we'd become Hajj buddies. We marveled for a moment at the unlikelihood of finding each other in these immense crowds. "I have something to tell you," he said. I listened. He proceeded to come out to me as a Sunni man.

"But I thought your wife and mother-in-law were Shia," I said.

"An unlikely marriage, but a very strong one," he replied. He asked me if I knew how to pray like the Shia. I told him I had spent months learning their customs before I came. When with the Shia group, I prayed like they did. When alone I prayed the slightly different Sunni way.

"A good compromise," he said. "It wouldn't be good to be found out as an outsider here." I already knew that Younes chose his words carefully. I wondered if he knew the shameful secret I carried. We sat in contemplative silence for a while. I had always been taught that where we sat was God's abode. And God detested liars, my mother used to say. My burden of deceit suddenly felt heavy.

"I have something to tell you, too," I whispered. "I am gay." The three words I have never even dared say to my father.

"I knew," he said. And then there was silence. Eternities passed. Younes gently put his arm around my shoulder.

"Why would you want to be a part of something that wants no part of you?" he asked.

The Kaaba gave me the strength to come out, I wanted to tell him. His kind gesture validated my very being. The sleepless nights spent here had changed me. By now I believed that I had received acceptance from a higher power than those who patrolled these walls with rifles and batons. Now, my Islam would forever be different. It would no longer be a faith of fear. It was no longer a question of whether Islam would accept me. It was a question of whether I would accept Islam.

And sitting there silent, with the nice Sunni doctor from Alabama, steps away from Islam's beating heart, I did.

CHAPTER 9

MUSLIM BOOT CAMP

O n my sixth night in Mecca, it was time for me to begin the rituals of my actual pilgrimage. Everything leading up to this point had been emotional preparation and spiritual tourism. It was the last month of the Islamic calendar, *Dhu al-Hijjah* ("Month of the Pilgrimage"). The Hajj is performed on the eighth, ninth, and tenth of this month. By this time, I had lost track of the Western calendar, and in a sense—all track of time. Everyone in my group had been talking for two weeks in terms of the Islamic calendar. This disconcerting effect contributed a deeper sense of timelessness to this place, as though it existed within its own spiritual realm.

It took me half an hour to complete the *ghusl*, the exacting ritual cleansing that must precede the putting on of the ihram, an act I'd performed upon first entering Mecca. In Islam, every minute action, down to the number of times you wash your armpit, is regulated by ritual. But by this time I was an expert. In the bathroom, unseen by the rest of my Shia group, I performed my ritual cleansing in the Sunni way. At this point I was breaking the solidarity I'd held with them since our arrival in Medina.

I must confess here that I performed another ritual in this sacred place, before performing the ghusl. This ritual was not part of my Hajj. In fact, it is forbidden in Shia jurisprudence. I performed *istimna*: I jerked off, which I reasoned to be OK, since I was following it with the ritual cleansing. It had been months since I'd experienced any sexual contact, and I was not looking forward to more abstinence. It was now or never.

I returned to the Masjid al-Haram to repeat the tawaf and saee. This time, I tried to touch "Hajjar's Skirt," the place where Hajjar and Ismael were buried, according to Sunni and Shia both. The manic crowds eager to earn extra credit points with Allah prevented me from getting anywhere near it. Almost overnight, it seemed, the crowds had ballooned with pilgrims. The population, by my estimation, had tripled since my arrival. Mecca was bursting at the seams, and the crowds were compelled by a stronger urgency, resulting in a Hajj experience that had diverged dramatically from that which had been commanded by the Prophet Muhammad. He argued that this experience was sacred and should be approached in a state of *tahara* ("purity"). Instead, I was elbowed, pushed, and pulled the whole day. The women had it even worse. Sometimes their screams felt louder than before.

Just as I exited Islam's holy mosh pit, my iPhone lit up. It was Keith, who must have sensed my fears. I told him the actual five-day rituals of the Hajj were beginning.

Walking out, I silently thanked the bin Ladens for what in this section was a surprisingly free Wi-Fi network. This imperfect network did work in some places. I was able sometimes to Facetime alongside hundreds of thousands of other users texting, emailing, tweeting, and more.

Exhausted and thirsty, I found one of the ubiquitous water containers throughout the mosque area. These fountains produced the holy Zamzam water, named after the magical spring that saved Ismael's life. Hajjis took home gallons of "healing" Zamzam for their loved ones. It is used during blessing ceremonies at weddings and births. I had my doubts that all of this water was sourced from a single well. I had Googled enough to know that the British Food Standards Agency alleged that the water contains dangerous levels of arsenic. The Saudis denounce this claim as Islamophobic propaganda. With apprehension, I drank my fill, reminding myself never again to be without sealed bottled water. At the time, I could not have imagined the H2O scarcity that was coming.

Sunni pilgrims had already departed in the thousands during the day, but some Shia dogma I didn't understand decreed that we travel at night. Under cover of darkness, we headed to the dusty plain called Arafat sitting at the base of *Jabal ar-Rahmah* (the Mount of Mercy). I hopped onto a bus for the fifteen-minute journey. What I thought would be a short jaunt turned out to be a seven-hour, bumper-to-bumper nightmare. The bin Ladens, like American planners they studied, had favored building roadways rather than public transportation, so traffic gridlock plagues this area during every Hajj season. I stood on the bus the entire time. My fellow pilgrims granted me no mercy. It was every pilgrim for himself.

Arafat is extremely important in Islamic exegeses. The Prophet had delivered his farewell sermon to the earliest Muslims here. This place is synonymous with the Day of Judgment. There is an urgency to Arafat and a sense of deep piety. Most Islamic scholars agree that this is one of the most important rites of the Hajj. The Prophet Muhammad himself said, "Hajj is Arafat." Pilgrims only had till before sunset to pray for redemption. The Sunnis stood in the merciless sun all day, sometimes holding umbrellas branded by Zain, the second-largest Saudi telecom. The Shia did it differently. We stayed in our tents, where the group leader led the rest of us in mournful chanting.

Every minute detail of the pilgrimage was ordained in two dense Hajj guidebooks we were given early on. Everything that was *wajib* ("recommended") was there and there was much dwelling on what wasn't. I had grown up afraid of a lot of *fard* ("obligatory") things good Muslims did. The Shia seemed to live in a similar black-and-white world of wajib and fard. These two books became my much-used companions in my struggle to perform a Hajj that would be accepted. I prayed for many *Hajj Mabroor* ("Accepted Hajj") greetings from fellow pilgrims and fellow Muslims when I got back home. Nothing less would suffice in my struggle to earn the status of a good Muslim.

My group leader reminded me why this day was important. I questioned him about a hadith I was told as a child about a successful Hajji being like a newborn.

"As long as you follow these," he said, pointing to the books. In the first book, he pointed to page 48: "The wuqoof there for this period is obligatory and whoever fails to do so by choice commits a sin." Wuqoof, a ritual central to Hajj, literally means to remain stationary at a place for a while. In Hajj-speak it's the plain of Arafat.

I did not dare ask him if the Shia wuqoof was similar to the Sunni one, which in the poetry that often speaks for Islam meant "to pause in contemplation of the divine."

I hurriedly leafed through the book. There were almost twenty pages about *Arafat* itself. And there were many "rules," the much-feared fard of my childhood. At one point it said we were supposed to recite:

100 times *Allahuakbar*
100 times *Alhamdulillah*
100 times *Subhanallah*
100 times *Chapter of Ikhlas*
And supplications of your choice

I couldn't possibly keep track.

The Meccan Surah of Ikhlas was one of my favorites, though, so it came easily. Al-Ikhlas meant "Pure Faith," which is why it had always been close to my heart.

In the name of Allah, most benevolent, ever-merciful.
SAY: HE IS God.
the one, the most unique,
God the immanently indispensable.
He has begotten no one,
and he is begotten of none.
There is no one comparable to him.

I will never be sure if I did the many other 100-this and 100-that the Hajj group mandated during my supplications that day. I am sure, however, that I found great redemption and succor for my soul by reciting Surah al-Ikhlas a hundred-ish times.

A young man scurried around the tents, passing out pieces of paper with Arabic text on one side and English on the other. He was the son of one of the men in our group. He was always hanging around the group leaders, performing little tasks like this. He looked and behaved like a teacher's pet—the type that you kind of want to bully and don't want to be caught red-handed by. He gave me one of his slips of paper and sat down next to me.

"I know you are Sunni," he whispered conspiratorially. "Let me explain this."

I turned the paper around.

"These are special *duas*," he continued. "If you are a Shia, you write your name before Maghrib while making all your wishes to Allah on this special day. Then you bury it, and your wishes will come true." And so I did.

All Sunnis were obliged to climb to the top of the Mount of Mercy. My group took the easy way out, supplicating tearfully in the comparatively cool shade of their tents. I never got to go to the Jabal ar-Rahmah. I joined my fellow pilgrims in prayers for redemption. The chanting started again. The group leader wailed in English, practically screaming, alongside a mellifluous voice in Arabic that laid out the entire lineage of Shia Islam, beginning with the Prophet's nephew and son-in-law Ali, wishing peace on the Prophet's prominent Shia descendants. If we'd been in a Sunni tent, they would not have dared to include these prayers.

The group leader spoke up between the Arabic chants, invoking the merciless Allah of my childhood:

> *Oh, forgive the sins of our fathers, our children.*
> *Too late to say Sorry, take me back, I'll be better.*
> *Then Allah says, "The only place you sit now is fire, it will not be your*
> *guardian."*
> *Then Allah says, "Look what a bad End. What a terrible, terrible End."*

But the prayer ended on a more hopeful note, saying that each one of us, upon performing our Hajj, with the right *niyat* (intention), would be blessed with a special place in Heaven. Of course, the implication was that the "terrible end" would befall the disbelievers like the Jews and Christians. These groups are specifically given preferential status in Heaven according to kinder strands of Islamic exegesis, because they're identified as *Ahl al-Kitab* ("People of the Book").

For a moment the entire place seemed to resonate with forgiveness, and yet mine felt incomplete. If any of these people had any idea who I was, they would not have wished me peace, or envisioned me alongside them in heaven. At dusk I left Arafat wondering if I was a good Muslim. Someone said it was the ninth day of Dhu al-Hijjah. I had lost all track of time, in either Muslim or Gregorian calendars.

Finally, we arrived at the open plain of Muzdalifah to collect forty-nine pebbles for stoning the devil at his domain in *Jamarat* (place of pebbles). My group leader had handed us little messenger bags to hold our pebbles and encouraged us to collect seventy, because we might lose a few on our way to the devil. Across the highway lay another plain exclusively for women to collect their pebbles. I wondered—if this ritual has been performed by millions of people every year for centuries, then how has Muzdalifah not yet run out of pebbles? Do the Saudis replenish the supply every year, trucking "used" stones back from Satan's domain at Jamrat?

I desperately had to pee. The Saudis, in what now seemed like typical disregard for pilgrim comfort, had provided only six toilets to relieve thousands of pilgrims. I was afraid even to enter—the stench was overwhelming. I turned to a friend from my Hajj group.

"The Ummah that pees together stays together," I said. He laughed. We held our noses and continued to wait in line. I knew that by Fajr time, it would be impossible to get into the restroom, because all the sleeping bodies around me would be awake and ready for their morning pee. Many Muslims like to believe they are the cleanest and purest people in the world. In that moment, as I gasped for air, it was hard for me to believe it.

The plain was littered with many thousands of white-shrouded bodies, many resting on sleeping bags. For me, there would be no sleep this night. It was lit up by thousands of smartphone screens being used as torches to aid in the search for pebbles. These gadgets gave the landscape an eerie, futuristic quality.

Confession is the first step on the path of redemption, and sinners have a way of finding each other. This is a land of secrets, and I found that many were comforted here by confiding in strangers. On this darkest of nights, I came across a modern-day Muhammad, whose sins are, in my mind, unforgivable. This pilgrim was praying and sobbing. This is considered un-Islamic. I wanted to remind him so he wouldn't get into trouble with the mutaween.

"Why are you crying?" I asked. We exchanged names. His name was also Muhammad, Muhammad Bashir, from Lahore, Pakistan.

"Brother Parvez, you must have heard these days in Pakistan there are killings for family honor," he said, with shame written across his face.

"I don't understand, brother," I replied.

"When someone is murdered in the name of honor, brother."

"Yes," I said. "I have heard and it makes me feel bad." I feared where this was going. "But it's the twenty-first century. Do you think murders happen in these times?"

Of course I knew they did. Saudi Arabia's most famous honor killing took place in 1977, when Princess Misha'al bint Fahd, a niece of King Khaled, was publically executed for her affair with a Lebanese businessman named Khaled al-Sha'er Mulhallal. She was blindfolded, forced to kneel, and shot. Her lover was forced to watch and then beheaded next to her bleeding corpse. More recently, British newspapers reported in 2008 that a woman was killed by her husband for chatting with another man on Facebook.

According to most interpretations of sharia law, an accusation of adultery can be made only when four male witnesses have testified in favor of the claim. The same applies to the act of "sodomy," which is often equated with homosexuality. In 2008, a twenty-six-year-old Turkish student was shot by his conservative Kurdish father five times when the young man left his apartment for some ice cream. While filming *A Jihad for Love*, I had visited gay cafés in Istanbul, and yet a spirit of intolerance ran deep throughout the country. In Saudi Arabia, homosexuals are routinely whipped, imprisoned, and executed by the mutaween. Vigilante justice is also common.

Muhammad confirmed that honor killings are common in Pakistan. "I personally know they happen, sir. That is the reason I am here. It was done in my house. Every time I try to pray, I see her face. I see her face when I look at my two nephews. My brother did not want to come on the Hajj. He doesn't think he did anything wrong. But I had to."

"Who is she?" I asked.

"My sister-in-law. Her name was Yasmin. Her family is asking for blood money. I don't know what we will do."

"Did you participate?"

"Yes, sir. This is the reason I am here on Hajj." I realized I was sitting next to a murderer. There was nothing left for me to say to him. I did not know how to bring him comfort. I did not want to.

The next morning, we walked from Muzdalifah to Mina, the world's largest tent city. Here there are more than 100,000 air-conditioned tents sprawling across twenty square kilometers. Historically, pilgrims brought their own tents. In the nineties, fires raged through sections of the city, so the tents that met my eyes were fiberglass coated with Teflon.

I felt awful. We hadn't showered in three days and had walked for miles in the dust. We walked bowlegged to avoid further chafing of our inner thighs. Our white ihrams had lost their made-in-China gleam. I had stopped eating and drinking sufficiently because I was terrified at the thought of having to use another overused Saudi toilet, the most disgusting I have ever seen in the world. A seasoned traveler, I had travelled to more than thirty countries *and* I came from India, a country that practically invented "disgusting toilets," enshrined for cinematic history in the opening sequence of *Slumdog Millionaire.* Our feet were calloused from our Hajj-mandated open-toed sandals. If it was good enough for the Prophet, it was supposed to be good enough for us.

Mina was divided into camps representing every country. "Welcome Russian Pilgrims," said one. "Caribbean Hajj," said another. I noticed flags from every corner of the world, from Fiji to the Maldives, and yet there were three glaring omissions: no Stars and Stripes, no Union Jack, and no Star of David. My majority-American group marched under the innocuous maple leaf of a less-controversial neighbor.

The inescapable call to Zuhr prayers resounded. In order to pray, I would need to perform the wudu, but that would involve a visit to the dreaded Saudi toilets. Imagine a port-a-potty with no seat—just a hole in the ground. In that enclosure, pilgrims are meant to defecate, piss, and then shower. No toilet paper, no flush. When showering, you are standing in a puddle of brownish water. Is it simply dirt and sand from the previous occupant, or something worse? Dirty water from adjacent stalls is flung over your head, and you can only hope that your neighbors are as clean as you imagine yourself to be. These are some of the most unsanitary conditions in the civilized world. Threats of pandemics hang over the Hajj ever year. The soundtrack of the Hajj experience is a cacophony of sneezing, coughing, and retching. Many pilgrims and Saudi guards wear surgical masks. With some shame, I opted sacrilegiously to skip the wudu. I pretended I had already done it by going for a short walk. I may have broken the letter of Islamic law by shirking the cleansing ritual, but in my mind I was all the cleaner for it.

Shahinaz texted me how she had sneaked an early-morning fag, post-Fajr, in one of those "shower-toilet combos from hell," as we both called them. At one point during Hajj, I stopped eating just so I would not need to use the bathrooms for anything but urination—they were loathsome.

While taking a smoke break outside my tent, I was approached by Abdullah Jaffar, the British doctor in my group, with a stern face.

"Brother Parvez," he said. "Do you understand the global network of smoking?"

"Yes," I said. "There are smokers everywhere."

His voice lowered, "Let me show you how it works." He drew a map of the globe in the air with his fingers, illustrating his conspiracy. "Here is America. And here is Britain. And here is Brazil. They all manufacture tobacco. Do you know where it ends up?" He jerked his hand across his map toward the Middle East and South Asia. "See? Where the majority of Muslims live?"

I let the kook rant.

The doctor traced a path between these countries, indicated a conspiratorial flow of tobacco from non-Muslim nations to the heart of Islam. "See?" He smiled, as though his irrefutable logic had fallen gracefully into place. "It's a conspiracy by the Jews of America."

I tried not to roll my eyes.

"They want the Muslims to die of lung cancer." His voice rose. "It's all connected! Be careful, brother. Not just for your health, but also for Islam!"

I hastily extinguished my cigarette.

The filthy alleys between the tents of Mina stretch for miles. The tents themselves are identical, and the only way to distinguish one from the other is to check the flag and group names. I lost my way easily before spotting someone from my group. Back in the tent I dared to pray in the Sunni way in front of all my Shia group members. At this point I had lost my desire to blend in, and my stubborn defiance was on full display. People stared and whispered to one another. I tuned them out and focused on the higher purpose that had brought us here in the first place.

As had happened many times now, women seemed to have disappeared suddenly and without warning. They must have had their own segregated tents apart from their husbands or male "guardians." I wondered if these women knew about the furor-ridden debates raging in the kingdom regarding women's rights, segregation, and equality.

While in Mina, I had seen a tweet from Al-Waleed bin Talal, one of the self-proclaimed reform-minded princes, arguing that women should be allowed to drive in order to abolish illegal work by undocumented immigrants. He claimed that this would lead to 500,000 fewer foreign chauffeurs. Critics, as they always did, screamed with outrage at this tweet. Sheikhs often appeared on Saudi television decrying the female driver: "If women started driving, what would they do if their car breaks down? They will be raped!" This and similar mindsets continue to prevent Saudi Arabia from entering the twenty-first century.

That night I went for a walk, because I was feeling claustrophobic. The men around me were taking up more than their fair share of space. I felt like I couldn't breathe. But the streets didn't bring much comfort. Excrement, trash, sirens wailing, and countless more pilgrims sleeping on the streets. These were another class of pilgrims—those who had come into the kingdom undocumented during the Hajj season. They had come looking for work. Many of them had found work, but many hadn't. So they whiled away their days, often begging. Many beggars had missing limbs; I assumed they'd been caught stealing. The landscape looked like the day after a bloody battle, with countless bodies, many broken, squirming and stretching across the landscape. There was a parallel Hajj going on.

I ran into one of my Hajj leaders, by now a regular smoking buddy. I complained to him about my tentmates. "My mother used to tell me that all good Muslims should take up the space of a coffin. You know, not encroaching on the personal space of the people around you," I said.

"Unfortunately, not everyone carries that morality," he replied.

"And what about these streets? Do they even realize that people like us sleep in air-conditioned tents? This is not the Hajj of equality that the Prophet envisioned."

"You're right," he said. "I've been bringing groups here for fifteen years. So much has changed even within that time. These people don't even have visas. I can't even tell you the things I've seen."

"What will happen to them when the Hajj season ends?"

"They will either find illegal jobs or end up in Saudi prisons to be deported."

Stomping out his cigarette, he looked into the distance. "I'm so glad they don't allow non-Muslims. The West shouldn't be allowed to see this side of us."

Satan's day had arrived with the next morning. On this day we were meant to confront Satan in a symbolic recreation of Ibrahim's confrontation with the devil. When Ibrahim left Mina, Satan appeared to him three times. Each time, the angel Jibreel showed up and told Ibrahim to pelt the devil with stones, which made him disappear. These three moments in which Ibrahim successfully confronted the devil are marked by three pillars at Jamrat. According to some traditions, the three pillars stand at the exact spots where Ibrahim threw stones at Satan and thus are representative of the temptations he needed to overcome to get God's blessings.

Our group leader corralled us into groups of about twenty. I was assigned to lead my group and given a tiny Canadian flag to wave. We began to chant alongside tens of thousands of other Muslims, *Labbaik Allah humma labbaik*:

> *O my Lord, here I am at Your service, here I am.*
> *You have no partner.*
> *Here I am.*
> *Praise be unto you*
> *Yours alone is all praise and all bounty*
> *And Yours is the sovereignty.*
> *You have no partners.*

We entered a series of tunnels, miles long, that shot through the many hills of Mecca. It never stopped—the shrieking noise of the chants that reverberated through this chaotic claustrophobia. Shahinaz was not with me. She had feigned illness to avoid the barbarity. This was just one example of an entirely Saudi-created Hell.

"Can't do it much longer," she pleaded. I acknowledged her and felt guilty. Thankfully her judgmental women would be gone all day.

"Take a Xanax and just sleep for a few hours," I advised.

"Perfect," she said.

For about three hours we trudged through the tunnels and the enormous roar. There were moments when savage behavior was common in the mini-stampedes that happened between tunnels. There were bodies sprawled on the rocks, mostly from dehydration or other medical problems. They tried to avoid the avalanche and fervor of the determined stoners.

"I need water. I will die," said a woman carrying a baby in a baby bjorn. She clearly lived in a Western country. I had bought many hydration packets of the kind used by sporty types, most of which I had given away. This was the last and I gave it to her, urging her to use it with thrift. "Shouldn't they have clean water for us?" she said. I nodded, helping her up. She was soon lost. My long walk to Satan was of a dehydration I had never experienced. Ahead a truck threw boxes of water bottles into a riot-like situation. I was going to be a savage like them. I grabbed two and hid them in my backpack.

We passed kiosks selling all manner of Islamic tchotchkes. But NOT ONE sold water. Was this a deliberate Saudi Satanic creation? Many in my group started yelling for water. It was nowhere to be found after that truck, which I believe was from God.

A group of clearly poorer pilgrims were wailing around a corpse. "He was my uncle," a young man cried. "He was pushed down and he had no water. It was too much for him," explained a youth, "but we lost everyone and his wife."

"It's a blessing to die in the holy city," said a loudmouth, showing no compassion.

I searched for a security guard and showed him the body. Cops came to the scene and put the body in their trunk. The nephew was not allowed to go with them. This dead man would forever be forgotten in one of their unmarked corpse holes.

This was an ideal environment for stampedes, which occurred with reliable frequency every couple of years. In 2015, over 2,000 pilgrims would be trampled to death here. If this particular part of the Hajj experience is intended to feel like a march to Hell, the Saudis have succeeded in constructing the perfect environment. The general vibe of the place evoked in my mind the heavy-metal song "Smoke on the Water" by Deep Purple. The grinding, malevolent guitar riff had always brought to mind the presence of evil.

In the mid-nineties, I had the opportunity to see Deep Purple play at the Nehru stadium in Delhi. By this time the band was several generations out of style in the West, but clearly not in the Third World. Clearly the only chance of recreating the fame of their heyday lay in these Third World tours. I fought hard to secure tickets. The massive stadium was sold out. As in the US, Muslim religious leaders in India were participating in "Satanic

Panic," but a few decades later. I felt like a real rebel at this concert. I've uncovered a 1995 *India Today* magazine clipping to give a sense of what these Muslim leaders faced:

> Deep Purple drummer Ian Paice has just rolled into a solo. At New Delhi's Jawaharlal Nehru Stadium, the band has been blasting full-throttle on adrenalin boosted by 40,000 watts of sound power for close to an hour. Rocked out, soaking in Paice's pulse, the metal sound filling up the stadium, a wild-eyed university student gushes: "These guys are gods, man."

The sounds of heavy metal, the music of my twenties, has always gone hand-in-hand with images of devilry in my imagination. *No matter what we get out of this I know, I know we'll never forget. Smoke on the water, and fire in the sky.* I reminded myself I was on a religious mission and tried to shake the lyrics out of my head.

When we arrived at the pillars, I readied my pebbles. As I threw my first stone, I remembered when Hossein had joked about the pillars' representing America, Israel, and England for some Iranians. The noise was too deafening for me to make out anything that was being said other than, "*Allahu Akbar.*" As pilgrims rushed past me in all directions, flinging their stones, I saw a manic look in their eyes, as though it were the end of days. I and many others were pelted by carelessly thrown pebbles, along with slippers, bedrolls, and other "cursed" or "unlucky" personal totems and objects that were poorly aimed at the pillars. There didn't seem to be anything godly about this place. I noticed that women were being pushed to the ground around me. Their sisters tried to hold them up. When I offered my hand to help pull a woman up, it was slapped away by another woman. Even here in Hell, gender segregation was self-enforced.

In the mad rush, I myself was pushed down by a phalanx of marching Indonesian pilgrims who inadvertently rammed me to the ground and walked over me ceaselessly and, more important, inhumanely. Was this the part where I die? I was rescued by a kind Nigerian beggar. She had no hands, but offered what little arm she had left. For me, her simple act of kindness, though it flouted the rules of Islamic gender segregation, would have had the Prophet's approval. As far as I could tell, only this butchered, humble beggar obeyed Muhammad's deepest calls for compassion.

In moments like this, I reminded myself that this was my journey of the spirit. I would focus on the Kaaba, the only place in Mecca that gave me spiritual succor. Being able to disassociate myself with the noise, the shoving, the heat, the dirt, the discomfort, and to transport myself to the black cube enabled me to remind myself continually of my purpose and realign my heart with the heart of the Prophet. I knew my reliance on the cube and the Prophet would be interpreted by the Wahhabis as idolatrous, but this secret devotion was the only thing that kept me from falling apart. As I walked, the Prophet always walked with me, with his hand on my shoulder. Blasphemously he took form in my imagination, just as Khala had described him in my childhood.

I staggered out of Hell and out into the sun. Although I had been tasked with keeping my group together, I had lost all of them. There was no way we could have stuck together in that madness. I headed to our planned meeting place: Gate 17. When I arrived, I was immediately scolded when a fellow pilgrim caught a whiff of my deodorant.

"Are you wearing perfume?" he said with a judgmental whisper, just loud enough for the whole group to hear. Pilgrims aren't supposed to wear anything that would constitute an adornment. This self-appointed ulema of Islam had decided this included perfume. I had never understood this commandment. I had been taught the Prophet was said to have loved perfume. So I ignored this stupid stricture. After three days without showering, trudging through the dust, I had allowed myself the tiny luxury of a swipe of deodorant, which barely made a dent in the odor emanating from my body. I ignored this guy's comment. Haters gonna hate.

I tried to find some strength and solace by thinking of the spiritual simplicity of my ancestors, and the lengths they went to perform their Hajj without any of the modern conveniences that I now enjoyed.

Not only did I smell awful, I emerged from Jamrat exhausted, bruised, calloused, dehydrated, and spiritually broken. I wasn't sure I could go on. The experience of the Hajj had stripped away everything about me that made me a modern civilized man. I felt newly in touch with whatever primal force that lay dormant in me—the caveman brain that thirsted for blood. It is at this point in the Hajj that pilgrims are commanded to sacrifice a goat, just as Ibrahim had done after sparing Isaac. When I was a child, the annual Eid ritual of blood sacrifice had always filled me with inexplicable fear and dread. Sacrifice was normal to me, but still seemed barbaric. In all my years, I'd never attempted to hurt another living being. But now, I yearned to spill blood. I have difficulty putting this feeling into words.

"Do you think you're really prepared for this?" said an uncle before I'd embarked on my Hajj.

"Yes," I said with confidence. "It's the right time in my life."

"Well, we shall see if you feel the same way when you have to kill an animal with your own hands."

For the first time in my life, I understood the cathartic power of the sacrifice. It no longer felt barbaric but essential. By releasing an animal into death, I would also be putting to death a sinful part of me that I desperately wanted to die.

But it wasn't meant to be. We trudged to the signs reading, "The Saudi Project for Utilization of Hajj Meat, Managed by the Islamic Development Bank." The words were accompanied by a little logo: a palm tree with two swords. Like many aspects of the Hajj, the slaughter was totally industrialized and housed inside a massive complex made up of many gates that were assigned to different groups. Pilgrims were corralled through the slaughterhouse, confused about where they were headed. My group walked forward with the other pilgrims, but officials screamed through bullhorns at us that we were not to continue. One of the guards told us in English, "You cannot come through because you are yellow." I never figured out why I was classified as "yellow," or what that color code signified. More Saudi gibberish, I thought to myself.

We weren't the only group that had been turned away. The slaughterhouse had run out of goats. The guards shouted, but pilgrims, desperate to complete this, one of the final rituals of the Hajj, were climbing on top of one another to try to get into the slaughterhouse.

"Leave, pilgrim!" shouted a guard. "No more goats!"

My group leader tried his best to pull all of us together. He shouted over the din, "For those of you who haven't been able to participate in the slaughter, write your name and phone number on a piece of paper. I will make sure that a goat is slaughtered in your name and call you to confirm that it has happened so you can shower and celebrate Eid."

We weren't supposed to shower until after our goats had been slaughtered. I had no idea that it was even an option, to have someone else spill the blood in my name. I'd been taught that the pilgrim had to do it with his bare hands. I felt robbed. This was supposed to be my great act of cathartic absolution, and I had been turned away. I had tried so hard to perform every ritual in the mandated way. I was devastated my Hajj felt incomplete.

I wasn't the only one who felt a sense of loss. As we walked dissolutely to our tents, riots formed behind us. Pilgrims were throwing punches at one another. The guards were outnumbered by these goat-less and blood-thirsty pilgrims. As we got closer to Mina, I saw men with freshly shaven heads strolling around in colorful *thobes* (tunics), arm-in-arm with their wives, celebrating the festival of *Eid al-Adha* ("Festival of the Sacrifice"). Millions of Muslims around the planet were doing the same. I was finally able to join the celebration later that night, when I received the call from my group leader.

"It's done," he said, like a Hollywood-style assassin calling in to home base to confirm a hit. I held my nose and showered in the abominable toilet-showers of Mina.

We returned the following day to stone the devil again at Jamrat. The end was nigh. We still had a few days left in Mecca, which gave me time to perform an Umrah (lesser pilgrimage) in honor of my mother. I took a cab outside the boundaries of Mecca and changed into a new irham with hard-earned expertise, Burmese style. And with confidence, I wore a belt with a fanny pack.

The Umrah only involved the circling of the Kaaba and running between the hills of Safa and Marwah: my two favorite rituals in Mecca. I was happy to repeat them. Being removed from the group, and performing the rituals on behalf of my mother, who never got to perform the Hajj, was spiritually satisfying. I felt as though I was performing an obligation. A sense of release came to me at the Kaaba, which helped to assuage the pain of missing out on the slaughter. Even though I was now able to lay my head in the comparative comfort of my hotel once again, I had trouble sleeping. So I turned to the Kaaba and prayed, night after night. I sat on the second level of the complex and reflected for hours. I watched pilgrims of all kinds—young, old, tall, short, colored, white, black, poor, disabled—all performing the tawaf. It was humbling to see the diversity of the Ummah on full display. Most humbling was the realization that many of these pilgrims had sold all their earthly possessions to get here in order to commune with Allah. Much more than New York, this was the city that never sleeps. I prayed for family, for friends, for forgiveness, and especially for Keith, my husband, who I loved more than life itself.

For the first time, the sense that I had killed my mother, having come out to her as she was dying of cancer, was lifted. I felt Allah's forgiveness. I was no longer a murderer.

Tawaf around the Kaaba

Swirl of activity around the Prophet's Mosque

Parvez in front of Kaaba and construction

Kingdom Tower looms over the Kaaba

Afghan pilgrim raises his index finger

Iranian pilgrim raises her hands

Pilgrims during the wuqoof in Arafat

A man in deep prayer in Medina

A man and his wife ride a motorcycle taxi in Mecca

African women pilgrims in Medina

A mutawa gazes at the Kaaba during tawaf

A young Hajj volunteer poses with the Saudi flag

Dangerous chaos in one of the many tunnels

A father and son stand at the second Jamrat

A young Indian boy performs self-flagellation

Communal Friday prayer in Parvez's hometown

CHAPTER 10

MECCA'S MANY MUHAMMADS

I t's made in China," said Muhammad. "The best things are always made there." The man working in a shop tried to sell me religious tchotchkes. In his hand was a little plastic keychain. Inside it stood a massive Kaaba and a tiny Kingdom Tower—a reversal of reality. The cube was filled with liquid like a snow globe, and little multicolored balls and glitter danced around when you shook the thing. A heart was etched into the cube, as if to say that the owner had left his heart in Mecca. The thing was hideous, but I loved it.

"Thirty riyals, but for you I'll do ten," he said with a grin.

"I'll take five," I told him. "I can give them out to my friends back home."

"Amreeka?"

I nodded. He rushed across the shop and pulled down a T-shirt for me.

"I heart Mecca!" he and the T-shirt said. It was designed like the ubiquitous "I heart New York" objects abundant in my city's many tourist traps.

Muhammad was dressed like a Bollywood star. Handsome and clean-cut, he was well-groomed in a way that seemed incongruous to his setting.

"Can you get me an Amreekan passport?" he said, half-jokingly.

I continued the joke. "It's a useless passport to have these days."

He laughed. "My name is Khan, and I'm not a terrorist!" He was referring to a recent movie quote by Bollywood megastar Shahrukh Khan. In the 2010 film *My Name is Khan*, his character is accosted by TSA officials doing a body-cavity search in a glammed-up, heavily stylized version of the bland, dated JFK airport. However, Khan's character has Asperger's syndrome, which prevents him from communicating easily. He comes to America to give a letter personally to President Obama in order to change the perception of Islam in the US. During his many adventures in a Bollywood-ized America, Khan nearly drowns during an unintentionally hilarious, extended, gospel-fueled Hurricane Katrina sequence. To his caricatured (though uncomfortably real) TSA detainers he says, "My name is Khan, and I'm not a terrorist." This phrase caught like wildfire and became part of the Indian and Pakistani zeitgeist. It was the equivalent of Forest Gump's saying, "Life is like a box of chocolates."

Muhammad proceeded to bust out a few lyrics from the soundtrack. I laughed heartily, for the first time in a while. With his Indian movie references, his Chinese tchotchkes, his I-heart shirts, and his probably illegal status in Saudi Arabia, he effortlessly reflected a kind of sophisticated global awareness, despite being nothing but an unskilled laborer. I bought a bunch of Muhammad's kitsch.

"Come again tomorrow," he said. "I will try to find the T-shirts in your size."

Hajj was over, but no one was in a hurry to leave Mecca.

I did return to Muhammad. Several times. We even shared a cigarette and a cup of tea once when I told him of the ubiquity of his name. I was drawn to him, and he was returning every subtle vibe I sent him. The needle on my gaydar hit "10." I bought more spiritual crap than I otherwise would have.

Several evenings later, Muhammad asked me to meet after Zuhr prayers, when his shift ended. I knew exactly what he was proposing, and despite my fear, I agreed to meet him. He led me up the ancient alleys and steep staircases of his slum. When he opened his door, I lost my confidence and felt a profound sense of spiritual unease.

I didn't want to shame him. "There is a place and a time," I said in Urdu. I later regretted my word choice. For me, there would be many other places and times, but for him stuck here in Saudi Arabia, there would probably not.

"*Khuda Hafiz*," he said, shutting the door. *May God be your protector.* I ran like I hadn't in a long time. Yes, I feared the mutaween and what might happen to me if we were caught doing what might have just happened, but my decision was driven more by piety. I wanted to be clean in this holy place.

I felt immense shame merely for having considered a carnal encounter in Mecca. Forgotten shames came alive. Right on cue, the call to Maghrib prayers began. I felt unclean, to the point where I irrationally thought the people in my group might be able to see the shame I felt for my carnal lust. I needed to go the extra mile in cleansing myself after this episode with Muhammad the shopkeeper. So although it otherwise wouldn't have been mandatory, I again performed the ghusl cleansing ritual instead of the simpler wudu.

I made the *niyat* (my intention) of a state of *tahara* (purity). I washed my hands three times while saying, "Bismillah," and washed my privates. Then I entered wudu mode. I cupped water in my left hand and spread it across my right arm, all the way up to my armpit. The same with my other arm. Then I cleaned behind my ears and poured water over my head and into the roots of my hair. I cupped water with my right hand and gargled three times. Then I washed my right foot, thoroughly scrubbing between my toes, and my left. Back to the ghusl. I washed my head again three times, then the rest of my body, right side and left, making sure to touch every inch of my skin with water. No one school of Islam agrees unanimously on the proper way to perform these rituals. In this moment of trauma, I tried to perform them as I'd been taught. But I am sure there were missteps.

I headed toward the Kaaba for the sunset prayer, followed by my version of a third mini-Umrah. I had already performed the Hajj, then an Umrah for my mother, and now a third pilgrimage for myself—just to be sure. After the near-sexual encounter with the shopkeeper, I thought this might earn me a few extra brownie points from Allah. Why not?

I performed the tawaf and set course for the saee. As I ran between the two hills, I noticed again a beggar woman holding a baby. I was immediately reminded of Hajjar and her child Ismael. I reached for my money belt and realized that I'd been pickpocketed, presumably during my tawaf. Thankfully my passport was in Saudi hands, having been confiscated at the beginning of my journey. I thanked God for the first time for the Saudis' authoritarian character. I was missing an expensive set of jade prayer beads and a little over $100 in riyal. I wondered how someone mere feet from the Kaaba could bring himself to steal. Only a most desperate poverty could drive someone to such depths of sacrilege and irreverence, not to mention risk—the wretched soul would easily lose a hand if caught. If he was a repeat offender, he could face execution by beheading.

The next day I indulged in a cab ride, asking the cabbie to "show me" Mecca. As was my habit in New York, I struck up a conversation with my Pakistani driver. His name was Muhammad Kasim. He lived in Aziziyah, in an area called "Little Pakistan." To make ends meet, Kasim also held down a second job in the mall, selling watches that told the wearer the direction of Mecca, wherever he was in the world. Kasim could tell I was interested in learning more about local life—he spotted me taking notes—so he offered to give me a driving tour of his neighborhood. There was no way to drive up to the entrance to his home, so we parked on the street—a steep slope. The garbage and sewage lining the narrow alleys reminded me of the worst slum in Bombay, Dharavi. We entered an apartment building and scaled the dank stairway. Kasim's apartment was exactly as had been described to me by Rahman, the floor sweeper I'd met in Medina—crowded, dark, smelly, dilapidated, no running water or flush toilet. Suitcases were piled up in a corner—a poignant reminder of their impossible hope to leave the country.

The Saudis utilized a system called *kafala* ("sponsorship") to monitor the activity of millions of unskilled migrant laborers. As part of the system, Kasim's passport was held by the owner of his taxi company. Kafala is, in reality, modern-day slavery, and as such has come under increased worldwide criticism.

"These Saudis think we're worse than dogs," said Kasim. "And they tell us as much. They say things like 'Animals are better than you,' and 'You belong under Saudi feet.'"

"How long have you been here?" I asked.

"Twelve years. I can't even tell you all the things I've seen here."

Kasim used a word that had been used to torture me in grade school. "*Gaandbazi*." It refers to someone who receives anal sex. The way Kasim used the word, he meant rape. He was telling me that his roommate had been sodomized by his employer.

I met others like Kasim and Rahman, unskilled laborers from South Asia. These indentured servants could be likened to Mexican migrant laborers picking strawberries in the California sun; however, these poor souls are treated with a much greater degree of spite. The "they took our jobs" refrain heard commonly in parts of the United States is a sentiment that is newly arriving in the Saudi kingdom. Oil revenues have steadily decreased over the last decade, and unemployment amongst young Saudis is high. It has gotten to the point where Saudi women have begun working at Victoria's Secret shops in malls, for example. Such service labor would have previously been considered far beneath them. Naturally their resultant animosity turns toward the outsider: growing in direct proportion to a slowing economy.

"How can you tolerate such conditions?" I asked him.

"*Alhamdulillah*," said Kasim. All praise be to God. "I am earning extra *sawab* (reward) for working near the Prophet's Mosque. That gives me strength to carry on."

I texted a Saudi friend in New York because I knew Adham wouldn't believe me. "There is forced gay anal sex going on in Mecca."

"Why are you surprised?" he replied. "The Saudis treat foreign workers like shit and Mecca for some is just another Saudi city."

"But it's Islam's holiest city?"

"Go around and look in the number of slums the city has. You saw City of Joy about your own country? No one knows how a large section of this country lives under the poverty line. Nobody!" I needed more proof than that, so I Googled that night. One website claimed a quarter of this country lived under the poverty line. How could this be in the world's most oil-rich nation? And how could the horrors of the poor in Calcutta relive here?

Back at my hotel I noticed a fifty-something man who'd been standing outside with a sign every day since I'd been in Mecca. His sign read, "Road to Makkah (Mecca)." Per habit, I wanted to talk to him.

"What's your name, brother? I've noticed you every day."

"Muhammad Jaffar," he said. He explained that he came from a Pakistani family of mutawif, a fast-disappearing profession of traditional Hajj guides who had lived in Mecca for generations. They were highly respected because their duty was seen as divinely appointed. Due to the modernization of the Hajj experience, these traditional gatekeepers had been largely displaced by elaborate tours.

"It's my last day here," I told him.

"Is there anything left you haven't seen?" said Jaffar. "Do you want me to take you?"

I thought for a moment. Only one place remained. It was not part of the traditional Hajj. However, it had been alive in my memory since childhood.

"The cave of Hira," I said. The place where the Prophet Muhammad received the first revelation of the Quran from the angel Jibreel.

"It will be very crowded," he said, "But I can take you there."

We hailed a taxi and headed to the mountain of Jabal al-Nour. We talked all the way.

"So much has been destroyed," I said, looking at the new, ever-expanding skyline.

"I used to work with Sheikh Angawi in the nineties. He fought so hard to preserve all the important places of our history. But he was no match for the power of the bin Ladens' bulldozers."

"Why do these Salafi Wahhabis destroy everything?"

"Don't say Wahhabi. They don't like that. Just call them Salafi," scolded Jaffar. "It's part of their religion. There can be no place of shirk so they constantly destroy." He said *their religion* with some contempt, separating his Islam from theirs.

We arrived at the mountain, crowded beyond belief.

"There's no way we'll make it to the top," he said.

Once again Saudi disregard for the safety of pilgrims was on full display. The crowd at Hira was similarly charged with passion, which increased the closer they got to the holy site. They were precariously perched across the mountainside, seemingly one faulty grip away from instant death.

I was disappointed not to be able to ascend the mountain to see the cave of Hira. The angel Jibreel's command to Muhammad to recite had always struck me as significant—Islam is nothing if not a call to the intellect.

Jaffar suggested that we share a cup of tea. We found a nearby tea stall serving piping-hot tea in tiny plastic cups.

"How has your Hajj been?" he asked.

"*Alhamdullillah*," I said. "I felt the greatest blessings at the Kaaba."

"I am so fortunate," he said, echoing my earlier cab driver. "I get to pray at it every day."

Jaffar told me how difficult it had become to support his family because of the commercialization of Hajj spiritual tourism. "Mutawifs like me used to be sought after. No more."

"If I had known, I would have approached you earlier." I handed him all the money in my new wallet, which he reluctantly accepted. "I have never seen so many kinds of Muslims from all over the planet in one place," I said. "I've never felt as safe as I have in Medina and even in Mecca."

"There couldn't be a better place for Muslims to meet. Jihadis like al-Qaeda can meet here easily. Hizbullah from Lebanon can meet Basij from Iran."

I was taken aback. "Have you ever been to a meeting like this?"

"If you've lived in Mecca as long as I have, you pretty much get a chance to see everything that goes on here. I was born here and then never left."

He pointed at graffiti on the surrounding rocks. One was a stencil of a woman's face covered in the PLO's revolutionary keffiyeh. It said, "I am a Saudi Citizen. Free and independent." Another simply read, "Who said I don't confess? I confessed everything to my God." Another, which seemed directly anti-Saud: "The government does not know love."

I pointed to another in ornate Arabic calligraphy.

Jaffar laughed. "What's the use of a virgin body when the mind is a whore?"

"How can they allow this to exist in such a holy city?" I asked rhetorically.

"The signs are all here," said Jaffar. "Where have we seen graffiti like this?"

"Egypt," I replied without missing a beat. I'd seen it with my own eyes.

He nodded. "Things like this were never said on the walls of Mecca until recently. You've seen Cairo, you've seen Tunis. You've seen Libya just a few days ago." Muammar Gaddafi had just been killed. "Wait till you see what's going to happen in Syria and Iraq."

What had this man heard? Syria and Iraq? Were there secret jihadi conclaves organized at the Mecca Hilton while unassuming pilgrims like me sat and sipped chai?

If the winds of change from the Nile were to blow eastward, it was but natural that Syria and Iraq would be next. The first had an Iran-supported dictator. The latter was in a state of constant fitna, originated by George W. Bush and gang and now characterized by a sectarianism that was almost unprecedented in Arab history. America's attempt to be a colonial power lay in dust. Democracy was not an outcome of the Iraq war, sectarian carnage was. Saddam Hussein, for all his evil, had at least held Iraq together.

I now know Jaffar was referring to the coming savagery of ISIS. I will never know how he knew.

In the streets of Mecca, there seemed to be a state of premonition. Jaffar had pointed out relevant graffiti to me to hint at it. And his words went even further. But was Jaffar the only Meccan to know about such matters? In the moment I was pretty sure he could not have been the only one. Other than in the Shia room 701 in Medina and sometimes in my group, politics was best left aside. It was clear, other than being the city that never sleeps, Mecca was also the only place in the world where extremist Muslims of all forms could meet and even strategize. I would even settle to be a fly on the wall of a violent jihad discussion. I was probably over-imagining these matters.

The post–Osama bin Laden world was still not in agreement about how to describe in English the coming scourge, known at different times as IS (for Islamic State) or ISIS (Islamic State in Iraq and Syria). Last there was ISIL (Islamic State of Iraq and the Levant). The Levant comprises Syria, Palestine, Jordan, Israel, Lebanon, Cyprus, and the Turkish province of Hatay. It's a post-colonial term that implies the bloody and hastily drawn geographical divisions constituting these modern "nations."

Calling them by any of the terms above created a unique problem that glib Western pundits, with their Wikipedia talking points, did not understand. All of these terms validate what ISIS wants: the recognition of statehood, the indivisible rise of and right to an unbreakable caliphate. On Arab streets they are called *Daesh*, which is an acronym of what they are actually called: *Dawlat al-Islamiyah f'al-Iraq w Belaad al-Sham* (roughly, "The Islamic State of Iraq and Syria"). Unknowingly the West, including the ISIL-spouting Obama, has given them greater power and geography than they have ever had. So for me, they are Daesh.

Saying "Daesh" to the likes of Chris Matthews of MSNBC hinted at a kind of superior knowledge, as if the paraded commentator of the moment knew an Arab secret that nobody else did. Using Daesh really pissed IS off. Their fatwa machines went into overdrive—those caught not saying the proper name of the group would have their tongues cut off. Daesh is similar to another Arabic word, *das*, which means "to trample down" or "crush." The cable pundits say IS for Islamic State, not knowing some of Daesh are said to like this classification. It undoes the slur-like possibilities of Daesh, taking, as they prefer, just the part that says *al-Dawla al-Islamiya* ("The Islamic State")—and, if pressed for time, the adherents to their savage ideologies could just say *al-Dawla* (simply "The State"). Most people don't know that saying ISIS, IS, and even ISIL gives this "group" greater geographical legitimacy than they actually possess. Arab governments have usually used Daesh to deny any legitimacy the organization craved. And when US Secretary of State John Kerry used the D-word, all hell broke loose for an entire news cycle. I texted my friend Adham in Jeddah about the semantics. I had read that it could also mean "stick it in" if pronounced as "Da'hesh." He said it was possible, yes.

"LOL! Just the way you like it Habibi! Just google it," he said.

"I don't have an Arabic keyboard," I replied. I did ask around some more and a consensus emerged amongst my Arab friends, at least. Daesh could be a pejorative because the way the letters were conjugated in Arabic made a difference. And that was not the end. Unfortunately for these terrorists that loathe being named Daesh, the "word" could also be used for a bigot, sectarian, zealot, or even fanatic or maniac who forces his view on others.

"Forcing their view on others" was exactly how the Ikhwan militias founded by ibn Saud during the eighteenth century had spread Wahhabism. Its roots in the Arabian Peninsula were all about savage war. While *Downton Abbey*'s Lady Mary was being deflowered by a ravishing Ottoman ambassador, Kemal Pamuk (who shared a first name with Turkey's Gandhi, Kemal Attaturk), the bloodthirsty Ikhwan had the run of the Arabian Peninsula. Although Ikhwan means "Brothers," they are not to be confused with Egypt's much-repressed Muslim Brotherhood.

Daesh had ignored a small part of Wahhabi ideology that was seen by many Islamic scholars as a "reform movement," and taken all the majority violent parts of it that suited them. Daesh and Wahhabism, or what the Wahhabis would prefer calling Salafism, were connected at the very birth of Daesh. The sword-wielding, all-black-clad, masked warriors on horseback conjured up images of the earliest, barbarically violent, Wahhabi Ikhwans set up by the early al-Sauds like the ibn Saud of that time during the demise of the Ottoman Empire. After much bloodshed, Saudi Arabia was formed into a nation in 1932.

Back at my group, there were whispered conversations. This same group also led Shia tours to prominent Shia religious places like Sham (a seventh-century name for Syria) and Karbala in Iraq. I have wondered why they would use a seventh-century word to describe what existed as a modern state. But I didn't dare ask because it would again highlight my ignorance, a product in their minds of my Sunni-ness. The ever-growing turmoil in the region would have to have undermined their business of Shia spiritual tourism. Many whispered fears that Syria as they knew it would not be around for much longer. In that they were right, just as Jaffar had hinted.

But there was even greater gossip to be heard. Their holiest shrines would begin to fall, they feared with familiar Shia fatalism. The Sayyidah Zaynab Mosque was named after the Damascus suburb of the same name, which according to Shia tradition is the grave of the Prophet's granddaughter Zaynab. In Shia exegesis, she was sister to Imams Husayn and Hassan and daughter of Imam Ali and the Prophet's daughter Fatima. There were fears that this sacred mosque could be blown apart. There had already been clashes in the region. A famous Shia ideologue of Iran's Islamic revolution, who wrote in a grand poetic style I admired, Ali Shariati, was also buried in those grounds. In the last five years, the suburb has come under heavy attack from Daesh, and my group leaders' fears of sectarianism becoming the new normal did come true.

I haven't dared to be in contact with them since, but I sometimes wonder how they negotiate Hajj and other Shia spiritual tourism in decimated cities filled with innocent dead, and when Iran and Saudi Arabia have cut off diplomatic ties once again. The 2014 version of the group the BBC called "the so-called Islamic State" were pleased with themselves. They had all the headlines they wanted and newer ready-to-radicalize Muslim youths to be plucked off what seemed like every corner in European and Arab streets. They had a "caliphate" and even a new *khalifa*, Abu Bakr al-Baghdadi, who could reach the entire planet on what I called the messy digital democracy of YouTube. A khalifa is Arabic for one who leads a caliphate—not to be confused with American rapper Wiz Khalifa, for those drawn to his music. Like Osama, Baghdadi does issue video and audio "sermons," but everything else he does or (increasingly) is done in his name is crafted using every available tech and cyber tool available in these last few years of the twenty-first century's second decade.

For me, Daesh were just "Al-Qaeda repackaged with Facebook, You-Tube, and Twitter," I posted as a Facebook status while sitting waiting in a doctor's office. I continued to wait as the number of likes and comments continued to grow—soon in the hundreds. It's nice to be liked on Facebook. My gadgets and I had been under US intelligence surveillance for years anyway, so I was not afraid to use the D word from my phone, on the social web, and often on my own laptop for research. This Daesh that the world was still figuring out claimed that their famous white-on-black flag came from the time of the Prophet. They called the flag *Rayat al-Uqab* ("Banner of the Eagle"). This was a dangerous repackaging of Islam and the question was of Islamic fact vs. Islamic fiction. Daesh seemed to prefer the latter. Islam's problem had always been that the majority of Muslims on the planet lived in extreme poverty and illiteracy. And for them words spoken at a sermon that seemed to legitimize Daesh could be a rallying call. Just as a few hundred humans could be rallied in Islamabad, Pakistan, against the Danish cartoons that offensively depicted the Prophet, an equal number could be produced supporting Daesh, as well. Not enough imams in Islam's many worlds were delegitimizing the organization using Quranic principles during Friday sermons, when they do have the bully pulpit. And that is exactly what was, and still is, needed.

Daesh had their own perverted logic on this, just as they did for all other matters Islamic. Prophet Muhammad did, according to most accounts, have a black standard, following in the Roman traditions of having standards. It was just what tribal leaders and leaders of nations fashionably did in his time. With many Muslim ulema who have an Armageddon-ish view of the world, the Prophet's flag indicates the coming of Islam's redeemer, the Mahdi. Many Muslims also believe that the coming of the Mahdi will be at the time of the resurrection of Jesus. The Mahdi will fight and defeat Dajjal, the Antichrist. So the Daesh claim (wrongly) to ape the Prophet with their standard bearing the obligatory Shahadah (Islam's super-short declaration of faith). They have added the "seal" of Muhammad also known as *Khatam-an-Nabiyyin*. *Khatam* in Urdu and Arabic means "finish" or "the end." *Nabi* is one of many words used for Muhammad and in this case literally means "Prophet." In their perverted flag they want to claim Islamic finality. There are centuries of theological disagreement on what did constitute the Prophet's standard, but Daesh has made this concocted version their own. By using it, Daesh is dangerously painting all of Islam with the color black, and saying the faith is monolithic, intolerant, and violent. Black because Islam is a dark force that can only evoke fear. And black does seem to enjoy worldwide revolutionary cred. "Revolting" anarchists from Seattle to London have often favored black scarves to conceal their identities. I wonder if Daesh has ever wondered about the fact that black is the most-used color in the rituals of the Shia they despise.

"They r already talking about this Daesh shit in Makkah?" texted Adham from Jeddah. For sanity and perceived safety, we texted out of my MMS. His extended family was rich and powerful. If I got into trouble, perhaps I could rely on his connections.

"Yes. Why, are they talking on TV?" I replied.

"Yup. I have seen a lot on al-Arabiya. I am assuming you haven't had time to watch our amazing variety of Saudi TV, Mr. Hajji!"

"LOL," I replied sending him a dramatic selfie and a dramatic sad-face emoji.

Toward the end of my time in Mecca, I spent entire nights at the Kaaba. Contemplating it from the bin Laden–built acres of a smooth, air-conditioned, and marbled second floor offered great succor. Would future history say that these greedy bin Laden contractors had done good instead of destruction? As I viewed the mesmerizing tawaf, I felt at peace. This circling had not stopped for centuries. Surely even my atheist husband would attest to the fact that an object like this, touched and grasped for centuries by generations of "sinners," had some kind of scientifically explicable power. Islam's canon, which is exceptional in science, mathematics, and more, offers little knowledge for much that is ineffable.

Brainpower lies in Islam's first revelation. At what point did a violent Muslim lose his or hers? What was the cause? Bad childhood? Indoctrination? Religion being the opiate of the (illiterate) masses? Muhammad was an iconoclast. He married a businesswoman, a decade his senior. She fed their family. They spat on him and said he was a "kept man." Mecca was nothing but misery without Khadija's unwavering love and belief in his Prophethood.

Intellectual command (Ikra!) should produce rational obedience. And centuries of Islamic thought has appealed to mortal rationality. But there is no rationality for the Al Saud or Daesh. *Jahiliyah* (literally, "time of ignorance") was an important concept used by Muhammad, the Quran, and Islam's canon to describe everything pre-Islamic, like the idolatry of the pagan Meccan tribes. Jahils were the ignorants.

For Muhammad, twenty-first century Islam would also be a time of jahiliyah. And every foot-soldier of Daesh, of al-Qaeda, of the Al Saud and bin Laden families, are jahil.

Many spokespersons of my faith disobey its command for intellectual engagement. I had hoped to find Muhammad's legacy in Saudi Arabia, but I didn't. Scholars learn to question faith, while believers just accept it. My adult self seemed to possess both abilities. My Hajj was a quest for knowledge and redemption. Sitting here, looking down at the Kaaba, I was bringing all my intellectual powers as a cultural historian, a reporter, a political analyst, and, primarily, a traveler of the spirit. Could I finally claim my own place at the table of the ongoing Islamic reformation that was forced upon Muslims post-9/11?

As the deep sea of circling believers moved in an ancient ritual all around me, I was realizing that if Islam was to change, change would come partially from people like the ones whom I had surrounded myself with in my years of study and travel. But in truth, only believers could become change-agents. Transformation in Islam would happen inside-out. And while a very minor dose of ijtihad, independent reasoning, could be a tool for many, it certainly would never offer a solution alone. In fact, the rulers of this land I despised praised ijtihad. How could I be one with them?

Will Muhammad still be a force to reckon with fourteen centuries from now? Probably. Will Daesh and their Wahhabi masters be mere footnotes? Hopefully.

As I prepared to leave Saudi Arabia, I reflected on just how deeply Wahhabi Islam had for years affected even my tiny world as a Muslim. The 96th Street mosque in Manhattan, where I often went for *Jummah* (Friday) communal prayers, was built with Saudi money. Newly created imams from Wahhabi-ization factories regularly rolled out for Friday prayer sermons. Manhattan had its share. And they always echoed medieval logic, such as how the only mandated place for women was at home. They were only to be baby-making and cooking machines. There were even methods to rein in "disobedient" wives. I was always stupefied. There in probably the world's freest city, my chosen home, in that little corner of Manhattan, the women had probably been relegated to some dark, dank corner of the mosque that I couldn't even spot. And they sat there as if obedient listeners to this perverted logic about their existence, coming as usual from Wahhabi-schooled men. And did they then go back to dilapidated apartments or projects in Queens and Brooklyn and set forth to do exactly that? Cook Pakistani-style biriyani (a South Asian rice dish) with a healthy amount of halal mutton for their cab-driver husbands?

In my youth, imams had often spouted unadulterated Wahhabi Islamic logic, which I didn't quite understand at the time. People who came back from working in the region or Hajj when I was growing up showed up with fancy electronics like shiny new color TVs, Akai sound systems, and Sony VCRs. I remember wondering if the Hajj was actually a shopping trip and Mecca a land of many modern gadgets. Their Wahhabi-ized brains manifested in other ways. Almost overnight, it sometimes seemed, women in their neighborhoods took to wearing the all-black burqas. My mother's carelessly thrown dupatta to cover her head was not for them anymore. Fathers would start sending my classmates and friends, little girls in eighth grade, to school wearing hijabs.

During recess, or "tiffin break," they would stand in their own circles and not interact with me as they always had in my girl-boy past.

Our gardener Saeed once visited with his wife after they had completed their Hajj. It had taken a lifetime of saving money for them to accomplish this sacred act they felt compelled to do.

"Assalamulaikum Hajji Saeed," I greeted him. He had now earned the highest title in the religion, that of a Hajji, one who has completed the Hajj. Used as a prefix to his name, it would immediately increase his standing in his own community. People would come and consult him on small religious matters. That's just how it worked. Saeed and Fatima had often together visited my parents. This time Fatima came dressed in a full-on blue burqa (the color the Taliban later favored). With the typical naiveté of my age, I asked Saeed why Fatima was dressed like this.

"I can't even see her face," I said.

"This is how it should be in our religion," said Saeed, adding, "This is how the Prophet wanted good Muslim women to dress."

The Wahhabi plague has not always spread in sinister ways. Our eyes have always been wide open.

As colonial powers fled Muslim lands in the twentieth century, religious organizing, zealotry, and fashionable "jihad" branding flourished. Wahhabi logic increasingly held it all together.

Muslims at the time were looking at a new world order. The loss of land was in part the natural outcome of the demise of the Ottoman Empire. But this change went deeper. It was the loss of culture, of entire histories and the advances of knowledge, discovery, and invention, architecture, poetry, and progressive thought that Muslim rulers had brought to their conquered lands. The loss of the idea of a caliphate was deep. It was a loss that was deeply mourned and never resolved. To add insult to injury, the departing colonizers butchered the centuries-old maps of Muslim regions into nation-states that suited them.

Was bereavement the primary characteristic of what the colonizers left behind? Not really. Just as it wasn't everything that an ascendant and colonial Islam of other times had left behind for those it colonized. Fourteen centuries proved it. Islam had always molded itself into the fabric of entire societies and cultures, creating an unprecedented religious syncretism. It left majestic legacies wherever it went. And it had never been an intolerant faith. If it were, then the immensity of empire would not have been the proof of its worldwide success. But the colonizers of Muslims rebirthed an essential Islamic problem. For centuries, Muslims were taught that their faith was not just spiritual. Just as it was rigid in its rules for the expansive universe of human behavior, it could doctrinally also be rigidly political. Political parties based entirely on religion are not a novelty. Just look at the Knesset of present-day Israel. Islam had the same skills of marrying religion and politics that its predecessor monotheisms had.

Here in Mecca, I was feeling a deep sense of loss, though mine was more of the kind brought about by the incessant and doubtful churning of the spirit. Daesh represented the worst kind of Islam. In Saudi Arabia's barren Wahhabi wastelands, a weed-like form of intolerance had been allowed to grow unhindered. And now its roots were too deep to chop. The eighteenth-century handshake between Wahhab and ibn Saud was now unshakable "truth." Wahhab preferred that his disciples be called Salafis, adherents who claimed to be superior to all Muslims. To this day, Saudi Arabia's Wahhabis disdain the term when it's used to describe them, which is exactly why I always try to use it in public. In the extremist Wahhabi mindset, the word itself would constitute idol worship, because it derives from the name of a real man. In their mind, they best emulated the Prophet Muhammad and his earliest followers, and subsequently the first three generations of Muslims known as *al-salaf al-salih*, the "pious ancestors." For these Salafis, this was also Islam's "ideal" period, during which Islam's canon, which a large percentage (but not all) of Muslims follow worldwide, would be crafted to perfection. For Sunni Muslims, one example was *Sahih Bukhari*, one of six *Kutub al-Sittah* (books of hadith and tradition) of the Islamic canon. The authenticity of these hadiths remains a subject of debate and disagreement. I knew Bukhari well, because I had been taught that this, after the Quran, was the most important book for Muslims. The word *sahih* in Urdu and Arabic means "correct."

Post-Hajj, for just a New York minute, I decided to try a different mosque than my usual one at 96th Street in the hopes that it would perhaps be a better fit. This much-smaller Bangladeshi East Village enterprise on 2nd Avenue and 11th Street, which used to be called Madina Masjid, now sported a new sign proclaiming "The Islamic Council of America." The prayer area had not changed much, but the imam had, at least on the few Fridays I went. It seemed he had been imported, supposedly from Bangladesh, the Islamic nation formerly known as East Pakistan—a country where I had filmed illegally for *A Jihad for Love*. Security agencies found out and we had to rush out of the country. I never went back. But I was fluent enough in the Bengali language, which made this mosque familiar. Bangladeshis worried how their country was increasingly "Taliban-ized." This imam was proof that it was. He used Wahhabi-style hadith in his sermon to buttress his arguments. This Friday, in late 2011, he decided to invoke Sahih Bukhari in his tirade against the *kafirs* ("disbelievers") and *murtads* ("apostates"). The former practiced *kufr* ("unbelief") and the latter were guilty of *riddah* ("apostasy"). "They should be killed," he almost yelled.

I wanted to challenge him. He was wrong, not just theologically but also Quranically. There were fifty to seventy-five congregants. I had addressed much-larger numbers at the talks I used to give in my speaking career. But I couldn't muster the courage. I had always been the good and obedient student, never daring to question my teachers with questions that I hadn't thought out completely. During school debates I would often lose to my fellow debaters, never quite finding the rhetorical flourishes they seemed to conjure easily. Our childhood selves never leave us.

If I had had the courage in the moment, I would have first invoked one of my favorite Surahs of the Quran. It was Chapter 109, *Surah Kafirun* ("The Unbelievers" or "The Disbelievers"):

> *In the name of Allah, the Beneficent, the Merciful.*
> *Say: Oh you who turn away*
> *I do not worship what you worship,*
> *nor do you worship what I worship.*
> *And I will not worship what you worship,*
> *Nor will you worship what I worship.*
> *Your way is yours, and my way is mine.*

The Quran, I would tell this ignorant man, was in part a call to religious tolerance. Allah, God, was saying, "Your way (faith) is yours and my way (faith) is mine." This was an unprejudiced, broad-minded Allah, who was respectful of religious diversity. I would not stop at that—I would take him up on jihad. I had, after all, put the words Jihad and Love in the same sentence for my previous film.

If able to gather even further courage in that moment, I would have taught him how I was a *mujahid* (a person engaged in jihad) and so were all other "good" Muslims. To dare to make this argument I would use semantics. In Arabic, *jihad* was often a noun and it was akin to "persevering, to struggling, to applying the self."

The imam then spoke at length about the disbelievers who surrounded us in Manhattan, never invoking Surah 109 and throwing in enough code about how we needed to stay away or convert them. His audience was typical NYC Bangladeshi cab drivers, a large minority in New York's yellow cab world, which is majority South Asian. How on earth would they convert a drunken passenger at 4 a.m. in, let's say, bar-heavy Hell's Kitchen? Did this idiot perched on his bully pulpit know his deranged rhetoric was one reason for Islamophobia? His arguments for an intolerant Islam would even manifest in the political candidacy of the vituperative (soon-to-be President) Donald Trump, who first called for a Muslim ban and then upon his second debate, confronted by a living Muslim woman, created the viral #MuslimsReportStuff. One tweet went: "Hello I would like to report a dangerous, racist, misogynist, demagogue on my TV . . . yes I'll hold." Anti-Muslim slurs emanating from mercurial, provocateur, reality show–style mouths like his are directly proportional to Daesh recruitment. In the recent past, when US soldiers kicked, stepped on, and urinated on Qurans, or when American evangelical pastors allegedly burned or flushed Qurans down the toilet, they generated a few thousand more recruits. But the East Village imam is also part of the problem.

Muhammad had favored *al-jihad fi sabil Allah,* or "striving in the face of God." It was this strife that was of paramount importance, because the struggle (jihad) was with oneself in order to reach a better rapport with Allah, God. Scholars through centuries tried to reason with the principle as ordained by the Prophet and the "Book" (Quran). Even I was a mujahid. But Jihad 2.0 favored by Daesh is of annihilation and barbarism. Their sword-waving, horsebacked, murderous Ikhwans behave exactly like their predecessors in the time of Wahhab and ibn Saud.

Daesh is never short of an endless supply of gullible and misguided youths, who have not even bothered to learn their mandated prayers. The *For Dummies* series of books has produced hundreds of guides to every aspect of life; naturally, the installment *Islam For Dummies* became a widely-read post-9/11 primer. Did would-be jihadis read it as much as bored housewives cruising Amazon or Walmart? Apparently yes, since it's been found amongst the tattered bodies of Daesh simpletons schooled by the likes of Daesh recruiter Salah Abdelslam. It seems that some suicide bombers do their crash courses in Islam this way. Many don't even know how to pray, having never been in the basement-style mosques favored in countries like France. They probably have been told that martyrdom would bring them their heavenly *houri,* or seventy-two virgins, and "wine-bearing" post-pubescent boys. Some scholars have tried to make the wider claim that all male believers will be rewarded with libidinous houris in paradise. If granted a one-way ticket to heaven, I'd choose the boys over the virgins any day.

But truthfully, a lone, suicidal, psychopathic, depressed, and deeply misanthropic individual with a laptop to trawl the dark web is all it takes.

Islam is the only difference between an Adam Lanza in the Sandy Hook massacre and Khalid El Bakraoui in the 2016 Brussels attacks. Out of 1.7 billion Muslims, the latter types are infinitesimal, but enough for savagery.

For Daesh, just like their Wahhabi Ikhwan ancestors, takfir (excommunication) is critical, thus the labeling of the Shia and Muslims like me as infidels. The one thing the Wahhabi and Daesh mind differs on is the idea of an Islamic monarchy. For Daesh, the House of Saud is un-Islamic; in fact, all monarchy falls outside of the much-sought *Dar al Islam* (House of Islam). For the codependent Wahhabis, it's a question of survival: They have long felt that without the Sauds they are nothing. In addition, there is *Dar al Harb* (House of War), which constitutes all lands that are not ruled by Islam. Daesh dares to say what Wahhabis won't say directly—even though many in their ranks believe it to be true—that there must be never-ending (till Judgment day) war with most of the planet, in addition to sectarian and infidel bloodbaths.

In Wahhabi and Daesh territory, anything outside of this kind of worldview, including mine, would be a serious deviation to be punished as *bida*, a religious innovation. As a filmmaker putting Islam and homosexuality together—something that had never been done before on film—I knew my inner state of struggle (the *Jihad al-Nafs*, "the struggle of the self") had become so challenging that it had brought me to the doors of Mecca, this ancient city, only for Muslims, and perhaps the keeper of all secrets of the Muslim world. Over the years, at Q&A sessions, I would always defend Muhammad and even emphasize how similar I tried to make my life to his. Sure, Muhammad was in part a warrior—but that was a regular condition in those times, often a legitimate outcome of monotheistic proselytizing, which for many Muslims included the Christian Crusades as just one example. The Holy Roman Empire was responsible for more than its fair share of violent warfare. One needed look only to the Torah for evidence of Jewish violence. The holy books of Jews, Christians, and Muslims were all tainted with blood. Muhammad was a reluctant warrior. Like Jesus, he was once a refugee. The similarities do not end there. Daesh religious history, however, is full of perversions. They, for example, exclude the fact that Jesus is mentioned ten times as often as Muhammad in the Quran. The book awards him, like Abraham and Moses, the status of a Prophet. The Quran rests firmly and respectfully on its predecessor monotheisms of Judaism and Christianity.

Tawhid, or the principle of the Oneness of God, is the fulcrum on which much of Islam rotates: *Allah al Ahad, al Wahhab* ("The God, the One and the Single"). In every single prayer a Muslim performs there is a period called *Tashahhud*, when the supplicant says, "There is no God but God and Muhammad is his Prophet." I was taught to raise the index finger of the right hand at the point where this central precept of one God comes up. Adham coincidentally texted one day, moments after my prayer, which included Tashahhud:

"Thanks be to Allah, Parvez! What if Muhammad had asked for the middle finger rather than the index one!"

I couldn't help but laugh at Adham's impiousness. And yet there was so much to be somber about. Muhammad's idea of a shared Tawhid for the entire Ummah lay in tatters. Not one of the early Muslims would recognize today's religion.

Parting from Muhammad Jaffar on that last day at the foot of Jabal al-Nour, after our failed expedition to Hira, I asked him, "There are millions of us here. So many kinds of Muslims. What kind are you?"

He laughed and made a sweeping gesture with his right hand from his heart to the sky above, "There is only one way to be Muslim. And that is mine."

Very simply he was describing many centuries of theological rigor that had debated this. At its crux, in Islam there were no intermediaries. It was just God and the believer. That is what the Quran and its Prophet intended. It is hard to prove whether Muhammad foresaw the fitna that through sectarianism and war Islam would create in future centuries. Notwithstanding sheikhs and ulema doing incredible damage to twenty-first century Islam, Muhammad had clearly and presciently revealed that there were no intermediaries between God and the believer. He in fact negated the idea of a clergy. Each Muslim, if he or she chose, would have a direct hotline to Allah, a kind of ongoing Whatsapp in today's terms. Despite his illiteracy, Muhammad became a vessel for the poetic and highly literary revelations of God because of his foresight.

Prophets become prophets because they can see things the rest of us cannot.

CHAPTER 11

MY PASSAGE TO INDIA

If you take Pakistan, India, and Bangladesh as a single South Asian entity, you come up with the world's largest number of Muslims (Indonesia is second in this configuration)—more than in the entire Middle East. This South Asian Trio used to be one single nation till the departing British colonizers split them into India and East and West Pakistan. They have shared languages, cultures, and histories. But the split (partition) led to history's bloodiest and biggest mass migration. Like their new names, East and West Pakistan sat on their assigned sides. The problem was that the world's second-largest population of Muslims contained at the time in Hindu India sat inconveniently in the middle. In 1971, India supported East Pakistan's war for independence, and it became its own nation of Bangladesh, as a result of a war that was as much about geography as it was about language and culture.

It was natural for me as an Indian Muslim to go back where I came from. One of Islam's truest legacies lives in South Asia, which was undivided not so long ago. Colonizers have always redrawn national boundaries with the blood of innocents. The US is new to colonial style behavior and the sorry results of its foolish attempts at it are fought on the streets of Iraq, Syria, Afghanistan, and Pakistan, to name just a few. More significantly I realize that America is not only bad at colonialism; it as a nation despises it.

Each time I go home, I get new insight into the "Islam problem," as one Pakistani TV pundit put it. For a while, Deobandi Islam enjoyed greater supremacy in South Asia than it does now, because of its strong influences on the Taliban. The primary reason for the lost influence is Wahhabi penetration. That dogma has meant the death of a carefully built syncretism that had been crafted over centuries between Muslim (Mughal) rulers, idol-worshipping (Hindu) subjects, and the meaningful numbers drawn to the Sufi way of life. The desecration of countless mausoleums of Sufi mystics is proof of the cobra-like ability of Wahhabi Islam to swallow all that comes in its path. The Deobandis, in fact, have always known the historical context for Daesh.

I first went back in 2006, when I was filming *A Jihad for Love*.

"Well, I can take you to the entrance, but promise that nothing will be seen and you are not filming me," insisted Zainab Alam. I had requested to meet her in the city of Lucknow, home to India's highest Shia population. Though a senior scholar at the University of Lucknow, she was not granted much prestige by her school, but Zainab had spent decades quietly studying the role of women in Islam, throughout history and today. On this day she was taking me and my Shia cameraperson to the Nadhwa madrassa (school) or to use the more officious name, Institute of Islamic Sciences. This school is directly linked to the Sunni Deobandi School of Islam that was born where I was and provided the ideological foundation for the Taliban. Several schools Deoband spawned either didn't allow women in at all, or if they were lucky enough to gain entry they had to be fully covered—Zainab's hair flew free.

In the West, "radicalization" toward global jihad happens by the flickering light of laptops belonging to hermetical psychopaths tuned in to the social-web-savvy Daesh. They hide behind undetectable browsing apps that promise to conceal or change IP addresses. But surely the NSA is able to overwrite those and join them on these midnight prowls of the dark web where Daesh partially lives?

Often these killing machines will never meet in person. There will never be contact with their *Emir*, Abu Bakr al-Baghdadi (rumored killed in 2016), or with his *shura* (counselors), or even a visit to their self-declared capital of Raqqa in Syria. But a few thousand have made the schlep to the "front lines."

But 2006 was a time when Osama was still alive, running his jihad chocolate factory. This jihad came packaged in different flavors. Entering Nadhwa, I wondered if "radicalization" happened in open sight here? I found the word problematic because I, too, was a radical Muslim, but of a completely different kind. So much Islam stood between al-Qaeda and me. Here, hundreds of Nadhwa schoolboys with white skullcaps bobbed their heads up and down in rote style recitation, its repetition intended to instill focus. They would never know the Quran's poetry or depth of meaning, or the context of its history.

"What are you learning about today?" I asked one.

"*Takfir,*" he said, one Muslim accusing another of being an infidel.

"Do you know what happens to a *kafir* (infidel)?" I asked. He giggled and shook his head. I wondered if he'd already been taught the un-Quranic principle that "all infidels should be killed."

"What else are you learning?" I asked, wondering further if he knew there was severe sharia punishment for using takfir lightly.

"*Taqlid,*" he said. This word means literally "to blindly follow." It is encouraged to follow a *mujtahid,* a scholar of sharia law, as per the majority Hanafi *madhhab* (school) opinion in India. Islam has four schools of thought. Hanafi, because of the Mughal and Sufi influences, has become more pluralistic than the Hanbali of the Wahhabi, the most puritanical. Just a year before I got to Nadhwa, the so-called "Amman" message had been delivered calling for unity and tolerance in the Muslim world. It had been endorsed by 200 ulema worldwide. It was a tedious document dealing with issues of Islamic *fiqh* (jurisprudence), but it formally stated that Sunni Islam comprised Hanafi, Shafi, Maliki, and Hanbali as the four schools of theology. The Shia got two schools—the Jafari and the Zaidi—and in addition there were two others that fit neither sect, Ibadi and Zafari. The unanimity they craved was not to be. I am pretty sure that neither Osama nor Baghdadi nor anyone here ever read the Amman message. I spoke to a bespectacled student after he had asked me Wahhabi-style to switch off my camera because it was "haram."

"We are learning about ibn Taymiyyah," he said. This, I knew, was treacherous territory. I asked him if he had been taught about Ayah 33 of *al-Ma'aidah*, the 5th Surah from the Quran. I quoted the Ayah. I had committed it to memory because I had been challenged about its specificity:

"The punishment of those who wage war against Allah and His Messenger, and strive with might and main for mischief through the land is: execution, or crucifixion, or the cutting off of hands and feet from opposite sides, or exile from the land: that is their disgrace in this world, and a heavy punishment is theirs in the Hereafter."

"I don't think such punishment can be used in modern times," the boy retorted, confidently. And he reminded me about the preceding (contentious) Ayah 32, which in part said: "We ordained for the Children of Israel that if any one slew a person—unless it be for murder or for spreading mischief in the land—it would be as if he slew the whole people: and if any one saved a life, it would be as if he saved the life of the whole people." The entire Bush administration would have qualified!

"Yes," I said, "I am glad you pointed that out. Killing even one innocent human is like killing all of humanity." It was one of my favorite Surahs and this young man's retort could have been mine. I knew he was a rarity. Western scholars ranting about "context" had probably never been to a school like this, where the use of context was selective yet available to students like him. They wouldn't find it in the Quran's classical Arabic. Yet this young man had. I hoped he became an *alim* (a learned one) and was not swallowed up by extremism. This lived Islam was so different from the faraway quad of a US campus—where reality doesn't really exist.

Alim is singular for ulema, the closest Islam got to clergy. For many Sunnis, they are the highest authorities. They are guardians of *fiqh* (Islamic jurisprudence) and *sunnah* (the traditions of the Prophet). Technically, Muhammad did not ordain a clergy.

Two abaya-wearing women had emerged from nowhere in the corridor. The teen made a great show of averting his eyes, even though there was nothing to be seen in their shapeless black forms with slits for eyes. He retreated back into his all-male world.

Nadhwa had a five-year curriculum such that after year one of Arabic, all teaching was in the language. Impoverished Muslims often see learning Arabic and the Quran as fortunate for their children, in a country where "English medium schools" proliferate but remain unreachable. A global network of charities based on *da'wa* (proselytizing) linked to *zakat* (charity), one of the five pillars of Islam, had always existed. It funded schools like Nadhwa and Deoband. It pre-dated al-Qaeda. But Muslims like me have long known that not all the moolah was sent to Islamic schools.

In the fourteenth century, the biggest scholar of Hanbali Islam (extremist school) was a man named Ibn Taymiyyah. This man issued a fatwa saying that violent jihad against disbelievers was permissible and encouraged. He was speaking of the Mongol invaders of his time. Scholars say they were so called because they didn't follow sharia. Centuries later Wahhab was a major fan. The puritanical Taymiyyah allegedly gave violent jihad a big thumbs up, saying:

> It is obligatory to take the initiative in fighting those people, as soon as the Prophet's summons with the reasons for which they are fought has reached them. But if they first attack the Muslims then fighting them is even more urgent, as we have mentioned when dealing with the fighting against rebellious and aggressive bandits.

For Daesh, who seem to have forgotten 9/11, this means neither Iraq nor Syria attacked the US or Western Europe first or at all. It was the other way around. In their perverted logic, Muslim land was attacked first.

Taymiyyah was making violent jihad against all non-Muslims a duty for all Muslims. "Those people" clearly meant "non-Muslims." It was a medieval time of banditry and mayhem in these deserts. They (the Mongols) were killing his people with highly trained armies. I wonder if a violence-loving imam in Islamabad can be convinced that because of ijtihad, independent reasoning, Taymiyyah's opinions need to be read in context.

Did the *jihad al-nafs* (struggle with the self) exist for him? I had always been intrigued by Taymiyyah's never marrying or having even a female companion in his entire life. Was he homosexual? I had dangerously and privately wondered while studying accounts of his life in the thirteenth and fourteenth centuries. Ibn Saud's savage Ikhwans must have looked up to Taymiyyah as an emulatory figure. Ditto Daesh.

It would be almost impossible to find a foot soldier of Daesh, sometimes even unschooled in the correct way to pray, who knows more than the name Taymiyyah or even the Islamic principles "really" favored by the Prophet and his companions. Those are the examples they claim to emulate. Yet their schooling has been quick. Your Islamic duty? Kill and Die. Your entire family gets salvation and so do you by ending up a *shaheed* ("martyr") in heaven where the *houris* (virgins—some say seventy-two of them) and other delights await. On that day at Nadhwa, a teacher directed his students to open Ayah 191 of Surah *Al Baqara* ("The Cow"), which said:

> And slay them wherever ye catch them, and turn them out from
> where they have turned you out; for tumult and oppression are
> worse than slaughter; but fight them not at the Sacred Mosque,
> unless they (first) fight you there; but if they fight you, slay them.
> Such is the reward of those who suppress faith.

Soon the couple of hundred little boys were bobbing their heads up and down in repetition.

"The Hindus don't eat cows. So should we kill them?" asked a curious student.

Aware of my presence, the teacher changed the topic. The question remained unanswered and the boy was reprimanded. Would he have answered with a yes were I not there?

More than 70 percent of the world's Muslims do not read, speak, write, or understand Arabic. They have learned the Quranic verses in classical Arabic by rote. Most have no idea what they say. The differences between classical and colloquial Arabic, with the latter coming in many regional forms, are enormous. The burden of learning placed on a student of the language is heavy. At a higher grade or probably further into this lesson itself, this teacher would possibly explain to his students what his idea of "they" was. He could arguably embellish his definition of kafirs by saying it was the Hindus, the Jews, and the Christians—pretty much the entire non-Muslim world, *Dar al Harb* ("House of War"). I am not sure he would engage in comparative theology to teach them what preceded this verse in Ayah 190: "Fight in the cause of Allah those who fight you, but do not transgress limits; for Allah loveth not transgressors."

Entering India in the seventh century, Indian Islam is as old as Islam itself. Most of the history of this time has been one of Hindus and Muslims coexisting peaceably, with both faiths even taking from each other. I was a product of that kind of doctrinal marriage, and in this room at Nadhwa, the ground beneath my feet seemed to slip.

The call to prayer rang out. I had often admired the musical variety of muezzins' *azaan* (call to prayer) in many countries. But here it felt strangely out of sync.

Wahhab would be pleased to learn just how far his ideology had spread, from 96th Street in Manhattan to Nadhwa and Deoband in India, even though he saw its early split between violence and nonviolence. To the horror of India's "secular" elite, the Wahhabi Deoband keeps on getting media attention with fatwas such as one declaring photography un-Islamic. India now has a right-wing Hindu government. Its influence on its Muslim citizens will be judged by time. During that 2006 trip, a Shia friend suggested being Muslim in India was like being black in America. Bang on, I remember thinking.

As children we were taught to seek the *ra'y* of elders. In Urdu and in Arabic, the word means "opinion." The elders included the scholars of sharia law, the mujtahid. They were qualified and led exemplary lives. Sahih Bukhari (the most influential Sunni canon of Muhammad's hadith) talks about how difficult it is to become a mujtahid. In my twenties I questioned how it was possible for the fluid concept of ijtihad to describe Islam's rigid and complex universe. Was personal effort the best way to describe jihad, as with the self? And was it OK to draw semantic links amongst the terms jihad, mujtahid, and ijtihad? Did a mujtahid have enough ijtihad-ic credentials to become a vessel of sharia to ordinary Muslims? Learning the Wahhabi-ijtihad relationship, over years of study, has made the latter less attractive.

Unfortunately, the majority of today's Ummah use *taqlid*, blind following. And that's perilous. The dangerous Hanbali school is only for al-Qaeda and Saudi types, some claim, wrongfully. But Wahhabi export has been so successful that most taqlid lands at Wahhabi/Hanbali doorsteps anyway.

For a moment, Nadhwa seemed otherworldly. MSNBC and CNN could never penetrate these walls with their logic of "moderate Muslims." America's punditry was planets away.

Was this curriculum a rehash of Deobandi, Wahhabi, and other dangerous theology? Were these elementary teachers adequately schooled? Ijtihad, to expand even further, needed a legal and scholarly interpretation of the Quran, of sharia, and of the canon. It was a lifetime of academic rigor. Achieving mujtahid-hood was as hard as getting into Harvard. Legal issues, for example, needed analogical reasoning and an ability to whip out a Surah or Ayah from the Quran as needed. Hafizs—those who memorize the Quran—were ideal. God's sharia was just, immense, and divinely ordained.

Unlike other religions, Islam decrees everything from how you clean your pubes post-heterosexual sex to how you arrange a table for *iftar* (Ramadan sunset meal) to what really is rightful jihad as the Prophet divinely understood and morally interpreted it. There needs to be *ilm*, or knowledge, of the precedent as well. Most important, every single thing a "good Muslim" does is rigidly prescribed in the canon and the Quran revealed to Muhammad. While almost none in the West has the qualifications to say so, many claim the doors to ijtihad closed in the tenth century. Others say no, with the Shia of Iran saying that they even allowed it through the Islamic Revolution of 1979. This makes them seem more in tune with the times than Sunni Muslims. The Saud-Wahhabi theology loves ijtihad. Hamas in Palestine favors ijtihad. Osama used it to invalidly claim mujtahid status.

"More chai?" interrupted a teacher, breaking my train of thought. The gaggle of teachers said they were all mujtahids. We sat there and discussed the semantics of the words ijtihad and thus mujtahid, deriving from the verbal roots of the word jihad. They remained silent as I spoke about how Osama, Egypt's Muslim Brotherhood, and the Wahhabi establishment of Saudi all claimed ijtihad, as well. I told them how dictatorial regimes throughout the Muslim world fear it because they think it will strengthen pluralism while undermining political unity, the latter being a necessity to subjugate their populations. Their response was unanimous: India is a secular country, so none of this mattered here.

My other thoughts I kept to myself. The dirty work of crafting a façade of "political unity" in the entire Arab Middle East is done by each country's feared Mukhabarat or intelligence agency, basically a Second World War Stasi-style secret police. They are used with equal and terrifying consequences by a wide range of dictators like Sisi in Egypt, the battered Bashar al-Assad of Syria, and even the supposedly Westward-looking King Abdullah II of Jordan. For these regimes ijtihad is allegedly akin to *bida*. In the past fourteen centuries, opinions on whether ijtihad is a continuing Muslim calling or not have been equally debated. As an individual I feel my ability to use independent reasoning is sacred to me. I believe that ijtihad is not a novelty for the progressive age, because it has been around for centuries. But arguments for its being a "solution" for the "troubles with Islam" are specious at best.

And who wants to sit in the same chair with al-Qaeda and the Wahhabis who condone the principle anyway? Not I.

More chai and another green room with a different cast of teachers. They had made it clear we couldn't film this conversation. One said that an Islamic caliphate was just around the corner.

"On September 11, 2001," said another teacher, "God's will became reality." A third argued that disbelievers like Jews and Christians created 9/11 as a conspiracy. Most of them bent over backward saying how they stressed "ijtihad" for their students from a very young age. Over endless cups of chai, this is the kind of hogwash these so-called ulema indulged in. And their bullshit homage to ijtihad was just that.

It was around that time I began to start thinking that ijtihad was just not what it was hyped up to be. Islam didn't just have one problem. And that's because there was no one kind of Islam. There were many, and each would have to be dealt with differently. Warfare, it could certainly be argued, would be a rightful jihad to annihilate the "disbelievers" for, let's say, an al-Qaeda "soldier"? I left them with a question: "So do you think America's war against al-Qaeda and Iraq makes violent jihad a justifiable duty for all Muslims?" Disturbingly, all of them nodded.

Pointing at me, one said, "Even upon you if you are a good Muslim."

I had come to Lucknow to film closeted but devout gay Muslims for *A Jihad for Love*. Lucknow had the largest Shia population in the entire Indian subcontinent. The gays called themselves *koti* (one who receives anal sex) *zenana* (one who acts like a woman), in a lighthearted, friendly way. Qasim, a Shia, was one of them.

The UK's Channel 4 had FedExed us press badges, thus granting us access to the mosque and home of Syed Kalbe Jawad, the most senior Shia cleric in South Asia, whose ante-room contained a giant portrait of Ayatollah Khomeini. The Syed was notorious and I, like Qasim, felt trepidation. This was the man who had organized 1 million people into the largest-ever demonstration by Muslims against the US, Israel, and Denmark when the Danish cartoons controversy erupted. This was a man who in 2016 compared Wahhabi Saudi Arabia to "the Jews." He went further to say that the Saudi execution of the venerable Saudi Shia Sheikh Nimr al-Nimr was a plot hatched by the US, Saudi Arabia, and Israel. The Shia syeds claim direct lineage from the Prophet Muhammad. India's many Islams were complicated and I had spent years studying them. Syed Ahmed Bukhari, the grand imam of one of the largest Sunni mosques on the subcontinent, Jama Masjid in Delhi, also claimed he was a syed. Neither of these men would ever reconcile their prejudices.

I had been filming the pious Qasim. Spiritual violence is a real thing and he was a victim. I hoped to capture a confrontation between this young man and the cleric. Sure enough, when we were granted our on-camera audience, Qasim displayed surprising candor.

"In Allah's house, the doors of forgiveness are always open," said the syed. The cleric wore a black turban and cloak, the uniform of his high rank. If he'd been Catholic, he'd have been wearing bright cardinal red.

Qasim persisted with his questions. "What if I had prayed for forgiveness already? Would that absolve me?" and "What if my attraction to men persists, even after I've been forgiven?" The syed grew irritated. The always-open "doors of forgiveness" seemed to be closing shut as the conversation grew heated. Finally, the syed encouraged Qasim to see a psychologist.

"You have a disease," said the cleric, after about twenty minutes of filming. On our rickshaw ride back, Qasim said, "It is God's will that I was born into this caste," adding, "He put the heart of a woman in a man's body, which is my misfortune." I tried to comfort him. Though unusual, this was not surprising to me. Qasim had used the English word *caste*. But why? Islam ostensibly had no caste system—the Ummah was equal, one God under one law. But Islam was also adept at adoption and blending in. Thus, the caste system that people assume is uniquely Hindu exists sometimes in many kinds of Indian Islams, as well.

Islamic *da'wa* (proselytizing) could only benefit from this unique ability of the religion, to both give to and take from other faiths. The Taj Mahal would not have existed if Hindus had been excluded from its creation, symbolically, culturally, or physically. More than two centuries of Islamic (Mughal) rule, which begun in the early sixteenth century, was initiated with violent warfare, like all including Christian civilizations and religions. But it did not lead to a constant state of "Islamic war" in South Asia. The opposite happened. A rich musical, artistic, architectural, linguistic, literary, cultural, and cinematic history emerged from the Islam-Hinduism marriage. Pervasive Indian Islamophobia was reserved for the twenty-first century. In 1582, the Muslim Mughal Emperor Akbar developed a new religion called *Din-I Ilahi* ("the Religion of God"). It was said to have taken the principles of all the faiths that divided his empire—Hinduism,

Islam, Sikhism, Zoroastrianism, and Jainism—and brought them together into a cohesive new whole whose primary principle would be mutual tolerance. Akbar was unique. He cherished intense debates on philosophical and religious matters.

"We are descended from the Mughals," my aunt Khala often used to say. She never produced any proof. Whenever my mother lamented the loss of her favored language, she explained that the Urdu that she wrote in was a language born from the Hindi of the Hindus and the Persian of the Mughal courts.

After our discussion with the syed, we rejoined Zainab. Over chai and biscuits in her meager apartment, we discussed the problems of contemporary Islam.

"Have you ever had access to women within Nadhwa-trained families?" I asked.

"No," she said. At this point I asked her about the Ayah 31 of Surah 24, *An Nur* ("The Light"), which in some translations seemed to clearly include "homosexuality" in one of its verses. Women were allowed to "show their finery" amongst many others to "male attendants who do not have any need for women."

"There you have it! Evidence in the Quran!" I said, believing at the time that this referred to kotis like Qasim as much as it referred to me.

"Most people you will meet on this journey will have little knowledge of the Quran," she replied.

I told her how every single "teacher" at Nadhwa had a *zabiba*—literally, "raisin," but used to identify the forehead of the pious, a kind of prayer bump. We both agreed they were hypocrites. Praying frequently does not a good Muslim make.

I knew she knew a great deal about my favorite subject.

"So as you know, in some parts of India Wahhabism is seen as a reform movement . . ." I began gingerly.

"Of course," she said, "In eighteenth-century Islam there were reform movements all over the place. Wahhab promised the same, including to people like my grandfather who used it to the very last day."

I challenged her about barbaric Wahhabi ideology that lay at the heart of Saudi sharia and was now everywhere. Zainab was a very learned woman, having earned her PhD in Islamic theology at India's famed Aligarh Muslim University.

"You have to study its appearance in context," she said, telling me what I already knew. Wahhab was a product of a time when Islamic empires were losing to colonizers. His pact with ibn Saud was necessary for "stability," she said. The man in his own lifetime saw his "reform" bastardized. It is true that a "split" between "peaceful" and "violent" occurred in Wahhab's lifetime. However, even his "peaceful" puritanical theology was destined to be a destructive force.

We discussed how Osama was in part a product of the violent part of Wahhabi logic. We assessed the immense anger and a sense of loss amongst empires of Muslims because their borders were being redrawn by colonizers like the British. For the Mughals and other Muslim powers, this political disintegration became a religious problem too. And then came the eighteenth-century Wahhab with his seventh-century logic.

"Yes, it was puritanical. It hated the Sufi style that the Mughals had encouraged and celebrated. It took away the freedoms of Muslim women, which they till then had taken for granted. But I still wonder if Wahhab thought he was on a divine mission to build what he viewed as an equal Ummah just like the Prophet had envisioned it," I said.

"That is worthy of research," said Zainab. "He was from the Nejd and thus walked the same sands the Prophet's early Muslims walked. He would have despised Hindus."

"But then why did it appeal to your grandfather?"

"Because even Deobandis embraced it. He was drawn to Wahhab's condemnation of idol worship, India's main religion. You see, he saw Wahhabi Islam as a reform movement. Which it was, in the eighteenth century." We both agreed that Wahhab himself had believed in Tawhid, the sunnah, and the Quran, and was probably not a violent man. His successors invoke his name "for horror," I said.

I was happy to find a Muslim woman scholar who said that Wahhab was no political ideologue. His transformation into the latter was the handiwork of Muhammad ibn Saud, eager to set up a divinely ordained monarchy.

We spoke about the contexts of those times. In 1744, post-treaty, Wahhab and the early ibn Saud deliberately moved tribes from nomadism to sedentary life, which allowed Wahhabi proselytizing. But even at the time, the ancient "ghazu" raids that had only involved the plunder of livestock for food morphed into takfiri and kafir human slaughter.

The Saud-Wahhab marriage was one of convenience. Wahhab would have no followers if ibn Saud did not conquer and bring them to him. Critically, Wahhab found no Islamic evidence for the ibn Saud–created Ikhwan's annihilation of humans. They were no martyrs, he said.

Was he an eighteenth-century Arab version of the sixteenth-century Protestant reformer Martin Luther? He preferred literacy, ijtihad, and Quranic exegesis. But he also favored public beheadings and taking away Quranic rights for women. For me, his "revivalism" is a bastardization of the Quran's comity. Sufi mystic ibn Arabi had said in the thirteenth century, "Do not praise your own faith so exclusively that you disbelieve all the rest." Wahhab would never have agreed. But surely he knew that a great deal of Islam's geographical expansion had used Sufi mythology, venerated by kings, mystics, and ordinary mortals alike.

"But Wahhab would have destroyed all the Sufi shrines here in Lucknow," I said to Zainab. Sufi mystics like India's syncretic "Chisti" Sheikh Nizamuddin Auliya was buried a few blocks from one of the homes where I grew up. In the thirteenth and fourteenth centuries it was normal for scholar-poets like him to say that he was neither a Jew nor a Christian, and not even a Muslim, because once the divine had been revealed to a believer, these manmade divisions no longer mattered.

She agreed about Auliya but added, "Wahhabization of this region is so complete that it's only a matter of time. Just look at Afghanistan and Pakistan." I could not imagine an India without a Nizamuddin. But twenty-first century Islam is increasingly suspicious of its Sufi mystical roots and legacy.

Wahhab's distaste for needless violence died with him. Future Sauds used jihad and takfir with equal ferocity to slaughter entire tribes. They plundered cities like Karbala, holy to the Shia at the turn of the nineteenth century. The ascendant Wahhabis were thrilled to see the evolving demise of the Ottomans they had warred with several times. However, there was relentless butchery in Arabia until Abdulaziz ibn Saud in 1932 formally established what Adham and I, like many, call KSA, the Kingdom of Saudi Arabia. This modern entity remembers the savagery at its roots full well and is never afraid to use it, even in our times.

I sometimes wonder what Zainab would think of Wahhabism's impact on Daesh? How would she view the wastelands of Syria and Iraq, and their connection to "end of days" logic? Daesh savages break bread with their own, and everybody else is up for death with lances and swords. Ignoring

Islam, they have routinely massacred "apostates" including unarmed villag-
ers in their thousands, thinking nothing of raping women and slaughtering
children, and routinely slitting the throats and even beheading male cap-
tives. Their cameras capture it all competently. In the late 1920s, Abdulaziz
al-Saud or ibn Saud (not the Saud who made the Wahhabi pact) was as
captivated as the Crawleys at Downton with telephones and the telegraph,
cars, cigarettes, and gramophones. His own itinerant Ikhwan said anything
modern (not used in the seventh century) was *bida*, heretical innovation,
and declared war on him. He finally defeated them in 1930, but they never
really went away.

Ibn Saud got his early ulema to say "militant jihad" was un-Islamic.
The rest of Wahhab's ideology became Saudi sharia. This official stance was
clearly never practiced. After 1979, Western governments including the
US, as afraid of revolutionary Shia Iran as the Sauds, gave their blessings
to the Saudi project of Wahhab-izing the planet.

I asked Zainab what she felt about this Wahhabi spread-ology.

"Islam has destroyed itself," she said sagely.

It has been years since we saw each other.

"I'm looking for the moon," said a little boy. "My father sent me to find it."

I was perched on a rooftop in chaotic Old Delhi, above the tangled
web of wires that were miraculously able to bring intermittent electricity
to the surrounding homes. It was winter 2012 and I was now a Hajji.
Celebration was in the air. This night was called *Chand Raat* ("The Night
of the Moon"). Shopkeepers cooked *mithai* (sweets). My favorite was the
sevaiyyan (toasted, sweet vermicelli noodles). Women applied henna, and
everyone wore new clothes. Ramadan was ending. For a month, I had
fasted from sunrise to sunset like millions of my fellow Indian Muslims
and began my renewed journey with faith and vigor. I joined tens of thousands of supplicants at New Delhi's Jama Masjid wearing a *kurta* (tunic)
my mother gave me. Just a year ago I had pounded Saudi sands.

That night we searched for the sliver of a crescent moon called *hilal*
that would signal Ramadan's end and assure the faithful that their prayers
had been answered. We waited for Delhi's highest cleric to proclaim the
hilal sighting through many loudspeakers. Often sectarian, south Asians,
like their TV channels, reported different times of the moonrise. Joyous

cries and firecrackers took over when he proclaimed the sighting. I suppose that seventh-century Muslims weren't aware of time zones. But finally the declaration was made. Tomorrow was Eid al-Fitr.

I retched on the stench permeating my second-class cabin on the train to Saharanpur. This stench brought back uncomfortable memories of childhood. I checked into the shabby Atlantis Hotel, which was far from even being a distant 1,000th cousin to its shiny sister in Dubai. My beloved *Real Housewives of Beverly Hills* frolicked and quarreled in nouveau-riche luxury in the latter. This one welcomed me with cockroaches scurrying about what the staff in Hinglish were calling a "suit" in lieu of "suite."

The next morning, I spoke with a local cleric at my childhood mosque about my intentions in Saharanpur.

"This is a complicated issue," I said, daring to explain that I went on the Hajj with Shia pilgrims and that their *madhhab* (doctrine) left the question of the method of goat slaughter as a matter open to the individual. I was never sure about what the various Sunni madhhab said on the issue.

"They ran out of goats," I explained. "I wasn't able to complete the final ritual of my Hajj. Our Shia group leader said he had done it on our behalf. I don't know if this is a matter of fiqh," or Islamic jurisprudence.

The junior cleric held his earlobes in imitation of a schoolboy's punishment. In India, disobedient children are told to clasp their earlobes. After a while, this hurts like hell, and is used as a common form of corporal punishment and public shaming.

"*Astaghfirullah!*" he exclaimed. The translation is "Forgive me, God," but it could be better understood as an outburst like "Oh, my God!" The melodramatic cleric was indicating his shock that I dared travel among Shia. He scurried into another room and retrieved a pile of books. "There are many religious opinions on this matter," he said.

I cut him short. "You just need to tell me if I can do a *qurbani* (sacrifice) after the Hajj is finished."

Sensing money, the mullah was eager to please.

"If you have the means, you can do it," he said. "Let me warn you—there's a lot of fiqh that will nullify your Hajj because you went with Shia apostates."

As I got up to leave his mosque, the cleric left me with a final question: "But can you make sure the meat is distributed here in this neighborhood?" I nodded and hugged him twice, as many Indian Muslims do when bidding goodbye to a same-sex member, slipping 3,000 rupees into his hands.

I wandered the streets of Saharanpur. For me these were streets of shame. My mother never forgave me for being gay. I looked all over the streets of the wood market, and there it was: our childhood halal butcher shop. To my disbelief, the same man was still running the family business. His wrinkles told the story of a difficult life.

"Do you remember me?" I asked him.

"Yes," he said. "I always cut the meat for your family on Eid."

"I need a qurbani."

"You want me to do it for you, you mean?"

I did not explain the circumstances that brought me to his shop. "I need to use my own hands, but I want you to be there to finish the job. Please don't ask too many questions." I handed him 10,000 rupees, a sum that would cover the cost of the sacrifice and quell any curiosity that might inspire him to get chatty with me. I associated this man with my past, which was marked by judgment and worse.

"How about eleven o'clock, tomorrow morning? I hope your wife and children are well!" It was inconceivable to this man that I could have reached adulthood without taking a wife and reproducing, as all good Muslims should.

The stink of daily death is particular. In the West, the smell born from animal slaughter is conveniently hidden away. Here in India, death in any form is out in the open. Slaughterhouses compete for space with every other kind of business, so one is never far from its unique odor. I met the butcher at the appointed hour the following morning. Together we procured a goat from a nearby market. The closer we got to the final act, the more I was plagued with inner conflict. On the one hand, I was dreading the experience. I had never performed an act of violence in my life. The sight of the slaughter was familiar to me, but I'd always kept a safe distance. Never before had I taken an animal's life with my own hands. On the other hand, I desperately craved the catharsis that I hoped would follow the sacrifice. I had left Saudi Arabia feeling that my Hajj was incomplete. My faith had been severely tested there, and having missed the chance to perform the sacrifice, I felt bereft. With the force of my own will, I had created a scenario that would enable me to find atonement.

Knife in hand, I stared at the goat I had personally nicknamed Ismael. As a child, my perception of the story of Ibrahim sacrificing his son Ismael was shaped by my fragile relationship with my own father. We were emotionally distant in both directions. The idea that Ibrahim was so ready and willing to sacrifice his own son struck me as an authentic portrayal of a father-son relationship. As a boy, I felt that if my own father had been given the choice, he, too, would not have hesitated to place me upon the altar. Would I find last-minute redemption as Ismael had?

No redemption for this thrashing animal was at hand.

"*Bismillah*," I said, as I brought the blade to the goat's throat. I struggled to break the skin.

"Push harder," said the butcher. The goal was to cut the jugular vein, the carotid artery, and the windpipe in a single clean swipe. Every aspect of Islam is carefully regimented. I summoned all my discipline to ensure that I performed the dreadful ritual correctly.

When it was done, I clutched the dead animal. My clothes were soaked with blood. My mind raced. Did I do it correctly? Had I been blessed with redemption? Were there certain supplications that I'd neglected? Would my mother have approved? What would my father think? The finality this brought was unfamiliar. With this animal, had I also killed my childhood?

I recited the first chapter of the Quran, which had always brought me comfort. Not this time. I felt like a murderer. I fell to the ground in a fetal position and lay there for what seemed like hours. I had never felt more unclean. Few Muslims would approve of what I did next. Covered in blood, I climbed to the rooftop and performed the *Namaz* (prayer) with extra *rakats* (prescribed movements). I was performing the wrong prayer at the wrong time, all while covered in animal blood, and thus in no state of *tahara*, or purity. In Islam, prayer had always been performance—a kind that is used to instill discipline and a retreat into the spiritual. Heavily ritualized, it's almost like the yoga of the Hindu religion.

As a child I had used the very expansive *Ayatul Kursi* ("Verse of the Throne") from the Quran to comfort me into sleep, and it unfailingly did that. But I had learned its meaning only as an adult. This is probably the most famous Quranic verse in the world, used for countless occasions, comforting me to sleep being one of them. I had often seen it etched in all kinds of wall hangings, silk, velvet, and more. Infinite styles of Arabic calligraphy, as seen in the Taj Mahal, were used for this verse, too.

"Allah. There is no god but He—the Living, the Self-subsisting, Eternal. No slumber can seize Him nor sleep. His are all things in the heavens and on earth. Who is there can intercede in His presence except as He permits? He knows what (appears to His creatures as) before or after or behind them. Nor shall they compass aught of His knowledge except as He wills. His Throne doth extend over the heavens and the earth, and He feels no fatigue in guarding and preserving them for He is the Most High, the Supreme (in glory)."

On that night in 2012 it still worked, better than any sleeping pill.

I was back in India, again. It was late January 2014. I sat on the verandah of the lavish Golf Links home of a prominent Delhi socialite. I was visiting her guest, a well-known Pakistani journalist called Ghalib Kidwai. He had just run in to "order" some more chai. I was in India, editing the film that would become *A Sinner in Mecca* upon its release in 2015. Delhi had not yet turned into a 50-degree-Celsius hellhole. Late January was still nice enough to sit outside. Ghalib and I had known each other for years from my early days as a cub reporter. He was always my ear to Pakistan, a country I had only once been granted a visa to. Visiting each other's country is nearly impossible for Indians and Pakistanis. Like many North Indians, my family had deep connections to Pakistan and vice versa. My grandfather had studied at a prominent Lahore college.

Ghalib, who is an atheist, knew the film I was editing and was afraid for me. We had been talking about a critical 2013 EU report that received scant media attention. "I just brought these pages; the whole thing is hard to get," he said. He knew I might quote him. His name and affiliation, like all others in this book, have been changed. Public knowledge of our long-standing friendship could do him and his career great harm—my name was notorious in Pakistan. Ghalib was my first Pakistani friend to discover that my first film was on Lahore's pirated DVD market.

It had taken some journalistic digging for him to find these quotes from the EU report. This usually comatose entity paying its bureaucrats hugely inflated salaries to manufacture miles of PowerPoint presentations seemed to have done something useful? I rifled through its tedious pages. It tried to explain the global network of finance using the Islamic principles of *zakat* and *da'wa*. It had started in the seventies with the Saudi oil boom that made

Osama's family rich beyond description. There were ibn Saud and bin Laden billionaires everywhere. This cash had fueled al-Qaeda and much other mayhem. Safe in their seemingly secure, lifelong desk jobs, these bureaucrats had finally woken up to a fact that Muslims had known for decades.

There it was on the photocopied page 74 of the EU report: Wahhabi and/or Salafi groups (depending on how you chose to name them—for me they were one and the same) based in the Middle East were closely involved in the "support and supply of arms to rebel groups around the world." Any Gulf returnee to Pakistan in the eighties could have told you that. We had known it for years but here was proof that the Sauds and their Wahhabi clerics had direct links to terrorism. It warned that, "No country in the Muslim world is safe from their operations . . . as they always aim to terrorize their opponents and arouse the admiration of their supporters." Ghalib returned with more chai.

"Oh, my God," I said. "Do you think that the Obama White House knows?"

"What do you think?" he said.

He said some English-language print media in Pakistan had written about it in 2013—because they were infested with this terror in their own backyards in Pakistani Punjab and its unruly NWFP. But why were the cable pundits and the Obama White House silent on this critical new finding? Bin Laden was dead, but al-Qaeda still existed and this is how Daesh and the remains of al-Qaeda were getting a great deal of their money. The EU nine-to-fivers would soon learn that "radicalization" was happening under their very noses in Brussels, just a few metro stops away. But there was a greater scourge that Ghalib and I had to discuss.

"Even a college sophomore with political science as a major would be able to tell the EU that the biggest example of this had already been the US and Saudi support of the early Afghan jihad against the Soviets—a phenomenon that created al-Qaeda," I said to Ghalib.

"It's simple, Parvez. Zakat fueling militants and building the Ummah (da'wa) can now happen online."

"Like a PayPal for zakat and jihad," I said, sipping my tea.

Were the little boys in Nadhwa and Deoband taught the philosophy that was the bedrock of the Talibs, al-Qaeda, Sarajevo jihadis, and more? Did they watch Daesh beheading videos? I had grown up with charities such as these in physical form.

Around Ramadan they would appear at our doorstep. "Even the smallest zakat is *fard* (obligatory) because God willed it," they would say. We always paid.

The EU report went further. The authors estimated that Saudi Arabia alone had spent more than $10 billion to promote Wahhabism through Saudi charitable foundations. The tiny and super-rich state of Qatar, primarily known for the creation of Al Jazeera, was the newest entrant to the game, supporting militant franchises from Libya to Syria.

Ghalib had more to tell me. They have known this since the Bush years, he said. Bush's own State Department in 2006 issued a report.

"It probably disappeared into some vault in the basement of the Harry Truman building in DC," I said, laughing.

Ghalib told me that the 2006 report had clearly said that Saudi donors and unregulated charities had been a major source of financing to extremist and terrorist groups over the past twenty-five years. Bush 43, as with his father's administration, had always been in bed with the Saudis. America's thirst for oil was unquenchable. The US dared not give State's own report much play publicly, hoping it would disappear. It did.

That Delhi afternoon chai extended toward dinner. Ghalib drew my attention to what was going on in the Pakistani side of Punjab. I remembered from my reporter years groups like Al-Khidmat, Jamaat-ud-Daawa, and Jaish-e-Mohammed having feet in both India and Pakistan. Every time the Indian government declared a group like Jaish terrorist, a new one popped up.

Both Ghalib and I surmised that now there were literally thousands of these groups, big and small, from all across Muslim countries and communities like Mali, Somalia, Syria, Afghanistan, Pakistan, India, Indonesia, and more. What did they do? They took Muslims of diverse traditions within Islam that are exceptionally moderate, like South Asian Sufi-enriched Islam, and flew in Wahhabi imams to preach intolerance.

After Hajj I no longer drank, so while Ghalib savored his favorite Black Label I asked for more chai.

"Pakistan finally a failed state? Which is why an Osama was able to hide there for years, not far away from the APS boarding school you went to?"

"You can't make such an expansive statement. You love nuance. You should know better," Ghalib said. He was right. Many in the Indian

Hindutva right wing did consider Pakistan a failed state and I did not want to share their rhetoric.

Osama made Pakistan one of the most important stops in global Islamic terrorism. It had, in my opinion, been in a state of civil war since its inception of being carved out of what was British-ruled India, the jewel in the crown. Notably, years of democracy were interspersed throughout. Pakistan had given the world a democratically elected female head of a Muslim state in Benazir Bhutto. It was also important to acknowledge that Bangladesh, which until 1971 was called East Pakistan, had almost always been an Islamic democracy, alternatively ruled by two women, Begum Khalida Zia and Sheikh Hasina Wazed, the latter being the only living female head of state who had the title of sheikh and used it. Islam was not incompatible with democracy, as bin Laden and his right-wing counterparts in the US liked to rage. Not many looked at the Islamic pluralism that allowed democracy led by women not once but several times. A glass ceiling that even America has not been able to shatter has forever been destroyed in Islamic democracies. Yes, Muslim women can be and have been heads of state and run them. And no, Islam is no stranger to or incompatible with democracy, as a self-satisfied BBC documentary producer had condescendingly said to me before a panel at a film festival.

I digressed, telling Ghalib about my time in Dhaka a few years before. I was invited to cocktails at the home of an "industrial giant" family made rich by the suffering hands of desperately poor Bangladeshis working in their clothes-manufacturing sweatshops. We were in a mansion in a rich neighborhood called Gulshan. Women dripping diamonds wore the region's famed sarees. My dying mother had cherished the two she had, when we used to live in Calcutta in what before 1947 was the Indian state of Bengal on its eastern edge. On its western end sat the State of Punjab. The British split both states, and millions were slaughtered in the name of religion. Lahore became the capital of the Pakistani Punjab and Chandigarh the capital of the Indian Punjab. Similarly, Calcutta became the capital of the Indian West Bengal and Dhaka the capital of what was called East Pakistan. In 1971, under the leadership of Indira Gandhi, another subcontinental female prime minister, India enabled a civil war that liberated East Pakistan and created Bangladesh. Bangladesh was immensely proud of its creation—the war had been amongst other things fought over language. Urdu from West Pakistan was being imposed on East Pakistan, while Bengali really was the language of their people.

On this night, the women at this mansion smoked and drank copiously just like the men. One who was rumored to be having an affair with a US diplomat shared a cigarette with me and was appalled I was living in the lower-middle-class neighborhood of Shanti Nagar (Neighborhood of Peace) in a hotel ironically called the White House.

"I am glad Gulshan is so close to the airport," she purred. "I have never been to such areas. They are not safe. I am sure we can find you a nice accommodation at the club or another hotel here." Unlike in Bombay and Cape Town, where the shantytowns were closest to the airports, Dhaka's geography put Gulshan closest. This Chanel No. 5 vision that stood before me had probably never left Gulshan to see the real Bangladesh, one of the poorest nations in the world. All she needed was this part of town to be chauffeured around in and then escape to Europe from the nearby airport.

An elderly intellectual-looking man approached me asking what kind of film I was making. I dared not tell him. I changed the subject and allowed him to launch into what seemed like a rare idea: "Have you seen how this country is being ruined by the Islam of the Taliban? I just wish India had never been separated."

I was surprised, but it was a sentiment my grandfather would have probably shared. Bangladesh was increasingly under the influence of Taliban, and thus Deobandi, philosophy. The women at this party proudly wore bindis, part of a cultural heritage they shared with the Hindu Bengalis of the Indian side. But the bindi wars had started. In mosque after mosque, sheikhs and imams railed against them, saying they were symbols of the shirk practiced by the Hindus, and Muslim women should not wear them. Some Bangladeshi Muslim women still wore bindis on their foreheads, though neither of the two alternating women prime ministers did. For Hindu women, the bindi was sometimes a religious signifier of being married, but more often than not it was just an accoutrement of beauty, and that's how Bengali women in this country used it.

"Lahore and Delhi are like that, too, Parvez," Ghalib told me that day in 2014. I knew that in our part of the world abject poverty lived right next to excess and opulence, but I disagreed.

"Come on, Ghalib. Delhi is hardly like that—this is the world's largest democracy. And the one time I went to Lahore, it was not like that either."

"Don't throw the world's largest democracy BS on me, my friend," he laughed, but I knew he was serious. For Pakistanis, Indian democracy had always been a sore subject.

Pakistan had suffered the worst kind of Wahhabi indoctrination and had the scars to prove it. In the late seventies Pakistani dictator Zia-ul-Haq, a US ally, put Wahhabi logic into his *hudood* (literally, "limits") ordinances for a sharia-compliant Pakistan. The Saudis were overjoyed, and the US looked the other way.

Ghalib had spent his teenage years in Zia's time. He had seen his country change almost overnight as these infamous ordinances were born. Overnight, stoning women to death was OK? Whose Pakistan was this? A sharia system parallel to the penal code was being established, and it was a circus. The delusional Zia wanted to recreate the raison d'être for Pakistan itself. In his head Pakistan was created to be an Islamic state. What he forgot was that his nation's famously alcohol-consuming founder Muhammad Ali Jinnah was partial to democracy and secularism; and worse, a Shia! In February 1948 Jinnah addressed "the people of the USA" on radio, saying in part:

> I do not know what the ultimate shape of the constitution is going
> to be, but I am sure that it will be of a democratic type, embodying
> the essential principles of Islam. Today these are as applicable in
> actual life as these were 1,300 years ago. Islam and its idealism have
> taught us democracy.

Islam teaching democracy? He meant it because he knew it was possible.

Zia, on the other hand, was a murderous dictator, who sentenced a popular prime minister, Benazir Bhutto's Soviet-leaning and democratically elected father, Zulfikar Ali Bhutto, to death by hanging.

"There was no way the CIA and the US were not involved in that," said Ghalib, echoing popular opinion. Once Zia was done with Bhutto, his newest idiotism was *Nizam e Mustafa* (literally, "Rule of the Prophet").

"But *whose* Prophet?" I asked Ghalib.

"Zia was a perfect partner for the Saudi Wahhabi machine," he said.

"Look at it this way, Parvez. Till 2006 you could stone a woman to death for adultery in the streets of Lahore or Karachi." *Zina*, or adultery, was punishable in the Wahhabi way. Rapists of women roamed free while the women victims languished in prison. I always viewed the rowdy Pakistani Muslims blessed with intellect superior to the Saudis'. I told Ghalib about Basheer, the "honor killer" I had met during Hajj.

"Thank God for my namesake," I said to Ghalib, referring to Pakistan's military ruler, General Pervez Musharraf, under whose watch a Women's Protection Bill was put into place in 2006. It made rape punishable by the more-stringent civil law. But Pakistan was Wahhabi-indoctrination paradise and the Federal Shariat Court remained—civil laws had to be "sharia compatible." Perhaps it was a sign of progress that a female justice in the form of Ashraf Jehan got to be one of the eight justices on this court.

"Good for her. I am thankful," he said sardonically as we discussed this strange legal system.

Political Islam and Pakistani identity were coalescing. To its credit, when not under military rule, Pakistan had functioned for brief periods as a working democracy with the exercise of real civic franchise. Islam is not democracy-averse. Pakistan, Bangladesh, Turkey, Indonesia, and Malaysia, all in their own ways prove it. And the world's third-largest Muslim population votes in the world's largest democracy (India).

I asked Ghalib if old-fashioned recruitment still worked.

"Why would it ever go away?" he said. My evolving thesis since Nadhwa was getting affirmed.

We were talking about a country that suffered endemic poverty. According to the UN Development Programme's 2013 "Human Development Index," Pakistan was number 146 out of 187 countries. The index had been developed as a marker measured by life expectancy, literacy, education, and standards of living.

As in India and Bangladesh, the rural poor made up two-thirds of the country. Pakistan was the world's second-largest Muslim nation and almost 70 percent of its population was poor? The statistics spoke for themselves. Poverty, illiteracy, and unemployment were the norm for South Asian Muslims who constitute the majority of Muslims on the planet.

"I cannot tell you how angry I feel at the handful of Muslim cable analysts who have completely NO idea of what they are dealing with," I said to Ghalib. "They throw about the one term they have learned—ijtihad. Many of these idiots even claimed that the failed revolution of Egypt was a social-media phenomenon."

We tried to connect the dots between the Saudis, the dead Osama, and the surging Daesh. The Sauds will never admit it, but they built an opaque and complex global network of bank accounts with links to Islamic charities, which in turn have links to terrorists. Post-9/11 the scion of the bin Laden family, Bakr, absolved his own vast clan of any responsibility because they had excommunicated Osama and cut off all financial links to him. Osama probably had withdrawn his share of the bin Laden annual dividends (millions) years ago, before he fled Sudan. It was comical. Post-9/11, Geneva was overrun by bin Ladens and Sauds trying to save their money. The latter reluctantly, in 1994, stripped Osama of his Saudi citizenship. They could get Osama out of Saudi Arabia, but they couldn't ever get the Saudi out of Osama. Days after 9/11, George W. Bush's White House cleared the secret evacuation of twenty-four prominent bin Ladens present on US soil, engaged in pursuits ranging from academia, real estate, and lobbying the capitol to just Rodeo Drive or 5th Avenue shopping. This was a time when millions of civilians remained unable to fly. Allegedly, a frantic King Fahd called his embassy in DC saying there were "bin Laden children all over America." It is logical to assume that a phone call between the Saudi king and George W. Bush made the entire bin Laden evacuation possible. The bin Ladens were no strangers to America and were, in fact, friends to the Bush White House.

After 9/11, Bush paid Saudi Arabia two visits, an obligatory, almost humiliating ritual of US presidential genuflecting at the feet of King Abdullah. Obama doubled that number, paying four. The absurdities continue: this country with no human rights became a member of the indolent United Nations Human Rights Council. As if that were not enough, in 2017, this, the most misogynist society on the planet, which treats its women as chattel, was appointed to the UN Women's Rights Commission. The hypocrisy of the UN could not be clearer.

And in less than a year, Donald Trump, a man whose very election was contested, would welcome the man who *really* ran Saudi Arabia, Deputy Crown Prince Salman, to the Oval Office—both men, members of the small club of the world's most dangerous leaders. Weeks later, during his first foreign trip, Trump would land in Riyadh for the optics of that familiar presidential genuflection to the now incapacitated eighty-one-year-old King Salman. It was a horrific "reset" to this parasitic relationship, which had become icy toward the end of Obama's second term.

Ghalib and I both knew of the twenty-eight pages about the Al Saud and bin Laden family links to al-Qaeda that were redacted from the 9/11 Commission Report about the (real, I believe) collusions between the monarchy and the bin Ladens with al-Qaeda—the question had haunted two presidencies. When Congress finally got the pages declassified in 2016, there was not much there. *The problem is, if it were not for Saudi Wahhabi Islam (taught to fifteen of the hijackers), there would have not been an al-Qaeda and a 9/11.*

"Whoever monitors the kind of websites I go to at the NSA in the US or even the government here in India is having lots of fun. At least it's for a good cause," I said.

"Don't joke about such things," admonished Ghalib, "these things have real consequences." It was almost certain that the notorious Pakistani Intelligence had him on its watch list.

We discussed how the majority in Egypt, the most populated Arab country at 82 million, lived in abject poverty. As in South Asia, it was endemic.

"Poverty is directly proportional to illiteracy, which in some cases is directly proportional to the number of times you pray or visit a mosque," I said. Ghalib agreed.

I knew that in spite of India's syncretic past, we were now sitting in the most Islamophobic nation in the world. Being Muslim in India was like being a young black man in America. Muslims filled Indian prisons. And the glass ceiling for highly educated Muslims was set to pretty low. And India could never have a "Muslim Lives Matter!"

For many of the world's almost 1.7 billion Muslims, smartphones were not a reality, and Facebook, Twitter, Instagram, and Reddit were things a few might have just heard about. The majority lacked easy access to the web, though they craved it. Most people had ordinary mobiles. iPhones and Galaxies? Not as much. A big part of the "radicalization" of Daesh happened mostly on the laptops of second- or even third-generation European Muslims. Muslims gathered in small Pakistani towns like Sialkot, along its terrorist highways, are a planet away from the "riches" of Muslims sitting in Brussels, Vienna, or Paris.

However, old-fashioned recruitment still works for Daesh, as it had for al-Qaeda. Always on the verge of economic collapse, Pakistan would turn up with its begging bowl at the doors of the Saudis. The "ever benevolent" Al Saud saw it as their zakat duty to help poor Muslim countries. So periodically free cash and oil were given to a Pakistan or a Bangladesh. But there is no such thing as a free lunch. Saudi oil and cash came with Wahhabi mullahs and curricula. Even Iran jumped into the donation spree, knowing that in the subcontinent lay the world's second-largest Shia population. Iranian cash came wrapped in militant Shia ideology.

Putting things in statistical context had always helped me. Muslims are a quarter of humanity. Six in ten Muslims live in Asia and not in Arab countries, which, including the often-forgotten North African countries like Algeria and Morocco, only get 20 percent of the global Muslim population. Ten to 13 percent are Shia Muslims and 87 to 90 are Sunni Muslims. Egypt is the only Arab nation that appears on the top-ten list of countries with the most Muslims. By 2050, India will be the country with the world's largest Muslim population. And yes, they will live within a majority-Hindu country. Is Eurabia a real threat? When you believe ludicrous statements like Germany has more Muslims than Lebanon, it can be. But Lebanon has fewer than 5 million people and only 55 percent of them are Muslim. Germany has 81 million people and in 2010 had 4.8 million Muslims. Only one in five Muslims lives in a non-Muslim country. Most important, two-thirds of the world's Muslims live in ten of the world's poorest nations. The tiniest fraction of these Muslim numbers lives in Europe. Of them, an infinitesimal number believes in driving trucks into celebratory crowds in Nice or Berlin.

Most Shias (between 68 and 80 percent) live in four countries: Iran, Pakistan, India, and Iraq. Iran has 70 million Shias; the rest are split between India, Pakistan, Bahrain, and Iraq. India and Iraq have almost similar Shia numbers. Iran's 70 million Shias constitute 40 percent of the world's Shia population. With the world's second-largest Shia population, India follows Iran. At number three is Pakistan with a sizeable 40 million. They are always the targets of violent Pakistani Wahhabism.

It's important to note that India has more Shias than Pakistan. This leads some to talk of the fortunate diversity of Islam—a statistical possibility, they say, only in this majority-Hindu nation, the world's largest democracy. In comparison, the US will remain majority white until 2043—interestingly, a year when Islam will become Ireland's second religion. Using the above, Muslim "rationalists" say Islam can be seen as decades ahead of the West. But they conveniently forget to mention that next to Islam's variety lies treacherous sectarianism, intolerance, and violence. Islamophobes are right that in countries like Saudi Arabia, Christians and Jews cannot openly pray. But Muslims can be sure they are surveilled in India, Europe, and the US.

Ghalib had another report about Islamic sectarianism for a talk he was going to give at New Delhi's rusty relic of the Raj called the IIC.

"I wish people would realize the greatest violence in the world is Muslim killing Muslim," I said to Ghalib. "I wish they did the math with due diligence."

"The streets of our cities flow with Shia and Sunni savagery," he replied.

For many Muslims, the oil-rich Saudi Arabia of the seventies was paradise. The desperately poor rushed to work, finding plenty of jobs, everything from being chauffeurs to construction workers and toilet cleaners. An entire nation with modern infrastructure including roads needed to be built. Saudis would never do this kind of lowly work—these were their Mexicans. The eastern, oil-boom flood came from India, Pakistan, Bangladesh, and Southeast Asia. From its west, Egyptians, Syrians, and Palestinians poured in. They raised entire families and returned home as devout soldiers of ibn Wahhab. Their women were sheathed in abayas and burqas, and their girls could now be married at puberty. This Islam was their legacy. In the twenty-first century, the Islamic charity network with its Saudi roots came to Pakistan's rescue repeatedly. The massive earthquake in 2005 and the floods of the year Osama was killed were proof.

"Not all that money went to survivors," said Ghalib. In reality a lot of that aid money was actually funneled to extremist groups that targeted India and the West with the support of Pakistan's Mossad, RAW (Research and Analysis Wing).

The fourth- and fifth-century Buddhas of Bamiyan were famously dynamited by the Taliban a few months before the West became the target of their al-Qaeda brothers. Immeasurable historic legacy was lost at the orders of Osama bin Laden's host and cohort, Mullah Mohammed Omar. He was fast turning the clock in Afghanistan back to the seventh century with beheadings, lashings, and limb chopping. The Buddhas were idols; destroying them was sunnah; the Prophet had done the same to the idols in the Kaaba. The irredentism of the Taliban and al-Qaeda was picked up by Daesh. The syncretic Islam of the region was dying. Any idols, including the graves of saints that had the misfortune of crossing paths with these marauders, had to be destroyed. The violence that the Urdu Deobandi Islam sanctioned for the Taliban was built upon the Arabic logic of al-Qaeda.

Ghalib and I also discussed Dr. Zakir Naik, a famous Indian Wahhabi zealot.

"I interviewed the bastard," Ghalib said. "As expected, he made no sense."

"Oh, boy, really? Because his YouTube lectures make a great deal of sense if you are his kind of person. He is very glib," I replied.

Like the extremist group, *Ahl e Hadith* ("People of the Hadith"), Zakir Naik had a long untrimmed beard and did not seem to prefer a mustache. In this, he was perverting Prophetic couture. His television channel, Peace TV, which had ratings in the millions, was banned. So he found love greater than he could imagine on YouTube. Naik spoke with Wahhabi piety. It was rumored that he had said all Muslims should be terrorists (I never found the video to prove it). He had claimed that George W. Bush engineered 9/11, and he openly advocated the death penalty for homosexuality and apostasy. India is proud of its constitutional freedom of speech, so the government allowed his other activities, including sermons in front of large audiences, and his YouTube sound-bites proliferated. Naik had huge audiences and did town-hall-style Q&As in which he opined on pretty much anything he was asked. Immensely popular in Pakistan as well, he was an Indian Joel Osteen, though his dogma would be very unchristian to most in the West.

As a delicious meal of biriyani was discreetly served, we discussed things we had spoken about before. "Let's switch to English," Ghalib said, sensibly. Our conversation was a charged one in the context we were in. Servants in India, while common, were no longer as servile as they had once been. Socialites in posh neighborhoods like Golf Links where *phirangis* ("foreigners") stayed still bitched about how hard it was to find any who stayed. It was obvious. Why scrub floors when you can work for a call center or deliver pizzas to the world's largest middle class? It was a nationwide "problem."

"These innumerable charities and groups are like cancers that have spread throughout the body of the nation," Ghalib said. He strangely foreshadowed the infamous characterization of Islam itself as a "cancer" and "not a religion" by Trump's short-lived appointee for the National Security Advisor, General Mike Flynn (a man of lies just like his master). Neither of us knew that in the next three years the world would turn upside down with just one election.

At the time, sometimes armed with almost $100 million split among violent jihadi groups, the "charities" targeted the poorest families. Violent jihad is what many of them drilled into the bobbing-up-and-down children's heads of the kind I had seen in Deoband and later Nadhwa. Under their governments' noses, in South Asia, money from these worldwide pots of zakat reached the hardline *maulanas* of local mosques who were very involved in the recruiting at ground level. A maulana was a respected religious leader, whose clout was earned with degrees from a *Dar-ul-Uloom* (literally, "House of Knowledge"). He knew both *kalam* (scholastic theology) and *fiqh* (jurisprudence). The derogatory "mullahs," on the other hand, were seen as rabble-rousers.

The best age to "catch" future soldiers of "the jihad" was between eight and fifteen. The trajectory was always the same, nurture and indoctrinate them till their late teens, then send them to the teeming terrorist "boot camps." It is here that they finally learned how to use AK-47s and newer assault weapons and hand grenades. For those *mujahideen*, it was Christmas all year round.

"So they still always target multiple-child families? Low income, poor-yield crops, and no access to 'real' education or jobs at call centers or delivering pizzas in Lahore?" I said. Ghalib nodded. Initial "identification" of potential recruits was done by the maulanas themselves, often accompanied by visitors from terrorist groups that had political fronts.

A maulana would arrive at the doorstep of a poor family saying their "condition" (poverty) was directly proportional to their un-Wahhabi actions, from visiting Sufi shrines for blessings or even listening to local Sufi peers, thus becoming one with the shirk of the idolators. These traditions went back generations, but a visit from a maulana was a huge honor. He would typically say that the fastest way to earn "God's favor" again was to devote the lives of one or two of their sons to Islam. They already knew the family's demographics. Muslim families tended to produce multiple offspring, so they were ripe for plucking. The maulana over cups of chai (the downtrodden are always hospitable) promised to educate the boys at his *madrassa* (school) and later find them work in "Islam's service."

A few weeks later, a second visit followed with a more ominous agenda. *Shahadat*, or martyrdom, was discussed. In the unlikely event that a son was "martyred" (they never used the words "death" or "killed"), there would be instant salvation not just for the son but for the family as well—in this life and in heaven. They moved between the celestial and the real world with ease. Each son had a price (obviously), all cash. The family was to receive compensation for their "sacrifice" to Islam. By the early 2000s, the going rate for a male child was about 500,000 Pakistani or Indian rupees (approximately $6,000 US). This was big money for the impoverished. Few families would refuse it. Plus, they got bragging rights that their sons were committed to the "cause" of Islam. Un-contextualized Quranic verses were often thrown about by the maulana in the recruitment process.

In the last few years, maulanas have also started recruiting young girls, which by its very nature, in a very patriarchal process, is messy and often involves child marriage.

The mood was somber as Ghalib lingered over his new peg of whiskey. "It never stops, does it?" I said.

"Their success is directly proportional to how poor the family is," he said.

We both knew that Pakistani and Indian RAW claimed they "watched" the larger urban madrassas. The Wahhabis knew how to outsmart them by keeping madrassas small, at less than 100 students. The indoctrinated children were left with almost no contact with the outside world. Videos of cowboy-style Daesh is what they now get as entertainment. In an earlier time, it was the less-sleek al-Qaeda videos. This was not a social-media universe with laptops and smartphones. But it was getting harder to ignore the power of the social web. This was not a "Grand Theft Auto" world equipped with Xboxes, either. But it was catching up. Both Nadhwa and Deoband, like many Pakistani counterparts, had websites. The curriculum was always Wahhabi. The Shia were not Muslim, just like the Hindus, Jews, and Christians, and it would take violent jihad to obliterate them. Democracy, Pakistani or Indian or Bangladeshi-style, was the enemy in a world where "Dar al-Islam" was the desired state. The recruiting maulana often visited the families who had offered their children, singing the praises of the progress they had made. Graduates often had two choices: become minor clerics themselves, of the kind I had met at Nadhwa, or go to local jihad boot camps. The latter was decided by the teachers, who carefully monitored a child's ability to engage in violence and an acceptance of "jihadi" culture.

"The real boot camps are in the FATA or the NWFP," said Ghalib. The former was the acronym for Pakistan's lawless "Federally Administered Tribal Areas," and the latter for the "North West Frontier Province," where Peshawar, a key city on the terror silk route, was located.

Successive Pakistani "governments" had done little about this. In India, the problem, though present, was not as widespread. Zia-ul-Haq, who was killed in a plane crash (which in rumor-rich Pakistan was "deliberate") had done his ungodly work carefully—the Pakistani bureaucracy is filled with his appointees, who remain sympathetic to these organizations and to militant Islam.

"Not an accident, Ghalib, that Osama bin Laden spent his last years living in Abbottabad right under the noses of that Pakistan Military Academy compound," I said as we parted that night.

"Be careful, Parvez. Even though we didn't speak much about it, I know the kind of work you are doing. It can have consequences, especially in this part of the world. When are you getting your US citizenship?" he asked, giving me a hug. I said it was at least a year away.

I was no stranger to fatwas calling for my death. But his words stayed with me as I was chauffeured back to my hotel on that chilly Delhi night, three years after my Hajj.

CHAPTER 12

ISLAM 3.0

After our Hajj 1432, as Shahinaz and I hugged tearfully, we knew the immensity of the dangers we had overcome. Even our hugging at Jeddah's King Abdulaziz airport was forbidden! By then we couldn't have cared less about the mutaween. Thousands of departing pilgrims were armed with gallons of Zamzam water and King Abdullah waved bye-bye from banners. It was as if the Saudis were eager to get rid of us.

"And who wouldn't?" texted Adham with his familiar sarcasm. "Now we have to go and clean the mess you all made in Mecca. Yuck!" This journey had changed me forever in ways I wouldn't understand for many years.

I texted Adham back, this time seriously, "Muslims leave Mecca, but Mecca never leaves them."

"I hope Hajj teaches you no more melodrama ;-)," he replied.

Young Wahhabis passed out flashy pink booklets of propaganda with titles like *The Life, Teachings, and Influence of Muhammad ibn Abdul-Wahhab*. Did they know putting a pink tint on the Kaaba might not be a good idea? Such books printed in all the languages Muslims speak exist in an infinite number of mosques worldwide. This was Saudi da'wa in action. They export Wahhabi Islam without raising a single saber.

During my thirteen-hour flight, I fully caught up with the Kardashians. It seemed that Kim was trying desperately hard to make another baby. Khloe and Lamar were headed to splitsville, Scott was back in rehab, and Saint was merely a glimmer in Kanye's eye.

My Pakistani cab driver cruised up the West Side Highway toward Harlem. A recording of the Quran droned from his stereo. A decorative disc dangled from his rearview mirror. I leaned forward for a closer look. Etched in its surface was the Kaaba. The stereo called out, "Pilgrimage thereto is a duty men owe to Allah, those who can afford the journey; but if any deny faith, Allah stands not in need of any of His creatures."

We passed a halal food cart on Sixth Avenue. It felt reassuring. I was getting home. Manhattan's "halal" food carts are now ubiquitous. I have always talked to their mostly Arab workers and wondered if their purveyors know that the "music" they play from their carts is nothing but Quranic recitations and that halal is just the Muslim equivalent of kosher.

The reciter was intoning from the third Surah of the Quran (*Al Imran*, or "The House of Imran") and its 97th verse. The *qari* (a Quranic reciter who follows the rules of recitation called *tajwid*) had a particularly beautiful voice.

I couldn't believe the serendipity. "I've just returned from my Hajj," I told my cab driver.

He turned around. "No way! I want to go so badly. I have been saving my whole life." I could hear the deep yearning in his voice. The name displayed on his ID tag was Muhammad Pervez.

"*Mashallah!*" he said, using an exclamation used by Muslims upon hearing good news. "What was it like?" I told him I shared his name.

"Oh, it was wonderful. A once-in-a-lifetime experience, so to speak."

He laughed. I rhapsodized at length. I deliberately omitted all of the garbage, the pickpocketing, the inequality—I accentuated the positive, just as my elders returning from Hajj used to do. The darker sides of the Saudi-controlled pilgrimage couldn't be told.

"How much did it cost you?" he asked.

"For me and a friend—we paid around $12,000, but that includes everything."

"Oh," he said. There were practically tears in his eyes. "I could never afford it. Surely there are cheaper ways?"

"I'm sure," I said. "The Hajj is meant for all."

"Listen, this is not an accident that I am in your cab and we share the same name. You are being called by Allah," I added.

"I always keep it in my heart," he said, guardedly revealing a life-long quest.

"Where do you pray?" I asked Pervez as he unloaded my bags.

"96th Street Mosque," he said.

"Maybe I'll see you there one day. I try and go every Friday, and maybe after Hajj now there will be new rigor and discipline."

"Inshallah."

I started walking toward the front door of my building when I turned back. "What day and year is it? I've been living in Mecca time, where it's 1432."

He laughed and told me. As tip, I gave him $40, all the cash I had. It was an action of zakat, I told myself.

When I reached my apartment, Keith and I embraced tearfully. Then we lay down and just spooned for hours silently. I wasn't able to describe my experience to him, and he didn't push me to. We'd been together for long enough to reach the stage of nonverbal communication taking precedence over the empty chatter new couples feel compelled to engage in. It was enough simply to be in each other's arms.

I had returned just in time for Thanksgiving. Keith cooked all day to prepare an elaborate feast. I understand Thanksgiving's violent roots, but it is such a uniquely American, nonsectarian celebration of pluralism. All Muslim and most Hindu festivals I'd experienced growing up were religious. But the turkey gets even avowed atheists like Keith to reflect on their lives and their gratitude in a way that you don't normally see outside of a mosque, church, or synagogue.

Our Thanksgiving table included a gay Hindu man, a transgender man from Berlin, his French girlfriend, and a black woman—Harlem-born and bred. We went around the table and gave thanks.

My Harlem friend had a terrific sense of humor. "Today I am grateful for the silent majority that kept my favorite Kenyan-born, socialist Muslim in office!" She offered me a glass of wine.

"I don't drink anymore," I said.

"Oh, that's what Saudi Arabia does to people, does it?" she joked. "What else did you change?"

"So much," I said. "And yet so little."

"Well, it definitely made you skinny. Hajj diet people! Hajj diet! Move over, Atkins, South Beach, and all the other blah blahs!" she exclaimed. There was mirth and gratitude at our table that night.

I had learned a lot in Saudi Arabia. And with all the years of study and real work, I felt I had *finally won* the right to sit at the table of Islam's ongoing reformation, forced upon it by 9/11. This is important. Islam didn't ask for a twenty-first century reformation. It's been forced to embrace one because of 9/11 and more. Post-Hajj, I can confidently say that the legacy of Saudi Arabia and Wahhab seen in history's vast moral arc will be destructive. And unfortunately the dogma (whatever you call it, Salafi or Wahhabi) has been more successful than oil in being the biggest Saudi export. Very few mosques in the world remain untouched.

Muhammad's legacy has been annihilated. Getting my hands dirty in many Muslim nations, living, studying, and filming with the most religious within my faith I believe gives me the authority to be one of those reformers. Wahhabi mindsets drool at ijtihad as a continuing tradition. But allowing Muslim pundits amongst us—let's say those in the West—to erroneously offer ijtihad as a solution would be a historical mistake.

How can it be a solution, in fact, when an ijtihad-loving Deoband issues illogical Wahhabi fatwas such as "all photography is un-Islamic" (2013)? Or that a family surviving on the earnings of a woman was un-Islamic, and that men and women should not work together (2010)? In modern India? Impossible.

The biggest problems in the Muslim "worlds," as I discussed with Ghalib, are illiteracy and poverty. Standard modern education is unavailable to the majority. And what's available in places like Nadhwa doesn't produce mujtahids—sharia-compliant scholars using independent reasoning (ijtihad). Does just being a gender-studies major lead to paying jobs? No. Nadhwa graduates face the same fate. Jobs for the ones not on their way to jihadist camps are pretty much impossible.

Therefore, for Islam's majority, their mujtahids are Wahhabi. Most are dangerous. And it's their style of ijtihad that a Wahhabi or Daesh mind seeks. No one cares about the "gay imam" in South Africa who offered ijtihad as a solution in my first film. I have come to disagree with the conclusion of my own *A Jihad for Love*. I wonder if he has finally learned to engage with world politics or if he is still lost in the Quran?

The House of Saud helped build a global terror network. In 2003, it arrived at the House's own doorstep when bombs exploded in Riyadh, killing thirty-nine. Osama berated the Sauds as un-Islamic in his frequent faxes and later Al Jazeera "interviews." After 9/11, the bin Laden family furiously began undoing any umbilical cord that would connect Osama to them or the House of Saud while shuffling their billions to offshore accounts. But how could they? 9/11 was a recent memory.

In the kingdom, its grand muftis serve at the pleasure of the king and, in return, the Saud monarchy survives only because of Wahhabi religious favor. Abdullah, then king, ordered the infiltration and monitoring of all Islamic charities that existed in his fiefdom and predictably ran to his always-obedient one-eyed grand mufti (Abdul-Aziz ibn Abdullah Al Shaykh), who was also chairman of the senior ulema, to produce a detailed fatwa-on-demand. In part, Al Shaykh said:

> Firstly: The recent developments in the United States, including hijacking planes, terrorizing innocent people, and shedding blood, constitute a form of injustice that cannot be tolerated by Islam, which views them as gross crimes and sinful acts.
>
> Secondly: Any Muslim who is aware of the teachings of his religion and who adheres to the directives of the Holy Quran and the sunnah will never involve himself in such acts, because they will invoke the anger of God Almighty and lead to harm and corruption on Earth.

There was more, including a subtle reference to the media's "defaming" Islam.

Not one Saud or ulema mentioned that fifteen of the nineteen hijackers held Saudi passports.

Saudis like Adham laughed. Had the monarchy forgotten that it had created and funded Osama's jihad? Didn't the Saudis know how much support he and now Daesh had amongst their own?

The nineties' Grand Mufti ibn Baz made jihad-lite fashionable. Young Saudis were encouraged to go for jihad against the Soviets in Afghanistan. They had to learn Islam's "challenges." It was like a semester abroad, and the jihadi-fied returnees strutted around like peacocks in their fatigues and military accoutrements at the Jeddah corniche. Didn't girls love men in uniform? Islam and violence? Never a novelty for the Saudis.

"Jihad of the Sword" is not unfamiliar to most Saudis or me. It has always had discreet support amongst some ordinary Saudis, many scholars, and even within the Saud and bin Laden families. Officially, the Sauds were partners in George W. Bush's "global war of terror." Ties between Dar al Bush and Dar al Saud went way back. Soon after his election and a few months before 9/11, Bush had asked the CIA and FBI to "back off" investigating the bin Ladens and Saudi royals. At the time of writing, Zacarias Moussaoui, the infamous al-Qaeda operative who is under life imprisonment, told lawyers that members of the Saudi royal family, including former intelligence chief Prince Turki al-Faisal Al Saud, "supported" al-Qaeda to carry out its attacks.

I had arrived in Saudi Arabia just a few months after Obama got Osama. Getting rid of the body was urgent. No one in the Obama administration wanted this man to achieve "martyr" status. Did they not realize that for many he was anyway? WikiLeaks has claimed that his body was brought to the US for pathological analysis and then cremated (against Islamic doctrine). Others say he really was dumped off the USS Carl Vinson, wrapped in a shroud and 300 pounds of chains. CIA head honcho Leon Panetta said in his book, "Bin Laden's body was prepared for burial according to Muslim traditions, draped in a white shroud, given final prayers in Arabic, and then placed inside a heavy black bag."

A few Muslim scholars disagreed with how Obama did it. Did they want a funeral procession? Even Amnesty International made the ridiculous claim that since he was found unarmed he should have been taken alive.

It was also a few months after the fires of an Arab Spring were lit. The Shia in the East were predictably protesting and this Hajj season had to be monitored carefully. When I was there, the mutaween were on edge and particularly proliferating. I was often in trouble with them. I had chosen Hajj 2011 deliberately.

In his lifetime Osama bin Laden had learned to detest his home-land, and yet conveniently both he and now Daesh take much of their logic from the Wahhabi Islam that is indistinguishable from the nation of its birth. The abominations of the Wahhabi state continue and often resemble Daesh and what remains of al-Qaeda. Many Saudi tweets said by mid-2015 that the Saudis had beheaded more than twice the number Daesh had. This airing of dirty laundry on Twitter and infuriated the monarchy and its new King Salman, who obdurately proclaims a new era. How? No one knows. His subjects are busy tweeting, the densest user base for Twitter along with Kuwaitis. Some say seven million Sau-dis are users. Do they know that this sophisticated surveillance state, built during the time bin Laden lived there, has moved with time—today policing Twitter, like daily life?

King Salman heads a shaken yet rigid state unlike any other. In Octo-ber 2016, the *New York Times* reported that the long-named Prince Turki bin Saud bin Turki bin Saud al-Kabeer had been executed for murder, probably by beheading. The Al Saud and grand mufti were in warning mode: If we can behead our own blood, a prince, imagine what can happen to an ordinary mortal. It had been four decades since a royal had faced the sword. The fear spread virally. Adham, like other young men, began to wonder if this meant a return to the brutal past. In reality, the brutality had never gone anywhere.

The Al Saud are famously opaque, yet the younger royals continue Instagramming their lavish lives, much like the Kardashians and the Real Housewives of everywhere. Probably the second-most-powerful man in Saudi Arabia is the thirty-one-year-old deputy crown prince Salman, who is the king's son. He sees his path to kingship clearly, while obliterating any power that the first in line to the throne—the diabetic, doddering, fifty-seven-year-old crown prince Nayef—has. Salman has his hands in practically every national matter in the kingdom. Yet his love of objection-able excess led to his purchase of a 440-foot yacht he had spotted while vacationing on the Riviera. This profligate spending does not sit well with the always-tweeting Saudis, who were shocked to learn of its $550 million cost. This is a time when the regimented "clergy" has been ordered to pro-claim frugality. It's an Islamic virtue, they say, and helps the country remain stable in uncertain times. The government has slashed the state budget, frozen government contracts, and cut civil employees' pay at a time of low oil prices. But the Al Saud, as per tradition, never stop shopping.

Even so, if Salman Junior emerges victorious in the collusion-filled palace intrigues, friends like Adham point out how he is seen as a palatable and young choice, as if he were the ascendant Saudi Obama. Salman poses in royal threads on the website of his pet project—Vision 2030. The site claims the project will kill Saudi dependence on oil and save the flailing economy. Big text on the website says, "Our Vision: Saudi Arabia, the heart of the Arab and Islamic worlds, the investment powerhouse, and the hub connecting three continents."

The prince also established an "Entertainment Authority" to placate his majority young subjects with things like comedy shows. Does the future of young Saudi Arabians lie in the hands of this charismatic man in his thirties who purportedly understands them? Will his subjects question what in great part was his decision for the misguided Saudi-Iran proxy war in Yemen? What would he do to hypocritically curb his enormous family's excesses? Princess Maha from the powerful Sudairi wing of the family infamously fled the ultra-luxurious Paris Shangri-La Hotel in the middle of the night to avoid paying a $7.5 million hotel bill.

"Everyone loves him," texted Adham. There are more than 10,000 royals in the kingdom, and depending on rank, each gets his or her share of the depleting moolah.

On October 15, 2016, the *New York Times* reported, "The White House got an early sign of the ascent of the young prince in late 2015, when—breaking protocol—Prince bin Salman delivered a soliloquy about the failures of American foreign policy during a meeting between his father, King Salman, and President Obama."

Saudi tweeters don't tweet against the monarchy or religion, and thus the heavily monitored Twitter is good for the royals. It allows their young subjects to vent, and a Trump-like state of distraction seems to have formed.

Not with the regularity of Trump, but for similar reasons of diversion, King Salman tweets frugally to his couple-of-million followers. Everyone knows about the disappearing petrodollars. And even economists like Adham's well-liked uncle says privately that at least a quarter of the population lives under the poverty line. Surely this number includes the immigrants in servitude? A Saudi version of poverty porn, à la the favelas of the film *City of God*, exists for Hajjis who look for it. My trip into Mecca's fetid by-lanes, like the one I had taken with my almost-trick Muhammad, was proof.

I believe that affluent Saudi youths got used to this peculiar nanny state. Every king threw subsidies at every problem. Most still believe the Al Saud will never let them down.

"We are too lazy for revolution," Adham said.

When the Muslim Brotherhood won Egypt's only real election by a landslide, I was one of the unsurprised few. This Ikhwan was nothing compared to Wahhabi ones, I reasoned. Egypt's demographics are clear: majority poor, illiterate, and thus devout. Their Ikhwan built decades of ingratiation and goodwill amongst these grassroots. For them, at the time, Mohamed Morsi's becoming president was a legit outcome. Moral policing was not number one on their agenda. So Egypt continued to be a kind of Saudi Riviera for those who were not rich enough to rent villas in France. Therefore the annual summer ritual of gaudy and vulgar Saudi excess in Beirut or Cairo has never stopped, even through dictators and revolutions. I have seen both women in "burqinis" and women in full-on abaya floating in the pool of the Four Seasons. Words cannot describe the comicality of a bloated black sack with a human under it in a five-star swimming pool. Yet another example of Saudi patriarchy.

With the oil drying up the House of Saud, try to take some comfort in this: The Hajj economy, at least, is never going away.

Adham had done his bachelor's in Islamic theology, which he said was "convoluted." In 2009, he enrolled in an engineering program at the controversial King Abdullah University of Science and Technology in Jeddah. KAUST made headlines because ikhtilat was halal—a key Twitter igniter. The ikhtilat is just one reason why conservative Saudis stayed away, keeping Saudi enrollment relatively low. In addition, like in Mecca, women at KAUST allegedly don't need to cover their faces. As long as their ungodly hair is covered, it's all halal. But foreign students clamored for admission, imagining degrees from here would lead to high-paying jobs in the region. Meanwhile, a quote from Sheikh Ahmad al-Ghamdi, the puritanical head honcho of Mecca's cruel mutaween, circulated like wildfire, and Adham texted me a link to the report in *Okaz*, the Saudi newspaper version of the *New York Post*.

Ghamdi said ikhtilat should be allowed. There was no need for gender segregation.

"Here comes change!" texted an obviously jubilant Adham. The *Ha'ia* (another name for the religious police) freaked out.

Ghamdi was fired.

But he built his own cult on Twitter and TV. He has at various times said it was OK for women to drive and shops didn't need to shutter at prayer times. He said that in the Prophet's time women rode camels, which was way more provocative than veiled women driving SUVs. Ghamdi is sly, and he, unlike most, knows the loopholes in religious laws that allow him his chutzpah. He is an insider gone rogue. In a July 10, 2016, *New York Times* article, Ghamdhi said about the mutaween: "Often, people were humiliated in inhuman ways, and that humiliation could cause hatred of religion." He said false eyelashes were OK and he appeared on TV with his made-up and facially uncovered wife.

Ghamdi's views are probably shared by the majority in Saudi society and even by the royal family. This man comes from Islam's very heart, Mecca. And perhaps policing morality there actually helped him realize how diverse Islam really is. Still, addressing these matters in public is rare. And his statements forced Salman to put the mutaween in line. But how will someone like Ghamdi make a living now?

Adham sent a picture of a KAUST cinema. "A land of no cinemas now has one. Wahhabi logic?"

"They will keep their mouths shut because the Saud built it," I replied.

Any reform there will be glacial. A strictly government-scrutinized and -patrolled film industry is forming. At least two fiction films, *Wadjda* (2012) and *Barakah Meets Barakah* (2016), have been submitted to the Oscars as "Saudi films." I am proud that my film, *A Sinner in Mecca*, is the world's first foreign-produced documentary set in Mecca and Medina, portraying the Hajj and the country from deep inside, warts and all. It's not a government-approved junket film but an unprecedented guerrilla-style documentary made on an iPhone. This, too, makes me an active participant in the ongoing revolution forced upon Islam after 9/11. Muhammad, though, would not hesitate to say that we live in a time of *jahiliyah* (ignorance). He would quickly realize the biggest problems that ail twenty-first-century Islam are poverty, illiteracy, and joblessness.

Muhammad would have favored what would have shocked suffragettes of decades past: Saudi women finally voted, after getting franchised in 2015. Twenty-one women candidates were even "elected" to municipal office. I put "elected" in quotation marks because in this land of no music, cinemas, or political parties, this sorry attempt at democracy is farcical. In the minds of many Wahhabis, we are still in the three centuries that followed Muhammad's death. Usually, they don't open their mouths when the king periodically pays lip service to reforms and human rights, conditions they have never lived in or understood.

Like every grand mufti, Baz's successor, al Shaykh, is "House of Saud compliant." He famously issued fatwas saying chess was un-Islamic and he banned Pokémon Go, the smartphone virtual-reality game phenomenon, because it was "gambling." Relatively early in his tenure, in 2007 he had aroused universal uproar in the Muslim world by issuing plans to destroy the Prophet's Mosque in Medina, the tombs "around it," and the Green Dome above it. This was perhaps the pamphlet my group leader in Medina had spoken about. Truth is, the Saudis know they dare not touch the dome. Worldwide (imagine more than 1.6 billion outraged Muslims) fitna is assured.

Palestinian extremist Abdullah Azzam, his former Saudi student Osama, and the still-alive Egyptian Ayman al-Zawahiri fathered the deliberately named al-Qaeda. It means "foundation."

They were all influenced by a radical ideology that Egyptian Islamist Syyed Qutb wrote about in his prolific career. Qutb was seen as influenced by a theologian called Hassan al Banna, who fathered the Muslim Brotherhood (*al-Ikhwān al-Muslimūn*), which has no connection to the Daesh-style Ikhwans of today. Regardless, all these men at different points in history have been experts at using the Quran and our canon, producing violent and illogical material.

The success of Daesh, unlike an al-Qaeda of a different time and space, has been its prowess at using the social web. Even in 2011, Daesh couldn't have dreamt of "recruiting" in European capitals from London to Brussels. But, in truth, all it takes is a lonely room, no job, a pre-existing psychopathic mindset, and a laptop. The glossy new mujahideen of this disparate entity the world has taken to calling ISIS or the more sensible Daesh carry

European or even US passports. And because of them, people like me, with my name, my beard, and a still-new US passport, are profiled at airports.

A recent victory, therefore, felt especially sweet. Traveling to Europe and stuck in one of the horrendous TSA lines at JFK, I ended up with a TSA official who recognized me from my film *A Sinner in Mecca*. I was flabbergasted as he said how much he loved the film, which he found while zipping through Netflix.

"You are a brave man, sir," he said and directed me to the TSA Pre-Check line, where you zoom through security and don't have to take your shoes off. I still wish I had taken a selfie with him. His nametag said "Julio," so I imagined he was Latino.

With each issue of *Dabiq*, Daesh's very own *Vanity Fair*, becoming sleeker, and every HD beheading or thrusting off a building uploaded on YouTube, Daesh are empowered almost daily to be the spokespersons for Islam, and I can understand why this leads to Islamophobia. The world's richest and most influential (Wahhabi) Muslim ideology from Saudi sands has done the gravest harm to modern Islam. The West is seeing its macabre consequences, sponsored by the Kingdom of Saudi Arabia.

As the "Christian West" (misleadingly) cowered, the filmmaking and typesetting skills of the uber-savvy media arms of Daesh only got stronger. *Dabiq* spawned a new, shorter, sharper, and more "global" online rag called *Rumiyah*. TV pundits quoted from it: "Mow the infidel down like grass." The Islam supremacist logic of Daesh remained. The videos, too, got sleeker—a particular one of two Turkish "soldiers" being burnt to death stuck with me. This was cinematic. There were clearly multiple cameras and cinematic concepts like cutaways and pull-focus used. The jittery, low-res shakiness of handheld phone shots was gone. The very latest in directorial skill and technology was being deployed.

"Rumiyah" was no accident. It meant Rome. This new rag, notably published in many more languages, titled itself (*Dabiq*-style) on obscure logic. Daesh's "media arm" Al-Hayat Media Center (named after the region's biggest newspaper) had dug up some questionable Islamic prophecy from the fifteenth century. It said Rome—and, by extension, the West—would fall after the Muslims took Constantinople and presumably restored the glory of the long dead Ottoman Caliphate. The idea of Christendom (the Vatican-containing Rome) being Dar al-Harb (House of War) suits the Muslim supremacists of Daesh just fine. Christianity at war with Islam?

Tried, tested, trusted, and thus dusted from historic obscurity into being front and center, on stages built by either Al-Hayat or the Trump White House.

Al-Qaeda had always been obsessed with Bollywood-style spectacle. How many can you kill and how (3,000 had perished in a hundred minutes on 9/11, the visual component the planet lived horrifically on live TV). Trucks driving into crowds would never replicate that spectacle. But for a historic minute, it did seem Daesh just wanted massacre, never mind the optics. Massacres of Muslims right up to current times no doubt get less or no airtime in the West.

The secretive monarchy though seems to get stronger: The Wahhabization of the planet is complete and Salman deceptively claims a great non-oil-related economic future. Just like Trump, they have no problem lying shamelessly. In June 2016, Twitter founder Jack Dorsey met with a high-level Saudi prince visiting New York. It was hardly a courtesy visit. Prince Alwaleed bin Talal, the forty-first richest man in the world according to *Forbes* magazine, owns much more of Twitter than Dorsey does. Talal is at 5.2 percent and Dorsey is a poor third at 3.2 percent. The latter was being obsequious out of necessity. Talal had been public about his desire to see the newly re-minted Dorsey replaced. And this cruel irony had brought one of America's greatest innovators to his knees in front of a corrupt Saudi prince. He needed to keep his job.

"The Sauds probably run the damn thing by now!" I texted Adham, who predictably had no idea of the Al Saud-Twitter connection. In the meantime, millions of ordinary Saudis, princes and princesses, the king, and crucially the ulema (religious scholars) fight for space in the Saudi Twitterverse. Following their traffic is critical.

These are times of social-web sheikhs and Twitter fatwas. Saudi Wahhabi cleric Mohammed al Arefe claims to be the most influential Arab Islamist ever with more than 15 million followers on Twitter. Some of Arefe's Twitter fatwas are bizarre, many dangerous. About the always red-hot topic of women driving, Arefe tweeted it was wrong because it would lead to more accidents. He must have missed the memo that statistically Saudis are amongst the world's worst drivers. He said it was OK for husbands to "Quranically" beat their wives, but the "beatings should be light and not make her face ugly." Many followers were not amused. "How," I texted

Adham after the beatings-fatwa tweet, "is this man allowed to even exist in this century? Why do people follow him?"

"You have no idea how many people love him." Adham said, adding that what his friends really needed was legal ikhtilat, not "this joker Arefe." They are "at breaking point," he said. The cruelly enforced Saudi misogyny makes modern Iran, where women drive and run in elections, feel like a paradise.

Other powerful Twitter sheikhs include Nasser al-Omar (1.8 million followers) and Saud al-Shureem (1.25 million followers). Each one of them can be rabble rousers and some, like Arefe, are.

Arefe once tweeted at the Emirati music diva Ahlam, asking her to become pious and use her fame to preach Islam since Ramadan was approaching. She politely refused. Gulf newspapers quoted Arefe at a conference, "The Shia are nonbelievers who must be killed." Arefe survives because he says things the Al Saud want to but cannot.

But profound perversion also lives within the religious establishment. TV preacher Fayhan al Ghamdi raped, tortured, and killed his five-year-old daughter Lama in 2012. He paid more than a million Saudi riyal to Lama's already divorced Egyptian mother as blood money. The barbarian was released. The hashtag #AnaLama (#IAmLama) proliferated and died. The beheading-needing Ghamdi is alive.

For me, the voice of Amr Khaled, the idolized Egyptian televangelist, held in high esteem by millions, with more than 7 million Twitter followers, had more promise. He was one of *Time* magazine's 100 most influential people and was the sheikh of *rawshaha* (hip and cool) who unimaginably made religion "fun."

Meanwhile in Saud-land, a newly moderate, sixty-year-old Sheikh called Salman al-Ouda is closing in on Arefe with 10 million followers. Ouda is also director of the popular, some say extremist, *Islam Today* website. He was once admired and quoted by Osama bin Laden and he returned the favor. In the nineties, the Sauds had imprisoned him for five years after he publicly attacked them for hosting infidels (American troops). Later, he did a 180, scolding Osama in a famously melodramatic "letter" broadcast by MBC (Saudi State TV):

> My brother Osama, how much blood has been spilt? How many
> innocent people, children, elderly, and women have been killed . . .

in the name of al-Qaeda? Will you be happy to meet God Almighty carrying the burden of these hundreds of thousands or millions of victims on your back?

Notably, Ouda was still calling Osama a brother though this was the perfect moment for takfir.

In 2016, Ouda allegedly spoke to a Swedish reporter. The story got picked up by CNN Arabic, *Huffington Post,* and more. It was the stuff of sensation. Ouda allegedly said, "Even though homosexuality is considered a sin in all the Semitic holy books, it does not require any punishment in this world." Alluding to Daesh, he added, "By condemning homosexuals to death, they are committing a graver sin than homosexuality itself. Even though homosexuality does not distance oneself from Islam, Islam does not encourage individuals who have same-sex attraction to show their feelings in public." He added, "homosexuality doesn't mean a person is not a Muslim."

There followed a Twitter storm in the majority-homophobic Middle East. Ouda was cleverly killing his two birds, Wahhabis and Daesh (which is busy pushing homosexuals to their deaths) with one (homosexual) stone.

"A former hero of Osama bin Laden saying homos are OK! Is this possible?" I texted Adham.

"If this is true, Parvez, his words matter," texted Adham.

With Daesh ever close to Saudi borders, Ouda tweets with fanatical zeal against them and extremism. Ouda went on Rotana, a TV channel owned by Prince Talal. A YouTube video of that interview was uploaded on June 21, 2015, in which Ouda said armies and wars were not the solution. Daesh have a strong media presence and use rhetoric that appeals to the uneducated, he said. For the poor masses, said Ouda, Daesh represent victory and power.

My thesis was getting stronger. The Twitter sheikhs proved that Muhammad created not just a spiritual Islam. In many ways (especially with the Medina constitution), Muhammad was also creating a political Islam. The marriage of the two would evolve differently wherever Islam went. Iran loved it. Al Saud fear it.

Adham sent hilarious videos of the Saudi comic-sheikh Amr Khaled in Ahmad al-Shugairi. He is the self-described "Elvis" of televangelists. He has almost 6 million followers and tweets about his bland TV show

Khawater ("Thoughts"). In a 2009 piece about him, the *New York Times* said, "(He) effortlessly mixes deep religious commitment with hip, playful humor."

"Like you call the Kardashians your Xanax . . ." Adham texted.

"And . . . ?"

"That's how I use Khawater!"

Shugairi claims he is interested in spreading the ideas of da'wa and *jihad al-nafs* ("struggle with the self"). The Islam of Khawater is sugar-coated. Lying as comfortably as Trump, Shugairi says he is the "only" nonsectarian Muslim.

These Twitter sheikhs are influential state actors. For cultural cues, Muslims, especially Arabs, have always looked toward India's Bollywood and the music, cinema, and culture of Egypt. For religious cues, they sadly emulate their Wahhabi clerics. The Saudi Project of the export of its Wahhabism is clearly bigger than its oil exports.

In comparison, Egypt, with its relatively low Twitter population, produces modern Islamic leaders like Islam Behery, whom Egypt's newest dictator, Abdel Fattah el-Sisi, sentenced to one year in prison in 2015 for "contempt of religion." Behery's TV show was cancelled but not his voice. He was released in six months and said, sarcastically, "Many thanks to President Sisi and his religious revolution . . . I am thankful for freedom of expression in Egypt." He remains an open critic of many hadith quoted in *Sahih Bukhari* among much else that needs to change in Islam. A Behery in Saudi would be sentenced to death, probably by the preferred public beheading.

By 2013 I had started taking Daesh very seriously. It made sense that my time in Saudi Arabia had a sense of premonition, of the coming plague. Muslims like me tuned in to all the chatter on the Arab, Persian, and Urdu social webs. I perused the sleek issue of Dabiq magazine. Its cover showed Shia mourners at Karbala. The title said, "The Rafidah: From Ibn Saba' to the Dajjal." That title made perfect sense with the accompanying picture. Karbala in Iraq is the second-holiest city for Shia, the scene of the momentous Battle of Karbala. It claimed the life of Shia Islam's most revered imam, Husayn. It's always been a Sunni target. The pejorative Rafidah (for Shia) are enemies for Daesh and Wahhabi alike. Ibn Saba is the name of a seventh-century Yemeni Jewish convert to Islam, and Dajjal is the Antichrist.

There is historic logic to *Dabiq*, the Daesh magazine title. Dabiq is a humble little town in the north of Syria. Most maps don't include it and Daesh is close to losing it, and thus the need for a Rumiyah to eventually replace Dabiq. Some Wahhabi eschatology believes that this will be the location of the final "end of days" battle between "forces of Islam" and the "forces of 'Rome.'" Daesh claims Quranic validity to this obscure if real mention and Rome for them represents the "armies of Christianity and America." Page one warns the rag will "also contain photo reports, current events, and informative articles on matters relating to the Islamic State."

These barbarians are masters at using the social web, and also graphic design, cinematography, typesetting, video editing, and photography. Final Cut Pro, Vimeo, WeTransfer, and Google Docs are probably used, too. *Dabiq* editors and content producers could be sitting anywhere in the world, even America, using free IP address–changing apps like TunnelBear.

With perilous economic indicators, the endless flow of fully state-funded Saudi students to American schools has ebbed. In addition, their monarchy has not changed its habits. In 2015, the usual Saud gravestone annihilators did a hypocritical about-face and remodeled the grave of ibn Wahhab in Diriyah, a suburb of Riyadh, now a tiny Muslim Disneyland with three museums, of which one was solely dedicated to Wahhab. These paragons of no-shirk virtue were hoping no one would notice. Adham sent me pictures. To me it looked like a theme park of terrorism.

At this point, 90 percent or more of Islamic history has been bull-dozed. Because it was yet another construction site in dug-up, crane-filled Mecca, I didn't realize I had witnessed the aftermath of the destruction of the home of an important *Sahaba* (companion) of the Prophet called Abu Bakr, reduced to rubble for a new Hilton hotel—allegedly the world's largest hotel. More destruction. The bill will be $3.5 billion. Anything that is antediluvian is destructible in Wahhabi-sanctioned bin Laden hands.

This Hilton was going to be called the Abraj Kudai, not far from the Abraj al-Bayt with its Starbucks where I once prayed and hung out. Paris Hilton had joined the nouveau riche melee, opening a store in Mecca Mall, which she had tweeted a picture of, saying, "Loving my beautiful new store that just opened at Mecca Mall in Saudi Arabia!"

Cranes busily sifting centuries of sand, oblivious to what might lie beneath, had filled the site even when I was there. Rumors had it that the Saudis were commissioning 10,000 rooms, a helipad, many malls, and more than fifty restaurants. It would include twelve towers, "royal suites," a "convention center," and "prayer rooms." The bin Ladens of 2016 had gained even more power. They still held the contracts for the continuing $21 billion expansion of the Masjid al-Haram, the "Haramain" high-speed rail-rink, which was open in Saudi-style apartheid only to Arab citizens of the Gulf Cooperation Council in 2011, and the contract for the "world's tallest building," the other Kingdom Tower in Jeddah.

The vulgar excess of the Al Saud has always been transformed into reality by the bin Ladens.

Adham explained a new malaise, "Waithood," often also a hashtag. Getting wives was impossible. Parents demanded larger *mehr* (dowry) for their educated daughters. More women than men have been abroad to get their hard-fought degrees. Costs of weddings and new homes are astronomical.

"I just wish you could have gotten out of Mecca and Medina," Adham said, adding, "You would find so much more material here in Jeddah. I could have introduced you to all the angry, young, and broke Saudis you want—tayyib as many! And they love to talk and tweet all the fucking time. There's even a couple of cool graffiti guys. We have our own Banksy of Jeddah! Have you seen the 'No Woman, No Drive' video?"

"What was I to do?" I replied. "They took our passports away."

"Can we have two tickets for *Jihad* please?"

Two older men were at the ticket booth of the IFC Cinema in New York's West Village. My film *A Jihad for Love* played to usually packed houses for five weeks at this movie theater in the summer of 2008. In the late afternoons, I would often hang out around the box office to see how many people were there for the film. I was overjoyed when audience members said just "*Jihad*" while buying tickets. By putting jihad and love together, had we made a dent in Islamophobia? Even a little bit mattered.

I was taking away the horror of jihad's other Islamic definition when I answered journalists everywhere, "In the Quran, jihad is understood as a struggle with the self in a path towards God." My film company was called Halal Films, because in my deepest self, I believe Muhammad would approve of what I had done. And *halal* literally meant permissible, the opposite of *haram* (if it was being used and pronounced as "forbidden"). Years later I would call the film company for *A Sinner in Mecca* Haram Films, using the word with its other (more important) meaning, "noble sanctuary."

At the end of *Jihad*, Zahir, the gay imam, conducted a PowerPoint workshop for about fifteen "straight," "devout," Muslim social workers in Cape Town. Debating Quranic semantics, they were mere drops in Islam's vast oceans of "homophobia." His solution to what I call the "problem of homosexuality" was ijtihad, and he got the last word in *A Jihad for Love*. I have now come to disagree with his logic.

Knowing what I know now, I would also not dismiss jihad so easily, and I would not say "in the Quran" but "in Islamic exegesis." I started to study my religion with adult vigor only in the mid-nineties. I began with what would become a heavily dog-eared copy of Yusuf Ali's translation of the Quran, full of marginalia in my bad cursive. It traveled with me to KSA. Most Muslims I knew then would say jihad was a Quranic calling to strive as a better Muslim. But the other jihad, only to be used in self-defense, does exist both in and out of context. As Muslims, it is our responsibility to acknowledge both kinds. Quranically, violent jihad is often the last option. But the Quran sometimes seems to sit on the precarious wall between an offensive vs. defensive jihad.

If a Daesh terrorist sat across from me, I would use the verse below. The problem is that he could find one for his argument, too. *Al-Hajj* ("The Hajj") 22:78 partly says:

> *And strive in His cause as ye ought to strive (with sincerity and under discipline). He has chosen you, and has imposed no difficulties on you in religion; it is the cult of your father Ibrahim. It is He Who has named you Muslims, both before and in this (Revelation).*

The Arabic word *jihad* as "strive in His cause" subsumes striving in the way of God entirely in this chapter above. I know it is dangerous to parse the Quran. But if Daesh and backward imams worldwide are doing it, so can we.

In Ayah 39 of the same chapter, God gave the Sahaba, then refugees to Yathrib (Medina), permission to fight back. This, again, for some
scholars is a nod toward the pacifism they claim is inherent in the Quran.
War is sanctioned only in self-defense, they say, quoting 22:39: "To those
against whom war is made, permission is given (to fight), because they are
wronged and verily, Allah is most powerful for their aid."

Many say that the Quran revealed the importance of this principle to
Muhammad. Surah 3, Ayah 159 (*Al Imran*, "the Family of Imran") says:

It is part of the Mercy of Allah that you dealt gently with them;
Had you been severe or harsh-hearted, they would have broken away
from you: so pass over (their faults), and ask for (Allah's) forgiveness
for them; and consult them in affairs (of moment).

The spoils of war in seventh-century Arabia must have included non-
combatants, women, and children, and the Quran was encouraging dealing
with them "gently." POWs in Vietnam, the Second World War, and even
Iraq have never been dealt with gently.

Was the Quran the best defense for itself? Yes, except for a few
instances where it contradicts itself.

The Quran I had loved today faces grave challenges. Islam apologists
(usually Muslims raised in the West) come equipped with hastily crammed
parts of the Wikipedia canon of Islam. They love to "quote" a cable-ready
fragment from a parsed 2:256 (*Al Baqarah*, "The Cow") verse. I, too, have
used it.

"There is no compulsion in matters of faith, says the Quran," they
quote, smiling benignly. This is the kind of "good Muslim" cable likes
to parade. Are we as Muslims living in the West guilty of not practic-
ing Quranic exegesis? Unfortunately true. In addition, our best efforts are
drowned out by the din of Islamophobia.

Some Islamophobes have done their homework. They point to more
than 100 verses in the Quran that they claim sanction violence. We need
to find a larger number and demolish their arguments verse by verse. Has
the violence inherent in all monotheisms been studied and compared
fairly? It has. But the academy of the West speaks to no one in Deoband,
for example.

Let's try exegesis in verses 190 to 193 of the same second chapter.

2:190 says, "Fight in the cause of Allah those who fight you, but do not transgress limits; for Allah loveth not transgressors."

2:191 says, "And slay them wherever ye catch them, and turn them out from where they have Turned you out; for tumult and oppression are worse than slaughter; but fight them not at the Sacred Mosque, unless they (first) fight you there; but if they fight you, slay them. Such is the reward of those who suppress faith."

2:192 says, "But if they cease, Allah is Oft-forgiving, Most Merciful."

2:193 says, "And fight them on until there is no more Tumult or oppression, and there prevail justice and faith in Allah. But if they cease, let there be no hostility except to those who practice oppression."

This part of the Quran seems to make clear that if there is a fight at all, it should be against the aggressors. A Medinan verse, it must surely allude to a period after Muhammad's Hijra forced by the Quraysh who had devised his gruesome assassination. There is an emphasis on not fighting unless attacked. The same Ayah 191 that uses "slay" as a verb also says, "Tumult and oppression are worse than slaughter."

"Those who suppress faith," also in Ayah 191, refers to the Quraysh and other Bedouin tribes Muhammad had yet to convert, not Jews and Christians, as is wrongfully interpreted. The Quran, Islamophobes need to be told, goes to great lengths to command kinship with the *Ahl al-Kitab* ("The People of the Book"), Jews and Christians.

This messy but poetic book has some answers, not all. But the contradictions of the book and its canon need to be used in its favor. An ideal world would be a Saudi-free curriculum at every school where Muslims learn.

Does Islam have a problem with violence, carried out in its name, using as justification verses from its book, the Quran? Any reasonable Muslim (and I hope I am one) would answer yes.

It seemed I had grown up with a faith of fear. Mecca killed my fear of faith. Post-Hajj I feel a blessing always in propinquity. I was glad that my Hajj was not a product of mere taqlid, or blind following. It was born from a centuries-old, innate Muslim thirst for knowledge. And perhaps it was my solitary attempt to become a mujtahid, even if to a very small extent.

In addition, my thesis that poverty and illiteracy are Islam's biggest problems has never been stronger. I am even able to admit that most Muslims I grew up with would not understand most of this book's content.

Europe is once again home to massacres of the innocents. The carnage in Paris was just five days old, and this particular film festival that had invited me asked if they should go ahead with the screenings. When I said yes, they added two. Sold out every time and long debates afterward.

"Is this a battle of civilizations?" asked a reporter from *Le Monde*.

I told him I couldn't answer him with a soundbite, adding, "But what I can say to you is that I am not willing to make statements like 'Islam is a religion of peace,' because they are reductive."

"So you are saying Islam is not a religion of peace?" he persisted.

"I never said that. You are twisting my words. I said the time to make such reductive statements has run out." I was wearing a "Je Suis Paris" T-shirt, numbers of which were probably being hastily manufactured in Bangladeshi or Chinese sweatshops and sent by shiploads to the West. I wore it thinking it protected me from xenophobia, which is now rampant in contemporary Europe.

I was protecting myself, in my own little way. It was a Friday and I found a dingy little basement mosque to go and perform Zuhr prayers. It was almost empty. I had never been surrounded by fewer than 150 people at any Jummah I ever attended. Did the Daesh suicide bombers realize that they had launched a full on attack on Islam as well? Was this even an organization, or was it open season for any psychopath to find guns, commit massacres, and invoke "ISIS"? Paris disturbed me deeply. It was so hard to buy guns in Europe. Mass murder was gun-obsessed America's expertise.

I was traveling to many EU nations (including what was then pre-Brexit UK) with my film, *A Sinner in Mecca*. Traveling in and out of the US with frequency to Europe, I was detained by US Customs more than once, agents even recalling my checked bags to examine every article of underwear I possessed. I felt violated. Was I racially or religiously profiled? Probably both. Did my new status as a US citizen make me feel safer? Not for a minute.

Fear of Muslim refugees was rampant. At one film screening in Copenhagen, an older gentleman showed up with a sheaf of papers. He had waited to talk to me, so we sat down for a coffee. He waved printouts from a website I knew well called religionofpeace.com. It was an extreme right-wing attempt at molding Islam the way one group saw it: the single biggest threat to humanity. The Islamophobic "David Horowitz Freedom Center" had been incredibly smart to grab the name while it was still available. Why would Islam and peace connect, anyway? Islam's apologists literally fed this website's raison d'être.

I decided to go to a section of his sheaf, "What would Muhammad do?" I took it from him and said, "OK, let's try to look at it reasonably. It says Muhammad would have sex with a nine-year-old girl, behead people, require women to cover their faces, own slaves, marry his daughter-in-law, approve of prostitution, gluttonize, recommend wife-beating, beat his own wife, kill prisoners of war, advocate suicide attacks, tell sick people to cure themselves by drinking camel urine, beat children for not praying, have boys as young as thirteen beheaded, have eleven wives at one time, approve of sex with children, lie, enslave women and children, stone adulterers to death, torture someone out of greed, steal, kill someone for insulting him, extort money from religious minorities, keep women as sex slaves, force conversions to Islam, encourage acts of terror, kill a woman, capture and rape a woman, and encourage the rape of women in front of their husbands! Wow, what a long list!" I said, knowing where I needed to go with him. I asked him if he considered the majority of humanity as reasonable human beings. He replied yes.

"OK, so now let's take Islam. Did you know there are 1.7 billion Muslims? Almost a quarter of humanity is Muslim." He knew.

"OK, let's look a little further into this religion. It has been there for fourteen centuries. It created many worldly empires. It did so much for mathematics. It has always had intellect, arts, poetry, architectural wonder, and so much more." He grudgingly agreed.

I said I wished I had more time but ended by saying, "Let us be in a situation where we take a majority of these contemporary 1.7 billion Muslims as reasonable human beings. If you consider that their faith has survived so long and given so much to the world, then, my friend, nothing on this irrational site would make any sense." I named a few basic books I remembered and asked him to read them instead. I even said he should read *Islam For Dummies*. In him, I had one more reason to believe that future scholars of Islam could rightly claim that the twentieth and twenty-first centuries were a second Islamic jahiliyah. Meanwhile, "Eurabia" fears in this continent were being stoked with renewed vigor. Xenophobia was being normalized. A hijabi woman (now almost the norm in some cities) was becoming a symbol of the oppression, violence, and darkness of Islam. Mere ijtihad was not going to solve this intractable problem.

A film festival in Prague gave me a "guide" for the day. As we strolled the beautifully preserved streets of this ancient capital, she made her feelings clear.

"I saw your film and you are very brave, so don't get me wrong," she said, adding, "We don't want those refugees here. The Czech Republic is a very small country. We need to preserve our values and our social structure." Almost immediately we came across graffiti that said, "Who wants to destroy Europe?" I had seen the very same in German scrawled on a Vienna wall.

I pointed at the graffiti and said gently, even though I was seething inside, "When the poor, the disenfranchised, the homeless, the hungry are literally washing up on the shores of Europe, some dying instantly, is it not the responsibility of the 'civilized' world to look after them?"

Her answer to that was, "Why don't the rich Saudis or the rich Gulf countries take them in? Why should it be us?"

Everywhere I went from Warsaw to Stockholm to Vienna, I seemed to be thrust into the uncomfortable position of speaking for the refugees just because I was Muslim. In hindsight, it is the product of the real xenophobia that walks the streets of the endangered, post-Brexit continent. In these small countries live eerie signs, from right-wing election-winning politicians to increasing numbers of hijab-embracing women. The chauvinistic right has longed for this time. I was exhausted being a Muslim on display, yet I did Q&A after Q&A for my film.

"Do you think your film will promote Islamophobia?"

"How can you defend Islam when all these Muslim refugees bring intolerance and homophobia with them?"

On the latter, I cannot be duplicitous: The majority of Muslims in Europe, either settled or coming in, are presumably homophobic.

"What will happen to our values of freedom, of peace, of equality?" asked another.

I answered, "Well, the Fifth Republic right here in the heart of Western Civilization said it best. *Liberté, égalité, fraternité.* Keep that close to your heart and maybe you will know what to do when a downtrodden refugee shows up at your doorstep."

Daesh "soldiers" have no Quran-study time. They hang at a McDonald's drive-through of Islam, where they pick and choose—an affront to fourteen centuries of learning. I was not surprised when I read reports that copies of *Islam For Dummies* was found in possessions belonging to the bombers in Paris and Brussels. For the ignorant, unemployed, semi-literate "radicals" of this imaginary caliphate, books such as these help cram basics like, "How do Muslims pray?" Replacing pray with prey, in this case, would induce the black humor Adham and I share. On their website, the *Dummies* people say, "*Islam For Dummies* helps you build bridges of understanding between you and your neighbors in the global village." Destroying rather than building bridges is what Daesh clearly prefer. And their "global village" would be the delusory caliphate.

Their "Emir" Abu Bakr al-Baghdadi, the head-honcho of horror, notably said:

> Islam was never a religion of peace. Islam is the religion of fighting.
> No one should believe that the war that we are waging is the war of
> the Islamic State. It is the war of all Muslims, but the Islamic State
> is spearheading it. It is the war of Muslims against infidels. Muslims,
> go to war everywhere. It is the duty of every Muslim.

Even Baghdadi invoked the specious Islam-apologist argument! Any lone ranger can claim allegiance to Daesh with the latter only learning about a new carnage via the media. In addition, unlike in Europe, Daesh recruitment in fortress America protected by the Atlantic has been sparse at best. The pattern is clear. Islam is being invoked to kill innocents. The perpetrators usually possess EU passports and were born and bred in Europe. I used to joke with friends that the UK is now Englandistan. But the time for jokes is over. A Wahhabi extremist like Anjem Choudary wants sharia in the UK, where he was born and raised. He openly praises Daesh. America has its own version in Maryland-based "Imam" Suleiman Anwar Bengharsa.

Men like these are the products of post-colonial mass migrations, where their poor parents or grandparents reliably fled to the countries that had once ruled them—not a historic novelty. They got what are now EU or British passports but little else. Decades of state-sanctioned disenfranchisement followed. Naked and systemic racism prowled the streets in Western Europe where the children of these immigrants went to schools, never colleges, and then grew up with no access to jobs. The glass ceiling in Europe is much lower than in the UK, where the mega-city of London elected a Muslim mayor, Sadiq Khan. But the England that elected Khan also has extremist South Asian Muslim voices like Choudary. Majority atheism was Europe's primary religion for decades. But ironically that very same Europe created a few young Muslims ready to blow themselves up in the name of Daesh. Many never got to meet the (allegedly killed) Baghdadi or had even been outside Europe. Like Trump, Baghdadi needs no recruiters.

Daesh is more than happy to be linked to any terrorist attack. Not being state actors, they behave like the famous hacktivist collective that no government has yet been able to defeat.

Daesh is the Anonymous of Islam.

Islam's war against itself isn't unusual in the history of the religion. But twenty-first-century Islam doesn't possess its historical correctives. It is too late to turn the clock back on worldwide Wahhabi indoctrination.

Some Western scholars have (rightfully) said that combat is ordered only against those who are attacking or killing innocent Muslims or fighting against a Muslim state. Do they know "radical Islamic extremists" use the same argument? The West declared war on Muslim lands like Afghanistan and then Iraq, and therefore "combat" against these "aggressors" is justified, Quranically. Daesh recruitment grows exponentially each time Trump says he won't let Muslims into America.

In classical and Quranic Arabic, the word *fitna* was used to denote trial and affliction. As is common with the many differences between classical and colloquial Arabic, in modern times today, depending on context, the word can mean charm and enchantment. I am interested in its use as a Quranic principle, and have often used it in this book to mean a state of "strife" or "chaos" that is feared by modern-day Arab power structures and invoked often by them, when challenged by people power.

In a very different time (2008), a Dutch politician, Geert Wilders, got worldwide fame with a poorly produced anti-Islam video called *Fitna*. There was precedent. In 2004, a little-known Dutch filmmaker named Theo Van Gogh and his subject, Ayaan Hirsi Ali, had done similar Islam-bashing with their video *Submission*. Van Gogh was savagely murdered and his subject gained instant stardom in the US, writing several books. It was said that she, labeled an infidel, became a paid pawn of the right-wing in the US. To me, the video was distasteful because verses of the Quran were written all over Hirsi's naked body. Cinematically like the former, it offered no particular vision and rudimentary filmic skills.

In 2005, a Danish newspaper published twelve editorial cartoons mocking the Prophet, one even depicting him with a bomb in his turban. I saw those again as a deliberate attempt to create controversy and stoke anger. Islamic aniconism was not a novelty. It had been known for centuries. *Charlie Hebdo,* whose consequences I personally view as a carnage, was using familiar European anti-Muslim provocation. The aftermath was savage, because Daesh is. It is interesting that the most visible "attacks" for "Islam" happened in Europe. An enormous chunk of the Muslim world was rightfully fearful because riots and savage murder could not be condoned. But the idea of a "backward" religion, a trope used against Islam repeatedly, was back in fashion. These "attacks" are seen as "war" in the world of Daesh. Only in these instances do they avoid universal condemnation. But is modern Islam in an almost ceaseless struggle with itself in addition to fitna? Unfortunately, that is true. But to make simplistic statements like "Islam is several centuries behind" reveals a problematic Orientalist mindset. Because historically Islam was always ahead.

Unlike the "glorious" Islamic history of wealth—be it material, physical, or intellectual—today reliable figures are often thrown around at economic conferences saying that half of the world's poor are Muslim. Muslims form a quarter of humanity, and a sizeable majority live in abject poverty. The most poverty-stricken countries on the planet include Sierra Leone, Afghanistan, Cambodia, Somalia, Nigeria, Pakistan, Mozambique, and, importantly, India. So eight of the poorest nations in the world include seven with Muslim majorities. The numbers are really mind-boggling and get worse. I highlight India because by 2050, it will have the world's largest Muslim population and is now at number three. The right-wing Hindutva brigade that rules India today often blames Muslim-poverty statistics similar to these as the reason that "Islam is bringing India down." What will really happen in 2050 when India has the world's highest number of Muslims—who will rule whom?

Almost 800 million of the world's 1.7 billion Muslims are illiterate. More than six in ten cannot read. For the Christian West, literacy is at 78 percent.

In 2009, a very pessimistic assessment of the usually self-satisfied Arabs was offered by the UN's Arab Development Report:

- Half of Arab women cannot read;
- One in five Arabs live on less than $2 per day;
- Only 1 percent of the Arab population has a personal computer, and only half of 1 percent use the Internet;
- Fifteen percent of the Arab workforce is unemployed, and this number could double by 2010;
- The average growth rate of the per capita income during the preceding 20 years in the Arab world was only one-half of 1 percent per annum, worse than anywhere but sub-Saharan Africa.

Statistics can be boring. But they are important. I had always believed that poverty and illiteracy are directly proportional. These statistics are proof. Egypt, the Arab world's most populous and desperately poor nation, is evidence. More than a quarter of almost 82 million Egyptians live in abject poverty. And they were never busy tweeting or updating their statuses on Facebook. They were simply trying to put food on the table. While mobile phone penetration was almost at 100 percent, the vast majority of those phones were not smart and were used only for calls. Only forty-four out of 100 Egyptians even know how to use the Internet or have any access to it. The majority of Muslims live in the once undivided but now three different countries of Pakistan, Bangladesh, and India—in other words, the Indian subcontinent has the world's largest Muslim population. And these three countries have enormously high rates of poverty and illiteracy. Who are the victims of this twin scourge? Muslims. In short, the luxurious hyper-connected Saudis are a rare exception to the average and majority Muslim "condition."

Six in ten Muslims not being able to read? Are they unknowingly disobeying the call to intellect at the heart of Islam? Are they so wretchedly poor that they literally have no choice? Where is the FDR-like figure for Muslims who could lift an entire generation out of poverty? Do Muslims have a right to call out for a pan-Islamic leader who could unite them under Islam's original promises, which include basic dignity and literacy (and also available jobs)?

Poverty and illiteracy, both al-Qaeda and Daesh and many before them had found, were ideal and potent breeding grounds for terror. Islam doesn't need an ijtihad that a quarter of humanity would agree to in this time of ignorance. What it needs are schools and jobs to counter the perverted rhetoric espoused every Friday in millions of mosques, that are *not* in the West. Muslims around the world also need to teach and learn from their very own "millennials," an enormous, ever-growing demographic.

Much happened during the year of *A Sinner in Mecca*'s European tour. The most important was the savagery of the 2015 Paris carnage. Soon after, I took a Thalys train from Amsterdam to Brussels. I was going all the way because two of the national Belgian TV networks needed a "Muslim of the moment" to explain the often inexplicable to their Dutch, French, and German (Flemish) audiences.

For the first TV interview, the anchor asked me how the Hajj changed me.

"How to deal with claustrophobia," I said, laughing. "But more seriously it was a life-transforming journey because in Mecca I killed the part of me that questioned whether Islam would accept me. In its place was the certainty that it was up to me to accept Islam."

"Do you?" he asked.

"Yes, with confidence and on my own terms. Not on the terms of the equally dangerous House of Saud and Daesh."

"Who speaks for Muslims?"

"They speak for themselves. 99.9 percent of Muslims," I told the anchor who was trying to corner me, "are just like you and me. Decent, hard-working people trying to make their lives work, to feed their families." I managed to engage him in a discussion about how Europe really needed to win the ideological battle with Wahhabi Islam. He asked me to stay "after the break."

By now I had done a lot of European press in small European countries. The bloodbath in Brussels was still a few months away, but the city was in complete shutdown because the alleged mastermind of the Paris massacres, Salah Abdelslam, whom his lawyer later famously called an empty ashtray and asshole, had allegedly been found in this city, the home of the ineffectual bureaucracies of the European Union.

I had disembarked into a station with soldiers and canines everywhere. When I got to my hotel a battle tank stood at its entrance. I told them that I was an American filmmaker who had been invited for an interview by a major broadcaster. They searched my backpack and ran some kind of quick background check on my passport. The latter seemed silly because the Belgians and the EU in general were notorious for not sharing intelligence. I asked one of the soldiers if I could have a cigarette before checking in. He turned out to be a fellow smoker and we shared my lighter. Here it was in action: the International League of Nonviolent Smokers, helping each other, as always. Inside, the lone receptionist looked frightened and refused to check me in. The Belgian producer had to be called and thankfully she answered her mobile. I was in.

Later that night, a taxi arrived to drive me to the second TV studio through what I had expected to be a desolate city but was now mired in traffic created by escapee panicked citizens probably expecting a Paris-style terrorist attack. Luckily for them the next day would be off. My Moroccan cab driver complained about Uber. I asked him if he was racially or religiously profiled in "these days."

"What's new about that? That's always been true," he said. He asked me what film I was promoting. I dared not tell him the title.

"Oh, it's a documentary about the Hajj," is what came out of my mouth, and he answered with the expected, "*Alhamdulillah*."

The second TV anchor was obsequious, and expectedly I was asked to opine about the refugees and then Abdelslam. I dutifully did. For this interview, I felt I managed a small victory by saying, "To make illogical statements like Islam is the religion of peace only perpetrates a falsehood. Yes, at least 99 percent of the world's Muslims are not terrorists. But it's that 1 percent or less that we should have saved from what is ultimately Saudi dogma. We didn't. And last I checked Obama and King Salman were still BFFs."

I was hungry that night and the abandoned hotel had no room service or chefs. I walked outside for a cigarette. Thankfully it was the same soldier on duty.

I told him how during previous trips to Brussels I had always "looked for my own people." I described how I had once made my way from Maelbeek metro station to the neighborhood of Molenbeek during Ramadan. They say today that Brussels' "Muslim problem" lives in the suburb of Molenbeek, which is 41 percent Muslim. As its notoriety spread, the *New York Times* even called the neighborhood "The Islamic State of Molenbeek."

I told the soldier about one old pre-terror Ramadan trip. The neighborhood was alive with festivity, lights, and lanterns, shops selling all kinds of Ramadan goodies, and everywhere the smells of Indian and Pakistani spices. Everyone was out and about that night, I told him, because it was *iftaar* (breaking of the fast) time.

"I can even smell those wonderful smells," I said.

"I've been there during Ramadan too," he said. "It has the best shawarma."

Sharing a cigarette with this armed soldier, standing next to a battle tank, and learning he appreciated Molenbeek's shawarma, felt oddly comforting.

Within a few months every single reporter, on the ISIS/IS/ISIL/Daesh beat in the world would learn how to correctly pronounce both Molenbeek and Maelbeek.

Exactly how the West learned to spell, pronounce, and find Afghanistan on a map after a sunny, cloudless September morning in what now seems like a faraway time.

GLOSSARY*†

Abaya: A black, thick, cloak-like garment that women in Saudi Arabia are required to wear in public. The abaya is opaque and its comfort level in extreme heat depends on whether it is from a couture house or is a nylon/polyester "made in China" garment. It has several moving parts, including a full-face veil called the niqab, which covers everything but the eyes, and the hijab or headscarf. Some women also choose to wear black gloves and socks with it. Its use outside Saudi Arabia is varied.‡

Ahl al-Bayt: Literally, "Family of the House." In this case, the family of the Prophet Muhammad. This family is very central to the sectarian split in Islam between

---

* It is important to remember that there is no universal system for transcription between English and Arabic. Arabic writers must transliterate when using computers and devices with a Latin alphabet keyboard. There are no English counterparts for several Arabic letters of the twenty-eight consonant characters that characterize the basic Arabic *abjadiyah* (script). Therefore, numbers are used. 7 is close to the Arabic equivalent that is ha'a (h). The numbers 3, 5, and 6 also refer to Arabic letters with no equivalent on an English keyboard. This style of transliteration is most used in text messages. A Saudi example for a basic greeting, "How are you today?" in text could be *kaif al7al? wsh Btsawoon el youm?* Finally, most people don't realize there are many different kinds of colloquial Arabic. Lebanese and Egyptian Arabic are good examples.

† The Arabic words *al* and *Al* appear frequently through the book. *Al* with a capital "A" and without a hyphen denotes "family" or "house of," as in *Al Saud*, "the House of Saud," as the Saudi monarchy is officially called. When this changes to *al-*, a lowercase letter followed by a hyphen, it becomes a definite article. Two examples would be how a small minority of Islamic extremists view the world divided into two: *Dar al-Islam* ("the House of Islam") and the rest of the world, *Dar al-Harb* (literally, "the House of War").

‡ Many Muslim women "cover" because of choice (the majority), morality, tradition, culture or religiosity. Some are forced. Others argue that covering is not a Quranic commandment. Regardless, the idea of dressing "modestly" applies to both men and women in the Islamic canon. In recent years in the West, the hijab has been the subject of heated debate and xenophobia.

Shia and Sunni. For the Shia, the family comprises the Prophet's daughter, Hazrat Fatima; her husband and the prophet's cousin, Ali (also their first caliph); and their sons, Hassan and Husayn. For Shia Muslims this is the rightful line of succession, with Imam Ali being the first leader. For Sunni Muslims, the family's composition has been contentious. For them, Abu Bakr, the Prophet's father-in-law, is the rightful successor to the Prophet, and they take a completely different lineage. Some Shia believe that after Muhammad's death, in a coup d'état against the Prophet's rightful successor, Ali, Abu Bakr usurped power.

Ahl e-Hadith: Also Jamiat Ahle Hadith. Literally, "People of the Hadith." Founded as a religious movement, it is considered by many (including an EU report cited in this book) to be a charitable/educational/political front for terrorism. The movement's beliefs, like the Wahhabi/Salafi doctrines, are puritanical. Notable beliefs include denouncing *taqlid* (blind following) and promoting *ijtihad* (independent reasoning).

Al-Fatiha: Literally, the "Opening" or "Beginning," referring to its being the first chapter of the Quran. It is used often, including during every prayer.

Alawite: A sect of Shia Muslims. The Syrian dictator in the middle of a catastrophic civil war, Bashar al-Assad, and his family are prominent examples. The Wahhabi thought behind Daesh would not even consider the Alawites to be legitimate Muslims.

Allah: The Arabic word for God.
- Inshallah: "If God wills."
- Alhamdulillah: "Praise be to God."
- Astaghfirulla(h): "I ask forgiveness from Allah."
- Mashallah: "What Allah wanted has happened." Often used when hearing good news.
- Subhanallah: "Glory be to God."

Arafat: Arafat is a plain about twenty miles from Mecca surrounding Mount Arafat, which is where the Prophet Muhammad is said to have given his farewell sermon. This is why the mount (hill) is also called Jabal ar-Rahmah (Mount of Mercy). Muhammad said, "Hajj is Arafat," and millions of pilgrims climb the mount and stay in the plain to deliver supplications before sunset. The day spent at Arafat is the most important ritual of Hajj. Pilgrims then head to another plain called Muzdalifah for a short rest (sleeping bags on very rocky ground) and to collect pebbles.

Ashura: The first month of the Islamic calendar is Muharram, and its tenth day, called Ashura, is of enormous ritualistic significance for Shia Muslims. Ashura marks the anniversary of the death of Imam Husayn in battle at Karbala in modern Iraq, an act they call his martyrdom which they mourn centuries later. One Ashura ritual involves public flagellation with rope-like metal chains on bleeding bare male torsos, carried out in a procession called *Tazia*. Women are not encouraged to go out publicly. In India and Iran the day is a national holiday. Shia consider it as the ultimate symbol of the resistance their religion commands and place it centrally in the spiritual morality of the Shia universe. In modern times the day has been used for political resistance. Imam Sadiq allegedly said, "Every day is Ashura, every land is Karbala."

Ayatollah: Literally, "Sign of Allah/the divine." It is the highest possible ranking given to an Islamic scholar, master of sharia and all divine matters in "twelver" Shia exegesis. This is a very exclusive club. Only the most exclusive list of ayatollahs appears in the *Marja-e'Taqlid* (source of emulation) category. These are the grand ayatollahs—in Iran, Ayotallah Khomeini and his putative successor, Ayatollah Khameini, and in Iraq, Ayatollah Ali al-Sistani. For Shias these ayatollahs are comparable to a pope. In Iran, which is a theocracy, the Ayatollah is the ultimate arbiter for all matters.

Bismillah: The word extends to *Bismillah ar Rahman ir Rahim* (literally, "In the Name of Allah, Most Gracious and Most Merciful"). Arguably the most-used phrase in Islam, Bismillah begins all prayer and every chapter of the Quran (but the ninth). It is uttered a great deal in daily Muslim life, for example, at mealtime.

Burqa: Widely worn in Central and South Asia, this garment has a purpose similar to that of the *abaya*—to ensure the shapelessness and invisibility of women. It is said to be uncomfortably heavy and difficult to maneuver in. Instead of the niqab, it usually has a rectangular piece of semi-transparent cloth with its top edge attached to a portion of the headscarf so that the veil hangs down covering the face and can be turned up if the woman wants. Around Kabul, light-blue burqas came into prominence when the Taliban were in power. Many Afghan women still use them, calling them *chadri*. It has semantic roots with its cousin in Iran called the *chador*, which many women say is less claustrophobic and only requires the wearer to clutch fabric. In the Indian subcontinent, burqas are mostly black.

Burqini: Islamically acceptable swimwear for Muslim women. The copyright for the terms Burqini and Burkini is held by an Australian firm that claims it came up with the concept and says 40 percent of its customers are not Muslim but include Hindus and conservative Jews. Wearing a burqini is like wearing a whole-body wetsuit with a hood attached. Interestingly, many municipalities in France (as they have done with the hijab since 2009) banned the garment in 2016.

Caliph: *Khalifa* in Arabic, this man controls sizeable geography called the caliphate (*khilafat*) that is "Islamic." For many Islamic schools, the caliph is supposed to be a descendent of the Prophet Muhammad. This idea that Daesh has made so dreaded and fearful today is something the world coexisted with and accepted for almost fourteen centuries. A caliphate allows for many principles that would be acceptable in this century, including a *Majlis al-Shura* (consultative assembly), basically a parliament. Until Daesh announced itself as Islam's new caliphate, using sadistic and un-Islamic logic, it was widely assumed that the end of the Ottoman Empire was the death of the Islamic Caliphate and of caliphs.

Da'wa: The proselytizing or preaching of Islam. A Muslim who is engaged in this is called a *da'i,* and, as in other religions, is basically a missionary.

Dabiq: A small town/village in northern Syria, important to a small number of Muslims whose Islamic eschatology holds it as a possible location for a war against Christians that Muslims will win. This is why the first Daesh online magazine is called *Dabiq.*

Darul Uloom (Deoband): Literally, "House of Knowledge." Located in a suburb called Deoband in India's Saharanpur district, it is the birthplace of the influential school of Deobandi Islam. It claims it follows Hanafi doctrine and Islamic sciences, but others have condemned its curriculum as heavily Wahhabi-ized, with great influence on the Taliban, among others. It regularly issues fatwas, which the elite in India treat with derision and scorn.

Eid al-Adha: Literally, "the Festival of the Sacrifice" and called "the greater Eid" by some scholars. It occurs on the tenth day of the month of Dhu al-Hijjah, the month designated for the Hajj, as well. It commemorates Ibrahim's willingness to sacrifice his first-born son, Ismael, at God's command, a sacrifice that was averted at the last moment, with Ismael replaced by a goat. The meat from the goat is traditionally split into three parts: for family, for friends and neighbors, and for the poor. It marks a moment when Hajj pilgrims are finishing their rites of Hajj by also making the sacrifice. There is difference of opinion on how this Eid is to be observed.

Eid al-Fitr: Literally "the Festival of Breaking the Fast." It is the big festival to mark the end of the holy month of fasting called Ramadan. It is the ninth month in the Hijri calendar. Celebratory traditions vary, just as Islam does, but feasts and gift exchanges have become common. Seemingly, there is no sectarian divide on the festival, though there is often disagreement on the sighting of the new moon. The sighting of the crescent moon (*hilal*) heralds the beginning of Ramadan. Eid al-Fitr arrives when the new moon is sighted, marking the end of Ramadan and the beginning of the month of Shawwal. It is said that the first revelations of the Quran to the Prophet happened during the month of Ramadan. This revelation came on a night called *Laylat al-Qadr* (an odd numbered night during the last ten days of Ramadan).

Fatwa: Literally, "legal opinion," with the "legal" aspect itself contested amongst scholars, some of whom have said a fatwa is no more than an "Islamic opinion." Some argue that only outstanding scholars of Islamic sciences can issue such opinions. Others say all qualified jurists can. Some even say that anyone trained in Islamic law (*sharia*) can issue them. As this book proves, fatwas have been variously used, fluctuating from the treacherous and divisive to the absolutely hilarious.

Fiqh: Islamic jurisprudence. Enormous rigor and scholarship are called for in the person who interprets it, the *faqih*. Required abilities include the human understanding of sharia (divine law) and the discipline of scholarship that needs to precede it. For Sunni Muslims there are generally four schools (*madhhab*) of fiqh: Hanbali, Hanafi, Shafi, and Maliki. The first is said to be the most puritanical and lies at the foundation of Wahhabi ideology in Saudi Arabia. For Shia, the most used are Jafari and Zaydi.

Five Pillars of Islam: Also known as *Arkān al-Islām*, these are:
1. Shahadah: Being able to recite the Muslim profession of faith, which is brief: "There is no god but God and Muhammad is his messenger." This relates to the very core of Islam, known as *Tawhid*, which is the oneness of God. In Urdu, it is called the *Kalima*.
2. Salah: Performing the ritual prayers in the proper way (Islam dictates pretty much every act a good Muslim is supposed to do), five times each day.
3. Zakat: A tax for alms, requisite for all Muslims. Muhammad's intent was to not have desperately poor Muslims, and thus this principle of

charity towards Muslims who live in wretched poverty was established. Clearly, this principle is not followed in present times. When it is followed, an example would be during the Festival of the Sacrifice (Eid al-Adha) when all extra meat is given to the poor.

4. Sawm: Fasting during the holy month of Ramadan. It usually lasts thirty days and it can be broken only if certain conditions are met. It is said the Quran's revelations began in the last ten days of this month.

5. Hajj: A mandated, highly ritualized religious journey to Mecca, once in a lifetime and incumbent on all Muslims, if they are willing and able and meet certain other requirements. It is said that Muhammad only did one Hajj in his lifetime and the Quran mentions it about twenty times in different verses.

Grand mufti: Used differently in different nations. In most Sunni countries, the term is used for the highest official arbiter of Islamic law (even if there is no sharia in the country). In sharia nations like Saudi Arabia, the grand mufti assumes great stature, becoming the foremost religious and legal authority. Unlike Catholicism, Islam has no pope-like figure to unite under.

Hadith: Used to describe the actions, habits, traditions, and sayings attributed to the Prophet Muhammad. Compilations of hadith, with the Quran, are the primary canon of Islam. It is of note that the hadith compilations in books such as *Sahih Bukhari* are enormously larger than the Quran itself. Within Islamic jurisprudence, and to this very day, the veracity of scores of hadith remains contested.

Hafiz: A hafiz (hafiza for women) is someone who has memorized the Quran. The person is treated with great respect and the word is deliberately chosen because it can mean "the guardian." It is said they are the carriers of the holy book, should there ever come a time of Islam's destruction. Memorizing the Quran is a hard task because it has 114 chapters containing 6,236 verses (about 80,000 Arabic words), and to do so requires Quranic study at a very early age with the rules of recitation (*tajwid*). Since so much of the Quran relies on recitation, a hafiz is a title so respectable that it is used as a prefix to a name. Interestingly, the deceased Saudi King Abdullah used the term to label his 2011 signature unemployment program.

Hai'a: Used for the Saudi-created "The General Presidency of the Promotion of Virtue and the Prevention of Vices," a government agency set up to police morality (usually cruelly). This agency employs the notorious and feared religious police called the mutaween (singular, mutawa), who are the ground enforcers of sharia law. There are about 4,000 of these barely literate men who can usually be identified because they wear their *ghutrah* (the Arabian peninsula–style headscarf) without an *egal*, the black cord that is usually used to keep the ghutrah in place. They often harass women for attire transgressions, enforce gender segregation, force shopowners to down their shutters at prayer times, or arbitrate actions they deem un-Islamic. The mutaween, set up in the eighties by King Fahd, behaved like state-sanctioned bullies with fearsome powers they abused. In 2016, they were stripped of most of their powers.

Hajj: The enormously desired annual pilgrimage to Mecca, which is one of the Five Pillars of Islam. All Muslims, if financially and physically capable (and meet a few other requirements) are mandated to make this pilgrimage at least once in their lifetime. Usually it lasts five days, beginning on the eighth and ending on the twelfth of the month of Dhu al-Hijjah. It is considered the largest gathering of humanity on the planet with a singular religious objective. It is highly ritualized. Many Muslims choose to use Hajji as an honorary prefix to their names upon successful completion of the pilgrimage, which is considered a big accomplishment.

Halal: Literally, "permissible." In Islamic theology, halal denotes deeds and objects that are permissible to engage in or use. Like its opposite, *haram*, this is a principle of significance and has often been disagreed upon by theologians coming from different cultures, geographies, and times. The term is so critical that it even includes food and drinks. *Mubah*, "Islamically OK," is another term used for basically the same ends.

Haram: In Arabic, there can be two meanings to haram, depending on the way it is written and pronounced. One is "sacred," as in the *Masjid al-Haram* (the Noble Sanctuary), a phrase that is used (amongst others) to identify the holiest mosque in Islam, in Mecca, which contains the Kaaba. In this pronunciation there is no emphasis on the second "a" (or *alif*, the first letter of the Arab alphabet). This pronunciation creates a sacred zone that cannot be violated. The other meaning of the word haram, with particular emphasis on the second alif, denotes the very highest level of Islamic prohibition. Muslims generally assume that sharia law includes many prohibitions against actions considered haram. Scholars also say that in addition to denoting what is divinely forbidden, the use of this word in this context is one of five commandments of Islam that are used to define what is moral and what isn't. Different schools of Islamic thought have differed on what acts they consider to be haram enough to merit punishment.

Hijab: A veil used by many Muslim women when in male company that is outside of family and friends. In reality, it is just a hair- and neck-covering scarf-like garment worn by many women by choice for reasons that can include cultural identity, modesty, and piety. There are also instances when it is not worn by choice. In the West, the choice factor is the most prevalent. It is seen by many Muslim scholars as an extension of the Prophet's command for both men and women to dress modestly. A hijab is not an abaya or a burqa. Its equivalent in South Asia, where the majority of the world's Muslims live, is called a *dupatta*. In countries like Egypt, magazines like the bestselling *Hijab Fashion* have transformed this simple scarf into an object of haute couture.

Hijra: The emigration of Muhammad and his earliest followers, facing persecution, from Mecca to Medina in the year 622. This year assumes great significance because that journey marks the beginning of the lunar Islamic calendar, which is also called the Hijri calendar.

Hira: A cave that sits on the mountain called Jabal al-Nour, about two miles from Mecca. It is the cave where Muhammad received his first Quranic revelation.

Hizbullah: Literally, "the Army of God." In the West, the group is considered a terrorist organization. But many in the Middle East and Shias everywhere view it as a freedom movement. Born as a result of Israeli occupation of southern Lebanon in 1982, Hizbullah is based in the southernmost part of Beirut, in a vast area called Dahieh. Its influential secretary general is Hassan Nasrallah. Hizbullah is also a political party that has won legitimate seats in the Lebanese Parliament in elections. Worldwide opinion swings from labeling it a terrorist group, to a legitimate resistance movement, to a political party. The EU and UK, for example, differentiate between the group's militant part and its political-party status, with the latter being affirmed. For the Russians, Hizbullah is a legitimate social and political organization.

Hudood: Literally, "limit" or "restriction," in both Urdu and Arabic. In 1977, Pakistani dictator Zia-ul-Haq implemented the infamous Hudood Ordinances in his attempts to make the penal code left behind by the British sharia-compliant. Offenses are either *hadd* (fixed) or *tazir* (discretionary). Until the 2006 "Protection of Women Act," rapists could roam free in Pakistan, and sometimes the victims ended up in prison, saying it was they who were guilty of *zinna* (adultery). The most horrific consequences range from public lashing to amputation of hands, death by stoning, and crucifixion. In modern times, sharia states like Saudi Arabia and Iran routinely enforce these punishments, claiming sharia compliance.

Ihram: Foremost a state of purity of mind and piety of spirit that a pilgrim performing the Hajj (the major pilgrimage) or the Umrah (the lesser pilgrimage) must enter. Like almost all of Islam, there are many rituals before a pilgrim dons the ihram, which for men is two unstitched pieces of white cloth. For women, the clothing is modesty ordained, and they must wear hijab on their heads, though their faces must be exposed. In Mecca, men and women should not even be separated and pray in the same lines. The geographical, cultural, and other diversities and immensity of Hajj, however, mean that both genders do not follow all the rules of attire in the absolutes of rituals Islam prefers.

Ijtihad: Literally, "effort" or "independent reasoning," during and after Wahhab's lifetime. The concept is not a novelty. Early Muslims learned that not all problems had a solution in the Quran, in the hadith (sayings/traditions attributed to Prophet Muhammad), or even *ijmā ʿ* (scholarly consensus). Thus came ijtihad, a principle as old as Islam itself. Many modern American or European scholars speaking on behalf of Islam see it as a quick fix and proof that Islam has "independent reasoning." Yet violent ideologies like the Wahhabis, and thus their ideological partners in Daesh, claim they favor and still exercise the principle. Post-revolutionary Iran has also embraced it. Ijtihad therefore remains fraught and cannot be seen as a quick bandage for Islamic exegesis. Due to Islam's pluralism, a unanimity of commandments applicable to 1.7 billion people cannot be assigned easily, not even if it is explicitly from the Quran.

Ikhtilat: The intermixing of men and women. It is the opposite of gender segregation, which most Islamic scholars say is mandated by sharia and should apply to Muslims everywhere. What we take for granted in the West (men and women working together, living together, etc.) is an enormously charged issue in countries that impose sharia, the biggest examples being Saudi Arabia and Iran. It has always been difficult for these regimes to implement gender segregation culturally. The majority population in both countries is below age thirty. Unsurprisingly, in the age of the social web, ikhtilat is increasingly desired by them and cannot be policed on the web. It often trends on Saudi Twitter as a hashtag.

Imam: The leader of a Muslim community, most commonly a "worship leader," a man who can lead prayer for a congregation and can even have a pastoral role in communities. For Shia Muslims the term is decidedly more sacred.

Iqama: There are not many ways to enter Saudi Arabia. This is one, and it means a work permit/residence visa valid for up to two years. In a country where corruption is endemic, employers have been known to extend iqama indefinitely because of whom they know, thus creating a kind of indentured servitude for the recipients, who cannot leave the country. Some have said it's akin to a modern-day slavery system.

Jaish-e-Mohammed: The banned Pakistani terrorist organization, whose name literally means "Army of Mohammed." It is most active in Indian-controlled Kashmir. It is primarily influenced by the teachings of the Deobandi school of Islam. The group also has connections to both al-Qaeda and the Taliban. Even though the United Nations has named Jaish-e-Mohammed a terrorist group, it keeps on springing up with different names and allegedly with support from Pakistan's primary intelligence agency, ISI.

Jamaat-ud-Daawa: The front for what the Indian and US governments view as a terrorist organization, *Lashkar-e-Taiba* (Army of the Pure), which was blamed for the Bombay terror attacks in 2008. It is claimed that Pakistan's ISI continues to give both Lashkar and Jamaat logistical and perhaps financial support. The Jamaat continues to work as the Lashkar's "charitable arm."

Jamarat: A critical ritual of the Hajj, it represents the act of the Prophet Ibrahim when he stoned three pillars representing Shaitan (Satan) and his attempts to distract him from God's will, that Ismael be slaughtered. The stoning happens thrice, ending with the tenth day of the month of Dhul al-Hijjah. The total number of pebbles to be used, according to most Sunni scholars, is forty-nine. After many stampedes and casualties, the Saudis replaced the walls surrounding the pillars with eighty-five-foot concrete walls. Today it is possible to engage in the stoning ritual from three levels, with the topmost being the most accident-free. However, this remains the most dangerous of all Hajj rituals. It is used as both a noun and a verb.

Jannat: Urdu and Arabic word for paradise.

Jannat al-Baqi: Literally, "Garden of Paradise." An enormous cemetery of unmarked graves in Medina that borders the second-most-important mosque in Islam, Masjid al-Nabi or the Mosque of the Prophet, where Muhammad, many of his family, and other Islamic ancestors are buried. The cemetery suffered great destruction at the hands of the violent Ikhwan (literally, "brothers," in this case a Wahhabi religious militia) in 1806 and 1925. All Shias and many Sunnis have denounced the Wahhabi destruction of what is essentially Islamic history. Muslims who die during Hajj are sometimes buried here, which is considered a great honor for the deceased.

Jannat al-Mu'alla: Literally, "Garden of the Mu'alla (judge, follower)." A cemetery in Mecca where the Prophet's first wife, the older businesswoman called Khadija, his grandfather, and other Islamic ancestors are buried. The graves here met the same fate as those at Medina's Jannat al-Baqi in 1925.

Jihad: Literally, this Arabic noun means "struggling, persevering, striving." Some scholars claim its primary motive is proselytizing, a dual religious duty for all Muslims to keep the faith intact and to convert others. Other scholars use the term *jihad al-nafs*, or "struggle with the self," presumably toward a better religious self. But there is also its association with an offensive concept: struggle or battle with the "enemies" of Islam. There are scholars who try to simplify it into just two compartments: the greater jihad, which they say is the inner spiritual struggle, and the lesser jihad, which is the struggle with the enemies of Islam. The word really entered global consciousness post-9/11, so much so that now it is seen as an almost English-language word. The concept of jihad remains one of ongoing global debate.

Kaaba: The cube-shaped building that is Islam's ground zero. It is Islam's version of something as holy as the Jewish tabernacle. Technically, 1.7 billion Muslims are commanded to perform Islam's ritualized prayer five times a day in its direction. That direction from anywhere is called the *Qibla*. A black silk cloth inlaid with (literally) gold verses, called the Kiswa, covers it and is changed annually.

It is said that the original Kaaba was built by the Prophet Ibrahim and his son Ismael twenty-one centuries before Christ. Clearly they would not recognize its current grandeur. Hundreds of thousands of Muslim homes, prayer beads, and prayer rugs have some sort of pictorial representation of the Kaaba, and thus it is a very emotional experience for the millions lucky enough to see it in reality.

Kafir: A nonbeliever (disbeliever, infidel, apostate).

Karbala: A city in central Iraq, which many Shia Muslims regard as their second-holiest city after Mecca. This is because of the 680 battle of Karbala that claimed the life of the revered Imam Husayn, who is buried here in a grand mausoleum. They regard it as his martyrdom and mark his death on the tenth day of the Islamic month of Muharram. This battle and martyrdom are additional proof that Shiism needs to be treated as a distinct religion, one with separate rituals and identity. Husayn was "martyred" at Sunni hands, in Karbala by the despised alleged Caliph, Yazid. Husayn's martyrdom at Karbala is Shia Islam's raison d'être.

Mahdi: Literally, "the Guided One." In Islam's eschatology, he is the redeemer of the faith to appear on the Day of Judgment. Sunni scholars vary on the duration of his rule: five, seven, ten, or nineteen years. Some schools of Islam says the second coming of Jesus will also happen simultaneously. The mainstream Sunni view holds that the Mahdi has not yet been born. The majority Shia view is that he went into occultation and will return as Muhammad al-Mahdi, their Twelfth Imam. The first Daesh magazine, *Dabiq,* claimed such end-of-times logic and said the time for the Mahdi to come and the place would be a small town in northern Syria, also called Dabiq. Throughout history many have claimed Mahdi-hood. The Mahdi rhetoric has dangerously been used by terrorist organizations like Daesh and al-Qaeda.

Madrassa: Urdu and Arabic word for school. Some (inaccurately) call them religious schools specific to Muslims.

Majlis al-Shura: Literally, majlis means "a place of sitting" and shura means "consultation." Therefore, this is an advisory council. It's a critical concept because such a majlis assumes its members as knowledgeable of the Quran and sharia. This is one of two ways of "electing" a caliph. The council exists in political terms in Egypt, Oman, Qatar, Pakistan, Bahrain, and even Iran (where it is called *Majles-e Shura-ye Eslami*). This concept is the closest that totalitarian Saudi Arabia comes to some form of legislature. It is said even al-Qaeda had such a majlis, and so does Daesh.

Marja, Marja-al taqlid: See *Ayatollah*.

Masjid al-Haram: Literally, "the Sacred Mosque." Some also say it means "The Noble Sanctuary." It is the holiest mosque in Islam, special because it contains the Kaaba, the heart of Islam, a structure that is said to predate Islam as we know it. The largest mosque in the world, it can allegedly accommodate 820,000 people, which is still not enough for Hajj numbers. The mosque has been in a constant state of expansion for decades. The reconstruction (destruction, say critics) is assigned to one of the world's largest contracting firms, the Saudi bin Laden group. Osama bin Laden was one of many sons in this family tree and for a while worked for his family's project of reconstructing the grand mosque.

There has been much criticism of the bin Laden family because the Ottoman and other historic architectural flourishes that formed a part of its history have been destroyed and replaced with faux gold and marble. It is common knowledge that in the mosque perimeters the bin Ladens, on Saud orders, destroyed the home the Prophet occupied with his first wife, Khadija, and built a row of toilets on top of it. The hills of Safa and Marwah, where the historically critical Hajjar ran to find water to save Ismael (who would lay forth Muhammad's lineage) have now been turned into air-conditioned marble corridors. When a crane collapsed onto the mosque on September 11, 2015, 111 people died and 394 were injured. It is said that when this set of renovations started by King Abdullah will be completed by King Salman in 2020, the capacity of the mosque will increase to 2 million.

Masjid al-Nabi: Literally, "the Prophet's Mosque." It is the second-holiest of the trinity of mosques that lie at the highest echelons of Islamic power. Located in Medina, the mosque went through a massive "redevelopment" project just like its counterpart in Mecca by the Saudi bin Laden family. The grave of the Prophet Muhammad and a few contested figures are contained within this mosque, where the exact location of the Prophet's grave is denoted by a green-topped dome that the Saudi monarchy and their real masters in the Wahhabi ulema have tried to demolish several times to prevent its becoming a place of veneration, which it actually has become. The Saudi king appends the title of "Custodian of the Two Holy Mosques") to his name.

Mawlid (Mawlid al-Nabi): The birthday of the Prophet Muhammad, which occurs in the third month of the Islamic calendar. Most Muslims celebrate it. In Saudi Arabia, though, it is forbidden, as is the celebration of any child's birthday. Celebrating birthdays is considered *bida* (an unnecessary religious innovation).

Mina: Three miles from Mecca, this valley is a behemoth tent city spread over twelve square miles. It is used only during the annual Hajj pilgrimage. It has been the scene of many stampedes, as recently as 2015, and even a giant fire in 1997. The Saudi government claims the 100,000 tents of this unusual city are now fire-proof. But the safety of up to 3 million pilgrims in areas like Mina and the Jamarat remains an intractable issue for the Saudi monarchy.

Mufti: A person who can opine on sharia law and issue fatwas. In Islamic hierarchies, a mufti is often near the bottom of a tall ladder of scholarship.

Mughal: This dynasty founded by Babur ruled most of India from the early sixteenth to the eighteenth century. Its fifth emperor gave the world one of its greatest monuments, the Taj Mahal. This originally Turkic-Mongol dynasty ruled over hundreds of thousands of miles and tried to create a united Indian state, a task only the British colonizers that followed them were able to finally execute. The Mughals were a Persianate society and brought that language and culture with them. This is why Urdu has so much in common with Persian. Akbar, one of the great Mughal Emperors, even tried to form a new religion called Din-i-Ilahi to unite the hundreds of ethnic languages, cultures, and religions of what some of them called Hindustan (the Land of the Hindus). The syncretism that existed between Hindus and Muslims for the most part under the Mughals lead to a great flourishing of architecture and the arts—an influence that can be clearly seen in contemporary India.

Muhajir: The Islamic word for an "immigrant." Even Prophet Muhammad and the earliest Muslims were muhajirun for a while when he had to escape Mecca and find shelter in Medina (then Yathrib). The word is connected by more than semantics to the name of Hajjar (mother of Ismael) and to Hijra. Most importantly, Muhammad, like Jesus, was a refugee.

Mujahid: One who wages jihad, plural is mujahideen, and it is contentiously used to describe terrorists who are Muslim.

Mukhabarat: The Arabic version of "intelligence agencies," used in many Arab countries to enforce state terror. Some of the countries are Egypt, Jordan, Syria, Iraq, Saudi Arabia, and Libya. Their tactics and victims have come under increasing scrutiny on the social web.

Mullah: A scholar who is educated and respected for his piety. It has Quranic roots in the word *mawla* (lord, vicar, guardian, trustee). The majority of Muslims in the world use it simply as a prefix for their local cleric. Interestingly, it is said that some Sephardic Jews have used the term to refer to a religious leader.

Mutawa, Mutaween: See *Hai'a*.

Niqab: See *Abaya* and *Burqa*.

Peer: Urdu word for a Sufi saint or wandering mystic, later revered with mausoleums (anathema for the Wahhabis).

The Pentad: Good Muslims are supposed to act within five commandments. This is a pentad into which all acts fall, varying sometimes slightly due to culture, geography, and the various other diversities of Islam. In Arabic, the phrase used is *al-'aḥkām al-khamsa*. Most scholars agree they can be divided into:

- farḍ or wājib - compulsory, obligatory
- mustaḥabb or sunnah - recommended, also known as *fadilah*, *mandub*
- mubāḥ - neither obligatory, recommended, disliked, nor sinful (neutral)
- makrūh - disliked, abominable (abstaining is recommended)
- ḥarām - sinful (abstaining is obligatory)

All of these terms assume particular significance under the rules of Hajj.

Qiyamah or Qiyamat: The Day of Judgment; different for different kinds of Muslims.

Raj: Literally, "ruler" in Hindi. Generally refers to the period between 1858 and 1947, when the British Crown ruled India. The British were very proud of their rule in India, calling the country the "jewel in the crown." The Raj ended when Gandhi and other "freedom fighters" established a unified post-British India. It was a time of history's largest and bloodiest migration and created the Muslim nations of East and West Pakistan. The former in 1971 would become Bangladesh.

Ramadan: The ninth month of the Islamic calendar, designated as the month of *sawm* (fasting), commemorating the first Quranic revelations to the Prophet in 622. The nature and number of restrictions during Ramadan depend on the kind of Islam being followed. Generally speaking, Muslims are commanded to fast from dawn to dusk. The predawn meal is called *suhur*; the post-dusk meal is called *iftar* and is often celebratory. Some of the prohibitions include drinking liquids, eating, and smoking, as well as refraining from any sexual relations. In some countries prohibitions also include gossiping, lying, insulting, fighting, or killing any living being. Ramadan is one of the five pillars of Islam.

Rasoolullah: Rasool means "Messenger," and Allah means "God." In South Asia Rasoolullah is used for Muhammad, as the Messenger of Allah.

Sahih Bukhari: Sunni Islam has four schools of thought: Hanbali, Hanafi, Sha'afi, and Maliki. They all developed under different circumstances. What many Sunnis agree on is the existence of an Islamic canon that comprises six *Kutub al-Sittah* (the Six Books). These very dense tomes are compilations of the Prophet's sayings (hadith) and actions (sunnah). *Sahih Bukhari* is considered to be one of the larger tomes, with 7,275 hadith. But even larger is *Sahih Muslim*, with 9,200 hadith. Of all six books these two (*Bukhari* and *Muslim*) are considered the most influential.

Salah/Namaaz: Salah (Arabic) and Namaaz (Urdu) refer to the daily mandated prayers for Muslims, who are to perform them facing the direction of the Kaaba in Mecca. There are five daily prayers: *Fajr* (dawn), *Zuhr* (noon), *Asr* (afternoon), *Maghrib* (sunset), and *Isha* (night).

Sharia: A body of religious and moral law derived from religious prophecy, as opposed to human legislation. Given Islam's diversity, with 1.7 billion vastly different adherents, sharia can be interpreted differently depending on history, geography, culture, the Muslim canon, and the Quran. The majority of the Muslim world does not live under any form of sharia. The implementation of religious law has been extremely contentious in Muslim communities around the world. Thus it is hard to pinpoint whose sharia is right in a sectarian faith with many schools of thought. Two major countries that are diametrically opposite and always in discord, Iran and Saudi Arabia, are the world's two most prominent examples where sharia is the law of the land.

Shaitan: Urdu and Arabic word for Satan.

Sufi: The expansive term for the mystical, present in many different forms of Islam in ways as diverse as the religion of Islam itself. In Arabic, the word is *tasawwuf* ("to dress in wool"), in Urdu *fakir*, and in Persian *darvish*.

Sufism: Mystical Islamic belief and practice in which Muslims seek to find the truth of divine love and knowledge through direct personal experience of God. It consists of a variety of mystical paths that are designed to ascertain the nature of humanity and of God and to facilitate the experience of the presence of divine love and wisdom in the world. It is often associated with ascetics who are worldly poor and spiritually divine. It usually conforms to diverse Islamic geographical, cultural, and spiritual practices. Muhammad ibn Abd al-Wahhab is said to have detested anything Sufi as *shirk* (idol worship). The Sufis through history have, however, been proselytizers of the faith. Disobeying the canon of Islam in their own unique ways, there are thousands of these mystics buried in Muslim lands from Morocco to Malaysia. They also remained repositories of all that is divine and ineffable.

Primarily through poetry, Sufi mystics made Prophet Muhammad an emulatory figure, thus influencing Islamic piety. In Urdu, Persian, Turkish, Arabic, Pashto, and Punjabi, their poetry has withstood the tides of times; though puritanical Wahhabi strains of Islam have destroyed their graves, they have not been able to contain their poetry and music. In the West, Rumi is erroneously presented as a singular Sufi figure and Sufism as religion. Both characterizations are wrong. Even in the seventh century, mystics wandered the sands of Arabia and even Mecca—perhaps it is them whose legacy the Sufis are.

Sunnah: Every Muslim is taught to follow and emulate the sunnah—in a sense, everything known from Muhammad's behavior and life. It takes all of Muhammad's known hadith (traditions), his actions, his disapprovals, his approvals, whether silent or verbal, and turns them into a very specific, ritual-heavy part of Islamic theology. In a sense, it spells out (part of) the essence of Islam's discipline, which is submission. The Quran itself is separate from this "path."

Surah, Ayah, Quran: A Surah is a chapter from the Quran, which has a total of 114 chapters. These chapters are divided into verses called *Ayah* (plural, *Ayat*). Literally, an ayah means "sign" or "evidence," which in a canonical context makes ayat divine revelations. Ayah can be Meccan (Makki) or Medinan (Madani), a geographical marker of where the Prophet was during revelation, since the Quran was not revealed sequentially. There is sectarian (Shia-Sunni) and scholarly dispute about the time of its compilation. Some scholars claim that what we know as the Quran today began compilation generations after the Prophet Muhammad died in 632. They claim this is partially because writing was not a common skill in seventh-century Arabia. There is, however, unanimity amongst all 1.7 billion Muslims on the planet that their illiterate Prophet Muhammad was the sole vessel of this ongoing revelation that took about twenty-three years. The holy book uses very sophisticated, classical, and poetic Arabic, and refers with great respect to its predecessors, the Old and New Testaments.

Takfir: It is Islam's version of excommunication. The dangerous practice of one Muslim's labeling another Muslim a disbeliever (*kafir*). Falsely accusing someone of *kufr* (disbelief in Islam) is considered a major punishable act in most schools

of Sunni Islam. There is widespread disagreement amongst Islamic scholars about
the concept of takfir and its usage.

Taliban: Taliban (singular, *talib*) in Pashto means "students." It refers to the
extreme and puritanical religious faction that emerged in Afghanistan and ruled
the country from 1996–2000. In a sense they turned the clock back so successfully that most of the world did not how to react to their consistent brutalities,
including the totalitarian misogyny that Afghan women suffered. They are notorious. Under the leadership of the deceased Mullah Mohammed Omar, they
took Osama bin Laden in as he escaped from Sudan, and al-Qaeda was born, in
a sense, on Afghan soil. Eager to destroy history, they famously obliterated two
sixth-century statues known as the Buddhas of Bamiyan. There have been recent
reports that Daesh has moved some of its "soldiers" to Afghanistan, which is
waging war with the still-active though vastly reduced Taliban. Their version of
Islam was, amongst others, much influenced by the Deobandi style from India.

Tawaf: The ritual counterclockwise circling of the Kaaba during Hajj and Umrah.
During Hajj there are different kinds of tawaf, but what is universal is that seven
circumambulations must be made upon entering Mecca and the same when leaving. Pilgrims often do more. This circling begins from the corner of the cuboid
Kaaba that contains the Al-Ḥajaru al-Aswad (see *Kaaba*). The tawaf is supposed to
signal that the pilgrims are all united under Islam's central precept of tawhid (see
Tawhid). Many scholars say that the ritual is older than Islam, dating to when the
Prophet Ibrahim laid the foundations for the Kaaba with his son Ismael. If those
scholars are correct, then Muhammad, till he was forty, must have participated in
the ritual, like his fellow Quraysh tribe, around a pre-Islamic Kaaba that at the
time contained idols.

Tawhid: This principle is the epicenter of this monotheism: There is only one
God, and God (Allah, literally *Al-Ilāh*, "the God") is One (*Al-'Aḥad*) and Single
(*Al-Wāḥid*). This is the very fulcrum around which the religion of Islam revolves. It
is even commemorated in prayer, when during a part of the prayer ritual, the supplicant raises the index finger of the right hand acknowledging Tawhid. Centuries
of Islamic theology and the building of its canon have rested on this wellspring.
For a Muslim to break from this principle is an unpardonable sin.

In Judaism a mirror principle called the shema exists, and the closest equivalent in Christianity is Unitarianism, which is not the norm in that religion. To
explain this sometimes complex principle, the 180th verse of the Quran's seventh

chapter (amongst others) alludes to the ninety-nine names attributed to a singular God: *The most beautiful names belong to Allah. So call on him by them; but shun such men as use profanity in his names: for what they do, they will soon be requited.*

Thobe or Thawb: A white robe worn by Saudi men and other Gulf Arabs. On the head they wear a piece of white cloth called the *ghutrah* (and sometimes the keffiyeh). The headgear is held in place by a circular cord called the *agal*. The robe itself is also called the *dishdasha*.

Ulema: Literally, the "learned ones." Semantically the word is connected to *alim* ("scholar") and *ilm* ("knowledge"). This is the closest Islam comes to having a concept akin to clergy, a council of learned men. Unlike Catholicism, Islam does not have a pope. Also the Quran and Muhammad agree that there is a singular relationship between the supplicant and God; no intermediaries are needed. Thus this term is particularly contested. There is the usual patriarchal dissent about whether or not women can be an *alimah*.

The ulema wield tremendous religious authority, which they say is earned from their scholarship. It is expected that an alim is at least a master of fiqh (Islamic jurisprudence) and sharia (Islamic law). History has often given them huge power in different regions of Islam (since Islam is not a monolithic entity), depending on their *ijma*, or consensus.

Ummah: The worldwide "community" of Muslims, which is a sacred concept handed down from the Prophet himself. This growing Ummah is 1.7 billion strong today.

Umrah: The lesser pilgrimage, to Mecca only. Unlike the Hajj it can happen at any time of the year (other than the month of Hajj) and involves fewer rituals.

Vilayat e faqih: This contested principle is at the center of the Iranian theocracy as it stands today. Literally, "guardianship of the jurist." Technically, *vilayat* means "rule" and *faqih* is a learned jurist with impeccable credentials. Ayatollah Ruhollah Khomeini, the father of the Islamic Republic, made this system a cornerstone of government, so Iran functions as a "republic" where absolute power rests with one man alone. Iran claims to possess a democracy where elections are held to a (religiously based) parliament and for the presidency. The final decision about most matters, however, comes down to one man: the faqih (supreme jurist), aka the supreme leader, aka rahbar (the supreme leader of the Islamic revolution). Many claim Iran's young population (with a majority under thirty) has wide disagreement with the current rahbar, Ayatollah Ali Khamenei, and his government.

Wahhabi Islam: The ultra-puritanical form of Islam practiced in Saudi Arabia. In 1744 a struggling cleric in the Nejd region of Saudi Arabia named Muhammad ibn Abd al-Wahhab made a pact with a local tribal leader, Muhammad bin Saud. Saud wanted religious backing for the monarchy he would build (Dar Al Saud) to rule what would become modern Saudi Arabia. In exchange for his political obedience, Wahhab wanted the protection and propagation of his Wahhabi movement, which would eventually lay the ideological and religious base of the country that would eventually (and brutally) form in 1932.

Many scholars see Wahhabism as a legitimate reform movement. Its followers reject being named Wahhabi (because that would be akin to being named after a person) and prefer the term Salafi, after the "Salafs," or early ancestors like those from Muhammad's time. Ironically, in Saudi Arabia's case they inhabit a country named after a person.

Wahhabi Islam is austere and particularly cruel, and has spread worldwide due to a sustained Saudi monarchical effort over decades. It has unfortunately become the most influential form of Sunni Islam worldwide. Extremists like the barbaric Daesh draw a great deal of their ideology from Wahhabi Islam, often modeling themselves after the barbaric horse-riding and sword-wielding early Saud Ikhwans present during Wahhab's time. The Wahhab-Saud pact has withstood centuries and remains the foundation of modern-day Saudi Arabia.

During and after Wahhab's time, for a brief while, the only destination outside of the Nejd region that the Wahhabis considered legitimate was India, where a Wahhab-style "reform" began almost simultaneously. In modern times the Indian subcontinent has been a particularly fruitful region for the dangerous spread of Wahhabi ideology.

BIBLIOGRAPHY

All quotations from the Quran in this book come from Abdullah Yusuf Ali's translation, universally acknowledged as the best English translation of the holy text:

Ali, Abdullah Yusuf. *The Holy Qur-ān: English Translation & Commentary* (with Arabic text), 1st ed. Kashmiri Bazar, Lahore: Shaik Muhammad Ashraf, 1934.

In addition, this book uses quotes from the six books of the Sunni Islamic canon called *Kutub al-Sittah*. They are primarily collections of the hadith (traditions) attributed to the Prophet Muhammad; the best known of these books is the *Sahih Bukhari*. It is said they were compiled in the ninth century, almost two hundred years after Muhammad died.

PROLOGUE

Ackerman, Spencer. "CIA has not found any link between Orlando killer and ISIS, says agency chief." *Guardian.* June 16, 2016. <https://www.theguardian.com/us-news/2016/jun/16/cia-orlando-shooter-omar-mateen-isis-pulse-nightclub-attack>

Onyanga-Omara, Jane. "Islamic State celebrates Donald Trump election victory." *USA Today.* November 10, 2016. <http://www.usatoday.com/story/news/world/2016/11/10/extremists-celebrate-donald-trump-election-win/93580822/>

CHAPTER 1: LI BEIRUT

Healy, Patrick. "Beirut, The Provincetown of the Middle East." *New York Times.* July 29, 2009. <http://www.nytimes.com/2009/08/02/travel/02gaybeirut.html>

CHAPTER 3: PUBE FACE, TOWELHEAD, CAMEL FUCKER, CAVE NIGGER

Al-Sharif, Imam. "Rationalizing Jihad in Egypt and the Modern World." *Islam Today*. <https://therearenosunglasses.wordpress.com/document-rationalization-of-jihad-in -egypt-and-the-world-imam-al-sharif/>*

Bergen, Peter and Paul Cruickshank. "The Unraveling." *New Republic*. June 11, 2008. <https://newrepublic.com/article/64819/the-unraveling>

Human Rights Watch. "Black Hole: The Fate of Islamists Rendered to Egypt." *Human Rights Watch*, 2005. <https://www.hrw.org/report/2005/05/09/black-hole/fate -islamists-rendered-egypt>

---. "In a Time of Torture: The Assault on Justice in Egypt's Crackdown on Homosexual Conduct." *Human Rights Watch*, 2004. <https://www.hrw.org/sites /default/files/reports/egypt0304_0.pdf>

---. "Trade-Off: The Rendition to Egypt of Sayyid Imam al-Sharif, `Issam Shu`aib, Khalifa Bidaiwi al-Sayyid al-Badawi, Ali`Abd al-Rahim, `Uthman al-Samman, and `Abd al-`Aziz Musa Dawud al-Gamal." *Human Rights Watch*, 2004. <https://www .hrw.org/reports/2005/egypt0505/10.htm>

Jones, Seth G. *Hunting in the Shadows: The Pursuit of al Qa'ida Since 9/11*. New York: W. W. Norton & Company, 2012.

MacAskill, Ewan. "Bhutto assassination could have been prevented, says UN report." *Guardian*. April 16, 2010. <https://www.theguardian.com/world/2010/apr/16 /benazir-bhutto-assassination-un-report>

Said, Edward W. *Orientalism*. New York: Vintage Books, 1979.

Shariati, Ali. *Hajj*. Translated from Persian by Ali Behzadnia and Najla Denny. Costa Mesa, CA: Jubilee Press. <http://www.ziyaraat.net/books/hajj_shariati.pdf>

---. *Hajj*. 2nd ed. Tehran: Free Islamic Literature, 1978.

---. *Hajj: Reflection on its Rituals*. Translated from Persian by Laleh Bakhtiar. Chicago: Kazi Press, 2007.

Wright, J. W. and Everett K Rowson. *Homoeroticism in Classical Arabic Literature*. New York: Columbia University Press, 1997.

Wright, Lawrence. "The Rebellion Within: An Al Qaeda Mastermind Questions Terrorism." *New Yorker*. June 2, 2008.

CHAPTER 4: THE GARDEN OF PARADISE

Armstrong, Karen. *Muhammad: A Prophet for Our Time*. New York: Harper Collins, 2006.

Dickey, Christopher. "The Fire That Won't Die Out." *Newsweek*. July 21, 2002. <http:// www.newsweek.com/fire-wont-die-out-147083>

Ismail, Raihan. *Saudi Clerics and Shia Islam*. New York: Oxford University Press, 2016.

Kramer, Martin. *Arab Awakening and Islamic Revival: The Politics of Ideas in the Middle East*. New York: Transaction Publishers, 2009.

---

*   Part of this historically important text is available on the extremist website *Islam Today*.

Mufti, Shahan. *The Faithful Scribe: A Story of Islam, Pakistan, Family, and War*. New York: Other Press, 2013.

Sciolino, Elaine. "A Nation Challenged: Ally's Future: U.S. Pondering Saudis' Vulnerability." *New York Times*. November 4, 2001. <http://www.nytimes.com/2001/11/04/world/a-nation-challenged-ally-s-future-us-pondering-saudis-vulnerability.html>

Sheikh `Abdul `Aziz Bin `Abdullah ibn `AbdulRahman ibn Bazz. "English Translations of Majmoo'al-Fatawa of late Scholar Ibn Bazz." *Portal of the General Presidency of Scholarly Research and Ifta'*. Vol. No. 9 of 30. <http://muslim-library.com/books/en_English_Translations_of_Majmoo_al_Fatawa_of_Ibn_Bazz_Volume_9.pdf>

CHAPTER 5: SHOOT ME IN HERE

Dabashi, Hamid. *The Green Movement in Iran*. Edited with an introduction by Navid Nakzadfar. New Brunswick, NJ: Tarnation Publishers, 2011.

Tait, Robert. "Iranian protesters' slogans target Khamenei as the real enemy." *Guardian*. June 17, 2009. <https://www.theguardian.com/world/2009/jun/17/iran-ayatollah-khamenei-protest-reaction>

Sahimi, Muhammad. "The Green Movement at One Year." *Frontline*. June 8, 2010. <http://www.pbs.org/wgbh/pages/frontline/tehranbureau/2010/06/the-green-movement-at-one-year.html>

Sharma, Parvez. "Memo from the streets of Tehran." *The Daily Beast*. June 18, 2009. <http://www.thedailybeast.com/articles/2009/06/18/memo-from-the-streets-of-tehran.html>*

CHAPTER 6: THE NAKED BELIEVER

Aslan, Reza. *No God but God: The Origins, Evolution, and Future of Islam*. New York: Random House, 2005.

Ramadan, Tariq. *In the Footsteps of the Prophet: Lessons from the Life of Muhammad*. New York: Oxford University Press, 2009.

CHAPTER 7: THE SATANIC VERSES

Armstrong, Karen. *A History of God: The 4,000-Year Quest for Judaism, Christianity and Islam*. New York: Ballantine Books, 1993.

---. *Muhammad: A Prophet for Our Time*. New York: Harper Collins. 2006.

---

*   Other articles I've written on subject: http://www.thedailybeast.com/contributors/parvez-sharma.html.

Gerard, Etienne. "Nicolas Sarkozy 'fier' de ses propos sur 'la racaille' et le Kärcher." *Le lab politique*. June 26, 2016. <http://lelab.europe1.fr/nicolas-sarkozy-fier-de-ses-propos -sur-la-racaille-et-le-karcher-2782717>

Literature, Migration and the "War on Terror." Edited by Fiona Tolan, Stephen Morton, Anastasia Valassopoulos, and Robert Spencer. Abingdon, Oxon: Routledge, 2012.

CHAPTER 8: MECCA VEGAS

"A beacon for pilgrims in the heart of the Holy City." *Fairmont.com.* <http://www. fairmont.com/makkah/?cmpid=google_mak_search-branded_branded-p-revsh>

Coll, Steve. *An Arabian Family in the American Century*. New York: Penguin Books, 2008.

Peer, Basharat. "Modern Mecca: The transformation of a holy city." *New Yorker*. April 16, 2012. <http://www.newyorker.com/magazine/2012/04/16/modern-mecca>

CHAPTER 9: MUSLIM BOOT CAMP

Coll, Steve. *An Arabian Family in the American Century*. New York: Penguin Books, 2008.

Nomani, Asra Q. *Standing Alone: An American Woman's Struggle for the Soul of Islam*. San Francisco: Harper Collins, 2005.

Smith, Lewis. "Fate of another royal found guilty of adultery." *The Independent*. June 19, 2009. <http://www.independent.co.uk/news/world/middle-east/fate-of-another -royal-found-guilty-of-adultery-1753012.html>

CHAPTER 10: MECCA'S MANY MUHAMMADS

Brown, Jonathan A. C. *Misquoting Muhammad: The Challenge and Choices of Interpreting the Prophet's Legacy*. London: Oneworld Publications, 2014.

Shariati, Ali. *On the Sociology of Religion: Lectures by Ali Shariati*. Translated from Persian by Hamid Algar. Berkeley, CA: Mizan Press, 1979.

CHAPTER 11: MY PASSAGE TO INDIA

Aygle, Denise. "The Mongol Invasions of Bilād al-Shām by Ghāzān Khān and Ibn Taymīyah's Three 'Anti-Mongol' Fatwas." *Mamluk Studies Review* XI (2), 2007.

Haider, Murtaza. "European Parliament identifies Wahabi and Salafi roots of global terrorism." *Dawn*. July 22, 2013. <http://www.dawn.com/news/1029713>*

---

* The entire EU report mentioned in this article is available at http://www.europarl.europa.eu /RegData/etudes/etudes/join/2013/457137/EXPO-AFET_ET(2013)457137_EN.pdf.

Ibn Taymiyyah, Ahmad ibn 'Abd al-Ḥalīm Kitab Al-Iman. Kuala Lumpur: Islamic Book Trust, 1999.

Khan, Yasmin. *The Great Partition: The Making of India and Pakistan.* New Haven: Yale University Press, 2008.

Usmani, Taqi Mufti. *The Great Scholars of the Deoband Islamic Seminary.* London: Turath Publishing, 2008.

CHAPTER 12: ISLAM 3.0

"Arab Human Development Report 2009." *United Nations Development Programme.* May 26, 2009. <http://www.undp.org/content/undp/en/home/librarypage/hdr/arab_human_developmentreport2009.html>

Cohen, Roger. "The Islamic State of Molenbeek." *New York Times.* April 11, 2016. <https://www.nytimes.com/2016/04/12/opinion/the-islamic-state-of-molenbeek.html>

Esposito, John, L. *The Future of Islam.* New York: Oxford University Press, 2010.

Gardner, Frank. "Islamic state releases al Baghdadi message." *BBC News.* May 14, 2015. <http://www.bbc.com/news/world-middle-east-32744070>

Hikek, Ismat. "What does Islam say about killing an innocent person?" *Fountainhead Magazine.* Issue 56: October-December 2006. <http://www.fountainmagazine.com/Issue/detail/What-does-Islam-say-about-killing-an-innocent-person>

Hubbard, Ben. "A Saudi Morals Enforcer Called for a More Liberal Islam. Then the Death Threats Began. *New York Times.* July 10, 2016. <https://www.nytimes.com/2016/07/11/world/middleeast/saudi-arabia-islam-wahhabism-religious-police.html>

Hubbard, Ben and Mark Mazzetti. "Rise of Saudi Prince Shatters Decades of Royal Tradition." *New York Times.* October 15, 2016. <https://www.nytimes.com/2016/07/11/world/middleeast/saudi-arabia-islam-wahhabism-religious-police.html>

Hubbard, Ben. "Saudi Arabia Executes a Prince Convicted in a Fatal Shooting." *New York Times.* October 18, 2016. <https://www.nytimes.com/2016/10/19/world/middleeast/saudi-arabia-prince-executed-salman.html>

Maayan, Groisman. "Saudi Cleric: Homosexuality not a deviation from Islam, should not be punished." *Jerusalem Post.* May 3, 2016. <http://www.jpost.com/Middle-East/Saudi-cleric-Homosexuality-not-a-deviation-from-Islam-should-not-be-punished-452957>

Sykes, Tom. "Why Saudi Arabian Prince Turki bin Saud al-Kabir Was Executed." *The Daily Beast.* October 24, 2016. <http://www.thedailybeast.com/articles/2016/10/24/why-saudi-arabian-prince-turki-bin-saud-al-kabir-was-executed.html>

Tahir-ul-Qadri, Muhammad, Shaykh-ul-Islam. *Fatwa on Terrorism and Suicide Bombings.* London: Minhaj-ul-Quran Publications, 2010. <http://www.quranandwar.com/FATWA%20on%20Terrorism%20and%20Suicide%20Bombings.pdf>

THANK YOUS

First, my husband, who makes everything possible.

Second, Robert Guinsler, my ever optimistic, prescient, and superb agent at Sterling Lord: a man who is intensely loyal and never gives up. Dr. Yousuf Zafar, you are undoubtedly a good doctor, but foremost you are the best photographer I know and I am honored to showcase some of your work. A big thank you to my brilliant author friend Cole Stryker, who suffered more than most have to in the creation of this book and who I hope, now married, spends less time on the dark web. A big thank you to my diligent, patient, and smart editor Vy Tran, who allowed herself to enter a world that was completely unknown and then make sense of it. So grateful for Glenn Yeffeth, Adrienne Lang, Aida Herrera, Jennifer Canzoneri, Monica Lowry, Sarah Avinger, Alicia Kania, Rachel Phares, and Aaron Edmiston—the outstanding team at BenBella who worked so hard to put this together. A big thank you is also due to Rona Vail, Juliet Widoff, Mark Mankoff, Jeff Hoffman, Loveleen Tandan, Sajid Akbar, and Vivek Mansukhani for their unflinching support. So many friends and colleagues have lived this journey with me and I don't know where we would be without them. So thank you A. T., H. V. A., P. Austin, and E. Goldstein. Aseem Chhabra and Cynthia Biboso, a special thank you. And Andrew Herwitz, Firoozeh Khatibi, Laila Jarman, Mallika Dutt, Lopa Banerjee, Vivek Rai, William O' Connor, Ambassador Rufus Gifford and his lovely husband Stephen DeVincent, Scott Long, A. A., Anni Zonevald, Adam Berman, Rhoda Kanaaneh, Nuzhat Leedham, Alia Younes, Asif Kamal, Aroon Shivdasani,

Ahmed Moor, Adam Horowitz, Raed El Khadem, Hiba Haidar, Mark Berthold, Layla Al-Zubaidi, Rabbi Sharon Kleinbaum, Hamid and Melissa Rahmanian, Philip Weiss, Brian Whitaker, Sourena Parham, Alison Amron, Sarah Masters, Zahir J., Shakeel V., John Murphy, Ross Posternak, Sandip Roy, Yassir Islam, Mike Galaviz, Geoff Burkhart, Leena Jaiswal, Lucas Verga, Michelle Hua, Peter Friedman, Michael Sanzone, Amy Goodman, Daayiee Abdullah, Tula Goenka, Faisal Alam, Muhsin Hendricks, Nadia and Shahinaz, Mazen el-Fares, El-Farooq Khaki, Vivek Rai, Sandi Dubowski, Max Carlson, Michelle Hua, GMHC, Mahdis Keshavarz, Bilal and Irum Musharraf, Steven Kopstein, Reza Aslan, Asra Nomani, Ensaf Haidar, Bonte Minnema, Bertho Makso, Georges Azzi, Brent Alberghini, John Avalon, Kevin Sessums, Cleve Jones, and so many more, including the folks in the Obama-era US Department of State and the US Department of Homeland Security (those were the days!). Also thanks to the EU and German Green friends, Amnesty International, and Human Rights Watch. And Rokhsareh Ghaemmaghami for listening and teaching from more countries than I can count.

This book would not exist without many friends and colleagues, some whose full identities cannot be revealed for safety reasons. They have often let me into their lives and secrets that I would normally not be privy to. Thank you Aisha, Zaffar, Rokhsana, Safa, Rafik, and so many others in Beirut. Thank you Adham and Salman in Jidda, Saudi Arabia. Nora in Riyadh and Zafar and Sadeem in Al-Qatif and al-Awammiyah, Saudi Arabia. In Cairo, much gratitude to A. A.; Garth O'Connor; Razia and Rausha at Al Azhar and Naseem at the American University of Cairo; the Younes, Asfour, Malouf and Khoury families; and the many nonprofits that have helped me over the years in Egypt. In Tehran, I would like to thank Arash Afsanian, Behrouz Farrokhzad, Arash Aryan, N. S., and the Hooshang and Jehangir families. In Pakistan, some of my own family and also Afzal, Karim, Khalida, Afsheen, Mehak, Ghalib, Tahir K., and the NGOs I worked with in Lahore, Islamabad, Dhaka, Syria, Lebanon, Egypt, and Jordan over the years, teaching me invaluable lessons about the region and information that I otherwise would not have been able to get access to. In India, my own family, Imam Khalifa and Maulana Hasan at the Nadhwa seminary in Lucknow, Zainab Bakhtiar, Maulana Syed Kalbe Jawad Naqvi, Ahsan, and Qasim. In Bangladesh, S. K., S. D.,

Bandhu, and the many NGOs that have taught me so much. In Lahore, Islamabad, and Karachi, Ghalib, K. A., T. K., R. R. and S. Jahangir, G. A., R. F., R. T., and yes, even the "deplorables" at the Lal Masjid in Islamabad.

To every single voice that needs an *Inquilab Zindabad* ("Long live the revolution") in the Indian subcontinent.

To each voice that dared to call for *"Marg Bar Diktator!"* ("Death to the dictator!") in Iran's unfinished 2009 Green Revolution.

To the courageous warriors that yelled in unison *"Ash-shab yurid isqat un-nizam"* ("The people want to bring down the regime") on the streets of Cairo in 2011 and now face the consequences of so many unfinished Arab Springs.

And to my fellow soldiers Adham and Shahinaz.

So much remains unfinished in the business of freedom.

ABOUT THE AUTHOR

PARVEZ SHARMA makes fearless, multiple-award-winning films about faith, identity, religious extremism, and social justice. Two of the best known are *A Jihad for Love* and *A Sinner in Mecca*. In the latter, shot mostly with an iPhone, guerrilla-style, Parvez travels to Mecca to reveal a side of Islam that's literally never been seen before. "We emerge from the film more enlightened," writes the *New York Times*, naming it a Critics' Pick. He has been hailed as a "gifted filmmaker" (the *Wall Street Journal*), "frankly brave" (NPR), "provocative" (*San Francisco Chronicle*), and as carrying out "an attack on Islam" by Ayatollah Khamenei's regime in Iran.

Parvez's writings on Islamic, racial, and political issues have appeared on the *Huffington Post*, the *Daily Beast*, the *Guardian*, and elsewhere. He is a prominent speaker on Islam, politics, extremism, personal identity, and the media, having spoken at more than 200 live events around the world and conducted workshops with the United Nations, European Union, US State Department, and the Department of Homeland Security. He reported actively about the "Green Movement" in Iran and about the revolution in Egypt. The *New York Times*, in a profile on the filmmaker, said, "After 'Jihad,' Mr. Sharma was labeled an infidel, and in the intervening years, he has gotten more death threats than he cares to recall." Parvez was named one of "50 Visionaries Who Are Changing Your World" in a list headed by the Dalai Lama.

For direct bookings and/or speaking events for Parvez, email info@asinner-inmecca.com. You can also contact his agency, Lavin, at http://bit.ly/2npO0uR.

Caruso, Enrico,
    59, 164, 165, **214**, 217
    Carmen, 32, 63-64, 67, 69, 154
    "'ell of a place!," 114-115, 214
"Caruso on the Earthquake," 214
Casino, The, 304
cattle, **98**, 97-99, 138
census records, 24, 146, 268
Central Emergency Hospital,
    61, 73, 86-89, 91, 92, 158
Central Theater, 60, 94, 306
Century Magazine, 200
Cerf, Myrtile, 37, 101
Chapman, Edyth, 289
Chicago, 47, 288
children,
    126, 143, 156, 209, **275**, 276-278
Chinatown,
    119-120, 160, 161, 203, 204, 236
Chinese,
    118-123, 128, 137, 203, 204, 265
    servants, 60, 126, 158, 169, 272
    vaudeville, 123
Chinese Historical Society of
    Greater San Diego, 118
Christensen, John, 189, 190
Chronicle building,
    29, **52**, 75, 153, 181
    on fire, 158, 159, 160, 165, 278
Chutes, The, 34, 212, 306
City Beautiful movement, 28
City Hall
    before quake, **36**, 37, 61
    quake damage, 33, 101, 102,
        127, 137, 165
    fire damage, **36**, 47, 158,
        240-243, **244**, 307
    police station, 72
    See also Central Emergency
        Hospital; treasurer's office
City Hall (new), 57, 221

City Hall Avenue, 88, 89
City of the Golden 'Fifties, 280
Civic Center, 57
Clabrough, Golcher & Co., 268, 271
Claus Spreckels Building
    See Call building
Cliff House, 28
Coffroth, Jimmy, 59, 61
Cohen, George M., 288
Coleman, Harry J.,
    58, 90, 162, 168, 240, 243, 244
Collier's magazine, 132, 161
Columbia Coffee & Spice Co., 199
Columbia Theater, 60
Commercial Hotel, 192
Committee of Fifty, 38, 39, 103
Committee of History & Statistics
    See Earthquake History Committee
Congress, U.S., 288
Conlan's, 106
controversies
    army, 42, 44, 46, 246
    dynamite, 42, 43, 44, 192
Cook, Jesse B., 70-71
cooking in the streets
    See stoves in streets
Coppa's Restaurant, 303
coroner's figures, 43
Cosgrave, Millicent, 237
Cosmos Club, 305
Court of Appeals, U.S., 235
cover-up campaign, 140
Cowdery, Frank, 237
Coxe, Charles, 146, 147
Coxe, Ella, 149
Coxe, Ella (Mrs.), 146, 148, 150
Coxe, Frank, 146, 149, 150
Coxe, Mabel, **146**, 150
Crafts and Arts, 148
Crocker building, 160
Crocker, Henry J., 116

Crocker School, 272
Crown Paper Mills, 193
curfew, 270-271
Curry, Charles, 46
Cushing, William, 77
Custom House, 196

D
Dailey, Pete, 288
"Dance, thumbykin, dance," 303
Dargie, W., 166
de Mille, Cecil, 237
de Young, Michael, 166
dead, the, 35, 42, 43, 160, 209
Delaney, Billy, 225
Delmonico's Restaurant,
    59, 64, 114, 301, 305
Desmond, Grace, 289
Dewey Monument, 110
Dinan, Jeremiah,
    86, 101, 102, 103, 159, 242
Dixon, L. Maynard,
    124, 125, 126, 127, 129, **308**
Dixon, Lilian, 124, 125, 129
Dolores Lake, 34
Dondero, George, 196
Dougherty, John, 46
drunkenness, 54, 55, 117, 264
Dunn, Allan and Mrs., 127, 128
Dwyer, J.M., 72
dynamite controversy,
    42, 43, 44, 192
dynamiting
    Van Ness Avenue, 131, 138, 251
    elsewhere, 115, 134, 142, 170,
        189, 203

E
Eagle, The, 140
Earthquake History Committee,
    24, 25, 26, 38

Earthquake Information Center, 29
earthquake of 1989, 57, 235
earthquakes of 1865 and 1868, 29
earthquakes in world, 29, 30
Eichbaum, Ed, 274
Eichbaums, the, 269, 274
Eiffel Tower Restaurant,
    193, 196, 197
Elliott, Captain (cadet corps), 263
Emerson, Edwin, Jr., 24, 298
Emporium, The, **145**, 165, 175
Enewold, Elmer, 256
Enewold, Lawrence, 256
Episcopal Church, 165
*Episodes of the San Francisco
    Catastrophe...*, 62
Erskine, Douglas, 171
Everybody's Magazine,
    66, 108, 138, 152
Examiner building
    136, **151**, 153, 163-164
    on fire, 157, 159, 165

F
Fairmont Hotel,
    22, 27, 60, 107, 160, 161
"Fall of San Francisco: Some
    Personal Observations," 206
Ferguson, David Miller, 253, 254
ferries, 48, 54, **144**, 217
    no fares, 48, 274
Ferry Building, **22**, 41, 48, 164, 241
Field, Charles K., 116, 188, 238
Fiesta Restaurant, 33
Finke's Widow, A, 196
Fior d'Italia Restaurant, 305
fire, 34-35, 47
    breaks, 47, 115, 138
    fighters, 154, 246-249
    Hayes Valley, 47, 157-158, 161
    See also Sullivan, Dennis

Fire Department, 41, 46
Fireman's Fund, 79
fires of 1849-1851, 30
fires, heat of, 43, 141
Fischer's Theater, 60
Fisher, Lucy B., 90, 95
Fisk, Arthur G., 231
Fitzpatrick, Colonel, 59
Flood, Mrs. James, 164
Flood building, **145**
Fly in the Pudding Restaurant, 126
Flynn, Jack, 61, 88
folding bed, 149
food distribution,
    136, 149-150, 202, 269, 271, 273
food, overpricing of, 147, 259, 263
Fort Mason, 129, 131, 149, 193, 258
Fort Miley, 41, 176
Fort Point, 204
"Frankie and Johnnie," 60
Franklin Hall, 56, 161
Frawley, Daniel, 289
Frawley, Tim, 290
free lunch, 59
free postage
    See postage-free mail
free transport, 48, 56, 241, 274
Freeman, Frederick Newton 54, 192
Fremstadt, Olive, 32, 67, 164
"French restaurants," 31, 55
Fugazi Bank Building, 192
Funston, Frederick,
    35, 37, 42, 43, 54, 101, 102

G

Garchik, Jerome M. , 146
Garchik, Leah, 146
Garnett, Porter, 129
Garratt, W.T. & Co., 97
Geary building, 110

Genthe, Arnold,
    53, 66, **112**, 214, 236, **238**, **239**, 241
Germans, 130
Girls' High School, 272
Give Us a Little Smile, Baby,
    58, 162, 168
Golcher, Bennie, 268
Golcher, Catherine, 268
Golcher, Catherine (Mrs.), 272
Golcher, Elise, 268
Golcher, Henry, 268, 271, 273
Goldberg Bowen & Co., 147
Golden Gate Park, 95, 238
    refugees, 117, 209, 227, 258, 259
Golden Pheasant, 309
Golf Club, 106, 186, 187
Goodwin, Nat, 288
Gorovan cottages, 252, 253
graft and corruption,
    31, 32, 55, 100
Grand Hotel,
    77, 136, 159, 160, 164, 182, 257
Grand Opera House
    before quake, 32, 59, 62-64, **65**, 67
    after quake, 127, 154, 164
Grau, L.H., 142
"Great Fire of 1906, The," 25
Greek Theater, 307
Greely, Adolphus, 37, 42
Griswold, Mary Edith, 24, 124, 298
grocery saloons, 262, 263-264
gun cotton, 43
Gunn residence, 252
Guthrie, Mrs., 187

H

Hackett, James K., 288
Hales (store), 277
Hall of Justice,
    37, 39, 101-103, 159-160, 257
Hall of Records, **244**

Hall, Blanche, 289
Ham and Eggs Fire
    See Hayes Valley Fire
Hamada, 113
Hamilton, Frank, 171
Hamlet, O.C., 189
Hansen, Gladys, 35
Hanson, Harry, 71
Happy Hooligan, 218, 220, **221**
Harbor Emergency Hospital, 99
Harbor View, 56
Harbor View Baths, 169, 170
Harvard Alumni Bulletin, 47
Harrell, O.R., 88
Harte, Bret, 117
Hawes, T.W., 175
Hayes Valley Fire, 47, 157-158, 161
Hayward Fault, 29
Hearst Building
    See Examiner building
Hebrew cemetery, 224, 225
Helms, Captain, 248
Heney, Francis J., 32
"Heroic San Francisco," 200
Hertz, Alfred, 164
Hittell, Frank, 246
Ho, Jimmy, 120, 121
Hobart residence, 309
Hoffman House (New York), 59
Home Telephone Co., 55
Hopkins, Mark, 137, 161
Hopper, James M.,
    66, 69-70, 108, 138, 152, 161
Horace, 116
horses,
    67, 75, 89, 98-99, 131, 136, 157
hospital, emergency
    See Mechanics' Pavilion
Hotaling, A.P. & Co., 188-189, 304
Hotaling's whisky,
    188-199, **199**, 304

Hotel St. Nicholas
    See St. Nicholas Hotel
*How the Army Worked to
    Save San Francisco*, 44
Huntington, Dr. (Presidio), 266
Huntington residence, 238
Hutchinsons, the, 272

I

Idora Park, 306
impressment of men,
    45, 46, 194, 230, 241, 273
infectious diseases, 49
International News Photos, 243
Irvine, Margaret,
    75, 77, 105, 184, 185
Italians, 128, 130, 131, 137, 257, 267
    See also Latin Quarter

J

Jacobson, Pauline, 280
Jacoby, Josephine, 165
jail, Broadway, 257
James, Henry, 53
James, William, 53, **292**
Janis, Elsie, 288
Japanese, 113, 137, 265
Jefferson Square, 220, 258, 265
Jeffries, Jim, 289
Jones, C.C., 253
Joosts, the, 269
Jordan, David Starr, 298
Journet, Marcel, 64

K

Kahn, George, 115
Kane, Rose, 87, 88
Kansas City, 288
Keith, William, 296
Kelly's livery stables, 106
Kennedy, Grace, 149

Kirkpatrick, John C., 181
Kirkpatrick, Thomas, 189
kitchens, street
    See stoves in streets
Kleaberger, Frank, 264
Kodak 3A Special, 115
Kohl Building, 160
Kohl, Mrs. Frederick, 164
Koster, John A., 41
KRON-TV, 204
Kwon Kong, 119, 120
Kwong Chow Temple, 119, 120

L

Lafler, Henry Anderson, 44, 154
Lane Hospital, 265
Langdon, William H., 32
Latin Quarter,
    126, 154, 157, 159, **267**, 305
Laurie, Annie, 24, **218**, 221
Leach, Frank A., 164, **174**, 179
Lee, Frank, 83
Leslie (tug), 164, 193
Levings, Bill, 242
Levison, Charlie, 79
Levison, Jacob B., 79
Levison, John, 79
Levison, Robert, 79
Lewis, Sinclair, 161
Liang, Hugh Kwong, **118**, 123
library, main, 57
Lick House, 60
Lick Observatory, 293
Lind, Edward M., 85, 188
Ling Yoke Ping, 123
liquor sales ban,
    38, 102, 170, **199**, 257, 270
Lohengrin, 164
Loma Prieta earthquake, 57, 235
London Hospital, 51
London, Charmian, 132, 138

London, Jack,
    85, **132**, 138, 161, 241
looters, shooting of, 38, 39, 44, 102
looting, 38, 102, 143
Lorraine, Robert, 288
Los Angeles Relief Camp, 202
Lotta's Fountain, 126, 163
Lowell High School, 272, 274
Lucchetti's Restaurant, 59
Lung Tin, 119, 120
Lyceum, The, 140, 142

M

Mackay, Clarence, 287
Maguire's Opera House, 192, 193
Maguire, John, 97
Maguires, the, 269
Majestic Theater, 60
Major Bowes Amateur Hour, 123
Mannering, Mary, 288
Mansell, Maria, 26, 77
Mansell?, Harry, 26, 77-79
Manson, Marsden, 56
Manx Hotel, 60
Marchand's Restaurant, 27, 59, 301
Mare Island Navy Yard, 41
Marina district, 56
marines, 192, 193, 194
Mark Hopkins residence, 137, 161
Marlowe, Julia, 288
marriage licenses, 51, 302
martial law, 39, 256, 260, **261**
Martinez, Xavier, 129, 154
Maskey's Fine Candies, 309
Matias's Restaurant, 305
McAdie, Alexander, 47
McCullough's burlesque house, 60
McCullough, Captain
    (harbor pilot), 34
McGinty, Arthur, 61, 87, 91, 94
McKinnon, Alfred, 191

McManus, Bernard, 88
Mechanics' Pavilion, 57, 59, 61
    hospital, 88-89, 90-95, **93**, 158, 168
    fire, 47, 94-95
Meese & Gottfried Co., 74, 96, 97
Menninger Foundation, 292
Menninger Perspective, 292
mentally ill patients, 86-89
Merchants' Exchange, 160
Merrill residence, 252
Metropolitan Opera Company, 165
Miller, Charles, 89, 94
Miller, Joaquin, 5
Mills Building, 160
Mint, U.S.,
    41, 54, 137, 157, 164, 174-179
Mission High School, 223, 225
Moller, John, 98, 99
Monaco, Dante, **267**
Monaco, J.B., **208**, **267**
Monaco, Katherine, **267**
Montgomery Block, 303
morgue, 102, 103
Morris, Charles, 37, 102
Morrison, "Scotty," 154
Mott, Frank K., 48, 286
Murger, Henri, 304
Mutual Bank Building, 71

N

Napa, 122, 123, 278
National Archives, 54
National Guard, California,
    41, 42, 44, 46, 256-260, 274
Navy, U.S.,
    41, 48, 54, 192-193, 230
Neill, James, 289
Nelson, "Battling," 289
Neptune Hotel, 67, 69, 158
Neustadter residence, 252

Nevada House, 82-84
New Mexico, 288
New Western Hotel, 192
New York City, 288
New York Times, 217
News Building Hotel, 77
Newspaper Row, **151**
Nile Club, 305
Nob Hill, 60, 107, 137, 161, 237, 241
North End Police Station, 161
Norton, Homer, 171
Nourse Auditorium, 57

O

Oakland *Tribune*, 166
O'Connor, Kathleen, 54
O'Dea, Jimmy, 61
O'Farrell, Jasper, 55
Oberon Building, 71
Occidental Hotel, 211
Oelrichs, Mrs. Herman, 164
Ogden (Utah), 48, 202
Ohio House, 84
Old Kirk Whisky, 188-199
Older, Fremont, 32
Olympic Club, 163
"On Some Mental Effects of
    the Earthquake," 292
Orpheum Theater, 60, 306
"Our San Francisco," 66
Owl Drug Store, 89

P

Pacific Mail Steamship Co., 29, 158
Pacific Union Club 106, 184, 185, 186
Palace Hotel, 27, 59, 214-215
    Palm Garden, 27, 33, **60**, 75,
        104-106, 126
    quake damage, 77, 104-107,
        136, 277, 304

continued …

Palace Hotel (continued)
  fire, 157, 159, 160, 164,
    180-183, **183**, 257
Palo Alto, 296
Panama Pacific International
  Exposition, 28, 56, 57
Paquette, Mary Grace, 62
Pardee, George C., 48, 191, 286
Paris of the West, 28
Parquette, Edmond F., 61, 73, 86
passes, **45**, 46, 103, 230, 241
Patek & Co., F., 198
Peacock, 309
Peters, Charles Rollo, 238
pets, 114, 128, 130, 156, 283
Phèdre, 307
Phelan Building, 71, 140, 142
Phelan, James, 32, 38
Pierce Rudolph Storage, 148
Pierce, H. & W., 193
Pinkham, Charles B., 89
plague, danger of, 49
Platt, Horace, 106
Plume, Edward J., 72, 73
Polhemus, Eric, 149
police, 31, 39, 41, 68, 70-76,
    156, 222, 271
police, citizen, 38, 103, 168, 171-172
Poodle Dog Restaurant,
    27, 60, **145**, 301, 305
"Portals of the Past," 238, **239**, 241
Portsmouth Square, 39, 159, 160
Post Office (Seventh Street),
    41, 137, 165, 226, **229**, 235, **244**
postage-free mail
    48, **50**, 228, 235, 274
postal service, 48, 56, 197, 226-235
Postal Telegraph, 287
postmaster, 227, 228, 230
Postum Cereal, 150
Powell, Henry N., 80-82

Pratt and Tierney's backroom, 60
Preble (destroyer), 41
Presbyterian Church, 251, 252
Presidio, 41, 43, 305
  hospital, 43, 158, 265-266
  camp, 49, 120-121, 227-218
prisoners, 103, 159, 160, 258
property damage,
    35, 37, 39, 69-85, 113-114, 148
prophesy, 128
Pup Restaurant, 59

Q

Queen of Sheba, 32, 164
Quinn, Frank R., 35

R

Railway Mail Service, 227
rats, 49
reaction of survivors,
    51-55, 134-135, 143, 220, 271-272,
    280-285, 292-297, 300
  See also drunkenness
Reagan, Thomas F., 89
*Recollections of a
  Newspaper Man*, 174
Recollections of the Fire,
    25, 104, 180
Red Cross, 225
Reflections of the Fire, 184
refugees,
    40, 41, 48, 114, 115-116, 127, 130,
    134-135, 149, 155-157, 201-202
  camps, 208-209, 220, 224, 225,
    227, 241, 258, 300
  Chinese, 120-121, 128, 137
  feeding, 49, 136
  shacks, 56
  See also breadlines
Reid, Constance, 26
Reinhardt, Dr. (Presidio), 266

relief supplies, 150, 202, 230
   funds, 48, 286-289
   See also breadlines
"Revelry of the Dying," 303
Revenue Cutter Service, 189
Rincon Hill, 54, 159
Roberts, Florence, 289
Rockefeller, John D., 287
Rogers, H.H., 287
Roosevelt, President Theodore,
   32, 48, 165, 298
Root, Jack, 289
Rosenstein, Mr., 271
Rossi, Archangelo, 165
Ruef, Abraham,
   30, 31, 32, 37, 38, 55, 192
rumors, 51, 94, 117, 166, 219

S
sailors
   See Navy, U.S.
Saint Francis (the saint), 130
"Sam, Sam, the Lavatory Man," 61
San Andreas Fault, 29
"San Francisco at Play," 298
San Francisco *Bulletin*,
   32, 160, 166, 280
San Francisco Call, **151**, 160, 166
San Francisco *Call=Chronicle=
   Examiner*, 166, **167**
San Francisco Chronicle,
   107, 146, **151**, 160, 286
San Francisco City Directory, 1905,
   268
"San Francisco During the
   Eventful Days of April," 250
San Francisco Examiner
   151, 166, 168, 169, 242, 243
"San Francisco (From the Sea)."
   117
San Francisco Newspapers Index, 23

San Jacinto Fault, 29
San Quentin, 55
Sanguinetti's Restaurant, 59
sanitary conditions, 49
Saunders', the, 274
Savoy Hotel, 110
Schaffers, the, 269
Scheff, Fritzi, 288
Schmitt, Henry C., 222
Schmitt, Mrs. Henry C., 225
Schmitz, Eugene, **100**, 171-172, 211
   election, 30-31
   graft, 31-32, 55
   actions, 37-39, 42, 100-103, 159
Schwabacher residence, 253
Scotti, Antonio, 59, 165
Search for Eric Bell ..., The, 26
Secretary of War, 42, 48
Sedgwick, Charles B., 206, 210
Sembrich, Marcella, 165
Sequoia Club, 128
servants, 113, 126
shacks, refugee, 56
Sharpes, the, 149
Shaw, George Bernard, 302
Sheehy, Margaret, 61, 87
Shortridge, Samuel M., 169, 170
Shreve's, 186
sightseers, 41, 54
Simpson, Ernest, 107
Sinclair, Upton, 161
Sisters of Charity, 91
Sketch, The (London), 214
Skinner, Otis, 288
smallpox, 49
Smith, George, 271
Smith, Grant, 271
social barriers obliterated,
   48, 49, 143
Sothern, E.H., 288
Sotomoyo (tug), 41

Southern Pacific Co., 54, 140
Southern Pacific Hospital, 155
"spirit of San Francisco," 53
Sports, the, 271, 273, 274
Spotorno, Mr., 269, 270
Spreckels, Claus, 32, 252, 253, 254
Spreckels building, Claus
    See Call building
Spreckels, Rudolph, 32, 38
St. Francis Hotel,
    27, 60, 77-78, 114-115, 214
    fire, 136, 161
St. Luke's Church, 251
St. Mary's Cathedral,
    165, 203, 204, **275**
St. Mary's Church, 120
St. Mary's Hospital, 159
St. Nicholas Hotel, 60, 92, 149
St. Patrick's Church, 71, 72, 164
Stafford, W.G., 186
Standard Oil Co., 287
Stanford Axe, 66
Stanford University,
    53, 142, 292, 293, 296, 298
Starr King Cadets, 274
Stehr, William F. , 82-85
Stephens, Henry Morse, 24, 26
"Steps That Lead to Nowhere," 238
Sterling, Gary, 24, 25
Sterling, George, 138, 161
Stetson, James B., 250, 254, **255**
Stevens, Ashton, 164
Stevenson, Mrs. Robert Louis, 298
Stevenson, Robert Louis, 203
    monument, 160, 203
stock yards, 97
Story of Cheerio by Himself, 188
Stoupe, Mr., 273
stoves in streets,
    116, 223-225, 269, 278, 300
Strathmore Hotel, 72

street kitchens
    See stoves in streets
streetcars, 55, 56, **139**
    no fares, 56
streets, cracked, 33, 70-71, 74, **76,**
    80, **139,** 141, 155, 165
Sullivan, Dennis, 181
    his plans, 30, 46
    killed, 35, 155, 265
Sullivan, Mrs. Dennis, 35, 155
Sunset Magazine,
    32, 124, 127, 217, 298, 308
Sunset Press building, 127
Sutro Baths, 28
Swiss American Wine Co., 196

T

Taine, John,
    See Bell, Eric Temple
Tait's Restaurant,
    27, 33, 59, 248, 301, 304, 305
Tanners, the, 269
Techau Tavern,
    33, 59, 301, 304, 305
telegraph messages, 48, 56, 227, 287
Tenderloin District, 55, 257
Theater, The, 214
"There'll be a hot time in
    the old town tonight," 211, 300
Third Congregational Church, 272
"Three Days Adrift," 298
Tillman, Tilton E., 89
Torney, G.H., 49
Tortoni's Restaurant, 60
Towart, Rob, 129, 130
Towne, Albion N., 237, 238
trains, no fares, 48, 241
transportation costs, 119, 154
treasurer's office, 38, 102
trunk pullers
    110, 116, 127, 129, 135, **213**

Tufts, Bronson, 274
22nd U.S. Infantry, 159, 189
28th Coast Artillery, 253
Twin Peaks auxiliary salt water
    system, 30
typhoid, 49

U
underground cisterns, 30
Underwriters Fire Patrol, 88, 89
Union Square,
    60, **110**, 136, 161, 165, 216, 217
United Railroads, 55
U.S. Geological Survey, 35
United Undertakers, 157
University of California, Berkeley,
    44, 66, 123, 262
    cadets, 44, 262-266
    faculty club, 305

V
Valencia Street Hotel,
    34, 80-82, **81**, 156, 165
Valencia Theater, 60
Varney, Mr., 272
Volkman, C.M. & Co., 198

W
Walker, Edith, 164
Walker, Meriweather, 37, 101
Wall, Louise Herrick, 200
Wallace, Richard R., 248
Walls of Jericho, The, 288
Walsh, Harry F., 74-75, 96
Walter, Mrs. Solly, 128
Walton, James, 253
Wanamaker, Mr., 270
Ward, James W., 95
Warfield, David, 288, 289
Washington Square, 208
waterfront, saving of, 48, 54

Watsons, the, 269, 270
Weber, Joe, 288
wedding, 24, 302
Wellington (ship), 33
Wenban residence, 253
wharves, 27, 164
Whitmans, the, 148
Whitney, Mr., 128
wholesale district, 159
Willamette Pulp & Paper Co.,
    193, 198
Willard, E.S., 288
Williams, John T., 37, 101
Wilson, Francis, 288
Winchester Hotel, 165
wind conditions, 47, 159, 195
Wolfe, Orrin R., 189, 190
Woodward's Pavilion, 165
wounded, care of,
    54, 87-89, 90-95, 155, 159
Wright, Frederick G., 198

Y
Y.M.H.A., 269
Ye Liberty Playhouse, 306

Z
Zellerbach Paper Co., 198
Zellerbach, Isidore, 198
Zinkand Cafe, 27, 59, 75, 301